lonely planet

CANADA

TOP SIGHTS, AUTHENTIC EXPERIENCES

Brendan Sainsbury, Ray Bartlett, Oliver Berry, Gregor Clark, Shawn Duthie, Steve Fallon, Anna Kaminski, Adam Karlin, John Lee, Craig McLachlan, Liza Prado, Phillip Tang

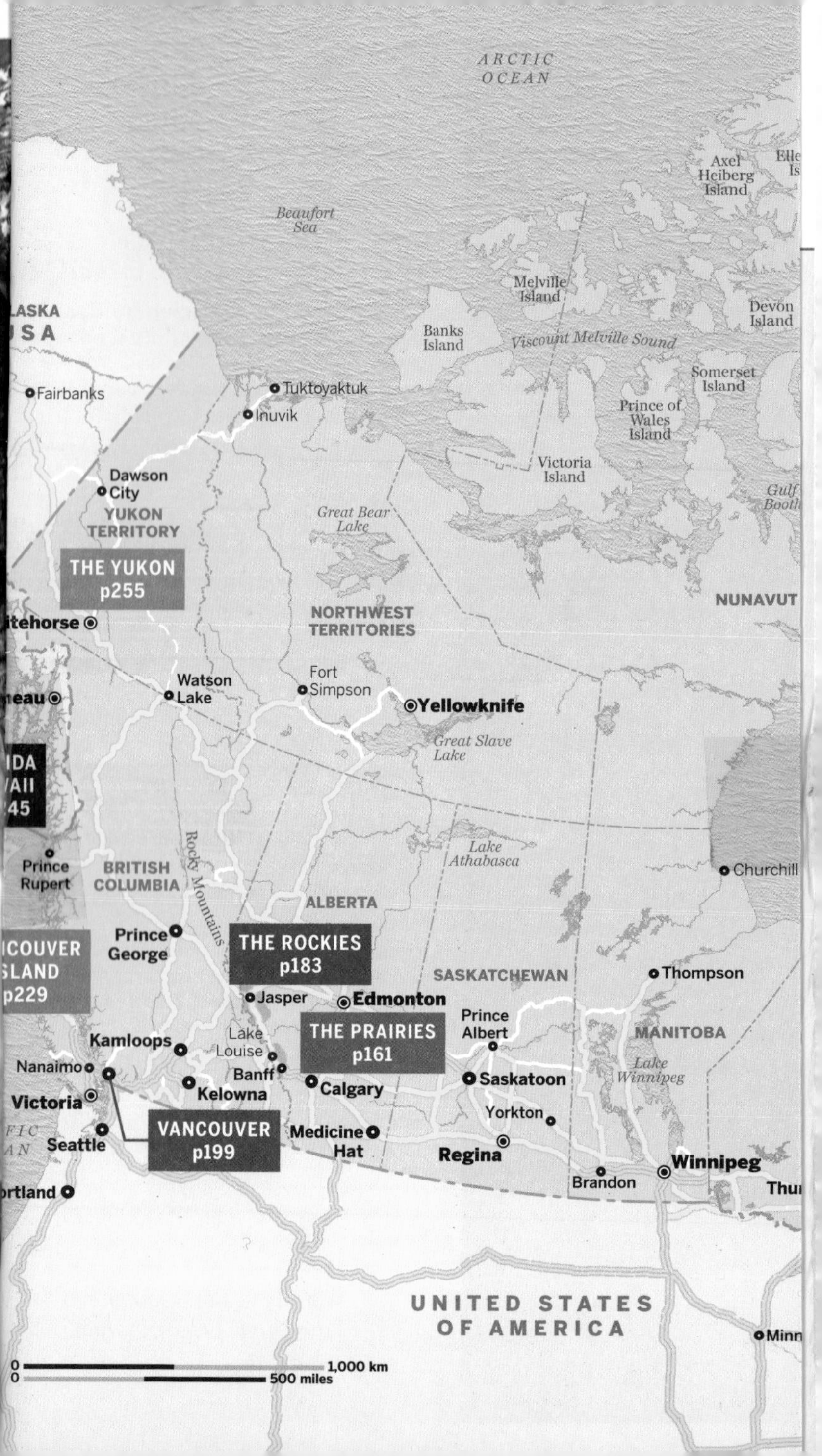

ARCTIC OCEAN

Beaufort Sea

Axel Heiberg Island

Elle Is

Melville Island

Devon Island

LASKA

USA

Banks Island

Viscount Melville Sound

Somerset Island

Fairbanks

Tuktoyaktuk

Inuvik

Prince of Wales Island

Victoria Island

Gulf Booth

Dawson City

YUKON TERRITORY

Great Bear Lake

THE YUKON p255

NUNAVUT

itehorse

NORTHWEST TERRITORIES

Watson Lake

Fort Simpson

neau

Yellowknife

Great Slave Lake

IDA
AII
45

Lake Athabasca

Churchill

Prince Rupert

BRITISH COLUMBIA

Rocky Mountains

ALBERTA

Prince George

THE ROCKIES p183

COUVER ISLAND p229

SASKATCHEWAN

Thompson

Jasper

Edmonton

Prince Albert

THE PRAIRIES p161

MANITOBA

Kamloops

Lake Louise

Lake Winnipeg

Nanaimo

Banff

Saskatoon

Kelowna

Calgary

Victoria

Yorkton

FIC AN

Seattle

VANCOUVER p199

Medicine Hat

Regina

Winnipeg

Brandon

Thu

rtland

UNITED STATES OF AMERICA

Minn

0 — 1,000 km

0 — 500 miles

In Focus

Survival Guide

Polar bear (p290)
ROBERT POSTMA / DESIGN PICS / GETTY IMAGES ©

Plan Your Trip
Canada's Top 12

The Rockies

The brawny backbone of the nation

The sawtooth, white-topped mountains (p183) straddling the British Columbia–Alberta border inspire both awe and action with ribbons of hiking trails, rushing white water and powdery ski slopes. The train provides another popular way to experience the grandeur: luminous lakes, jumbles of wildflowers and glistening glaciers glide by as the steel cars chug up mountain passes and down river valleys en route to points east or west. Above: Icefields Parkway (p188); Right: Moraine Lake (p187)

MATTEO COLOMBO / GETTY IMAGES ©

1

Montréal

2

Canadian cool with a certain je ne sais quoi

Witness a French-infused city that's in love with festivals, the arts, good food, living well and enjoying life to the hilt. Toronto may be Canada's economic capital, but Montréal (p93) remains the country's cultural juggernaut. A standard-bearer for an entire linguistic-cultural identity, the city lives for public celebrations of the arts, architecture and food. Top: Montréal Jazz Fest (p96) puppet parade; Bottom: St Lawrence River

EB ADVENTURE PHOTOGRAPHY / SHUTTERSTOCK ©

Vancouver

3

Urban sophistication collides with feral wilderness

Vancouver (p199) always lands atop the 'best places to live' lists, and who's to argue? Sea-to-sky beauty surrounds the laid-back, cocktail-lovin' metropolis. With skiable mountains on the outskirts, beaches fringing the core and Stanley Park's thick rain forest just blocks from downtown's glass skyscrapers, it's a harmonic convergence of city and nature. Above: False Creek (p208)

4

The Atlantic Provinces

Acadian, Celtic and Viking culture

Home to Canada's craggiest coastline, loneliest lighthouses and fiercest tides, in the Atlantic Provinces (p135) you can feel the full force of nature at work. They call Newfoundland 'the Rock', a fitting name for an island of thoroughly elemental attractions and aesthetics. Under-the-radar New Brunswick hides culturally rich Acadian villages, Nova Scotia is a place that's steeped in the sea, while Prince Edward Island presents a postcard-worthy picture of pastoral Canada. Right: Peggy's Cove (p138)

Québec City

French-speaking and deliciously seductive

Québec City (p115) is one of North America's oldest and most magnificent settlements. Its picturesque old town is a Unesco World Heritage site, a living museum of narrow cobblestone streets, 17th- and 18th-century houses and soaring church spires, with the splendid Château Frontenac hotel towering above it all. Just walking down the street here is an aesthetic treat, unlike anywhere else in North America. Right: Terrasse Dufferin (p122) and Old Québec

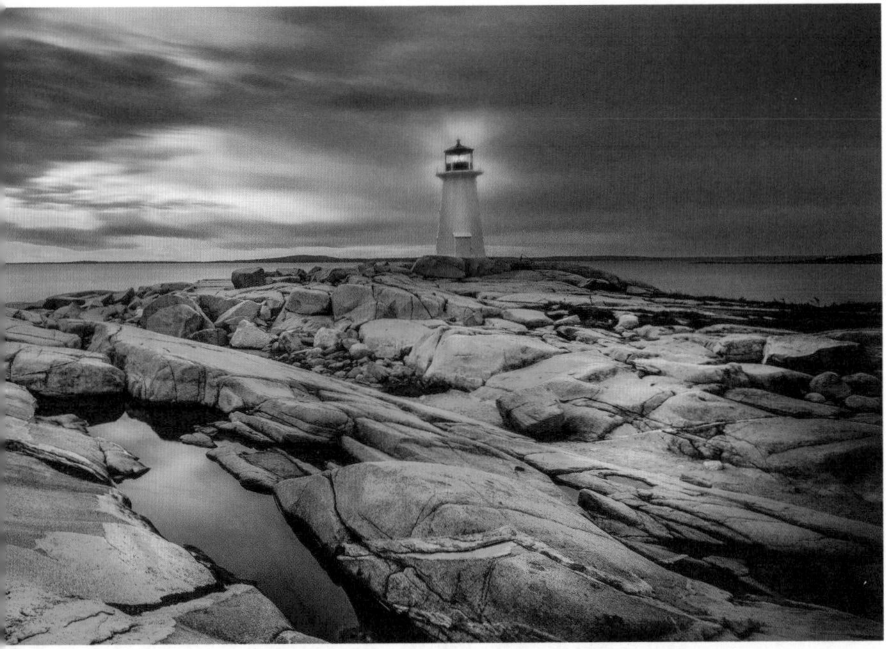

PAULO COSTA / GETTY IMAGES ©

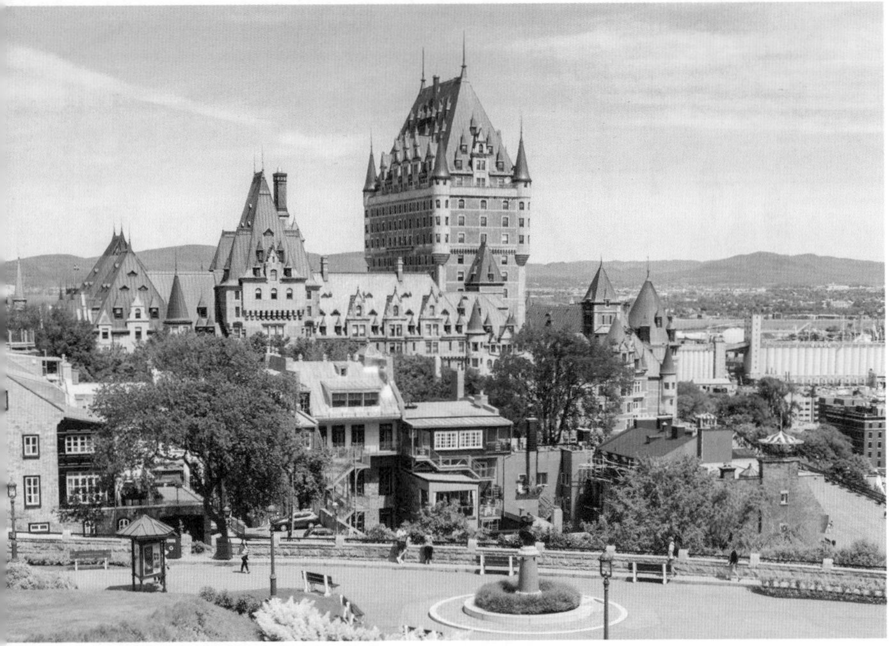

UPDOGDESIGNS / GETTY IMAGES ©

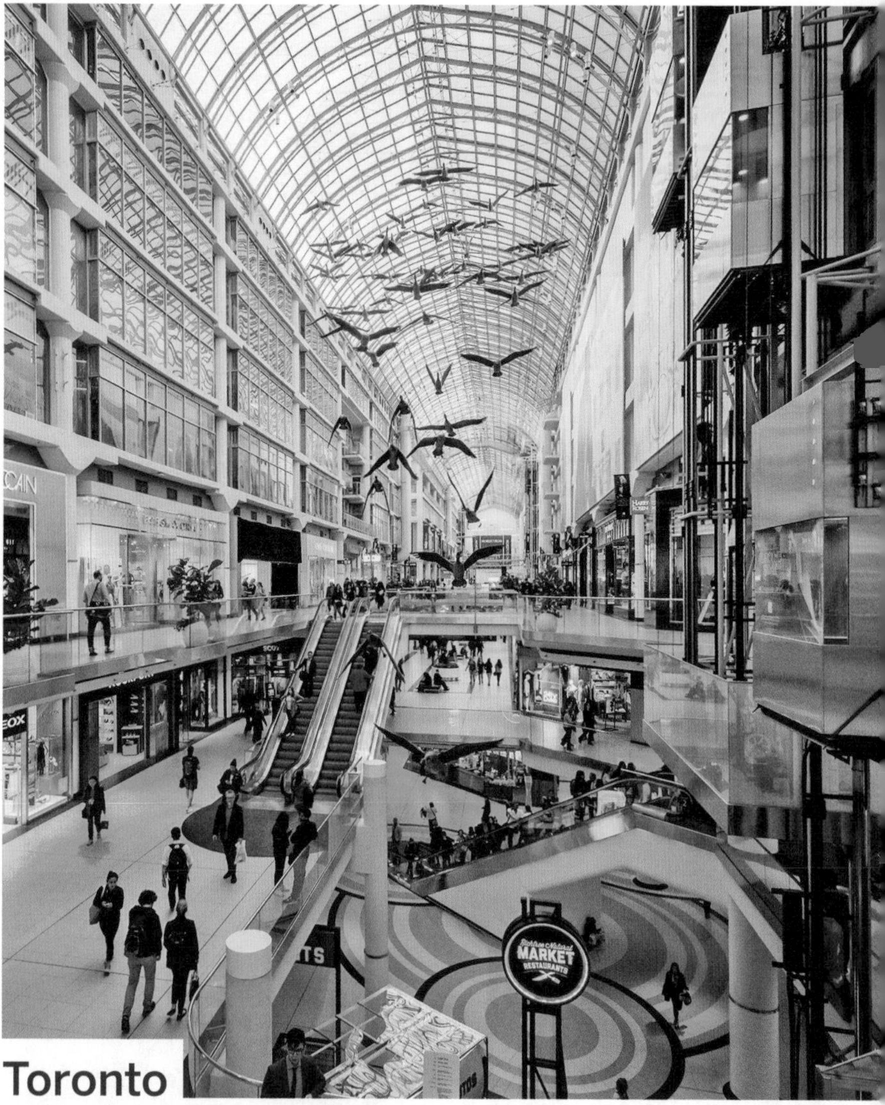

JON BILOUS / SHUTTERSTOCK ©

Toronto

Canada's largest and most diverse city

A hyperactive stew of cultures and neighborhoods, Toronto (p35) strikes you with sheer urban awe. Will you have dinner in Chinatown or Greektown? Five-star fusion or a peameal-bacon sandwich? In Ontario's cool capital, designer shoes from Bloor-Yorkville are accessorized with tattoos in Queen West, while mod-art galleries, theater par excellence, rockin' band rooms and hockey mania add to the megalopolis. Above: Eaton Centre (p50)

6

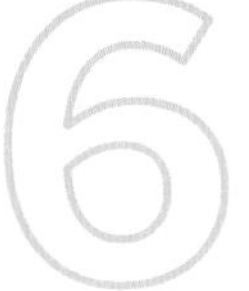

Haida Gwaii

Witness the magic and mystery of pre-colonial Canada

Haida Gwaii (p245) forms a dagger-shaped archipelago of some 450 islands lying 80km west of the BC coast, and offers a magical trip for those who make the effort. Attention has long focused on the many unique species of flora and fauna that populate lonesome Gwaii Haanas National Park, which makes up the bottom third of the archipelago, but each year it becomes more apparent that the islands' true soul is the Haida culture itself. Above: Totem pole by artist Christian White

7

Vancouver Island

Echoes of England in a west-coast setting

Kissing the Pacific Ocean, Vancouver Island (p229) is Canada's 'wild' west. Regally refined Victoria is the island's heart, beating with bohemian shops, wood-floored coffee bars and a tea-soaked English past. Brooding Pacific Rim National Park sports the West Coast Trail and the mist-shrouded surfer beaches of Tofino. Then there's journeyman Port Alberni at the head of a narrow inlet, hemmed in by giant trees beyond which lie welcoming organic farms and boutique wineries. Right: Victoria (p236)

JOSEF HANUS / SHUTTERSTOCK ©

JENIFOTO / GETTY IMAGES ©

JOSEF HANUS / SHUTTERSTOCK ©

9

The Yukon

Where gold-rush dreams are made

Few places in the world today have been so unchanged over the course of time as the Yukon (p255). Indigenous people, having eked out survival for thousands of years, hunt and trap as they always have, and even the well-documented Klondike Gold Rush of 1898, the Yukon's high point of population, retains an ephemeral heritage. Come to the north and lose yourself in a vast Arctic wilderness with few modern trappings. Far left: Dawson City (p264); Left: Moose (p290)

VLADONE / GETTY IMAGES ©

AQNUS FEBRIYANT / SHUTTERSTOCK ©

DENNIS MCCOLEMAN / GETTY IMAGES ©

Ottawa

Canada's culture-heavy bilingual capital

Toronto is larger, Montréal is certainly cooler and Vancouver is objectively more attractive but, lest we forget, underrated Ottawa (p75) is Canada's classy capital. Herein lie the country's Gothic parliament buildings, along with ample parks, impressive public spaces, a canal that becomes a 7.8km-long winter skating rink and a cache of nation-defining museums. If you want to understand the modern success story that is Canada, Ottawa is the best place to start.

OLESYA BARON / SHUTTERSTOCK ©

The Niagara Region

Wine, history and a spectacular cascade

Crowded? Cheesy? Well, yes. Niagara Falls (p64) is short, too – it doesn't even crack the top 500 worldwide for height. But c'mon, when those great bands of water arc over the precipice, roaring into the void below, as you you sail toward it in a mist-shrouded little boat, Niagara Falls impresses big time. Beyond it stretches a region (p61) speckled with vineyards and home to one of the country's best-preserved 19th-century towns. Above: Horseshoe Falls

SHYLAMA PRODUCTIONS / GETTY IMAGES ©

The Prairies

Fields full of wheat and dinosaur bones

12

The flatlands – boring? No way. Drive through uninterrupted fields of golden wheat in Manitoba, Saskatchewan and Alberta and you'll encounter stiff winds, bruised clouds and a horizon punctuated by old grain elevators and famously friendly prairie towns. In between lie the real highlights of the Prairies (p161): dinosaur bones, wind-eroded hoodoos, unexpected canyons and echoes of a stalwart Ukrainian heritage.

Plan Your Trip
Need to Know

When to Go

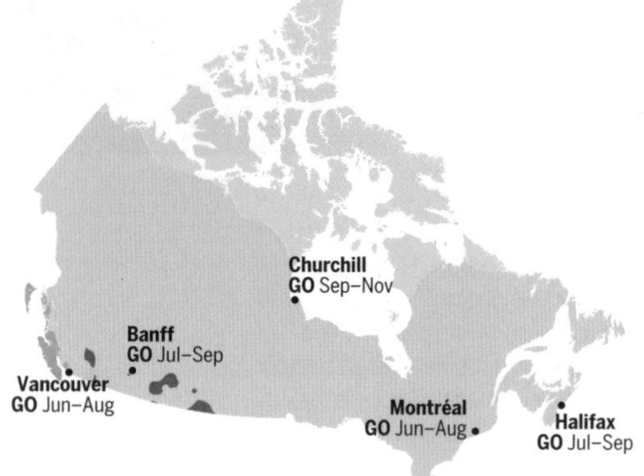

High Season (Jun–Aug)

- Sunshine and warm weather prevail; far northern regions briefly thaw.
- Accommodation prices peak (up 30% on average).
- December through March is equally busy and expensive in ski resort towns.

Shoulder (May, Sep & Oct)

- Crowds and prices drop off.
- Temperatures are cool but comfortable.
- Fall foliage areas (eg Cape Breton Island and Québec) remain busy.

Low Season (Nov–Apr)

- Places outside the big cities and ski resorts close.
- Darkness and cold take over.

Currency
Canadian dollar ($)

Languages
English, French

Visas
Visitors may require a visa to enter Canada. Those exempt require an Electronic Travel Authorization (eTA; $7), with the exception of Americans. See the Visit page on www.cic.gc.ca.

Money
ATMs are widely available. Credit cards are accepted in nearly all hotels and restaurants.

Cell Phones
Local SIM cards can be used in unlocked GSM 850/1900 compatible phones. Other phones must be set to roaming. Coverage is spotty.

Time
Canada spans six of the world's 24 time zones. The time difference from coast to coast is 4½ hours.

Daily Costs

Budget: Less than $100

- Dorm bed: $25–40
- Campsite: $25–35
- Self-catered meals from markets and supermarkets: $12–20

Midrange: $100–250

- B&B or room in a midrange hotel: $80–180 ($100–250 in major cities)
- Meal in a good local restaurant: from $20 plus drinks
- Rental car: $45–70 per day

Top end: More than $250

- Four-star hotel room: from $180 (from $250 in major cities)
- Three-course meal in a top restaurant: from $65 plus drinks
- Skiing day pass: $50–90

Useful Websites

Destination Canada (www.destination canada.com) Official tourism site.

Environment Canada Weather (www.weather.gc.ca) Forecasts for any town.

Lonely Planet (www.lonelyplanet.com/canada) Destination information, hotel bookings, traveler forum and more.

Government of Canada (www.gc.ca) National and regional information.

Opening Hours

Opening hours vary throughout the year. We've provided high-season opening hours; hours will generally decrease in the shoulder and low seasons.

Banks 10am–5pm Monday to Friday; some open 9am–noon Saturday

Restaurants breakfast 8–11am, lunch 11:30am–2:30pm Monday to Friday, dinner 5–9:30pm daily; some open for brunch 8am–1pm Saturday and Sunday

Bars 5pm–2am daily

Clubs 9pm–2am Wednesday to Saturday

Shops 10am–6pm Monday to Saturday, noon–5pm Sunday; some open to 8pm or 9pm Thursday and/or Friday

Supermarkets 9am–8pm; some open 24 hours

Arriving in Canada

Toronto Pearson International Airport Trains (adult/child $12.35/free) run downtown every 15 minutes from 5:30am to 1am; taxis cost around $60 (45 minutes).

Montréal Trudeau International Airport A 24-hour airport shuttle bus ($10) runs downtown. Taxis cost a flat $40 (30 to 60 minutes).

Vancouver International Airport Trains ($7.95 to $10.70) run downtown every six to 20 minutes; taxis cost around $40 (30 minutes).

Land Border Crossings The Canadian Border Services Agency (www.cbsa-asfc.gc.ca/bwt-taf/) posts wait times (usually 30 minutes).

Getting Around

Air Regional and national carriers crisscross the country, taking days off travel time and reaching northern towns inaccessible by road.

Car An extensive highway system links most towns. The Trans-Canada Hwy stretches from Newfoundland to Vancouver Island. Away from the population centers, distances can be deceivingly long and travel times slow due to single-lane highways. All the major rental car companies are readily available.

Ferry Public ferry systems operate extensively in British Columbia, Québec and the Maritime provinces.

Train Outside the Toronto–Montréal corridor, train travel is mostly for scenic journeys.

For more on **getting around**, see p308 

Plan Your Trip
Hotspots For...

SETH K. HUGHES / GETTY IMAGES ©

Wildlife Watching

Up here in the wild North, humans are still but a small cog in a food chain patrolled by whales, polar bears, moose and elk.

The Yukon (p255)
Sparsely populated, this province is text-book wilderness: salmon, grizzlies, golden eagles soar overhead.

Paddle it!
Join Kanoe People (p261) for a Yukon River excursion.

Icefields Parkway (p188)
Watch for bears, bighorn sheep and mountain goats along this scenic route through the Rockies.

Cycle it!
Cycle and camp along the 230km highway.

Gros Morne (p140)
They say there are six moose per square kilometer in Newfoundland's premier park.

Hike it!
Hop Green Gardens trail for wildflowers and wild sheep.

STOCKSTUDIOX / GETTY IMAGES ©

Adrenaline Activities

The wilderness here is not just about good looks. Locals have been jumping in head first – sometimes literally – for decades.

Whistler (p206)
If you want to ski or snowboard Canada's best, Whistler reigns supreme.

Whistler & Blackcomb
Ski both mountains, taking the gondola between them.

Banff (p190)
Queen of the Rockies, Banff has it all: skiing, hiking, rafting, horseback riding, mountain biking...phew!

Banff Canoe Club
Paddle (p191) around Vermilion Lakes.

Tofino (p234)
Little Tofino packs big adventure with its Pacific Coast surfing, kayaking, hiking and storm watching.

Pacific Surf School
Rent a board or take a lesson.

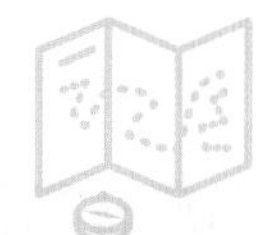

Historic Sites

Indigenous people, Vikings, the French, British, Americans and others have all left a lasting imprint on Canadian soil. Follow in their footsteps.

MEETING OF TWO WORLDS BY LUBEN BOYKOV AND RICHARD BRIXEL; SEBASTIENLEMYRE / SHUTTERSTOCK ©

Québec City (p115)
History is palpable throughout the walled city where the French put down stakes in 1608.

Les Tours Voir Québec
Sample history and food on a walking tour (p126).

Dawson City (p264)
Preserved structures in Dawson City tell the tale of the 1897–98 Klondike gold rush.

Parks Canada Walking Tours
Learn about the gold rush with a costumed guide (p265).

L'Anse aux Meadows (p141)
Poke around the Viking vestiges that Leif Erikson left behind in Newfoundland around 1000 CE.

Norstead
See modern-day interpreters living the Viking life.

Art

It's not just outdoor action: Canada serves up unique art ranging from Indigenous sculpture to the landscape musings of the celebrated Group of Seven.

ALASTAIR WALLACE / SHUTTERSTOCK ©

Ottawa (p75)
With a thriving creative scene and numerous contemporary galleries, culture is close at hand in the capital.

National Gallery of Canada
World's largest collection of Canadian and Inuit art (p82).

Toronto (p35)
All kinds of art forms can be found: film, theater, fine art, street art, dance, poetry, music and more.

Art Gallery of Ontario
Québecois statuary, Inuit carvings and Group of Seven (p45).

Vancouver (p199)
Choose from independent galleries, a blockbuster gallery, and an Insta mix of eye-popping public art.

Museum of Anthropology
Spectacular Indigenous totem poles (p211).

Plan Your Trip
Essential Canada

Activities

While the great Canadian outdoors is undeniably postcard pretty, the wilderness here has more than good looks, with activities ranging from hiking and kayaking to cycling and snowboarding. For the daring, there's ice-climbing and caving, and for those after something a little quieter, strap on some snowshoes or hop in a canoe.

Canadians aren't fooling around when it comes to hockey. They play hard and well, and if they're not playing, they cheer and catcall like they mean it. Grassroots hockey, aka pond hockey, takes place in communities across the country wherever there's a frozen surface. All you need is a puck, a hockey stick and a few friends to live the dream. If you'd rather watch than play, Vancouver, Edmonton, Calgary, Toronto, Ottawa, Winnipeg and Montréal all have NHL (www.nhl.com) teams who skate tough and lose the odd tooth.

Shopping

Streets such as Robson in Vancouver and Yonge in Toronto are Canada's retail hubs, with plenty of high-end shops. For something more authentically Canadian beyond the typical maple syrup or vacuum-packed smoked salmon, check out Indigenous art shops and the many markets that are the highlight of summer weekends for work by local potters, jewelry makers and other artists. The nation's major museums often have excellent gift shops with quality, locally inspired products.

Eating

Canadian cuisine is nothing if not eclectic, a casserole of food cultures blended together from centuries of immigration. Poutine (French fries topped with gravy and cheese curds), Montréal-style bagels, salmon jerky and pierogi jostle for comfort-food attention. For something more refined, Montréal, Toronto and Vancouver have well-seasoned fine-dining scenes, while regions

P.F.MAYER / SHUTTERSTOCK ©

across the country have rediscovered the unique ingredients grown, foraged for and produced on their doorsteps – bringing distinctive seafood, artisanal cheeses and lip-smacking produce to menus.

Tastemakers may not tout Canadian food the way they do, say, Italian or French fare, so let's just call the distinctive dishes and fresh, seasonal fruits and veggies our little secret. Ditto for the award-winning bold reds and crisp whites produced from the country's vine-striped valleys.

Drinking & Nightlife

Canadian nightlife is as varied as the landscape. Cities have packed pubs serving microbrews, cocktail bars for the well-heeled, clubs catering mainly to the young, and live music bars for their parents. In small towns, you'll mostly find at least one pub, which is as much a meeting place as a drinking establishment. Cafes are everywhere, although espresso machines are used with varying success in far-flung locations.

★ Best Breweries

Powell Brewery (p221), Vancouver

Griendel Brasserie Artisanale (p130), Québec City

Shelter Brewing Co (p176), Saskatoon

Bellwoods Brewery (p54), Toronto

Craft Beer Corner (p153), Charlottetown

Entertainment

Maybe it's the long, cold winters that drive teens into their basements to play music, but Canada has more local bands than you can shake a (hockey) stick at. Consequently, finding live music is not a challenge. Rock, folk and pop are the mainstays, while clubs have a steady stream of local and international DJs. In major cities, you'll also find a smattering of opera, dance and drama.

From left: Robson St, Vancouver (p216); Poutine

Plan Your Trip
Month by Month

MARC BRUXELLE / SHUTTERSTOCK ©

January

Ice Wine Festivals

British Columbia's Okanagan Valley (www.thewinefestivals.com) and Ontario's Niagara Peninsula (www.niagarawinefestival.com) celebrate their ice wines with good-time festivals. The distinctive, sweet libations go down the hatch alongside chestnut roasts, cocktail competitions and cozy alpine-lodge ambience.

February

Chinese New Year

Dragons dance, firecrackers burst and food sizzles in the country's Chinatowns. Vancouver (www.vancouver-chinatown.com) hosts the biggest celebration, but Toronto, Calgary, Ottawa and Montréal also have festivities. The lunar calendar determines the date.

Québec City's Winter Carnival

Revelers watch ice-sculpture competitions, hurtle down snow slides, go ice fishing and cheer on their favorite paddlers in an insane canoe race on the half-frozen, ice-floe-filled St Lawrence River. It's the world's biggest winter fest (www.carnaval.qc.ca).

Vancouver Wine Festival

Vancouver uncorks 1700 wines from 200 vintners at the Vancouver International Wine Festival (www.vanwinefest.ca), a rite of spring for oenophiles. You're drinking for art's sake, since the event raises funds for the city's Bard on the Beach summer Shakespeare festival.

March

Sugar Shacks

Québec produces three-quarters of the world's maple syrup, and March is when trees get tapped. Head out to a local sugar shack and do the *tire d'érable* (taffy pull), where steaming maple syrup is poured onto snow and wound around a popsicle stick once it's cooled.

JIMFENG / GETTY IMAGES ©

April

World Ski & Snowboard Festival

Ski bums converge on Whistler for 10 days of adrenaline-filled events, outdoor rock and hip-hop concerts, film screenings, dog parades and a whole lotta carousing (www.wssf.com). Heed the motto: party in April, sleep in May.

☆ Hot Docs

Want to learn more about Ontario's Hwy 7? Millionaires who live in Mumbai's slums? Belly dancers working in Cairo? Toronto hosts North America's largest documentary film festival (www.hotdocs.ca), which screens 170-plus documentaries from around the globe.

May

Tiptoe Through the Tulips

After a long winter, Ottawa bursts with color – more than three million tulips, made up of 200 types, blanket the city for the Canadian Tulip Festival (www.tulipfestival.ca). Festivities include parades, regattas, car rallies, dances, concerts and fireworks.

★ Best Festivals

Montréal Jazz Festival, June

Québec City's Winter Carnival, February

Toronto International Film Festival, September

Dark Sky Festival, October

Calgary Stampede, July

June

☆ Luminato

For 10 days in early June, big-name musicians, dancers, artists, writers, actors and filmmakers descend on Toronto for a celebration of creativity that reflects the city's diversity (www.luminatofestival.com). Many performances are free.

From left: *Tire d'érable*; Canadian Tulip Festival

✩ North by Northeast

Over its 25-year history, NXNE (www.nxne.com) has become a must on the music-industry calendar, with around 1000 emerging indie bands taking to the stages of Toronto's coolest clubs. You might catch the rock stars of tomorrow. Film screenings and comedy shows add to the mix.

✩ Montréal Jazz Festival

Two million music lovers descend on Montréal in late June, when the heart of downtown explodes with jazz and blues for 11 straight days (www.montrealjazzfest.com). Most concerts are outdoors and free, and the party goes on round the clock.

Pride Toronto

Toronto's most flamboyant event (www.pridetoronto.com) celebrates diversity of sexuality and gender identity with a month of festivities, climaxing with a triple whammy: the Trans March, Dyke March and Pride Parade. Rainbow-coated Church-Wellesley Village is ground zero.

July

✩ Country Music in Cavendish

Some of the biggest names in country music come to Prince Edward Island for the Cavendish Beach Festival (www.cavendishbeachmusic.com). This is one of the largest outdoor music festivals in North America, and the island swells with people.

Calgary Stampede

Raging bulls, chuckwagon racing and badass, boot-wearing cowboys unite for the 'Greatest Outdoor Show on Earth'. A midway of rides and games makes it a family affair well beyond the usual rodeo event, attracting up to 1.5 million yee-hawin' fans (www.calgarystampede.com).

August

Canadian National Exhibition

Akin to a state fair in the USA, 'The Ex' (www.theex.com) features more than 700 exhibitors, agricultural shows, lumberjack competitions and outdoor concerts at Toronto's Exhibition Place. The carnivalesque 18-day event runs through Labour Day and ends with a bang-up fireworks display.

Newfoundland Rowing Regatta

The streets are empty, the stores are closed and everyone migrates to the shores of Quidi Vidi Lake for the Royal St John's Regatta (www.stjohnsregatta.org). The rowing race began in 1825 and is now the continent's oldest continuously held sporting event.

September

PEI Fall Flavors

This island-wide kitchen party merges toe-tapping traditional music with incredible seafood over the course of three weeks (www.fallflavours.ca). In Charlottetown, don't miss the oyster-shucking championships or the chowder challenge.

✩ Toronto International Film Festival

Toronto's prestigious 10-day celebration (www.tiff.net) is a major cinematic event. Films of all lengths and styles are screened, as celebs shimmy between gala events and the Bell Lightbox building. Buy tickets well in advance.

October

Dark Sky Festival

In late October, Jasper's Dark Sky Festival (www.jasperdarksky.travel) fills 10 days and nights with events celebrating space. Hear talks by astronauts, astronomers and astrophotographers, listen to the symphony under the stars, see the aurora borealis reflected in a glacial lake and gaze through a telescope into the great beyond.

December

Niagara Festival of Lights

From November to January, the family-friendly Winter Festival of Lights (www.wfol.com) gets everyone in the holiday spirit with two million twinkling bulbs and 125 animated displays brightening the town and the waterfalls themselves. Fireworks occasionally light up the skies, too.

Plan Your Trip
Get Inspired

ALEXANDER HOWARD / LONELY PLANET ©

Read

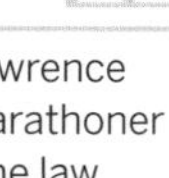

The Illegal (Lawrence Hill; 2015) A marathoner running from the law takes on issues of race and immigration.

Indian Horse (Richard Wagamese; 2012) An Ojibwe man in rehab recalls his life as a hockey star, touching on Ojibwe rituals and spirituality.

Dear Life (Alice Munro; 2012) A collection of stories by the 2013 Nobel Prize laureate.

Alias Grace (Margaret Atwood; 1996) Drama set around the real-life 1843 murders of a gentleman and his housekeeper.

Barkskins (Annie Proulx; 2016) Riveting epic novel of two penniless woodcutters ('barkskins') in 17th-century New France.

Watch

Room (Lenny Abrahamson; 2015) Canadian-Irish film about a mother and son finally released after years of captivity.

Sleeping Giant (Andrew Cividino; 2015) Teens deal with boredom in an isolated Ontario cottage community.

Bon Cop, Bad Cop (Eric Canuel; 2006) An Anglophone and Francophone join forces.

C.R.A.Z.Y. (Jean-Marc Vallée; 2005) A gay teen growing up in a large Catholic family in 1970s Montréal tries to fit in.

I Confess (Alfred Hitchcock; 1953) Hitchcock's lens caresses Québec City in this old-world film-noirish suspense thriller.

Listen

Fully Completely (Tragically Hip; 1992) This album is as Canadian as a maple-syrup-drenched hockey puck.

Views (Drake; 2016) This singer put Toronto back on the music map.

Songs of Leonard Cohen (Leonard Cohen; 1967) Debut album from one of the best-known Canadian musicians.

A Tribe Called Red (Electric Pow Wow; 2012) This incredible debut sparked a whole new genre, mixing Indigenous heritage and electronic music.

Come On Over (Shania Twain; 1997) The best-selling studio album by a female artist in any genre, from country music's Canadian queen.

Above: Lake Louise (p186)

Plan Your Trip
Five-Day Itineraries

Wild West Coast

Sandwiched between sea and mountains, the west will wow you with its beauty. Take in cultured Vancouver with its museums and parks before heading to Vancouver Island to explore picturesque Victoria and the wilds of Tofino.

1 **Vancouver** (p199) Spend two days exploring the art gallery, Stanley Park and Granville Island's food market.

1 hr to Tsawwassen, then 2 hrs to Swartz Bay, then 30 mins to Victoria

2 **Victoria** (p236) Explore Chinatown, the Royal BC Museum and Craigdarroch Castle. Take a whale-watching tour from Fisherman's Wharf.

2½ hrs to Port Alberni

3 **Port Alberni** (p243) Wander through enormous, centuries-old trees in Cathedral Grove.

2 hrs to Tofino

4 **Tofino** (p234) Spend two days at Long Beach, visiting the Roy Henry Vickers Gallery and hopping a boat to Meares Island.

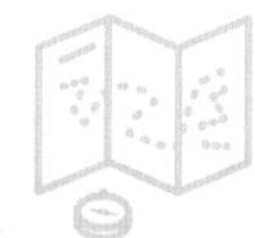

Mountains & Prairies

Get in touch with your inner cowboy in surprisingly hip Calgary before crossing the prairie to the towering Rockies. Explore Banff and then drive one of the world's most stunning roads to Jasper, hopefully catching a glimpse of some wildlife en route.

1. **Calgary** (p170) Visit the new National Music Centre, buy a Smithbilt cowboy hat and then take in Calgary's impressive restaurant scene. 1½ hrs to Banff Town

2. **Banff Town** (p190) Take in the Whyte Museum and then canoe down the Bow River, watching for elk and moose. 40 mins to Lake Louise

3. **Lake Louise** (p186) Admire Lake Louise and hike to Lake Agnes for alpine tea. Take the gondola and watch for grizzly bears below. 3 hrs to Jasper

4. **Jasper** (p194) Visit Maligne Lake and take a boat trip out to iconic Spirit Island.

FROM LEFT: ALEXANDER CHLUM / SHUTTERSTOCK ©, AIVRAD / SHUTTERSTOCK ©

Plan Your Trip
10-Day Itinerary

City-Hopping

Urbanites will love taking in the world-class museums, arts scenes and nightlife of Canada's cities. From buzzing Toronto to Québec City's old-world charm, with the vineyards of Niagara in between, you could easily stretch this itinerary out to a few weeks or more.

Ottawa (p75) Take in Ottawa's impressive museums, particularly the Canadian Museum of History and the National Gallery. And don't forget Parliament Hill. 🚗 2½ hrs to Montréal

Toronto (p35) Spend two days exploring Toronto's museums and galleries, taking a ride to the top of the CN Tower and browsing the markets. 🚗 1½ hrs to Niagara Falls

Niagara-on-the-Lake (p68) Soak up the atmosphere of this 19th-century town and enjoy its neighboring vineyards. 🚗 5½ hrs to Ottawa

Niagara Falls (p64) Take in the falls from different points, including tunnels and boats. Visit the Daredevil Exhibit. 🚗 30 mins to Niagara-on-the-Lake

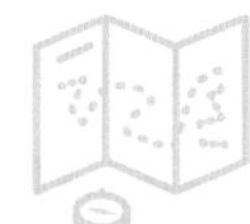

6 **Québec City** (p115) Stroll the picturesque old town, visit the Musée de la Civilisation and cycle the city's scenic paths.

5 **Montréal** (p93) Explore Old Montréal and the Musée des Beaux-Arts. Take in the parks, the markets and some live music.

🚗 3 hrs to Québec City

Plan Your Trip
Two-Week Itinerary

Atlantic Highlights

Wild, windswept and whale-riddled, a trip through the Atlantic provinces unfurls sea-and-cliff vistas, Viking vestiges and Celtic heritage. From foot-tapping music to buttery lobster feasts, this is satisfying traveling.

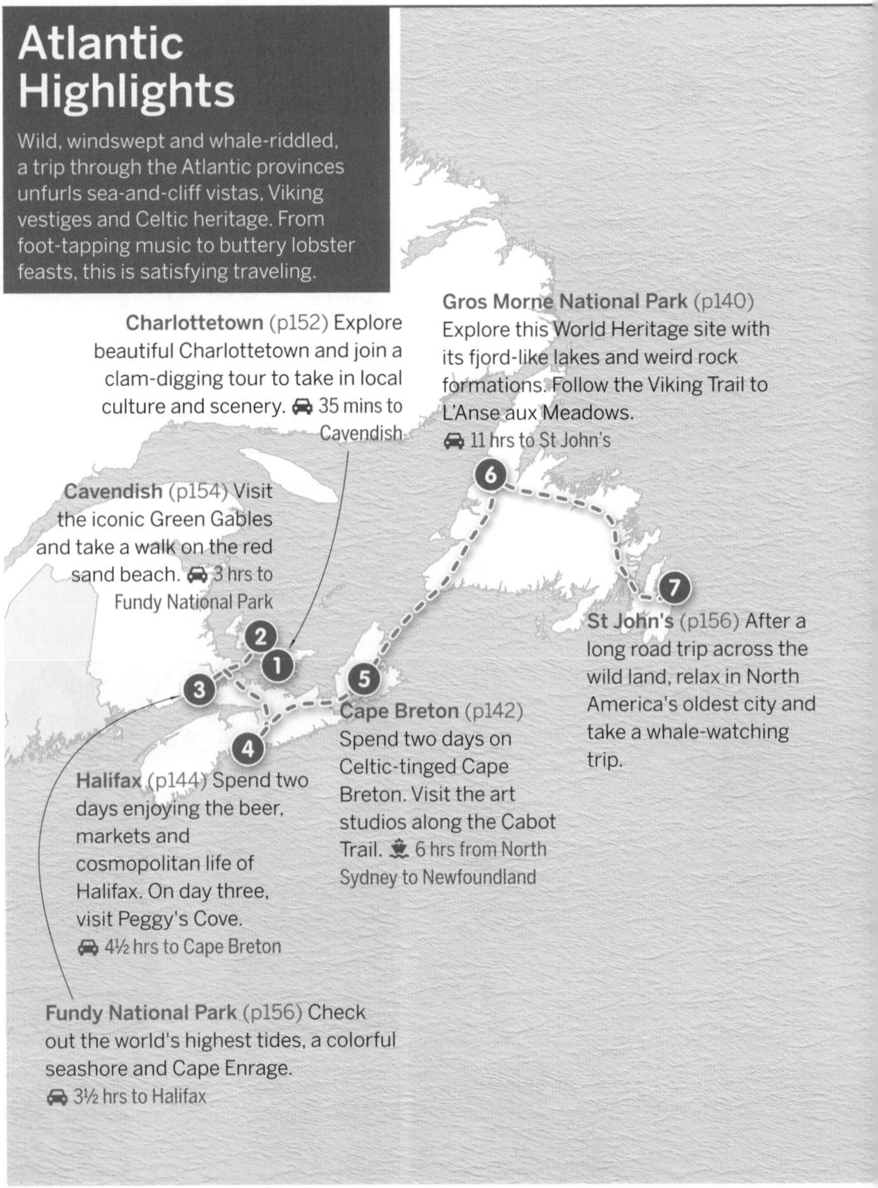

Charlottetown (p152) Explore beautiful Charlottetown and join a clam-digging tour to take in local culture and scenery. 35 mins to Cavendish

Cavendish (p154) Visit the iconic Green Gables and take a walk on the red sand beach. 3 hrs to Fundy National Park

Fundy National Park (p156) Check out the world's highest tides, a colorful seashore and Cape Enrage. 3½ hrs to Halifax

Halifax (p144) Spend two days enjoying the beer, markets and cosmopolitan life of Halifax. On day three, visit Peggy's Cove. 4½ hrs to Cape Breton

Cape Breton (p142) Spend two days on Celtic-tinged Cape Breton. Visit the art studios along the Cabot Trail. 6 hrs from North Sydney to Newfoundland

Gros Morne National Park (p140) Explore this World Heritage site with its fjord-like lakes and weird rock formations. Follow the Viking Trail to L'Anse aux Meadows. 11 hrs to St John's

St John's (p156) After a long road trip across the wild land, relax in North America's oldest city and take a whale-watching trip.

5

Plan Your Trip
Family Travel

ELENA ELISSEEVA / SHUTTERSTOCK ©

Choosing Your Destination

Deciding where to go with your kids in Canada can be a daunting decision. Mountains, prairies, beaches and easygoing cities are strewn across six time zones. Luckily, between wildlife sightings, cowboy encounters, hands-on pirate history, hunting for dinosaur fossils and ice-skating on mountain lakes, it's impossible to make a bad choice.

Outdoor Activities

Canada is all about open spaces, fresh air, rivers, lakes, mountains, snow, sand and wildlife.

Most Canadian cities are endowed with parks and promenades set up for even the tiniest of cyclists, while the Canadian National Parks system contains easy strolls as well as longer hiking trails. Horseback riding can be especially fun in cowboy country around Calgary.

Most lake areas offer canoe rentals perfect for family outings, and seafront regions are packed with kayak outfits. For a bigger adrenaline rush for older kids, try white-water rafting. On the coasts and the Bay of Fundy, whale-watching can be thrilling, and the small summer waves on the east and west coast are excellent for first-time surfers.

Skiing or snowboarding is an obvious family choice. Children under six often ski for free, and receive discounts up to the age of 18. There's also ice-skating, sledding and snowshoeing.

Museums & Monuments

Most large Canadian cities have science museums that specialize in hands-on activities, while at historic sites strewn across the country, costumed thespians get you right into the period and often give demonstrations of everything from blacksmithing to cooking. Teens usually enjoy these sites as well, since they are often large and diverse enough for self-exploration and touch on subjects they've studied at school.

Planning

Lonely Planet's *Travel with Children* offers a wealth of tips and tricks. The website Travel For Kids (www.travelforkids.com) is another good, general resource.

Note that children who are traveling to Canada without both parents need authorization from the non-accompanying parent. Sometimes this is enforced and other times not; play it safe with a notarized letter.

Accommodations

Some properties offer 'kids stay free' promotions, while others (particularly B&Bs) may not accept children. Ask when booking.

Camping is huge in Canada. Some campgrounds offer different options such as tipis or yurts, while others have swimming pools or minigolf. Cabins, which come with kitchens and other perks such as barbecues, are a great option. You can find full listings with each province's visitors guide online.

★ Best Destinations for Kids

Vancouver Island (p229)

The Rockies (p183)

Montréal (p93)

The Atlantic Provinces (p135)

Toronto (p35)

Eating Out

Everywhere you turn in Canada you'll find fast food and fried fare. A hurdle can be finding more wholesome options in small towns. Easy-to-find Canadian foods your kids will love if you let them include poutine (French fries topped with brown gravy and cheese), fish and chips, Montréal-style bagels (wood-fired, dense and slightly sweet), pancakes or French toast with maple syrup, bear-claw doughnuts, butter tarts and Nanaimo bars (crumb crust topped with custard and then melted chocolate).

Fort York National Historic Site (p42)

TORONTO

The Annex & University of Toronto
The gritty Annex neighbourhood is home to students from Canada's largest university, with its stately buildings.

Kensington Market & Chinatown
A dragon gate marks Chinatown's epicenter while Kensington Market is multicultural Toronto at its most interesting.

Financial District
Toronto's 'Wall Street' and the nicest of the skyscrapers are here, plus Union Station – Canada's busiest transport hub.

Toronto Pearson International (19km)

Billy Bishop Toronto City Airport

Lake Ontario

Entertainment District
Where you come to catch a baseball or hockey game, see a musical or comedy show, and spend a night on the town.

St Lawrence Market (p43)

Arriving in Toronto

Toronto Pearson International Airport The UP Express (adult/child $12.35/free) is the fastest way to get from the airport to downtown's Union Station; it leaves every 15 minutes from 5:30am to 1am. A taxi to downtown costs $60.

Billy Bishop Toronto City Airport A free ferry and pedestrian tunnel provide easy access to the mainland from this Toronto Islands airport. A free shuttle bus takes travelers to Union Station.

Where to Stay

Toronto has no shortage of accommodations, from high-rise hotels in the Financial District to boutique hotels in the West End. B&Bs are in residential neighborhoods, while hostels dot the city. Lodging can be expensive, especially in summer, when rooms sell quickly and at a premium. It's essential to book ahead, remembering that 13% tax will be added to the quoted rate. An additional 3% destination tax is sometimes levied too.

For more information on the best neighborhood to stay in, see p59.

CN Tower

This marvel of 1970s engineering – once the highest freestanding structure in the world – looks like a giant concrete hypodermic needle.

Great For...

☑ Don't Miss

The EdgeWalk, if you dare – a 20-minute outdoor walk around the unbounded perimeter of the main pod (356m).

The CN Tower's function as a communications mast takes a backseat to its role as a beacon to tourists. Even if you don't feel its pull, you're bound to catch a glimpse of the tower at night, when the entire structure puts on a brilliant free light show year-round. The best street-level vantage of the tower is at the intersection of McCaul St and Queen St W, due north of the tower.

Queues for the elevator can be up to two hours long in each direction.

History

The 1960s construction boom saw a surge in skyscrapers filling Toronto's skyline that dwarfed the city's transmission towers. The solution was rather extreme: 1537 workers toiled 24 hours a day for five days a week for over three years. In 1975, when a helicopter placed the final piece of the

ARCHITECT: JOHN ANDREWS; BOBNOAH / SHUTTERSTOCK ©

antenna in place, the CN Tower became the tallest free-standing structure in the world, a title it held until 2007. Built to withstand an earthquake of 8.5 on the Richter scale and winds of up to 420km/h, it continues to provide some of the clearest reception in North America.

Lookout-Level Views

A 58-second ride on a glass-fronted elevator leads to perhaps the most spectacular sight in the city: a 360-degree view of Toronto, spread below like a shimmering carpet. Floor-to-ceiling windows make it seem as though you could reach out and touch the skyscrapers. (The windows also make taking photos easier: their darkness adjusts relative to the sunlight.) Come at twilight to see the city transform from day to night, almost magical with its twinkling lights.

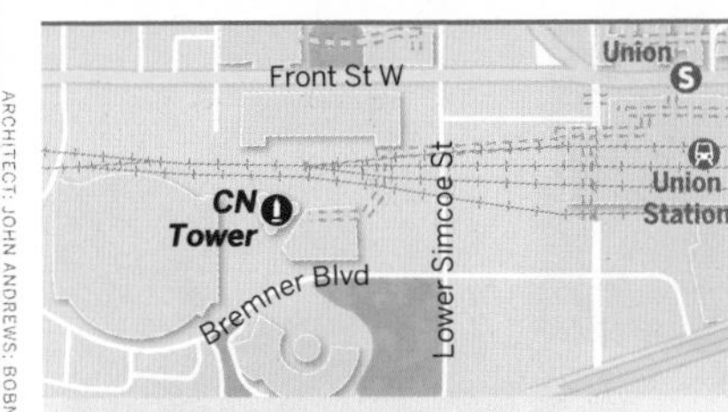

Need to Know

La Tour CN; Map p48; ☎416-868-6937; www.cntower.ca; 301 Front St W; Tower Experience adult/child $38/28; ⊙8:30am-11pm; 👪; Ⓢ Union

Take a Break

Take in views and a bite from **360°**, the obligatory revolving restaurant at the top. It's expensive, but the elevator price is waived for diners.

★ Top Tip

Buying tickets online saves 15%.

Outdoor Sky Terrace

The Outdoor Sky Terrace, 342m high, boasts the CN Tower's original glass floor – the world's first when it was inaugurated in 1994. (There's now another one a level up.) Walking across it, seemingly nothing between your steps and the city streets far below, is surprisingly difficult, even for those with no fear of heights. Don't worry, it won't break – designed to withstand the weight of 35 moose, each floor panel is 6.35cm thick, with four layers of clear tempered glass plus a layer of air for insulation to keep the room warm.

EdgeWalk

Those with nerves of steel can walk around the 1.5m-wide perimeter of the main pod, with no windows, no fence, no nothing between you and the city far below. Leaning forward over the tips of your toes is encouraged. (Gulp.) A tether to a metal rail keeps you safe.

Diverse Dining

From Azerbaijan to Zimbabwe, and everywhere in between, nowhere is Toronto's multiculturalism more potent and thrilling than on the plates of its restaurants.

Great For...

☑ Don't Miss

Following vitamin-D-starved locals to patio bars and restaurants when the sun peeks out.

Eating here is a delight – you'll find everything from Korean walnut cakes to sweat-inducing Thai curries, New York steaks and good ol' Canuck pancakes with peameal bacon and maple syrup. Fusion food is hot: traditional Western recipes spiked with handfuls of zingy Eastern ingredients and cooked with pan-Asian flare. British influences also linger – hearty lunchtime pints and formal afternoon high teas are much-loved traditions.

Eating by Neighborhood

Executive diners file into classy restaurants in the Financial District and Old Town, while eclectic, affordable eateries fill Baldwin Village, Kensington Market, Queen West, Ossington Av and the Yonge St strip. More ethnically consistent are Little Italy, Greek-town, Little India and Chinatown.

ROSANNA U / GETTY IMAGES ©

Old-School Diners

In a city where franchised everything is inescapable, and where restaurants come and go, it's refreshing to know that some things never change. We've sniffed out some of Toronto's classic diners, greasy spoons and cheap eats to transport you back to the golden age of tasty home cooking and vinyl and laminate booths.

Patrician Grill (☎416-366-4841; http://patriciangrill.com; 219 King St E; meals $5-16; ⏰7am-4pm Mon-Fri, 8am-2pm Sat; Ⓢ King)

Avenue Open Kitchen (Map p48; ☎416-504-7131; https://aveopenkitchen.ca; 7 Camden St; mains $5-12; ⏰7am-4pm Mon-Fri, 8am-3pm Sat; 🚊504)

Golden Diner (Map p44; ☎416-977-9898; 105 Carlton St; mains $7-16; ⏰6am-9pm; Ⓢ College)

ℹ Need to Know

Whenever possible, make a reservation – especially on weekends and for prime real estate on the patios.

✕ Take a Break

For people-watching (almost) 24/7, hit **Thompson Diner** (Map p48; ☎416-601-3533; www.thompsondiner.com; 550 Wellington St W; breakfast/mains from $11/14; ⏰6am-3am; 🚊504, 511).

★ Top Tip

Look out for good-value menus during the Winterlicious (www.toronto.ca/winterlicious) and Summerlicious (www.toronto.ca/summerlicious) food festivals, held in January and July respectively.

Gale's Snack Bar (539 Eastern Ave; meals $2-4; ⏰10am-6pm Mon-Fri, to 5pm Sat; 🚊501, 502, 503)

Senator Restaurant (Map p44; ☎416-364-7517; www.thesenator.com; 249 Victoria St; mains $18-36; ⏰7:30am-2:30pm Mon, to 9pm Tue-Fri, 8am-2:30pm & 4:30-9pm Sat, 8am-2:30pm Sun; Ⓢ Dundas)

Vegetarian Havens

Meat- and/or dairy-free eating options in food-obsessed Toronto run the gamut from gourmet to passé. These are sure-fire hits:

Govinda's (Map p44; ☎888-218-1040; www.govindas.ca; 243 Avenue Rd; meal platters adult/child $10/5; ⏰noon-2:30pm & 6-9pm Mon-Sat; 🖋; Ⓢ Rosedale)

Kupfert & Kim (Map p48; ☎416-504-2206; www.kupfertandkim.com; 140 Spadina Ave; mains $10-12; ⏰8am-10pm Mon-Fri, 9am-10pm Sat, 9am-9pm Sun; ❄📶🖋🐾; Ⓢ Osgoode, 🚊501) 🍃

Urban Herbivore (Map p44; ☎416-927-1231; www.herbivore.to; 64 Oxford St; mains $9-14; ⏰10am-7pm; 🖋; 🚊510)

SIGHTS

Downtown Toronto is an easy-to-navigate grid bounded by a hodgepodge of bohemian, cultural and historic neighborhoods. Yonge St, the world's longest thoroughfare, dissects the city: an East or West designation indicates a street's position relative to Yonge.

Most sights are found in the Waterfront, Entertainment and Financial Districts at the southern end of downtown.

Waterfront

Harbourfront Centre Arts Center

(Map p48; 416-973-4000; www.harbourfrontcentre.com; 235 Queens Quay W; 10am-11pm Mon-Sat, to 9pm Sun; P; 509, 510) An artistic powerhouse, this 4-hectare complex educates and entertains Toronto's community through a variety of year-round performances, events and exhibits. The center is made up of more than two dozen waterfront venues, including parks, outdoor stages, theaters and galleries. The main building alone houses the well-respected **Craft & Design Studios**, open studios where the public can watch artists-in-residence at work; the 1300-seat **Concert Stage**; and even the lakeside **Natrel Rink** (416-954-9866; 9am-10pm Sun-Thu, to 11pm Fri & Sat Nov-Mar;) FREE where you can slice up the winter ice.

Power Plant Contemporary Art Gallery Gallery

(Map p48; 416-973-4949; www.thepowerplant.org; 231 Queens Quay W; 10am-5pm Tue, Wed & Fri-Sun, to 8pm Thu; P; 509, 510) FREE Easily recognized by its painted smokestack, the Power Plant gallery is just that: a former power plant transformed into Toronto's premier gallery of contemporary art. Best of all, it's free and exhibitions change regularly. Free kid-centered tours and workshops are offered throughout the month; call to reserve a spot. It's part of the Harbourfront Centre complex.

Fort York National Historic Site Historic Site

(Map p48; 416-392-6907; www.fortyork.ca; 250 Fort York Blvd; adult/child $14/6; 10am-5pm Jun-Aug, 10am-4pm Mon-Fri, to 5pm Sat & Sun Sep-May; P; 509, 511) Established by the British in 1793 to defend the then-town of York, Fort York was almost entirely destroyed during the War of 1812 when a small band of Ojibwe warriors and British troops were unable to defeat their US attackers. Several structures – barracks, block houses and powder magazines – were immediately rebuilt and still stand on the 17-hectare site. From May to September, men decked out in 19th-century British military uniforms carry out marches and drills, firing musket volleys into the sky.

Entertainment & Financial Districts

401 Richmond Gallery

(Map p48; 416-595-5900; www.401richmond.com; 401 Richmond St W; 9am-7pm Mon-Fri, to 6pm Sat; 510) FREE Inside an early-20th-century lithographer's warehouse, restored in 1994, this 18,500-sq-meter New York–style artists collective hums with the creative vibes of more than 140 contemporary galleries, exhibition spaces, studios and shops representing works in almost any medium you can think of. Speaker series and film fests are held throughout the year. Grab a snack at the ground-floor cafe (open 9am to 5pm Monday to Friday) and enjoy it on the expansive roof garden, a little-known oasis in summer.

Hockey Hall of Fame Museum

(Map p48; 416-360-7765; www.hhof.com; Brookfield Pl, 30 Yonge St; adult/child $20/14; 9:30am-6pm Mon-Sat, 10am-6pm Sun Jun-Sep, 10am-5pm Mon-Fri, 9:30am-6pm Sat, 10:30am-5pm Sun Oct-May; ; S Union) Inside the rococo gray-stone Bank of Montreal building (c 1885), the Hockey Hall of Fame is a Canadian institution. Even those unfamiliar with the rough, super-fast sport are likely to be impressed by this, the world's largest collection of hockey memorabilia.

The Power Plant building

Check out the goalkeeping masks that are *Texas Chainsaw Massacre*–esque or go head-to-head with the great Wayne Gretzky, virtual-reality style. And, of course, be sure to take a pic with the beloved Stanley Cup.

Ripley's Aquarium of Canada Aquarium

(Map p48; ☎647-351-3474; www.ripleysaquariumofcanada.com; 288 Bremner Blvd; adult/child $32/22; ⏰9am-11pm; 👪; Ⓢ Union)
Arguably one of Toronto's best attractions for both young and old, it has more than 16,000 aquatic animals and 5.7 million liters of water in the combined tanks. There are touch tanks, a glass tunnel with a moving walkway, educational dive presentations...and even live jazz on the second Friday of each month. Open 365 days a year. Peak hours are 11am to 4pm.

Old Town, Corktown & Distillery District

Distillery District Area

(☎416-364-1177; www.thedistillerydistrict.com; 9 Trinity St; ⏰10am-7pm Mon-Wed, to 8pm Thu-Sat, 11am-6pm Sun; 🚌72, 🚋503, 504)

> *Toronto's premier gallery of contemporary art*

Centered on the 1832 Gooderham and Worts distillery – once the British Empire's largest – the 5-hectare Distillery District is one of Toronto's best downtown attractions. Its Victorian industrial warehouses have been converted into soaring galleries, artists studios, design boutiques, cafes and eateries. On weekends newlyweds pose before a backdrop of red brick and cobblestone, young families walk their dogs and the fashionable shop for art beneath charmingly decrepit gables and gantries. In summer expect live jazz, activities, exhibitions and foodie events.

St Lawrence Market Complex Market

(Map p48; ☎416-392-7219; www.stlawrencemarket.com; 92-95 Front St E; ⏰8am-6pm Tue-Thu, to 7pm Fri, 5am-5pm Sat; Ⓟ; 🚋503, 504)
Old To's sensational St Lawrence Market has been a neighborhood meeting place

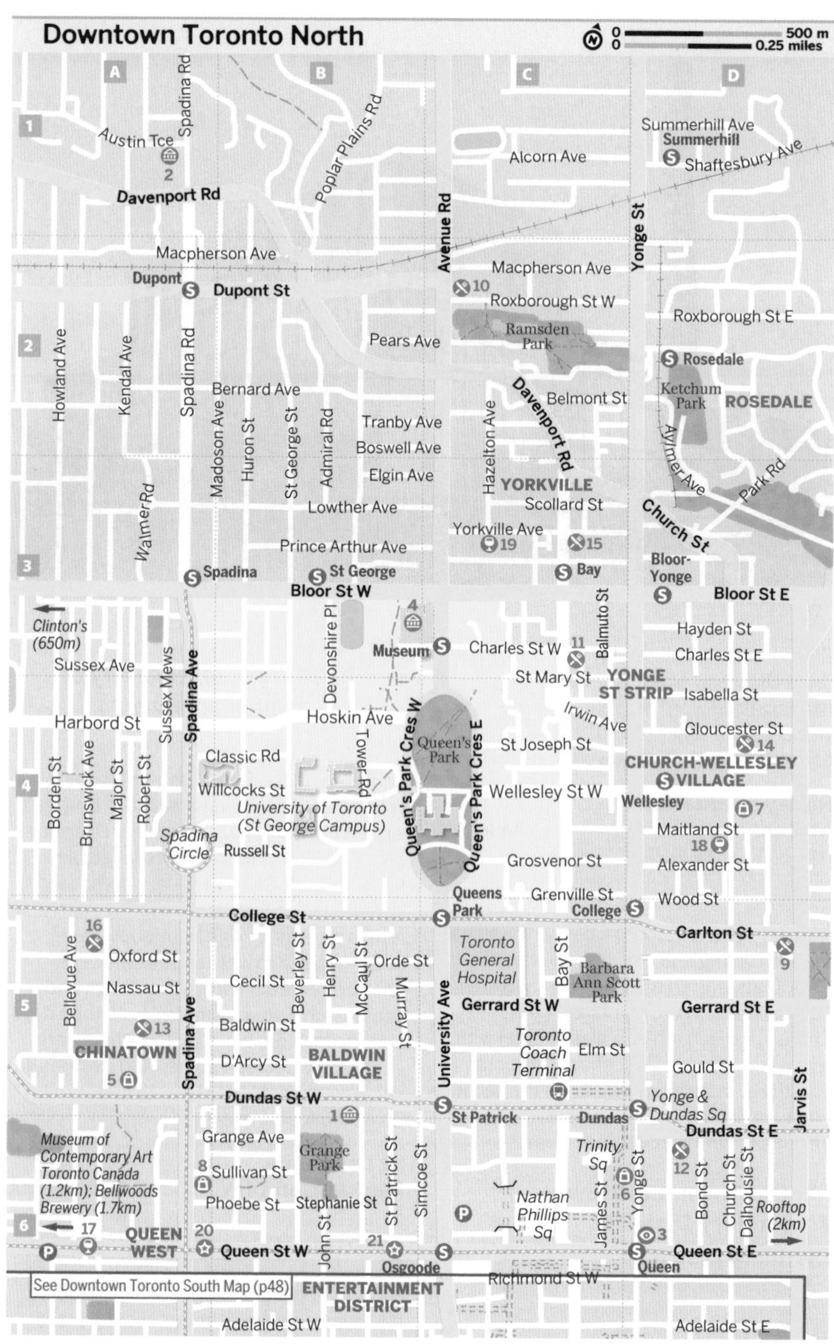

Downtown Toronto North
0 500 m
0 0.25 miles
Summerhill Ave
Summerhill
Shaftesbury Ave
Alcorn Ave
Austin Tce
Spadina Rd
Poplar Plains Rd
Davenport Rd
Avenue Rd
Yonge St
Macpherson Ave
Dupont
Dupont St
10
Roxborough St W
Roxborough St E
Ramsden Park
Pears Ave
Rosedale
Howland Ave
Kendal Ave
Bernard Ave
Belmont St
Ketchum Park
ROSEDALE
Madoson Ave
Huron St
St George St
Admiral Rd
Tranby Ave
Boswell Ave
Elgin Ave
Hazelton Ave
Aylmer Ave
Park Rd
Walmer Rd
YORKVILLE
Scollard St
Lowther Ave
Church St
Yorkville Ave
19
15
Prince Arthur Ave
Spadina
St George
Bay
Bloor-Yonge
Bloor St W
Bloor St E
4
Clinton's (650m)
Hayden St
Devonshire Pl
Museum
Charles St W
11
Balmuto St
Charles St E
Sussex Ave
Sussex Mews
Spadina Ave
St Mary St
YONGE ST STRIP
Isabella St
Hoskin Ave
Irwin Ave
Harbord St
Queen's Park Cres W
Queen's Park
Queen's Park Cres E
Gloucester St
Classic Rd
Tower Rd
St Joseph St
14
CHURCH-WELLESLEY VILLAGE
Borden St
Brunswick Ave
Major St
Robert St
Willcocks St
Wellesley St W
Wellesley
7
University of Toronto (St George Campus)
Maitland St
18
Spadina Circle
Russell St
Grosvenor St
Alexander St
Queens Park
Grenville St
College
Wood St
College St
Carlton St
16
Toronto General Hospital
Bay St
9
Bellevue Ave
Oxford St
Beverley St
Henry St
McCaul St
Orde St
Barbara Ann Scott Park
Nassau St
Cecil St
Murray St
University Ave
Gerrard St W
Gerrard St E
13
Baldwin St
Toronto Coach Terminal
Elm St
CHINATOWN
D'Arcy St
BALDWIN VILLAGE
Gould St
5
Jarvis St
Dundas St W
Yonge & Dundas Sq
1
St Patrick
Dundas
Dundas St E
Museum of Contemporary Art Toronto Canada (1.2km); Bellwoods Brewery (1.7km)
Grange Ave
Grange Park
St Patrick St
Simcoe St
Trinity Sq
12
8
Sullivan St
Phoebe St
Stephanie St
Nathan Phillips Sq
James St
6
Bond St
Church St
Dalhousie St
Rooftop (2km)
17
QUEEN WEST
20
John St
21
3
Queen St W
Queen St E
Osgoode
Queen
See Downtown Toronto South Map (p48)
ENTERTAINMENT DISTRICT
Richmond St W
Adelaide St W
Adelaide St E

Downtown Toronto North

Sights
1 Art Gallery of Ontario B5
2 Casa Loma A1
3 Elgin & Winter Garden Theatre D6
4 Royal Ontario Museum B3

Shopping
5 Courage My Love A5
6 Eaton Centre D6
7 Glad Day D4
8 Sonic Boom A6

Eating
9 Golden Diner Family Restaurant D5
10 Govinda's C2
11 Okonomi House C3
12 Senator Restaurant D6
13 Seven Lives A5
14 Smith D4
15 Trattoria Nervosa C3
16 Urban Herbivore A5

Drinking & Nightlife
17 BarChef A6
18 O'Grady's D4
19 Oxley C3

Entertainment
20 Horseshoe Tavern A6
21 Rex B6

for over two centuries. The restored, high-trussed 1845 **South Market** houses more than 120 specialty food stalls and shops: cheese vendors, fishmongers, butchers, bakers and pasta makers. The **Carousel Bakery** is famed for its peameal-bacon sandwiches, as is **St Urbain** for its authentic Montréal-style bagels.

Downtown Yonge

Elgin & Winter Garden Theatre Theater

(Map p44; ☎416-314-2871; www.heritagetrust.on.ca/ewg; 189 Yonge St; tours adult/student $12/10; SQueen) This restored masterpiece is the world's last operating Edwardian double-decker theater. Celebrating its centennial in 2013, the Winter Garden was built as the flagship for a vaudeville chain that never really took off, while the downstairs Elgin was converted into a movie house in the 1920s. Today it serves as a stage for traveling Broadway shows. Fascinating tours run at 5pm Monday and 10am Saturday.

Kensington Market & Chinatown

Art Gallery of Ontario Gallery

(AGO; Map p44; ☎416-979-6648; www.ago.net; 317 Dundas St W; adult/under 25yr $25/free, 6-9pm Wed free; ⊙10:30am-5pm Tue & Thu, to 9pm Wed & Fri, to 5:30pm Sat & Sun; 505) The AGO houses collections both excellent and extensive (bring your stamina). Renovations of the facade, designed by the revered Frank Gehry and completed in 2008, impress at street level: it's like looking at a huge crystal ship docked on a busy city street. Inside, highlights of the permanent collection include rare Québecois religious statuary, Inuit carvings, stunningly presented works by Canadian greats the Group of Seven, the Henry Moore sculpture pavilion, and restored Georgian house The Grange.

There's a surcharge for special exhibits, but there are also several highly recommended – and free – tours offered throughout the week, all leaving from the Walker Court. The most popular? Daily one-hour tours leaving on the hour from 11am to 3pm and on Wednesdays and Fridays at 7pm. If you don't want to commit that much time, 10-minute pop-up 'On the Dot' art chats are held in front of different works every day on the half-hour from 11:30am to 3:30pm and on Wednesdays and Fridays at 7:30pm.

Yorkville & the Annex

Royal Ontario Museum Museum

(ROM; Map p44; ☎416-586-8000; www.rom.on.ca; 100 Queen's Park; adult/child $23/14, 5:30-8:30pm 3rd Mon of month free; ⊙10am-5:30pm, to 8:30pm 3rd Mon of month; SMuseum) Opened in 1914, the multidisciplinary ROM is Canada's biggest natural-history museum and one of the largest museums in North America. You'll either love or loathe the synergy between the original heritage buildings at the main entrance on Bloor St and the 2007 addition of 'the Crystal,' which appears to pierce the original structure and juts out into the street like a massive shard. There are free docent-led tours daily.

Casa Loma Historic Building

(Map p44; ☎416-923-1171; www.casaloma.org; 1 Austin Tce; adult/child $33/23; ⏰9:30am-5pm, last entry 4pm; P; 🚌127, S Dupont) Toronto's only castle may never have housed royalty, but it certainly has grandeur, lording over the Annex from a cliff that was once the shoreline of the glacial Lake Iroquois, from which Lake Ontario derived. A self-guided audio tour leads visitors through the four levels of the Edwardian mansion as well as the 240m tunnel to the stables; the top floor houses a military museum. Head to the pool-turned-theater first, where a short film provides a good overview.

West End

High Park Park

(www.toronto.ca/parks; 1873 Bloor St W; ⏰dawn-dusk; P 👪; S High Park, 🚋501, 506, 508) Toronto's favorite green space is a wonderful spot to unfurl a picnic blanket, swim, play tennis, bike around, skate on 14-hectare **Grenadier Pond** or – in spring – meander through the groves of cherry blossoms donated by the Japanese ambassador in 1959. Several nature walks, workshops and talks are organized by the Nature Centre (www.highparknaturecentre.com) and led by rangers. **Shakespeare in High Park** (☎416-368-3110; www.canadianstage.com; suggested donation adult/child $20/free; ⏰8pm Tue-Sun Jul-Sep) has been produced in the park's amphitheater for almost 40 years.

Museum of Contemporary Art Toronto Museum

(MOCA Toronto; ☎416-530-2500; http://museumofcontemporaryart.ca; 158 Sterling Rd; adult/child $10/free, 10am-2pm last Sun of month free; ⏰10am-5pm Wed-Mon, to 9pm Fri;

Casa Loma interior

KIEV.VICTOR / SHUTTERSTOCK ©

P ♿; S Lansdowne, 306, 506) Housed in what was once Toronto's tallest building – a factory producing aluminum parts – MOCA exhibits innovative works by Canadian and international artists that address themes of contemporary relevance. Exhibits change four times per year, but all seek to provoke and engage viewers, whether they like what they see or not.

Toronto Islands

There's no better place to admire Toronto's scenic skyline and enjoy a day of biking and beach-going than the Toronto Islands. Just 2km offshore, on a clear day the islands offer spectacular views back toward the city. Several rustic beaches are accessible via lakeshore bike paths and simple roads; best of all, the islands are car-free except for a few service vehicles. With a historic amusement park and even a petting zoo, things definitely get jammed in summer – and especially on weekends – but indie-minded travelers can still find pockets of true getaway.

Ward's Island Island

(www.torontoisland.com; Ward's Island) The most residential of the Toronto Islands, Ward's has funky old houses crowded together and narrow pedestrian and cyclist-only streets. At the island's western end is an 18-hole **Disc Golf Course** (www.discgolfontario.com; dawn-dusk) FREE. An old-fashioned boardwalk runs the length of the southern shore, starting at **Ward's Island Beach** (beach hotline 416-392-7161; Lakeshore Ave) and passing the back gate of **Riviera cafe** (416-203-2152; www.islandriviera.com; 102 Lakeshore Ave; mains $12-17; 11am-11pm;) with its lovely patio.

East Toronto & Rosedale

Evergreen Brick Works Park

(416-596-7670; www.evergreen.ca; 550 Bayview Ave; 9am-5pm Mon-Fri, 8am-5pm Sat, 10am-5pm Sun; P ♿; 28A, S Broadview) FREE Famed for the transformation of its once-deteriorating heritage buildings into a prime location for all things geotourism,

Cycling Toronto

For cyclists, the **Martin Goodman Trail** (Map p48; Queens Quay W), a 56km-long paved recreational trail running along the Beaches and the Waterfront to the Humber River in the west, is the place to go. Head for the lake and you'll find it. On the way you can connect to the Don Valley mountain-bike trails at Cherry St as well as leafy High Par in the West End. On the Toronto Islands, the south-shore boardwalk and the interconnecting paved paths are car free. For a longer trek, the Martin Goodman Trail is part of the Lake Ontario Waterfront Trail (www.waterfronttrail.org), stretching 450km from east of Toronto to Niagara-on-the-Lake.

If you choose to explore Toronto by bike, stick to marked cycling trails when possible. Although many locals cycle to work, downtown is fraught with peril: aggressive drivers, streetcars and phone-blinded pedestrians. Cyclists do get hit by car doors, and rider accidents from connecting with streetcar tracks aren't uncommon. Though there's no legal requirement that adults wear a helmet in Ontario, anyone 17 and younger must wear one.

Essential information for cyclists can be found at www.toronto.ca/cycling/map. For real-time route planning, go to www.ridethecity.com.

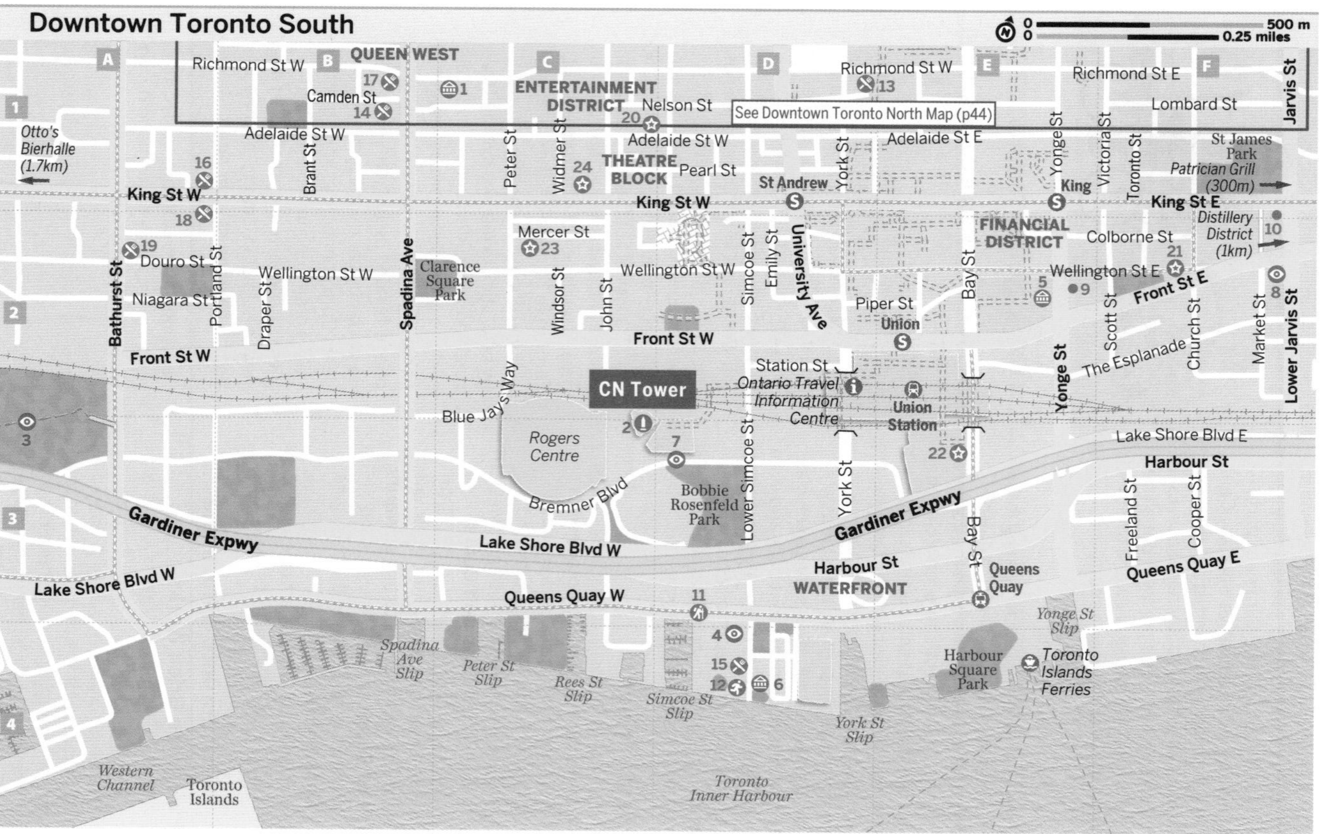

Downtown Toronto South
500 m
0.25 miles
QUEEN WEST
ENTERTAINMENT DISTRICT
THEATRE BLOCK
FINANCIAL DISTRICT
WATERFRONT
See Downtown Toronto North Map (p44)
Otto's Bierhalle (1.7km)
Patrician Grill (300m)
Distillery District (1km)
CN Tower
Rogers Centre
Bobbie Rosenfeld Park
Clarence Square Park
Harbour Square Park
St James Park
Ontario Travel Information Centre
Union Station
Union
St Andrew
King
Queens Quay
Toronto Islands Ferries
Toronto Inner Harbour
Toronto Islands
Western Channel
Richmond St W
Richmond St E
Camden St
Nelson St
Lombard St
Adelaide St W
Adelaide St E
Pearl St
King St W
King St E
Mercer St
Colborne St
Douro St
Wellington St W
Wellington St E
Niagara St
Piper St
Front St W
Front St E
Station St
The Esplanade
Blue Jays Way
Lake Shore Blvd E
Lake Shore Blvd W
Harbour St
Bremner Blvd
Gardiner Expwy
Queens Quay W
Queens Quay E
Bathurst St
Brant St
Portland St
Draper St
Spadina Ave
Peter St
Widmer St
Windsor St
John St
Simcoe St
Lower Simcoe St
Emily St
University Ave
York St
Bay St
Yonge St
Victoria St
Toronto St
Scott St
Church St
Market St
Jarvis St
Lower Jarvis St
Freeland St
Cooper St
Spadina Ave Slip
Peter St Slip
Rees St Slip
Simcoe St Slip
York St Slip
Yonge St Slip

Downtown Toronto South

Sights

1 401 Richmond C1
2 CN Tower C3
3 Fort York National Historic Site A3
4 Harbourfront Centre D4
5 Hockey Hall of Fame E2
6 Power Plant Contemporary Art Gallery D4
7 Ripley's Aquarium of Canada D3
8 St Lawrence Market Complex F2

Activities, Courses & Tours

9 Chariots of Fire E2
10 Heritage Toronto F1
11 Martin Goodman Trail D3
12 Natrel Rink D4

Eating

13 Assembly Chef's Hall D1
14 Avenue Open Kitchen B1
15 Boxcar Social D4
16 Buca A1
17 Kupfert & Kim B1
18 Lee A2
19 Thompson Diner A2

Entertainment

20 Adelaide Hall C1
21 Reservoir Lounge F2
22 Scotiabank Arena E3
23 Second City Toronto C2
24 TIFF Bell Lightbox C1
Toronto Maple Leafs .... (see 22)

this dynamic, LEED-certified environmental center and park hosts interactive workshops and community festivals on the themes of ecology, technology and the environment. There's a garden market, an ice rink and lots of nature trails, which can be explored on foot or by bike (rentals are available). Check the website to see what's going on. Take the free shuttle bus from Broadview subway station.

ACTIVITIES

Toronto Island SUP — Water Sports

(416-899-1668; www.torontoislandsup.com; 13 Algonquin Bridge Rd, Algonquin Island; 2hr tours from $79, yoga $49, rental 1st/additional hour $30/10; 10:30am-before sunset Mon-Fri, 10am-6pm Sat & Sun; Ward's Island) Join a paddleboard tour to explore the 14 islands that make up the Toronto Islands archipelago. Morning and afternoon excursions focus on flora and fauna, while night tours (with illuminated paddles) let you take in the city views. There are whimsical ukulele tours (yep, paddle and play) and yoga classes on the water, too. Rentals available. Launches are from Algonquin Bridge.

Boat House — Kayaking

(416-397-5166; Centre Island; 20min single kayak $19/43, double kayak $38/99, canoe $30/76; 11am-6pm Mon-Fri, to 7pm Sat & Sun; ; Centre Island) Explore the islands' waterways in a kayak or canoe. Look for the Boat House off Lakeshore Ave on the southern side of Centre Island, across the channel from **Centreville Amusement Park** (416-203-0405; www.centreisland.ca; all-day ride passes adult/child/family $36/27/118; 10:30am-8pm Jun-Aug, Sat & Sun only with earlier closing May & Sep;), a quaint park with an antique carousel, goofy golf course, miniature train and little-kids' rides.

TOURS

Chariots of Fire — Bus

(Map p48; 905-877-0855; www.tourniagarafalls.com; day tours $77; 7am-9pm Mon-Sat, 1-9pm Sun; King) This outfit offers low-cost day tours from Toronto to Niagara Falls, including free time in the historic village of Niagara-on-the-Lake and a winery tour. A boat ride on the *Hornblower Niagara* is available as an add-on. These guys are highly organized and comfortably present the best of the Falls, leaving from Toronto, for those who only have a day to experience it all. Highly recommended.

Heritage Toronto — Walking

(Map p48; 416-338-3886; www.heritagetoronto.org; 157 King St E; suggested donation $10; May-Oct) A diverse offering of fascinating historical, cultural and nature walks, as well as bus (TTC) tours, led by museum experts, neighborhood historical-society members and emerging historians. Tours generally last one to three hours. Check the website for a handful of downloadable self-guided tours too.

Toronto Bicycle Tours Cycling

(☎416-477-2184; https://torontobicycletours.com; adult/child from $46/75; ⏲8am-6pm) Offering year-round bike tours – even in winter (ponchos and gloves provided) – of downtown, 15 neighborhoods and the Toronto Islands. Excursions are for all levels and ages, and last 3½ to seven hours. Bike, helmet, water and snacks are provided (plus picnic lunch for longer tours). Multilingual guides or interpreters are available too.

SHOPPING

Shopping in Toronto is a big deal. When it's -20°C outside, you have to fill the gap between brunch and the movies with *something*, right? People like to update their wardrobes and redecorate their homes, or just walk around the sprawling **Eaton Centre** (Map p44; ☎416-598-8560; www.torontoeatoncentre.com; 220 Yonge St; ⏲10am-9:30pm Mon-Fri, 9:30am-9:30pm Sat, 10am-7pm Sun; 📶; Ⓢ Queen, Dundas). This habit continues through to summer, making boutique-hopping an excuse to hit the streets, or vice versa.

Arts Market Art

(☎416-778-9533; www.artsmarket.ca; 790 Queen St E; ⏲noon-5pm Mon-Tue, to 6pm Wed-Fri, 11am-6pm Sun; 🚋501, 502, 503) A collective of local artists displays and sells work at this eclectic shop. High quality and unique, there's everything from handcrafted cards and jewelry to pottery and portraits as well as a few vintage finds.

Courage My Love Vintage

(Map p44; ☎416-979-1992; 14 Kensington Ave; ⏲11am-6pm Mon-Sat, 1-5pm Sun; 🚋505, 510) Vintage-clothing stores have been around Kensington Market for decades, but Courage My Love amazes fashion mavens with its secondhand slip dresses, retro pants and white dress shirts in a cornucopia of styles. The beads, buttons, leather goods and silver jewelry are handpicked. Well stocked without being overwhelming.

From left: Kensington Market; glass decorations at a market stall; Eaton Centre

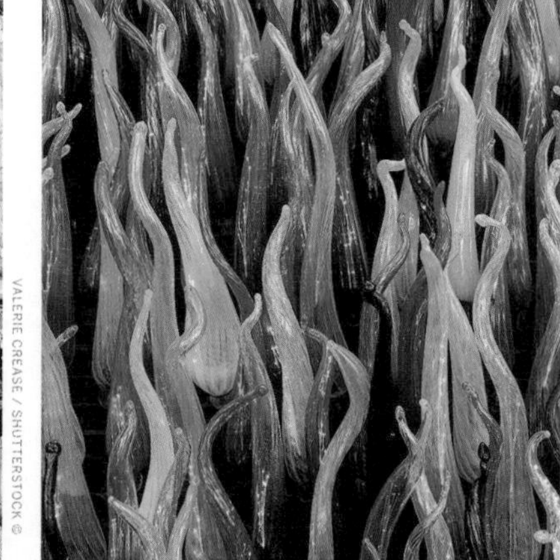

Sonic Boom
Music

(Map p44; ☎416-532-0334; https://sonicboommusic.com; 215 Spadina Ave; ⏰10am-10pm; 🚋310, 510) The largest indie record store in Canada, Sonic Boom has rows upon rows of new and used vinyl, CDs and even cassettes. Longtime staffers are deeply knowledgeable, offering direction and advice. Quirky T-shirts, irreverent souvenirs and coffee-table books (most with a musical bent) are sold at the front.

Glad Day
Books

(Map p44; ☎416-901-6600; www.gladdaybookshop.com; 499 Church St; ⏰10am-10pm Mon-Thu, to 2am Fri & Sat, 11am-7pm Sun; Ⓢ Wellesley) It's the oldest still-running gay bookstore in the world, making Glad Day an LGBTIQ+ landmark. The store has transformed from a place to defy censorship of LGBTIQ+ publications into an event and gathering space to promote creativity and further free speech. It's also a cafe and bar. Weekends mean Saturday-night dance parties and Sunday Drag Brunch.

EATING

Boxcar Social
Cafe $

(Map p48; ☎844-726-9227; www.boxcarsocial.ca; Harbourfront Centre, 235 Queens Quay W; mains $12-18; ⏰9am-5pm Mon, to 11pm Tue-Thu, to late Fri, 10am-late Sat, to 8pm Sun; 📶🍸; 🚋509, 510) An industrial-chic cafe/bar/coffee haven, Boxcar Social has enviable views of Lake Ontario. The menu matches the vibe, with fresh takes on salads and sandwiches (kale Caesar salad, anyone?). Mornings bring locals with coffee and computers; evenings bring drinks on the patio and twinkling lights.

Otto's Bierhalle
German $

(☎416-901-5472; www.ottosbierhalle.com; 1087 Queen St W; mains $10-16; ⏰noon-11pm Mon & Tue, to midnight Wed & Thu, to 2am Sat, to 10pm Sun; 🚋501) Garage doors, long communal tables, a wide selection of draft beers and ciders, huge platters of brats and schnitzels – it looks like Oktoberfest pretty much year-round here (the only thing missing is the oompah band). A popular spot with

an upbeat vibe, this place makes out-of-towners feel like part of the city. Reservations recommended on weekends.

Seven Lives Tacos $

(Map p44; ☎416-803-1086; 69 Kensington Ave; tacos from $6; ⏰noon-6pm Mon-Fri, to 7pm Sat & Sun; 🚋310, 510) What started as a pop-up taqueria is now a hole-in-the-wall place with lines of people snaking out the door, waiting to order Baja-style fish tacos: light and flaky mahi-mahi with pico de gallo, cabbage and a creamy sauce. Other seafood and veggie combos offered, too. Most diners eat standing or take their meal to nearby Bellevue Sq.

Okonomi House Japanese $

(Map p44; ☎416-925-6176; 23 Charles St W; mains $9-17; ⏰11:30am-3pm & 4:30-10pm Mon-Fri, noon-3pm & 4:30-10pm Sat; 🌶; Ⓢ Bloor-Yonge) Okonomi House is one of the only places in Toronto dishing up authentic *okonomiyaki* (savory Japanese cabbage pancakes filled with meat, seafood or vegetables). It's not fancy – just a step up from a diner – but it's a must for Japanophiles.

Smith Canadian $$

(Map p44; ☎416-926-2501; http://smithrestaurant.com; 553 Church St; mains $18-28; ⏰11am-4pm & 5-11pm Tue-Thu, to midnight Fri, 9am-4pm & 5pm-midnight Sat, 9am-4pm Sun; 🌶; Ⓢ Wellesley) Come to this bohemian-chic eatery in the heart of the Village for brunch, when the classics are served with flair: eggs Benedict with leek fondue, a short stack with maple cream cheese and candied lemon, or perhaps a Bloody Mary with a bouquet of bacon on top. Is your mouth watering yet? Reservations recommended.

Trattoria Nervosa Italian $$

(Map p44; ☎416-961-4642; www.eatnervosa.com; 75 Yorkville Ave; mains $17-33; ⏰11:30am-10pm Mon-Wed, to 11pm Thu-Sat, noon-10pm Sun; 📶; Ⓢ Bay) In the heart of fancy Yorkville, this restaurant is an attitude-free

> *less food court and more sprawling upscale eatery*

Eatery inside Assembly Chef's Hall

EQROY / SHUTTERSTOCK ©

oasis. The patio is a good corner from which to people-watch well-heeled passersby while you dig into simple, excellent pasta – the *mafalde ai funghi* has incredibly deep mushroom flavors without being overly creamy.

Assembly Chef's Hall Food Hall $$
(Map p48; 647-557-5993; www.assemblychefshall.com; 111 Richmond St E; mains $12-19; 7am-10pm Mon-Fri, 10am-10pm Sat; ; Osgoode) Home to a diverse set of global cuisines by some of Toronto's top chefs, this is less food court and more sprawling upscale eatery. There's everything from margherita pizza and pork *carnitas* tacos to *khao soi* beef. Weekday lunch hours are crowded with suits and professional attire (it's in the heart of the Financial District), but dinnertime is much more chill and relaxed.

Buca Italian $$$
(Map p48; 416-865-1600; www.buca.ca; 604 King St W; mains $17-55; 11am-3pm & 5-10pm Mon-Wed, 11am-3pm & 5-11pm Thu & Fri, 5-11pm Sat, 5-10pm Sun; 304, 504) A breathtaking basement-level restaurant with exposed-brick walls and a soaring ceiling, Buca serves artisanal Italian fare such as homemade pasta and nose-to-tail-style dishes such as *orecchio di maiale* (crispy pig ears) and *cervello* (lamb brains wrapped in prosciutto and sage). Ease into the experience with a charcuterie board of house-cured meats, flavorful cheeses and bread knots.

McMichael Canadian Art Collection

This **gallery** (905-893-1121; www.mcmichael.com; 10365 Islington Ave, Kleinburg; adult/child $18/15, Tue $15/12; 10am-5pm May-Oct, to 4pm Tue-Sun Nov-Apr; P; 13) comprised of handcrafted buildings (including painter Tom Thomson's cabin, moved from its original location) is set amid 40 hectares of conservation trails. It contains works by Canada's best-known landscape painters, the Group of Seven, as well as works by First Nations, Inuit, Métis and other acclaimed Canadian artists. It's a 34km, 45-minute drive from Toronto and totally worth the trip. A sculpture garden and the graves of gallery co-founders Robert and Signe McMichaels, as well as six of the Group of Seven artists, are also on-site.

Free tours are included with admission Wednesday to Sunday. Parking is $7.

First Nations mask

Ruby Watchco Canadian $$$
(416-465-0100; http://rubywatchco.ca; 730 Queen St E; prix fixe $58; 6-10pm Tue-Sat; 501, 502, 503) Creative farm-to-table comfort food is the game at this homey restaurant, run by two of Toronto's top chefs. (Chef Lynn even stars on the Food Network hit *Pitchin' In*.) A new menu is presented nightly, always four courses, always prix fixe. Expect dishes like fried chicken with rosemary honey and maple barbecue ribs; save room for the artisanal cheeses and decadent desserts.

Lee Asian $$$
(Map p48; 416-504-7867; www.susur.com/lee; 601 King St W; mains $16-38; 5-10:30pm Sun-Wed, to 11pm Thu, to 11:30pm Fri & Sat; ; 504, 508) Truly a feast for the senses, dinner at acclaimed *cuisinier* Susur Lee's self-titled flagship is an experience best shared. Slick servers assist in navigating the selection of East-meets-West delights: you really want to get the pairings right. It's impossible to adequately convey the dance of flavors, textures and aromas one experiences in the signature Singaporean slaw, with...how many ingredients?!

LGBTIQ+ Toronto

To say Toronto is LGBT-friendly is an understatement. That it embraces diversity more fully than most other centers of its size is closer to the mark. In 2003 Toronto became the first city in North America to legalize same-sex marriage. Just over a year later, an Ontario Court also recognized the first legal same-sex divorce.

Toronto's **Pride festival** (☎416-927-7433; www.pridetoronto.com; ⏲Jun) is one of the largest in the world, and lasts a month. At other times of the year, the Church St strip of the Village draws everyone from biker bears to lipstick lesbians to its modest smattering of sunny patios, pubs, cafes and restaurants for promenading and people-watching. After dark it's all about the dancing: whether for cabaret or drag, thumping Top 40 and R&B or queer alterna-punk.

Other gay-friendly neighborhoods include the Annex, Kensington, Queen West, Cabbagetown and Leslieville (aka 'Lesbianville'). Gay nightlife venues are abundant, and although men's bars and clubs vastly outnumber lesbian venues, Toronto is also home to drag kings, women-only bathhouse nights and lesbian reading series.

Toronto is a great place to be gay or to explore your sexuality. Head to the *Daily Xtra* (www.dailyxtra.com) online magazine for the latest scoop on LGBTIQ+ issues in the Village.

Toronto Pride Parade

DRINKING & NIGHTLIFE

O'Grady's Pub

(Map p44; ☎416-323-2822; www.ogradyschurch.com; 517 Church St; ⏲11am-2am; SWellesley) Come to this friendly Irish pub on Wednesdays for Dirty Bingo nights, when fabulous drag queens call out numbers and give winners risqué prizes from 9pm to midnight. On bingo-less nights, it's all about the patio – the Village's largest – which fills up as soon as the sun comes out. The kitchen, serving comfort food, stays open late.

Rooftop Rooftop Bar

(☎416-362-8439; www.thebroadviewhotel.ca; Broadview Hotel, 106 Broadview Ave; ⏲5pm-late Mon-Thu, 11:30am-late Fri-Sun; 🚋501, 502, 503) This rooftop bar with floor-to-ceiling windows and a wraparound patio affords guests a 360-degree view of Toronto and a breathtaking outlook on the city skyline. Shareables and finger foods – duck-fat popcorn with sea salt, anyone? – complement the cocktail and wine lists well. Sunsets are particularly busy. Reservations highly recommended.

BarChef Cocktail Bar

(Map p44; ☎416-868-4800; www.barcheftoronto.com; 472 Queen St W; cocktails $16-55; ⏲6pm-2am; SOsgoode) You'll hear 'oohs' and 'aahs' coming from the tables in the intimate near-darkness of this swanky bar as cocktails emerge alongside a bonsai tree or under a bell jar of vanilla and hickory-wood smoke. Beyond novelty, drinks show incredible, enticing complexity without overwhelming some unique flavors – truffle snow, chamomile syrup, cedar air, and soil!

Bellwoods Brewery Brewery

(www.bellwoodsbrewery.com; 124 Ossington Ave; ⏲2pm-midnight Mon-Wed, to 1am Thu & Fri, noon-1am Sat, to midnight Sun; 🚋505) Fresh, urban-chic Bellwoods pours award-winning beers, from pale ales and double IPAs to stouts and wild ales. With candles lighting up the main room and gallery, the brewery itself is decidedly cool and buzzing with locals. An elevated menu of small plates – cheese boards, chicken-liver mousse, mussels – complements the beers.

Oxley Pub

(Map p44; ☎647-348-1300; https://theoxley.com; 121 Yorkville Ave; ⏰11:30am-midnight Mon-Wed, to 1am Thu, to 2am Fri, 10am-2am Sat, to midnight Sun; 📶; Ⓢ Bay) A first-class British pub, the Oxley is located in a 19th-century row house in the heart of Yorkville. Two floors of leather seating, ornate wallpaper and Victorian-era decor attract business folk and the well-heeled hankering for a 20oz pour of craft beer, a glass of wine or a stiff drink. Classic English fare served, too.

✪ ENTERTAINMENT

As you might have guessed, there's always something going on here, from jazz to art-house cinema, offbeat theater, opera, punk rock and hockey. In summer, free festivals and outdoor concerts are the norm, but Toronto's dance and live-music scene keeps grooving year-round. LGBTIQ+ life is also rich and open, with plenty of clubs, groups, bar nights and activities for all.

Reservoir Lounge Jazz

(Map p48; ☎416-955-0887; www.reservoirlounge.com; 52 Wellington St E; cover $5-10; ⏰7:30pm-2am Tue-Sat; 🚋503, 504) Swing dancers, jazz singers and blues crooners call this cool, candlelit basement lounge home, and it has hosted its fair share of musical greats over the years. Where else can you enjoy a martini while dipping strawberries into chocolate fondue during the show? Tables are reserved for diners; prepare to drop at least $15 per person to sit down.

Horseshoe Tavern Live Music

(Map p44; ☎416-598-4226; www.horseshoetavern.com; 370 Queen St W; ⏰noon-2:30am; 🚋501, 510) Well past its 70th birthday, the legendary Horseshoe still plays a crucial role in the development of

> *This place oozes a history of good times*

Midnight Shine performs at the Horseshoe Tavern

local indie rock. This place oozes a history of good times and classic performances. Come for a beer and check it out.

Rex Jazz

(Map p44; ☎416-598-2475; www.therex.ca; 194 Queen St W; ⊙shows 6:30pm & 9:30pm Mon-Thu, 4pm, 6:30pm & 9:45pm Fri, noon, 3:30pm, 7pm & 9:45pm Sat & Sun; 501) The Rex has risen from its pugilistic, blue-collar past to become an outstanding jazz and blues venue. Over a dozen Dixieland, experimental and other local and international acts knock over the joint each week. Cheap drinks; affordable cover.

TIFF Bell Lightbox Cinema

(Map p48; ☎888-599-8433; www.tiff.net; 350 King St W; 504) Headquarters of the **Toronto International Film Festival** (TIFF; ⊙Sep), this resplendent cinema complex is the hub of all the action when the festival's in town. Throughout the year it's used primarily for TIFF Cinematheque, screening world cinema, independent films, directorial retrospectives and other special events. Try to see a film here if you can.

Toronto Maple Leafs Ice Hockey

(Map p48; ☎416-815-5982; www.mapleleafs.com; 40 Bay St; ⊙Oct-Apr; SUnion) The 13-time Stanley Cup–winning Maple Leafs slap the puck around **Scotiabank Arena** (Map p48; ☎416-815-5500; www.scotiabankarena.com; 40 Bay St; SUnion). Every game sells out with such fiery fans – hockey is intrinsic to the culture, after all – but a limited number of same-day tickets go on sale through Ticketmaster (www.ticketmaster.ca) at 10am and at the ticket window from 5pm. If you can score a ticket, it's worth the splurge.

Second City Toronto Comedy

(Map p48; ☎416-343-0011; www.secondcity.com/shows/toronto; 51 Mercer St; tickets $28-52, training-center tickets $5-15; SSt Andrews, 504) Running for decades, Second City has nightly improv and sketch-comedy

> *Every game sells out with such fiery fans*

Toronto Maple Leafs practice

STEVE RUSSELL / CONTRIBUTOR / GETTY IMAGES ©

shows that'll have you laughing all night long. Big-name comedians such as Catherine O'Hara and Mike Myers got their start here. Its training center, the **John Candy Box Theatre**, presents shows by students and budding comics with prices to match; the entrance is around the corner on Blue Jays Way.

Adelaide Hall Concert Venue

(Map p48; 647-344-1234; https://adelaidehallto.com; 250 Adelaide St W; 141, 143, 144, 145) One of the best small venues in town – its acoustics are tops – Adelaide Hall attracts both big-name and up-and-coming acts. On other nights, DJs and cover bands keep the place hopping. Look for the entrance tucked into an alley off Adelaide St (or just follow the line of people).

INFORMATION

Ontario Travel Information Centre (Map p48; 416-314-5899; www.ontariotravel.net; Union Station, 65 Front St W; 9am-6pm Mon-Sat, 10am-6pm Sun; Union) Knowledgeable multilingual staff and overflowing racks of brochures that cover every nook and cranny of Toronto and beyond.

GETTING THERE & AWAY

AIR

Most Canadian airlines and international carriers arrive at Canada's busiest airport, **Toronto Pearson International Airport** (YYZ; Lester B Pearson International Airport; Terminal 3 416-776-5100, Terminal 1 416-247-7678; http://torontopearson.com; 6301 Silver Dart Dr, Mississauga; UP Express), 27km northwest of downtown Toronto in the suburb of Mississauga: it's a giant and attracts one of the highest airport taxes in the world. (Don't worry, you'll have unknowingly paid that in the price of your ticket.) There are two terminals: Terminal 1 and Terminal 3; check the website or call your airline to confirm which one you'll be arriving into or leaving from to help with pickup/drop-off logistics. A free train connects the terminals as well as the Viscount Station, where car-rental-agency shuttles pick up customers.

The Beaches

The name says it all: the Beaches is a lovely part of Toronto where you can stroll along a broad boardwalk, dig your toes into the sand and even brave the chilly waters on a hot summer's day. It's no Turks and Caicos, of course, but it's still a scenic and relaxing escape from the city proper. And there's more: the Beaches is home to popular spots includ **Tommy Thompson Park** (416-661-6600; www.tommythompsonpark.ca; Leslie St; 4-9pm Mon-Fri, 5:30am-9pm Sat & Sun; 83 Jones S, 501), a birder's paradise, and **Woodbine Park** (www.toronto.ca; 1695 Queen St E; dawn-dusk; ; 501), home to various outdoor festivals. Meanwhile, Queen St E is loaded with shops and eateries catering to every taste.

REIMAR / SHUTTERSTOCK ©

BUS

Long-distance buses operate from the art deco **Toronto Coach Terminal** (Map p44; 416-393-4636; 610 Bay St; Dundas). Greyhound Canada (greyhound.ca) has numerous routes throughout the country from here, while Megabus (ca.megabus.com) has a smaller, and cheaper, selection of destinations. Advance tickets offer significant savings with both companies; online sales often close two hours before departure.

TRAIN

Union Station (416-869-3000; https://torontounion.ca; 140 Bay St; Union, 509, 510) downtown is Toronto's main rail hub. From here, **VIA Rail** (888-842-7245; www.viarail.ca) plies the heavily trafficked Windsor–Montréal corridor and beyond. Amtrak (www.amtrak.com) links Toronto with Buffalo, NY ($47, 4½ hours, two daily), and New York City ($131, 14 hours, two daily). GO Transit (www.gotransit.com) trains and buses also use the station, with an ever-expanding network of destinations, including Kitchener, Hamilton, Barrie and other Ontario locations, often with the cheapest rail fares.

 GETTING AROUND

TO/FROM THE AIRPORT

The fastest way to get downtown is the **Union Pearson Express** (UP Express; www.upexpress.com; 1 way adult/child/family of 5 $12.35/free/25.70, 1 way on PRESTO card $9.25; 5:30am-1am;) rail link. The comfortable trains leave every 15 minutes and take just 25 minutes to get to Union Station.

Taxis from Pearson to the city take anywhere from 40 to 70 minutes, depending on traffic. The Greater Toronto Airports Authority (GTAA) regulates fares by drop-off zone: it's $60 to downtown, $75 to destinations east of town. Don't pay more and remember to tip.

BOAT

From April to September **Toronto Islands Ferries** (Map p48; 416-392-8193; www.toronto.ca; 9 Queens Quay W; adult/child return $8.19/3.95; Union) services run from the terminal at the foot of Bay St to Centre Island (every 15 to 30 minutes from 8am to 11:15pm), Hanlan's Point (every 30 to 45 minutes from 6:30am to 10pm Monday to Friday, 8am to 10:45pm Saturday and Sunday) and Ward's Island (every 30 to 60 minutes from 6:35am to 11:15pm). From October to March services are slashed (to roughly hourly), only running to Ward's Island and Hanlan's Point.

PUBLIC TRANSPORTATION

Operated by the Toronto Transit Commission (TTC; www.ttc.ca), Toronto's antiquated subway, streetcar and bus system is adequate at best. Tickets, tokens, day passes and PRESTO cards can all be used on the TTC ($3.25/free per adult/child).

Bus Regular city buses run every 10 minutes from 6am (8am Sunday) to 1am daily. Check the TTC's website for maps and timetables.

Subway The two main subway lines are the crosstown Green line (Bloor–Danforth) and the U-shaped Yellow line (Yonge–University–Spadina).

Streetcars Run 24 hours daily. Service slows to every 30 minutes from 1:30am to 5am. Streetcars are notoriously slow during rush hours, stopping frequently.

TAXI

Taxis are abundant and easy to hail in downtown Toronto. Often, major hotels have a line of taxis outside. In outer neighborhoods you'll have to call a cab. In either case, metered fares start at $4.25, plus $1.75 per kilometer, depending on traffic. A tip of 15% to 20% is customary. Credit and debit cards are typically accepted.

Diamond Taxicab (416-366-6868; www.diamondtaxi.ca)

Maple Leaf Taxi (416-465-5555; www.mapleleaftaxi.com)

Royal Taxi (416-777-9222; www.royaltaxi.ca)

Where to Stay

Toronto has top-notch luxury hotels, but midrange rooms can feel drab and dated. There are some great hostels and plenty of B&Bs to choose from. Book in advance: the best digs fill up quickly in summer.

Neighborhood	Atmosphere
Waterfront	Outstanding views and amenities, and a little slice of resort-style living just minutes from the urban center; no midrange or budget hotels and few eating options.
Entertainment & Financial Districts	Killer views and a location that can't be beat, but prices can be prohibitive.
Kensington Market & Chinatown	Trendy neighbourhood with good food and thrift shopping and handy streetcars, Not many lodging options though and it can be noisy.
Old Town, Corktown & Distillery District	A plethora of restaurants, bars and sights readily accessible by foot, and close to public transit for trips further afield; few accommodations options.
Downtown Yonge	Home of the downtown core with plenty of midrange hotels; can feel a little sketchy, especially on Yonge St north of College.
Yorkville & the Annex	Residential areas near the museum district are home to B&Bs; Spadina Ave is packed with shops, restaurants and a few small budget options; can feel removed from some of the sights.
East Toronto & Rosedale	Gives you a neighborhood feel, yet with good dining and nightlife; removed from the major sights.

NIAGARA
REGION

In this Chapter

Niagara Region at a glance...

Jutting east from Hamilton and forming a natural divide between Lake Erie and Lake Ontario, the Niagara Peninsula is a legitimate tourist hot spot. A steep limestone escarpment jags along the spine of the peninsula, generating a unique microclimate. Humid and often frost free, this is prime terrain for viticulture: a fact not lost on the award-winning wineries of Niagara-on-the-Lake. Many visitors, of course, come to the peninsula to see just one thing – the staggering Niagara Falls – but there is plenty more to explore; consider a several-day visit to fully experience the delights of the region.

One Day in the Niagara Region

Spend the day exploring **Niagara Falls** (p64), starting early with a view of Horseshoe Falls from Table Rock. Don a plastic poncho and get up close with **Journey Behind the Falls** (p70), then feel the mist with **Hornblower Niagara Cruises** (p71). With your feet firmly back on the ground, check out the barrels at the **Daredevil Exhibit** (p70) and end with an interactive history lesson at **Niagara's Fury** (p70).

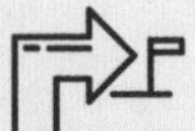

Three Days in the Niagara Region

Head out to **Niagara-on-the-Lake** and explore its history museums and quaint store-lined 19th-century streets. Dine at the classy **Prince of Wales Hotel** (p69) and stay in one of the charming local B&Bs. The next day explore the many top-notch vineyards of the surrounding **Wine Country**.

Previous page: Niagara Falls (p64)

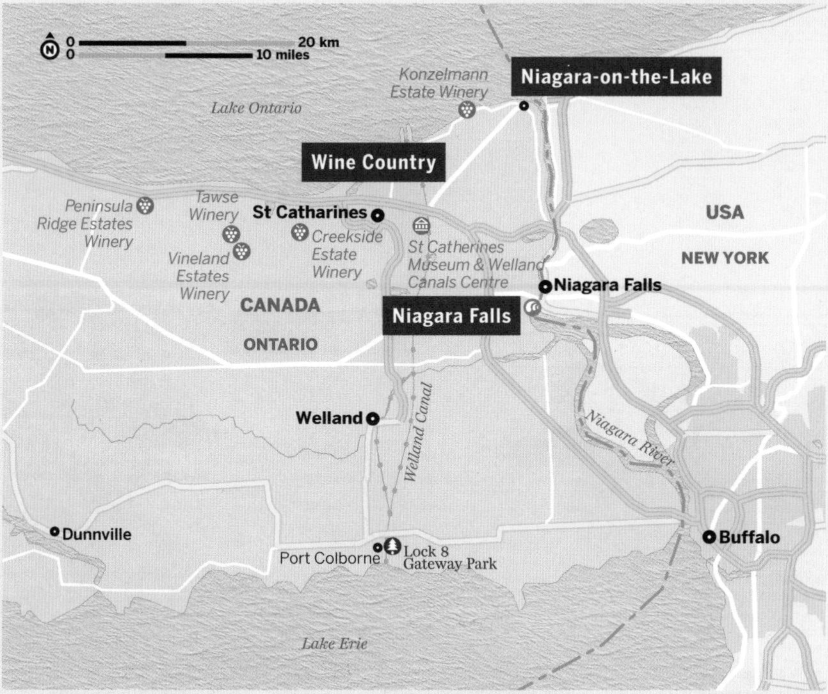

Arriving in the Niagara Region

Niagara Transportation Centre Greyhound Canada buses to Toronto ($23, 1½ to two hours, seven daily) and Buffalo, NY ($15, 1½ hours, five daily).

Niagara Airbus Door-to-door shared airport shuttle service to Toronto Pearson ($99, two hours) or Buffalo International, NY ($105, 1½ hours).

Niagara Falls Train Station Twice-daily services to Toronto ($23, two to 2½ hours).

Where to Stay

It isn't necessary to stay on the Niagara Peninsula if your goal is just to see the falls. There are usually more beds than heads in Niagara Falls, but the town is sometimes completely booked up. Prices spike sharply in summer, on weekends and during holidays. You might find you prefer waking in the town of Niagara-on-the-Lake more than next to the falls; when the local **Shaw Festival** (p69) is running, lodging is very tight, so plan ahead.

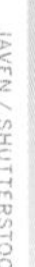

Visiting the Niagara Falls

Join thousands of onlookers who delight in the spectacle of this magnificent, unstoppable flow of water every day.

Niagara Falls forms a natural rift between Ontario and New York State. On the US side, Bridal Veil Falls crash onto mammoth fallen rocks. On the Canadian side, the grander, more powerful Horseshoe Falls plunge into the cloudy Maid of the Mist Pool.

Height & Volume

Niagara is not the tallest of waterfalls – at just over 50m (165ft) it is actually quite short in the waterfall stakes – but in terms of sheer volume, there's nothing like it, with some 2830 cu metres (100,000 cu ft) of water plummeting downwards every second. By day or night, regardless of season, the falls never fail to awe. Even in winter, when the flow is partially hidden and the edges freeze solid, the watery extravaganza is undiminished.

Great For...

☑ Don't Miss

Taking a virtual plunge over the falls at IMAX Niagara (p70).

Need to Know

Arrive early to beat the crowds. Visiting the falls is free, but parking access around the falls and Clifton Hill is expensive and limited.

Take a Break

Just a few blocks from the falls, Napoli Ristorante Pizzeria (p71) serves the best Italian in town, hands down.

Top Tip

The prime falls-watching spot is Table Rock, poised just meters from the drop of Horseshoe Falls.

Niagara Escarpment

The Niagara Escarpment, a 725km-long land formation that creates Niagara Falls, is a designated Unesco World Biosphere Reserve. Sweeping from eastern Wisconsin, through Ontario and ending in New York State, the escarpment is a combination of what was originally lime bed and ancient sea floor. The dolomitic limestone that makes up the land formation is more resistant than the land around it, which has eroded and left the bulge of limestone slithering around the Great Lakes.

Niagara Falls Daredevils

Surprisingly, more than a few people who have gone over Niagara Falls have actually lived to tell the tale. The first successful leap was in 1901, by a 63-year-old schoolteacher named Annie Taylor, who did it in a skirt, no less. This promoted a rash of barrel-stunters that continued into the 1920s, including Bobby Leach, who survived the drop, but who met his untimely death after slipping on an orange peel and developing gangrene!

In 1984 Karl Soucek revived the tradition in a bright-red barrel. He made it, only to die six months later in another barrel stunt in Houston. Also during the 1980s two locals successfully took the plunge lying head to head in the same barrel.

A US citizen who tried to jet ski over the falls in 1995 might have made it – if his rocket-propelled parachute had opened. Another American, Kirk Jones, survived the trip over the falls unaided in 2003. After being charged by Canadian police with illegally performing a stunt, he joined the circus.

Only one accidental falls-faller has survived – a seven-year-old Tennessee boy who fell out of a boat upstream in 1960 and survived the drop without even breaking a bone.

Konzelmann Estate Winery

Wine Country

A visit to Niagara Wine Country makes an indulgent day trip or lazy weekend, with vineyards both old and new to explore.

The Niagara Peninsula adheres to the 43rd parallel: a similar latitude to northern California and further south than France's Bordeaux. Here, the mineral-rich soils and a moderate microclimate create the perfect recipe for viticulture success.

Touring the vineyards by car is the best way to go. Regional tourist offices stock wine-route maps and brochures, which are also available at winery tasting rooms. Besides tastings, most places offer tours and dining. Parking is free at all vineyards.

Great For...

☑ Don't Miss

The week-long Niagara Grape & Wine Festival (www.niagarawinefestival.com) in mid-September.

Top Wineries

Tawse Winery (☎905-562-9500; www.tawsewinery.ca; 3955 Cherry Ave, Vineland; tastings/tours $8/15; ⏲10am-6pm May-Oct, to 5pm Nov-Apr) Elegant tasting room on a gorgeous landscaped vineyard that integrates organic and biodynamic farming.

Ice wine grapes

CHIYACAT / SHUTTERSTOCK ©

Creekside Estate Winery (☎905-562-0035; www.creeksidewine.com; 2170 4th Ave, Jordan Station; tastings from $10, tours $12; ⏰10am-6pm May-Nov, 11am-5pm Dec-Apr, tours at 2pm May-Oct) Hipster-ish winery, where you can tour the crush pad and underground cellars.

Peninsula Ridge Estates Winery (☎905-563-0900; http://peninsularidge.com; 5600 King St W, Beamsville; tastings $2-5, tours $15; ⏰10am-5pm Nov-May, to 6pm Jun-Oct) Includes a lofty timber tasting room, a restaurant and a magical hilltop setting.

Vineland Estates Winery (☎905-562-7088; www.vineland.com; 3620 Moyer Rd, Vineland; tours with tastings/purchases $15/7; ⏰10am-6pm) The elder statesperson of Niagara viticulture, almost all the wines here are excellent.

Konzelmann Estate Winery (☎905-935-2866; www.konzelmann.ca; 1096 Lakeshore Rd; tours $10-35; ⏰10am-6pm, tours May-Sep) One of the oldest wineries in the region and the only one to take full advantage of the lakeside microclimate.

Need to Know

The official Wine Route is signposted off the QEW, on rural highways and along backcountry roads. For more info, check out www.winecountryontario.ca.

Take a Break

Fill your belly with pizza or meat pies at **Pie Plate** (☎905-468-9743; www.thepieplate.com; 1516 Niagara Stone Rd, Virgil; sandwiches $16-20; ⏰10am-8pm Wed-Thu, to 9pm Fri-Sun; 🌶).

★ Top Tip

Avoid being the designated driver and join a Crush on Niagara (www.crushtours.com) winery tour.

Niagara Region Ice Wine

Niagara's regional wineries burst onto the scene at Vinexpo 1991 in Bordeaux, France. In a blind taste test, judges awarded a coveted gold medal to an Ontario ice wine – international attendees' jaws hit the floor.

To make ice wine, a certain percentage of grapes are left on the vines after the regular harvest is over. If birds, storms and mildew don't get to them, the grapes grow ever-more sugary and concentrated. Winemakers wait patiently until December or January when three days of consistent low temperatures (-8°C) freeze the grapes entirely.

It takes 10 times the usual number of grapes to make just one bottle. This, combined with labor-intensive production and the high risk of crop failure, often drives the price above $50 per 375mL bottle.

George Bernard Shaw statue by Elizabeth Bradford Holbrook

Niagara-on-the-Lake

One of the best-preserved 19th-century towns in North America, affluent N-o-t-L boasts tree-lined streets and impeccably restored houses.

Great For...

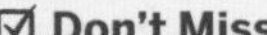

☑ Don't Miss

Queen's Royal Park – this sweet spot for a picnic beside the water is just a few blocks from Queen St.

Originally a neutral First Nations village, Niagara-on-the-Lake was founded by Loyalists from New York State after the American Revolution. It later became the first capital of the colony of Upper Canada. Today, lovely Queen St teems with shops of the ye-olde variety, selling antiques, Brit-style souvenirs and homemade fudge, and with stampedes of tour-bus guests. Stay past 5pm, however, and you'll discover this is a *real* town, not just a fairy-tale gingerbread lookalike.

Historical Sights

On the town's southeastern fringe, restored **Fort George** (☎905-468-6614; www.pc.gc.ca/fortgeorge; 51 Queens Pde; adult/child $11.70/free; ⏰10am-5pm May-Oct, noon-4pm Sat & Sun only Nov-Apr; P 👪) dates from 1797. The fort saw some bloody battles during the War

Morning parade at Fort George

JONATHANNICHOLLS / GETTY IMAGES ©

of 1812, changing hands between British and US forces a couple of times. Ghost tours, skills demonstrations and battle re-enactments occur throughout the summer.

South of Simcoe Park, the **Niagara Historical Society Museum** (905-468-3912; www.niagarahistorical.museum; 43 Castlereagh St; adult/child $5/1; 10am-5pm May-Oct, from 1pm Nov-Apr; P) has a vast collection relating to the town's past, ranging from First Nations artifacts to Loyalist and War of 1812 collectibles (including the prized hat of Major General Sir Isaac Brock).

Celebrating and honoring the contributions of Canadians of African descent to Niagara-on-the-Lake, the **Voices of Freedom Memorial** (www.vofpark.org; 244 Regent St) integrates West African and Underground Railroad symbolism with historical city footprints of Black neighborhoods and inspirational quotes.

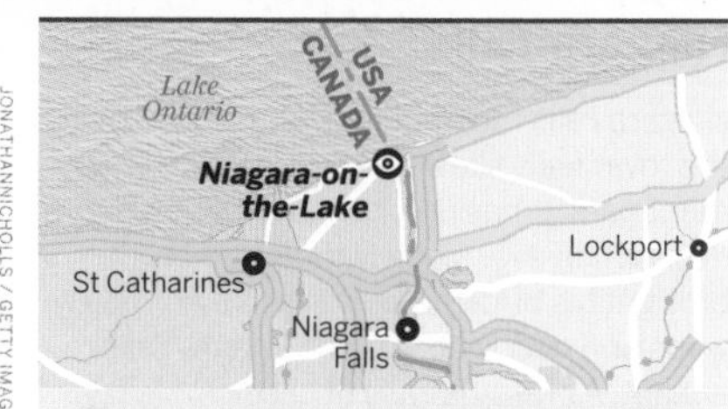

Need to Know

Chamber of Commerce Visitors Information Centre (905-468-1950; www.niagaraonthelake.com; 26 Queen St; 10am-6pm) Pick up maps and details on a self-guided walking tour.

Take a Break

Make time to dine at the opulent **Prince of Wales Hotel** (905-468-3246; www.vintage-hotels.com; 6 Picton St; d/ste from $370/510; P).

★ Top Tip

Cycling is a great way to explore the region. Rent a bike from Zoom Leisure (www.zoomleisure.com).

Shaw Festival

For more than 50 years, the theatrical **Shaw Festival** (905-468-2172; www.shawfest.com; 10 Queens Pde; Apr-Dec, box office 9am-9pm) has lured global audiences, who haven't been shy about issuing praise. Performances run from April through October, including a variety of works from Victorian drama to contemporary plays, musicals and classics from Wilde, Woolf and Coward. Specialized seminars are held throughout the season, plus informal 'Lunchtime Conversations' on selected Saturdays.

Actors tread the boards in three venues around town – the Festival, Royal George and Court House theaters. Rush seats go on sale at 9am on performance days (except for Saturdays). Students, under-30s and seniors receive discounts at some matinees; weekday matinees are the cheapest.

Niagara Falls

Niagara Falls might not be what you expect: the town feels like a tacky, outdated amusement park. It has been a saucy honeymoon destination ever since Napoleon's brother brought his bride here – tags like 'For newlyweds and nearly deads' and 'Viagra Falls' are apt. A crass morass of casinos, sleazy motels and tourist traps lines Clifton Hill and Lundy's Lane – a little Las Vegas! Love it or loathe it, there's nowhere quite like it.

SIGHTS

Skylon Tower Viewpoint
(☎905-356-2651; www.skylon.com; 5200 Robinson St; adult/child $16.25/10.50; ⊙9am-10pm Mon-Thu, to 11pm Fri-Sun; P) The Skylon Tower is a 158m-tall concrete spire with yellow pill-shaped elevators crawling up and down the tower's neck to the top. The interior itself is dated, but the views! They're eye-popping and simply picture perfect, with the falls to the east and, on clear days, Toronto to the north. The two observation areas – a glass-enclosed indoor deck and a wire-fenced outdoor one – give you 360-degree views of the region. Plus, there's a revolving restaurant and a family-friendly buffet.

Niagara Falls History Museum Museum
(☎905-358-5082; https://niagarafallsmuseums.ca; 5810 Ferry St; adult/child $5/4, Thu 5-9pm free; ⊙10am-5pm Tue-Wed & Fri-Sun, to 9pm Thu; P) A complete change of pace from the sights near the falls, this museum uses multi-media displays and artifacts to explore the history of Niagara Falls. The focus is on the War of 1812 as well as the transformation of Niagara Falls from an Indigenous settlement to one of the most touristed places in Canada. Things like colonial soldier dress-up areas and simulated tight rope walks make it fun for kids.

Niagara IMAX Theatre & Daredevil Exhibit Museum
(☎905-358-3611; www.imaxniagara.com; 6170 Fallsview Blvd; adult/child IMAX $13/9.50, Daredevil Exhibit $8/6.50, combo $15.50/13; ⊙9am-9pm; P) Hourly screenings of *Niagara: Miracles, Myth & Magic* give you an overview of Niagara Falls from the end of the Ice Age to modern day. The shots of the falls themselves are gorgeous, of course, but the romanticized history of the Aboriginal people who lived here and the modern-day tourists sporting mullets make you wish they'd give the film a refresh (it was made in 1986). Next door, the Daredevil Exhibit is worth a look.

ACTIVITIES

Journey Behind the Falls Walking
(☎905-354-1551; www.niagaraparks.com; 6650 Niagara Pkwy; adult/child $22/14; ⊙9am-10pm, hours vary by season) From Table Rock Information Centre, don a very unsexy plastic poncho and take an elevator through the bedrock partway down the cliff to the Cataract and Great Falls portals for an in-your-face view of the falls. Continue through 130-year-old tunnels to two observation decks – as close as you can get to the falls without hopping in a barrel. It's open year-round, but be prepared to queue.

Niagara River Recreation Trail Walking
(www.niagaraparks.com) The idyllic 3m-wide Niagara River Recreation Trail, for cycling, jogging and walking, runs parallel to the slow-roaming, leafy Niagara Pkwy. The trail can easily be divided into four chunks, each of which takes around two hours to pedal. The parkway meanders for 56km along the Niagara River, from Niagara-on-the-Lake past the falls and all the way to Fort Erie.

Niagara's Fury Amusement Park
(☎905-358-3268; www.niagaraparks.com; 6650 Niagara Pkwy; adult/child $16/10.25; ⊙half-hourly 9:15am-9pm;) Inside the Table Rock Visitor Centre, this Universal Studios–style interactive attraction is a 360-degree cinema-simulation of how the falls were created. Expect lots of high-tech tricks to suspend disbelief, including getting splashed, feeling snow fall and experiencing a rapid drop in temperature. (If it's

winter, taking a stroll next to the falls might just feel the same.) Aimed at kids.

TOURS

Hornblower Niagara Cruises Boating
(www.niagaracruises.com; 5920 Niagara Pkwy; adult/child $26/16, fireworks cruise $40; 8:30am-8:30pm May-Sep, to 5:30pm Oct) A classic Niagara Falls experience: boat tours that come so close to the spectacular Bridal Veil Falls and Horseshoe Falls that you'll be drenched (despite the rain ponchos). Hornblower offers two tours on its 700-person catamarans: a 20-minute daytime 'Voyage to the Falls'; and a 40-minute 'Fireworks Cruise,' on summer nights with live music and cash bar. Avoid the massive ticket lines and buy a ticket online.

Niagara Helicopters Scenic Flights
(905-357-5672; www.niagarahelicopters.com; 3731 Victoria Ave; adult/child $149/92; 9am-sunset, weather permitting) A fantastic 12-minute falls encounter takes you on a flight path along the Niagara River, over the Whirlpool past the American Falls and Bridal Veil Falls, with the grand finale over Horseshoe Falls. Learn facts about the sights via clunky headphones. A gorgeous and pricey (and not the most environmentally sensitive) way to see the falls.

EATING

Queen Charlotte Tea Room British $
(905-371-1350; www.thequeencharlottetearoom.com; 5689 Main St; mains $8-17, high tea $25; 11am-7pm Wed-Thu, Sat & Sun, to 8pm Fri) British expats craving a decent or even fancy cuppa, cucumber sandwiches, steak and kidney or fish-and-chips with mushy peas should head straight to this quaint establishment on Main St, near the intersection with Lundy's Lane, for a spot of tiffin! Reservations required for high tea; gluten-free options available.

Napoli Ristorante Pizzeria Italian $$
(905-356-3345; www.napoliristorante.ca; 5545 Ferry St; mains $16-36; 4:30-10pm) Head to Napoli for easily the best Italian in town.

Bruce Trail

For 900km, the **Bruce Trail** (800-665-4453; www.brucetrail.org) winds along the top of the Niagara Escarpment, from the **Queenston Heights Park** (905-357-7808; www.niagaraparks.com; 14184 Niagara Pkwy, Queenston; dawn-dusk; P) on the Niagara Peninsula to the Tobermory harbor on the Bruce Peninsula. This wide, well-maintained path is excellent for hiking during summer months, while those armed with cross-country skis take it through its winter paces. Day hikes along the trail are an appealing way to spend a sunny afternoon.

Opened in 1967, it's the oldest hiking trail in Canada and the longest in Ontario. The trail winds through public and private land, as well as along roadways. Wander past wineries, farmlands and forests, and marvel at Georgian Bay's shimmering azure waters from the escarpment's white cliffs. A multitude of campgrounds en route have budget accommodations for those on longer trips, and trail towns offer B&Bs galore.

Delicious pizza, rich pasta, creamy risotto and veal parmigiana all feature on the familiar menu.

AG Canadian $$$
(289-292-0005; www.agcuisine.com; 5195 Magdalen St; mains $18-38; 6-9:30pm Tue-Sun) Fine dining isn't something you find easily at the falls, which makes this lovely restaurant at the **Sterling Inn & Spa** (289-292-0000;

www.sterlingniagara.com; r from $221;) so refreshing. Service, decor, presentation and especially the quality of the food all rate highly. It has a seasonal menu featuring dishes like fennel-pollen pickerel and crispy-skinned trout, sourced locally.

Koutouki Greek Cuisine Greek **$$$**
(905-354-6776; http://koutoukiniagara.com; 5745 Ferry St; mains $22-42; 4-10pm Tue-Sun) A local favorite with an old-world feel, Koutouki serves classic Greek cuisine with a homey but elegant touch. Meals are beautifully presented and filling. Try, if you can, to save room for the baklava, a sweet phyllo dough dessert with walnuts and honey syrup. Worth the longish walk from the falls.

INFORMATION

Niagara Falls Tourism (905-356-6061; www.niagarafallstourism.com; 6815 Stanley Ave; 9am-5pm Mon-Fri) Offers information on the different neighborhoods and what's on around town. Located near the **Marriott** (www.niagarafallsmarriott.com; 6740 Fallsview Blvd).

GETTING THERE & AWAY

BUS

The **Niagara Transportation Centre** (905-357-2133; 4555 Erie Ave) is in the old part of town. Greyhound Canada (www.greyhound.ca) buses depart for Toronto ($23, 1½ to two hours, seven daily) and Buffalo, NY ($15, 1½ hours, five daily) from this bus station. Go Transit (www.gotransit.com) also provides service to Toronto by a combination of train and bus, via Burlington.

Niagara Airbus (905-374-8111; www.niagara airbus.com; 8626 Lundy's Lane; 24/7) operates door-to-door shared-shuttle services to Toronto International Airport ($99, two hours) and Buffalo International Airport ($105, 1½ hours). There are discounts for groups and/or if you leave from its bus depot.

TRAIN

Via Rail (888-842-7245; www.viarail.ca) and GO Transit (www.gotransit.com) provide daily rail services from Niagara Falls to Toronto ($23, two to 2½ hours, two departures). Service frequency increases on summer weekends.

Welland Canal

TONY MODA / SHUTTERSTOCK ©

GETTING AROUND

BICYCLE

The falls are perfect for cycling from site to site. If you're just looking to explore for a few hours, try **Zoom Bike Share** (☎905-468-3401; https://zoombikeshare.com), a self-serve bike share system. Download the app, go to a designated bike drop-off location, scan the code, and you're good to go. Rentals cost $5 per hour.

PUBLIC TRANSPORTATION

- Cranking up and down the steep 50m slope between Table Rock Visitor Centre and Fallsview Blvd is the quaint, gondola-like **Incline Railway** (☎877-642-7275; www.niagaraparks.com; 6635 Niagara Pkwy; one way $2.50, day passes $6.25). It saves you a 10- to 20-minute walk around, and is best taken uphill.
- **WEGO** (☎905-356-1179; www.wegoniagarafalls.com; adult/child 24hr pass $9/6, 48hr pass $13.50/10) is an economical and efficient year-round transit system, geared to tourists. There are three lines: red, green and blue; between them, they've got all the major sights and accommodations covered. For areas further afield, use **Niagara Transit** (☎905-356-7521; www.niagarafalls.ca; adult/student one way $3/1.75, day pass $7).

Welland Canal Area

Rebuilt four times between 1824 and 1932, the historic Welland Canal, running from Lake Erie into Lake Ontario, functions as a shipping bypass around Niagara Falls. It's part of the St Lawrence Seaway, allowing shipping between the industrial heart of North America and the Atlantic Ocean, with eight locks along the 42km-long canal overcoming the difference of about 100m in the lakes' water levels.

Before it shifted east to Port Weller, the original Welland Canal opened into Lake Ontario at Lakeside Park in **Port Dalhousie**. This rustic harbor area is a blend of old and new, with a reconstructed wooden lock and an 1835 lighthouse alongside bars, restaurants and ice-cream parlors.

Crossing the Border

The Canadian side of the Falls is considered by many to be the more spectacular. If you do wish to cross the border for a complete picture from the US side, you will need to arrange the normal visa requirements before arrival. You can not obtain a tourist visa at any of the border crossings at the Falls. US and Canadian citizens need to bring their passports, as usual.

SIGHTS

Lock 8 Gateway Park Park

(Mellanby St, Port Colborne; 24hr) Port Colborne, where Lake Erie empties into the canal, contains the 420m-long Lock 8 – the second longest canal lock in the world. Go to this park to get a view of it from an elevated viewing platform. South of Main St.

St Catharines Museum & Welland Canals Centre Museum

(☎905-984-8880; www.stcatharines.ca; 1932 Welland Canals Pkwy, St Catharines; by donation; 9am-5pm; P) For an up-close look at the canal, the Centre at Lock 3, just outside St Catharines, has a viewing platform close enough to almost let you touch the building-size ships as they wait for water levels to rise or fall. Ships sail through from April to December only. Check the ships' schedules online (www.greatlakes-seaway.com) to plan your visit accordingly.

EATING

Port Colborne has the best restaurant options along its quiet, attractive canal-side boardwalk on West St. Good for an afternoon stroll or evening meal.

GETTING THERE & AWAY

You need your own transport to get to the Welland Canal, and will pass interesting bridges along the way. The nearest town is St Catharines.

OTTAWA

In this Chapter

Ottawa at a glance...

Descriptions of Ottawa read like an appealing dating profile: dynamic, gregarious, bilingual, and likes long walks along the river. In person, the attractive capital fits the bill. For architecture buffs, huge Gothic parliament buildings anchor the downtown core, and for those seeking culture, the city's world-class museums house a variety of intriguing collections. Of course, average temperatures sit well below 0°C from December to March, but locals celebrate winter with outdoor pursuits and the Winterlude festival. When spring clicks to summer, tulips cheer downtown, while fall brings streets lined with trees in eye-popping shades of red and yellow.

One Day in Ottawa

If you're only here for a day, first get yourself to **Parliament Hill** (p80) for happy snaps with the Peace Tower (which is still photographic despite undergoing renovations until 2028). Next, be seduced by the shimmering glass spires of the **National Gallery of Canada** (p82), with its carefully curated collection of Canadian art. Pause for lunch at the **ByWard Market** (p89), where you'll uncover scores of vendors hawking farm-fresh produce, and sample a fried dough beavertail. Finally, walk or skate along the **Rideau Canal** (p85) and its 7.8km trail.

Two Days in Ottawa

On day two, cover the major sights flanking the **Ottawa Locks** (p83) or gravitate toward the awe-inducing architecture, city views and fascinating exhibits of the **Canadian Museum of History** (p78). Ogle taxidermic megafauna at the **Canadian Museum of Nature** (p83) before heading to **Wilf & Ada's** (p87) for a diner-style lunch. Choose another museum or two before cocktails and tacos at **El Camino** (p87) or *plats du jour* at **Métropolitain Brasserie** (p88).

Previous page: Parliament and Rideau Canal
VLAD G / SHUTTERSTOCK ©

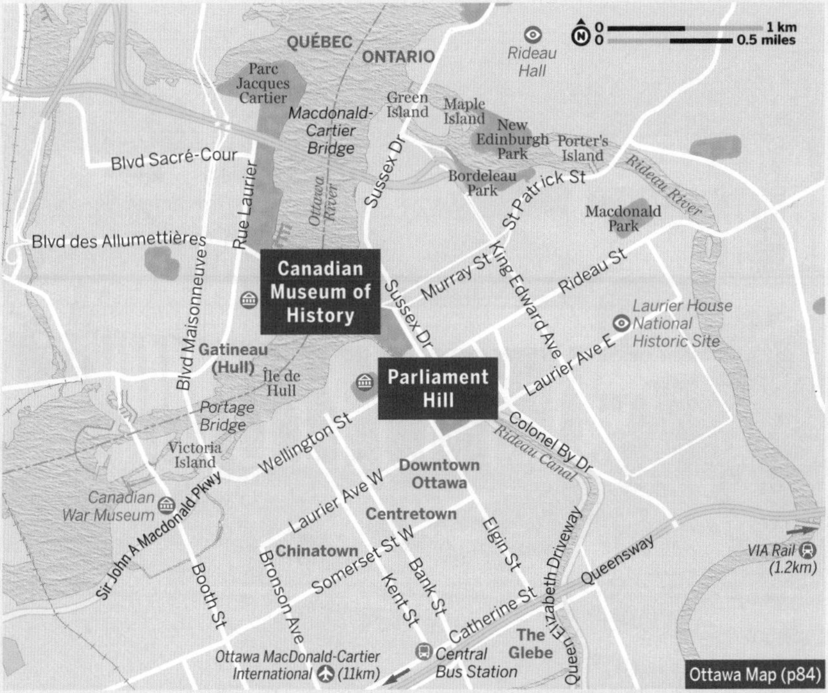

Ottawa Map (p84)

Arriving in Ottawa

Ottawa MacDonald-Cartier International Airport Take bus 97 from pillar 14 outside the arrivals area ($3.50, 40 minutes) or grab a taxi (around $30, 20 minutes).

VIA Rail Station Located 7km east of downtown; take a taxi or an OC Transpo bus (www.octranspo.com; $3.50).

Central Bus Station Located just off Queensway (Hwy 417), near Kent St.

Where to Stay

Ottawa has an impressive array of accommodations in all price ranges. Reservations are recommended during summer and over festival times, especially Winterlude. Downtown and Centretown offer numerous options, including boutique hotels, suite hotels, and hostels around ByWard Market. South of the market, the Sandy Hill district has pleasant B&Bs among its stately heritage homes and international embassies.

Building by architect Douglas Cardinal

MARC BRUXELLE / SHUTTERSTOCK ©

Canadian Museum of History

Through a range of spectacular exhibits, this high-tech, must-see museum recounts 20,000 years of human history.

Great For...

☑ Don't Miss

The museum's temporary events, hands-on exhibitions and big-screen films (check the website for details).

Situated across the river, in Hull, Québec, the museum boasts incredible views back to Parliament Hill.

First Nations

The museum's smooth stone exterior represents an organic, pan-Canadian landscape. Inside, the Grand Hall is said to have the world's largest indoor collection of totem poles. Wander along a boardwalk, getting an up-close look at the towering poles and the recreated facades of six traditional Aboriginal houses.

Next door, the First People's Hall is a permanent exhibit of more than 2000 incredible images, objects and documents that tell the story of the First Nations. This is where you'll find some of the museum's oldest artifacts; keep your eyes peeled for one of the oldest representations of the

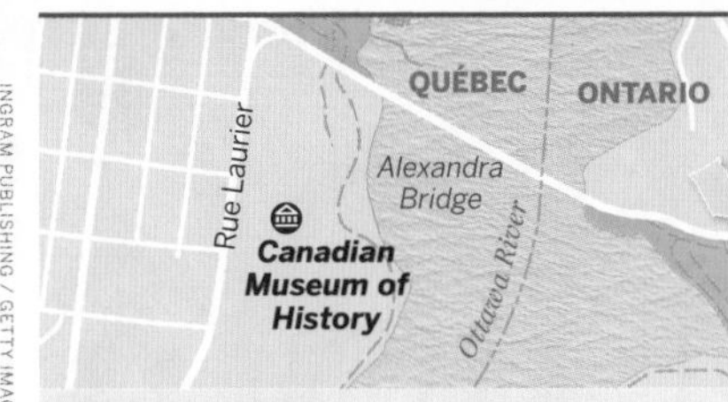

Need to Know

819-776-7000; www.historymuseum.ca; 100 Rue Laurier, Gatineau; adult/child 3-12yr $20/12; 9am-5pm Fri-Wed, to 8pm Thu Apr-Jun, to 6pm Jul & Aug, from 9:30am Sep-Mar;

Take a Break

The museum has two cafes and a bistro to keep you nourished.

★ Top Tip

Hop on an Aqua-Taxi ferry to get here from Ottawa Locks.

human face. There's also a fascinating section on the relationship of Canada's Aboriginal people with the land and their ongoing contributions to Canadian society.

Canadian History Hall

It's no small feat to fill more than 3500 sq metres of gallery space with authentic artifacts that stretch from objects recovered from Canada's very first inhabitants, all the way to more recent images of the arrival of 25,000 Syrian refugees. Rather than focusing on historical bigwigs, the hall spotlights the lives and experiences of everyday people through some 1200 images and 1500 artifacts. As well as a recreation of a 4000-year-old family who were found buried with 350,000 handmade beads, and the forensic facial reconstruction of the 800-year-old 'kayak man,' you'll find stories of Canada's 'dark chapters,' such as Japanese internment camps and residential schools, and current topics such as Canada's First Nations Idle No More Movement and the fight for LGBTQI+ rights.

Five years in the making, this gallery opened amid much fanfare on Canada Day (July 1) 2017, in celebration of Canada's 150th birthday.

Children's Museum

Fancy climbing aboard an extravagantly decorated Pakistani bus or a three-wheeled rickshaw from Thailand? Curious to step inside a Bedouin tent, or houses in India, Indonesia and Mexico? You can, in the Canadian Children's Museum, just around the corner from the History Museum. Over 30 exhibition spaces, based on a 'Great Adventure' theme, whisk kids off on a journey around the world. We're talking props, costumes, artifacts you can pick up and play with, and all sorts of toys and games. And the best part? Admission is free with your Museum of History ticket.

Library of Parliament

Parliament Hill

Set on the banks of the Ottawa River, this is the political and cultural heart of the city.

Great For...

☑ Don't Miss

Joining up to a thousand people on the lawns for a free yoga session on summertime Wednesdays at noon.

Parliament Buildings

Vast, yawning archways, copper-topped turrets and Gothic revival gargoyles dominate the facade of the stunning lime-and-sandstone Parliament buildings, the home of Canada's legislature. The main building, known as the Centre Block, supports the iconic Peace Tower (which is still photographic) and is undergoing renovations until at least 2028. Until then, visitors can still tour the House of Commons in the West Block and the historic East Block, and the grounds are still magnificent and worth a walk around. The Senate is now in a new building close to Parliament Hill.

Note that these are not the first Parliament buildings to stand on the site. The original was built between 1859 and 1866 in anticipation of the nation's birth, but all that remain are the East Block and the

Need to Know

☎613-996-0896; https://visit.parl.ca; 111 Wellington St; ⌚East Block tours 8:30am-4:30pm Jul-early Sep, West Block tours 8:30am-4:30pm FREE

Take a Break

Head to nearby Métropolitain Brasserie (p88) for delicious Gallic dishes.

★ Top Tip

On summer evenings, enjoy the free bilingual sound-and-light show on the lawns.

library. When a small fire broke out in the Centre Block's Commons Reading Room on February 3, 1916, it claimed seven lives and quickly consumed everything in its path. Thankfully, a quick-thinking employee closed the library's iron doors, saving the people inside and thousands of irreplaceable books.

Tours

Tours of the East and West block last around 40 to 50 minutes, depending on parliamentary activity, and may be subject to rigorous security checks going in. It's best to order your tickets in advance, but you can also get them on the day from the **ticket office** (⌚9am-7:30pm Mon-Fri, to 4:30pm Sat & Sun mid-May–Jun, 9am-4:30pm Jul-early Sep, to 3:30pm Mon-Fri, to 4:30pm Sat & Sun early Sep–mid-May).

Free tours of the grounds are also offered. There are paths behind the buildings with views across the river that rival the Ottawa Locks (p83).

Visitors are welcome to watch debates in the Senate and the House of Commons whenever they are in session. Check the calendars on the website to find out when the chambers will be sitting. Expect lengthy security checks.

Changing of the Guard

At 10am daily in summer, find a spot on the front lawns to witness the colorful changing of the guard. Originally a morning routine that began in 1959, it's now an iconic ceremony, complete with a regimental band and pipers. The Ceremonial Guard is comprised of two regiments – the Governor General's Foot Guards and the Canadian Grenadier Guards.

SIGHTS

Most of Ottawa's numerous world-class museums are within walking distance of each other. Some offer free general admission on Thursday evenings, and many close a day or two weekly (normally Monday) in winter.

National Gallery of Canada Museum

(☎613-990-1985; www.gallery.ca; 380 Sussex Dr; adult/child $16/free, 5-8pm Thu free; ⏰10am-6pm daily May-Sep, 10am-5pm Tue-Sun Oct-Apr, to 8pm Thu year-round) The National Gallery is a work of art in itself: its striking ensemble of pink granite and glass spires echoes the ornate copper-topped towers of the nearby parliament buildings. Inside, vaulted galleries exhibit predominantly Canadian art, classic and contemporary, including an impressive collection of work by Inuit and other Indigenous artists. It's the world's largest Canadian collection, although additional galleries of European and American treasures include several recognizable names and masterpieces. Interpretive panels guide visitors through the nation's history and cultural development.

Deep within the gallery's interior you'll find two smooth courtyards and the remarkable **Rideau Street Convent Chapel**. Built in 1888, the stunning wooden chapel was saved from demolition and rebuilt here 100 years later – quite extraordinary.

Canadian War Museum Museum

(☎819-776-7000; www.warmuseum.ca; 1 Vimy Pl; adult/child 3-12yr $17/11; ⏰9:30am-5pm Fri-Wed, to 8pm Thu Sep-Mar, from 9am May-Aug) Fascinating displays twist through the labyrinthine interior of this sculpture-like, modern museum, tracing Canada's military history with the nation's most comprehensive collection of war-related artifacts. Many of the touching and thought-provoking exhibits are larger than life, including a replica of a WWI trench. Take a look at the facade in the evening, if you can: flickering lights pulse on and off spelling 'Lest We Forget' and 'CWM' in both English and French Morse code.

Ottawa Locks

Canadian Museum of Nature Museum

(☎613-566-4700; www.nature.ca; 240 McLeod St; adult/child 3-12yr $15/11; ⏰9am-5pm Tue-Sun, to 8pm Thu Sep-May, to 6pm Jun-Aug; 🚌5, 6, 7, 14, 101, 103, 401) This imposing baronial building houses one of the world's best natural history collections, which the vast museum brings to life with modern and interactive exhibits. There's an impressive collection of fossils, the full skeleton of a blue whale and an excellent stock of dinosaur skeletons and models. Everyone loves the realistic mammal and bird dioramas depicting Canadian wildlife – the taxidermic creatures are so lifelike, you'll be glad they're behind a sheet of glass.

Laurier House National Historic Site Historic Site

(☎613-992-8142; www.pc.gc.ca/en/lhn-nhs/on/laurier; 335 Laurier Ave E; adult/child $4/free; ⏰10am-5pm daily Jul & Aug, Thu-Mon May & Jun) This copper-roofed Victorian home built in 1878 was the residence of two notable prime ministers: Wilfrid Laurier and the eccentric Mackenzie King. The home is elegantly furnished, displaying treasured mementos and possessions from both politicos. Don't miss the study on the top floor.

Notre Dame Cathedral-Basilica Church

(☎613-241-7496; www.notredameottawa.com; 385 Sussex Dr; ⏰9am-6pm) Built in the 1840s, this shimmering tin-topped house of worship is the oldest church in all of Ottawa and the seat of the city's Roman Catholic archbishop. Pick up the small pamphlet at the entrance outlining the church's many idiosyncratic features, including elaborate wooden carvings and the dazzling indigo ceiling peppered with gleaming stars.

Ottawa Locks Historic Site

The series of steep, step-like locks between the Château Laurier and Parliament Hill marks the north end of the 200km-long Rideau Canal, which flows all the way down to Kingston. Colonel By, the canal's visionary engineer, set up headquarters here in 1826.

Gatineau Park

Just across the river from Ottawa, Gatineau Park is a deservedly popular 360-sq-km area of woods and lakes in the Gatineau Hills of Québec. In summer, this green expanse of cedar and maple offers 150km of hiking trails and more 90km of cycling paths. In winter, you can explore dozens of cross-country skiing and snowshoeing trails.

Lac Lapêche, **Lac Meech** and **Lac Philippe** have swimming beaches (including Lac Meech's nude gay beach), which lure the landlocked locals for a refreshing dip. Before taking a swim, check with the park's visitor center; tiny larvae called cercariae that can cause 'swimmer's itch,' an uncomfortable skin rash, are occasionally present in the lakes.

Also in the park is the **Mackenzie King Estate** (www.ncc-ccn.gc.ca/places/mackenzie-king-estate; per car $12; ⏰grounds open year-round, buildings 10am-5pm Mon & Wed-Fri, 11am-6pm Sat & Sun mid-May–mid-Oct), the summer residence of a former Canadian prime minister. The **Fall Rhapsody** festival, celebrating the wonderful autumn colors, occurs in October.

Rideau Hall Notable Building

(☎613-991-4422; www.gg.ca/rideauhall; 1 Sussex Dr; ⏰10am-4pm Jul-early Sep, noon-4pm Sat & Sun May & Jun) FREE Home of the Governor General, Rideau Hall was built in the 1830s

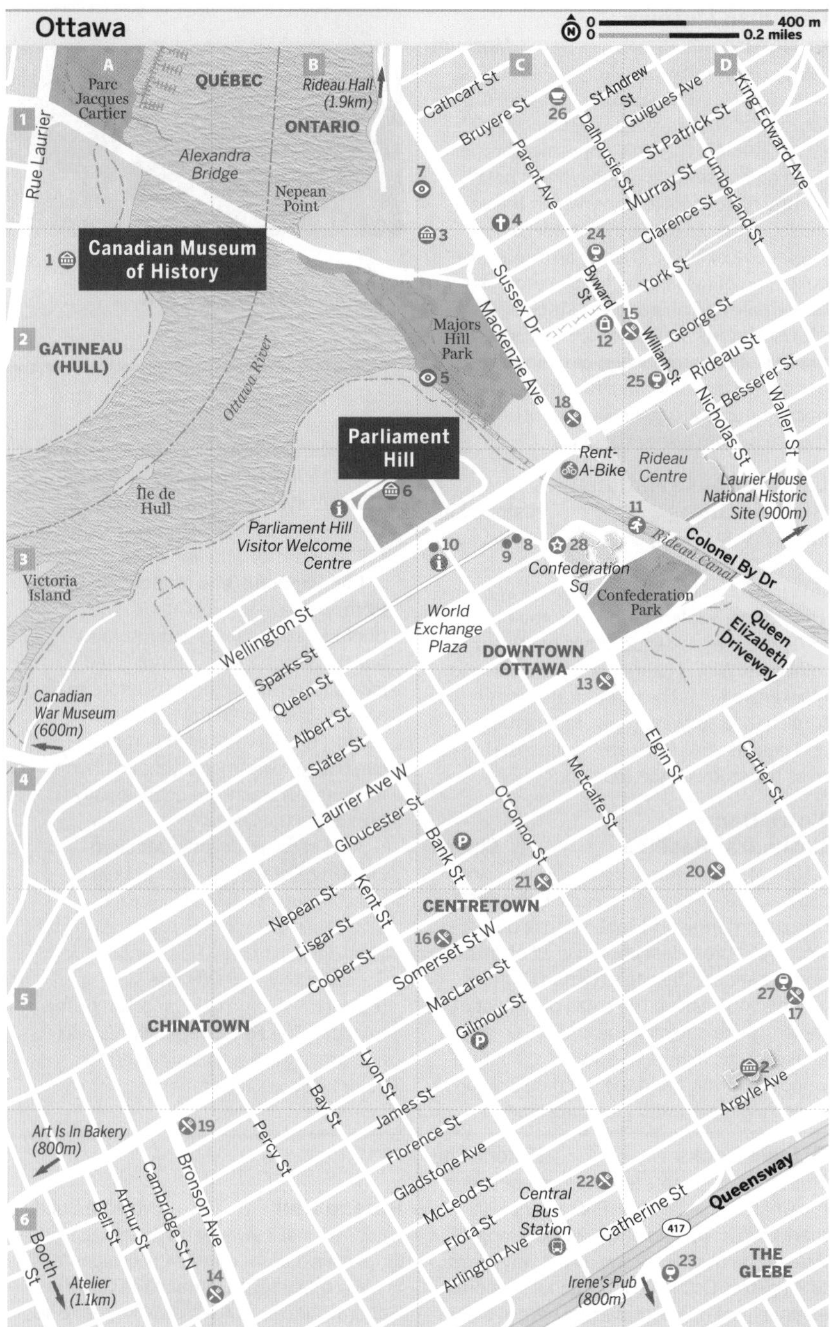

Ottawa
400 m
0.2 miles
A
B
C
D
1
2
3
4
5
6
Parc Jacques Cartier
QUÉBEC
ONTARIO
Rideau Hall (1.9km)
Rue Laurier
Alexandra Bridge
Nepean Point
Canadian Museum of History
GATINEAU (HULL)
Ottawa River
Majors Hill Park
Parliament Hill
Île de Hull
Parliament Hill Visitor Welcome Centre
Victoria Island
Canadian War Museum (600m)
Cathcart St
Bruyere St
St Andrew St
Guigues Ave
King Edward Ave
St Patrick St
Parent Ave
Dalhousie St
Murray St
Cumberland St
Clarence St
Sussex Dr
Byward St
York St
Mackenzie Ave
George St
William St
Rideau St
Besserer St
Waller St
Nicholas St
Rent-A-Bike
Rideau Centre
Laurier House National Historic Site (900m)
Rideau Canal
Colonel By Dr
Confederation Sq
Confederation Park
Queen Elizabeth Driveway
World Exchange Plaza
DOWNTOWN OTTAWA
Wellington St
Sparks St
Queen St
Albert St
Slater St
Laurier Ave W
Gloucester St
Bank St
O'Connor St
Metcalfe St
Elgin St
Cartier St
Nepean St
Kent St
Lisgar St
Cooper St
CENTRETOWN
Somerset St W
MacLaren St
Gilmour St
CHINATOWN
Lyon St
Bay St
James St
Percy St
Florence St
Gladstone Ave
McLeod St
Flora St
Arlington Ave
Central Bus Station
Catherine St
Queensway
417
Argyle Ave
THE GLEBE
Irene's Pub (800m)
Art Is In Bakery (800m)
Booth St
Bell St
Arthur St
Cambridge St N
Bronson Ave
Atelier (1.1km)
1
2
3
4
5
6
7
8
9
10
11
12
13
14
15
16
17
18
19
20
21
22
23
24
25
26
27
28

Ottawa

Sights

1 Canadian Museum of History ... A2
2 Canadian Museum of Nature ... D5
3 National Gallery of Canada ... C2
4 Notre Dame Cathedral-Basilica ... C1
5 Ottawa Locks ... C2
6 Parliament Hill ... B3
7 Royal Canadian Mint ... C1

Activities, Courses & Tours

8 Gray Line ... C3
9 Haunted Walk ... C3
10 Ottawa Walking Tours ... C3
11 Rideau Canal ... D3

Shopping

12 ByWard Market ... C2

Eating

13 Beckta Dining & Wine Bar ... C4
14 Blue Nile ... B6
15 ByWard Market Square ... D2
16 Ceylonta ... C5
17 El Camino ... D5
18 Métropolitain Brasserie ... C2
19 Saigon Boy Noodle House ... A6
20 Town ... D4
21 Union Local 613 ... C4
22 Wilf & Ada's ... C6

Drinking & Nightlife

23 Clocktower Brew Pub ... D6
24 Heart & Crown ... C2
25 Highlander Pub ... D2
26 I Deal Coffee ... C1
27 Manx ... D5

Entertainment

28 National Arts Centre ... C3

with grand additions made by successive governors. There are free 45-minute walking tours of the fancy residence, featuring anecdotes about the various goings-on over the years. Otherwise, from 8am to one hour before sunset, the grounds are available to be enjoyed at your leisure (as is the building between 3pm and 4:30pm in July and August).

Royal Canadian Mint Notable Building

(613-993-8990; www.mint.ca/tours; 320 Sussex Dr; guided tours adult/child $8/4.50; 10am-5pm) Although Canada's circulation-coin mint is in Winnipeg, the royal mint holds its own by striking special pieces. The imposing stone building, which looks a bit like the Tower of London, has been refining gold and minting since 1908. It's an interesting tour and children will enjoy watching the sheets of metal being spun into loads of coins.

Canada Science & Technology Museum Museum

(613-991-3044; www.ingeniumcanada.org/cstm; 1867 St Laurent Blvd; adult/child $17/11; 9am-5pm May-Aug, Tue-Sun Sep-Apr) The newly renovated science and technology museum reopened in late 2017, expanding its educational and fun exhibits, which both adults and children will enjoy. A walk through the 'Crazy Kitchen' is a blast: the lopsided galley makes you stumble from start to finish. There are trains out back to enlighten you on the science of coal and steam propulsion, and there is also a large display of space technology. There are daily shows during the summer months as well as various special exhibits.

ACTIVITIES

Rideau Canal Ice Skating

(www.ottawatourism.ca/ottawa-insider/rideau-canal-skateway) Ottawa's most famous outdoor attraction, the Rideau Canal, became Canada's 14th location to be named a National Historic Site in 2007. It's ideal for boating, with parks, small towns, lakes and many places to stop en route, and in winter, it turns into one of the world's largest skating rinks.

The 7.8km-long artery of groomed ice between downtown and Dow's Lake features numerous heated rest stops and changing stations, but most importantly, skaters can pause to purchase

Food 'Hoods

Follow Bank or Elgin Sts south for a surplus of less-touristy pubs, restaurants and cafes. After crossing Queensway (Hwy 417), there are more eateries along Bank St in the hip Glebe neighborhood, especially between First and Fifth Aves.

Ottawa's lively Chinatown, spread along Somerset St W around Bronson Ave, is a great spot to visit, with a tasty smattering of Vietnamese flavors around Booth St. Further west in Little Italy, take an evening stroll down 'Corso Italia' (Preston St) – adjacent to 'Via Marconi' (Gladstone Ave) – for a little slice of the homeland.

Even further out, over the Somerset St W and Albert St railway bridges, and about 3.5km from Parliament Hill, Hintonburg is Ottawa's latest up-and-coming 'hood with hipster cafes to rival the Glebe.

LINDA RAYMOND / GETTY IMAGES ©

scrumptious slabs of fried dough called beavertails. Huts all along the canal rent out skates for around $22 for two hours (with a $50 deposit).

TOURS

Gray Line Tours

(☎613-562-9090; www.grayline.com/ottawa; cnr Sparks & Elgin Sts; 24hr hop-on, hop-off tour from $29; ⊙Apr-Oct) Offers sightseeing tours including hop-on, hop-off bus services, bus-and-bike tours and Ottawa River cruises. Check the website or visit the sidewalk ticket booth for schedules and pricing. Bus tours depart from the booth, cruises from the Ottawa Locks.

Haunted Walk Walking

(☎613-232-0344; www.hauntedwalk.com; 46½ Sparks St; adult/child walks $24/20) Has several ghoulish walking tours including visits to the old county jail, now the **HI hostel** (☎613-235-2595; www.hihostels.ca/ottawa; 75 Nicholas St; dm members $37-41, nonmembers $43-53, jail rooms $61-141; P❄@).

Ottawa Walking Tours Walking

(☎613-799-1774; www.ottawawalkingtours.com; 90 Wellington St; adult/child under 11yr $15/free) These informative and fun two-hour tours with professional guides depart from the Terry Fox statue in front of the tourist office. Cash only unless you book online. There are free tours every day at 11am from May to August, though tips are appreciated.

EATING

Art Is In Bakery Bakery $

(☎613-695-1226; www.artisinbakery.com; 250 City Centre Ave; sandwiches $9-15; ⊙8am-9:30pm Mon-Fri, to 4pm Sat, to 3pm Sun; P☎) Start the day with a breakfast sandwich or croissant and an excellent cappuccino at this buzzy bakery cafe, occupying a warehouse space on an industrial estate. The gourmet sandwiches have fillings such as pickle melt and Thai chicken, with gluten-free options and salads available.

Blue Nile Ethiopian $

(☎613-321-0774; www.blueniIeottawa.com; 707 Gladstone Ave; mains $12; ⊙11am-10pm Tue-Sat, noon-9pm Sun-Mon) Undoubtedly the best place to satisfy any *injera* (flat, spongy bread) cravings, this small restaurant in Chinatown also offers homemade *tej* (honey wine) and a large selection of authentic Ethiopian dishes.

Saigon Boy Noodle House Vietnamese $

(☎613-230-8080; 648 Somerset St W; mains $13; ⏰11am-9pm) Locals rate Saigon Boy as the city's best choice for *pho,* a Vietnamese soup containing rice noodles with beef or chicken. Other dishes, such as grilled pork and rice, are also available.

El Camino Mexican $$

(☎613-422-2800; http://eatelcamino.com; 380 Elgin St; mains/tacos $15/7; ⏰5:30pm-late Tue-Sun, takeout noon-2:30pm Tue-Fri) With a hip industrial aesthetic underscored by Day of the Dead references, El Camino is either praised as Ottawa's taco joint of the hour or derided as overpriced. Come for chorizo and crispy fish tacos, eaten at benches or taken out, and cocktails ($13) such as the sweet and spicy El Fuego – and book ahead.

Town Italian $$

(☎613-695-8696; www.townlovesyou.ca; 296 Elgin St; mains $23; ⏰5-10pm Mon-Sat) Slick, smart and ineffably cool, this joint is always packed: arty-farty hipsters bump elbows with wealthy coiffured housewives. Ottawa foodies appreciate the use of local produce and northern Italian recipes, resulting in a short and seasonal menu of small and large plates, such as the mainstay ricotta-stuffed meatballs, with an abundance of Niagara wines to accompany them.

Wilf & Ada's Diner $$

(☎613-231-7959; www.facebook.com/wilfandadasascratchdiner; 510 Bank St; mains $16; ⏰7am-3pm Mon-Fri, from 8am Sat & Sun) This 'scratch diner' is one of Ottawa's hippest breakfast and lunch spots, with its retro art and everything made from scratch. Breakfast is home-cured bacon, buttermilk French toast, 'homies' (home fries) and maple syrup, while chunky sandwiches, soup, salads and poutine are served for lunch. If it's full, head round the back to the affiliated cafe Arlington Five.

> *Start the day with ... an excellent cappuccino*

Art Is In Bakery

DAVID GIRAL / ALAMY STOCK PHOTO ©

BILL BACHMANN / ALAMY STOCK PHOTO ©

Highlander Pub

Ceylonta Sri Lankan $$

(613-237-7812; www.ceylonta.com; 403 Somerset St W; mains $18; 11:30am-2pm Mon-Fri, from noon Sun, 5-9pm daily) Locals recommend this friendly neighborhood Sri Lankan restaurant, serving fresh and zingy dishes. Go for the fish *thali* or the chicken or mutton *kothu rotti*. Dinner only on Saturday.

There is also a location in Bayshore if you have a curry craving while out in the suburbs.

Union Local 613 Modern American $$$

(613-231-1010; www.union613.ca; 315 Somerset St W; mains $28; food served 11:30am-2pm Wed-Fri, from 10am Sat & Sun, 5:30pm-late Mon-Sat;) Sit among the low-lit decor of hummingbirds and hot-air balloons, and drink house beers and other local craft brews from screw-top jars. It's food with attitude, including southern-fried chicken and cornmeal-crusted catfish, and there's a 'speakeasy' behind a bookshelf in the basement (open 10:30pm to 2am Wednesday to Saturday).

Beckta Dining & Wine Bar Canadian $$$

(613-238-7063; www.beckta.com; 150 Elgin St; mains $32-45; 5:30-10pm Mon-Sat, to 9pm Sun) Book in advance for one of the hottest tables in the capital, if not the whole country. Beckta offers an upmarket dining experience with an original spin on regional cuisine. You can choose between à la carte dining or a five-course pairing with wine ($98, plus $54 with wine pairing).

Métropolitain Brasserie French $$$

(613-562-1160; www.metropolitainbrasserie.com; 700 Sussex Dr; mains $25-31; 11am-midnight Tue-Fri, to 11pm Mon, 9am-midnight Sat, 9am-11pm Sun) Métropolitain puts a modern spin on the typical brasserie with its swirling zinc countertop, flamboyant fixtures and Gallic soundtrack: you'll feel like you're dining on the set of *Moulin Rouge*. 'Hill Hour' (4pm to 7pm on weekdays and from 9:30pm daily) buzzes with the spirited chatter of hot-blooded politicos as they down *plats du jour*.

Atelier Fusion $$$

(☎613-321-3537; www.atelierrestaurant.ca; 540 Rochester St; menu $125; ⏲5:30-8:30pm Tue-Sat) The brainchild of celebrated chef and molecular gastronomy enthusiast Marc Lépine, Atelier is a white-walled laboratory dedicated to tickling the taste buds. There's no oven or stove – just Bunsen burners, liquid nitrogen and hot plates to create the unique 12-course tasting menu.

 DRINKING & NIGHTLIFE

Clocktower Brew Pub Bar

(☎613-233-7849; www.clocktower.ca; 575 Bank Street; ⏲11:30am-late) Enjoy homemade brews such as Raspberry Wheat and Bytown Brown in the newly renovated taproom. There is also a new taproom on Rideau St and three other locations around town, but nothing beats beer right from the source!

Heart & Crown Irish Pub

(☎613-562-0674; https://heartandcrown.pub; 67 Clarence St; ⏲11am-2am Mon-Fri, from 9am Sat & Sun) This ByWard Market stalwart is popular with young Ottawa folk for beers and big platters of pub grub. Several rooms and patios sprawl into each other, incorporating four other pubs along the way. Big screens show soccer matches. There's music from live bands to acoustic sets seven days a week.

Highlander Pub Pub

(☎613-562-5678; www.thehighlanderpub.com; 115 Rideau St; ⏲11am-2am) Kilted servers, 17 taps and 200 single malt whiskies all add to the wonderful Scottish appeal of this ByWard Market area pub. And the food is good too!

I Deal Coffee Coffee

(☎613-562-1775; www.idealcoffees.com; 176 Dalhousie St; coffee $4; ⏲7am-7pm Mon-Wed, to 10pm Thu-Fri, 8:30am-7pm Sat, 9am-6pm Sun) Ideal indeed; handcrafted blends are produced and roasted on-site. The decor is thin, with bins and sacks of 'light organic blend' and 'prince of darkness' stacked next to the roaster; it's all about rich, flavorful cups of joe (hot or iced). In the words of one happy customer, this might be Ottawa's best cappuccino.

ByWard Market Square

Anchoring the market district, this sturdy brick **building** (☎613-244-4410; www.bywardmarketsquare.com; ⏲10am-8pm) is the perfect place to stop when hunger strikes. Aside from the fresh produce and cheese, an array of international takeaway joints offer falafel, spicy curries, flaky pastries, sushi... the list goes on. Look for the stand selling beavertails, Ottawa's signature sizzling flat-dough dish. Located between William, Byward, George and York Sts.

There are also rich culinary pickings in the surrounding **outdoor market** (☎613-562-3325; www.byward-market.com; cnr York & ByWard Sts; ⏲6am-6pm), one of North America's largest outdoor farmers markets.

PHUONG D. NGUYEN / SHUTTERSTOCK ©

Manx Bar

(☎613-231-2070; www.manxpub.com; 370 Elgin St; ⏲11:30am-1am Mon-Thu, to 2am Fri, 10am-2am Sat & Sun) 'Ottawa's original sinkhole,' as this basement bar has called itself since Rideau St collapsed in 2016, offers a great selection of Canadian microbrews (including the beloved Creemore), served on copper-top tables. There's food, too (mains $14 to $16) – brunch here is popular at weekends.

Museums Passport

Capitalize on Ottawa's cache of fantastic museums with the **Museums Passport** (www.museumspassport.ca; adult $35), a discount card that grants carriers admission to three of the city's seven best museums. The card can be purchased at any of the participating museums or the Capital Information Kiosk (p90), and is valid for three days from your first museum visit. Accompanying children are given a 30% discount off the normal admission rate.

ENTERTAINMENT

Canadian Tire Centre Spectator Sport
(613-599-0100; www.canadiantirecentre.com; 1000 Palladium Dr, Kanata) Ottawa is a hard-core hockey town. It's worth getting tickets to a game even if you're not into hockey – the ballistic fans put on a show of their own. NHL team the Ottawa Senators (www.senators.com) play here, at their home ground, about 25km southwest of the center in Ottawa's west end. Big-ticket concerts also take place here.

Irene's Pub Live Music
(613-230-4474; www.irenespub.ca; 885 Bank St; 11:30am-2am) Friendly and funky, if a little grimy in the thick of a busy weekend, Irene's is the three-decade-old spiritual home for the Glebe neighborhood's artists and musicians. It offers live music, with a good line in Celtic, folk and blues, and other entertainment a few nights a week. Enjoy a great selection of whiskeys and local craft beers on tap.

National Arts Centre Theater
(NAC; 613-947-7000; www.nac-cna.ca; 1 Elgin St) The capital's premier performing arts complex delivers opera, drama, Broadway shows, and performances by its resident symphony orchestra. The grand building stretches along the canal in Confederation Sq.

INFORMATION

Capital Information Kiosk (844-878-8333; 90 Wellington St; 9am-5pm) This helpful office is the city's hub for information and bookings.

Ottawa Tourism (www.ottawatourism.ca) Offers a comprehensive online look at the nation's capital, and can assist with planning itineraries and booking accommodations.

GETTING THERE & AWAY

AIR

The state-of-the-art **Ottawa MacDonald-Cartier International Airport** (YOW; 613-248-2125; www.yow.ca; 1000 Airport Pkwy) is 15km south of the city and, perhaps surprisingly, is very small; almost all international flights require a transfer before arriving in the capital (normally in Toronto's Lester B Pearson International Airport).

BUS

The **central bus station** (613-238-6668; www.ottawacentralstation.com; 265 Catherine St) is just off Queensway (Hwy 417), near Kent St. Several companies operate bus services from the station, including **Greyhound** (1-800-661-8747; www.greyhound.ca) with services to Toronto (from $67, 5½ hours, eight daily).

TRAIN

The **VIA Rail Station** (888-842-7245; www.viarail.ca; 200 Tremblay Rd) is 7km east of downtown, near the Hwy 19/Riverside Dr exit of Hwy 417. Trains run to Toronto ($109, 4½ hours, 10 daily) via Brockville and Kingston, and to Québec City via Montréal ($114, two hours, four daily).

GETTING AROUND

TO/FROM THE AIRPORT

The cheapest way to get to the airport is by city bus. Take bus 97 from Slater St between Elgin St and Bronson Ave (make sure you are heading in the 'South Keys & Airport' direction). The ride takes 40 minutes and costs $3.50.

Canadian Tire Centre

Ottawa Shuttle Service (☎613-680-3313; www.ottawashuttleservice.com; 1 or 2 passengers within Ottawa $59; ⊙office 10am-10pm, shuttles 24hr) offers private and shared shuttles from downtown hotels.

Blue Line Taxi (☎613-238-1111; www.bluelinetaxi.com) and **Capital Taxi** (☎613-744-3333; www.capitaltaxi.com) offer cab services; the fare to/from downtown is around $30. During the week, if you're having a hard time snagging a cab, there's always a cluster on Metcalfe St between Sparks and Queen Sts.

BICYCLE

Right on the Rideau Canal bike path, the friendly staff at **Rent-A-Bike** (☎613-241-4140; www.rentabike.ca; East Arch Plaza Bridge, 2 Rideau St; rentals per hour from $9; ⊙9am-5pm) will set you up with a bike and offer tips about scenic trails. The Capital Information Kiosk has bike maps.

PUBLIC TRANSPORTATION

OC Transpo (☎613-741-4390; www.octranspo.com) operates Ottawa's useful bus network and a light-rail system known as the O-train. Bus rides cost $3.50 ($1.80 for children under 13) and you can pay on the bus. Make sure you have the exact change on you. You can also purchase a day pass ($10.50) from the driver. Be sure to take your ticket when boarding and paying; it allows you to transfer to other buses for a period of 90 minutes. The Capital Information Kiosk has bus maps.

The O-train's Confederation Line runs downtown via Parliament and the University of Ottawa and was finalising operations at the time of writing. The fare will be the same as the bus and riders will be able to transfer from the bus to train and vice versa for free.

Ottawa and Hull/Gatineau operate separate bus systems. A transfer is valid from one system to the other, but may require an extra payment.

MONTRÉAL

In this Chapter

Montréal at a glance...

Montréal is a slice of old Europe in a pie of contemporary design. The architectural sweep of the city takes in photogenic 18th-century facades as well as 20th-century icons. The city is also at the forefront of Canada's cultural juggernaut, with a fascinating blend of festivals and celebrations. The Québécois love their summers and autumnal colors, but it is the winter that defines much of their lives – get set to join them on the slopes of local mountains via ski, snowboard or toboggan, or warm up and fill up in one of their irresistible patisseries, cozy English pubs, venerable Jewish delis or magnificent food markets.

One Day in Montréal

Beeline to the stunning **Basilique Notre-Dame** (p100), then explore the old town and stroll up **Place Jacques-Cartier** (p101) with its many buskers and artists. Visit the excellent **Pointe-à-Callière Cité d'archéologie et d'histoire de Montréal** (p101), making sure to visit the archaeological crypt. Cap off the day with dinner at **Liverpool House** (p109) and a **Cirque du Soleil** (p110) show.

Two Days in Montréal

On day two, visit the **Musée des Beaux-Arts de Montréal** (p101), then head to **Marché Atwater** (p103) for croissants and local produce. Explore the **Canal de Lachine** (p104) either by bike with **My Bicyclette** (p104) or boat with **Le Petit Navire** (p104). In the evening catch some live music – perhaps go classical with the **Orchestre Symphonique de Montréal** (p111) or opt for a way-left-of-center gig at **Foufounes Électriques** (p111).

Previous page: Montréal in autumn

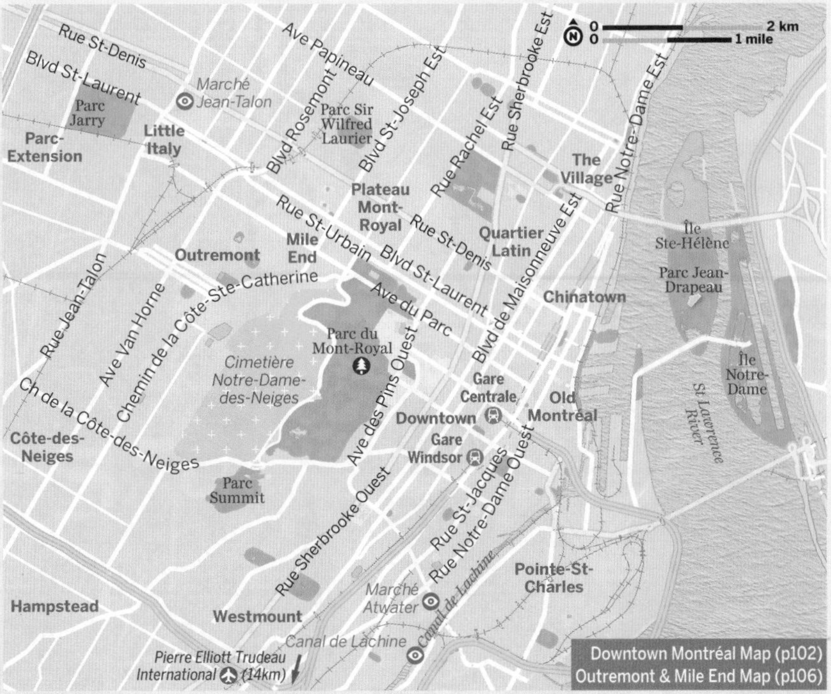

Downtown Montréal Map (p102)
Outremont & Mile End Map (p106)

Arriving in Montréal

Pierre Elliott Trudeau International Airport Take a bus ($10, 45 minutes) or taxi ($40, 30 minutes) downtown.

Gare Centrale Trains pulling into Montréal arrive at this convenient downtown terminus, well serviced by local taxis.

Gare d'Autocars de Montréal Most long-distance buses arrive here in the Quartier Latin, with handy connections to the Berri-UQAM metro station.

Where to Stay

Montréal's accommodation scene is blessed with a tremendous variety of rooms and styles. Though rates aren't particularly cheap, they are reasonable by international standards – or even compared with other Canadian cities such as Toronto or Vancouver. French- and Victorian-style inns and independent hotels cater to a variety of budgets.

For more information on the best neighborhood to stay in, see p113.

Montréal Jazz Fest

In a city that loves festivals, the Festival International de Jazz de Montréal is the mother of them all.

Great For...

☑ **Don't Miss**

Downloading the festival app for schedules, artist bios, tickets and even a pocket photo booth.

Erupting in late June each year and turning the city into an enormous stage, the festival is no longer just about jazz. Count on hundreds of top-name performers bringing reggae, rock, blues, world music, Latin, Cajun, Dixieland and even pop to audiophiles from across the globe.

It started as the pipe dream of a young local music producer, Alain Simard, who tried to sell his idea to the government and corporate sponsors, with little success. Now it's the single biggest tourist event in Québec, attracting nearly two million visitors to 400 concerts – many say it's the best jazz festival on the planet. Miles Davis, Herbie Hancock, Al Jarreau, Sonny Rollins, Wayne Shorter, Stevie Wonder, Al Dimeola, James Cotton, Dianne Reeves, Booker T Jones, Taj Mahal, John Scofield and Jack DeJohnette are but a few of the

JOSEPH S | TAN MATT / SHUTTERSTOCK ©

Need to Know

The festival runs for 10 days from late June to early July; the festival website (www.montrealjazzfest.com) provides all the details.

Take a Break

From terraces serving oysters and wine to fabulous food trucks, there are plenty of on-site places to recharge and refuel.

★ Top Tip

Book ahead for packages that include accommodations, show tickets, tours and even a T-shirt.

giants who have graced the podiums over the years.

Local Talent

In the 1940s and '50s, Montréal was one of North America's most important venues for jazz music. It produced a number of major jazz musicians, such as pianist Oscar Peterson and trumpeter Maynard Ferguson. The scene went into decline in the late 1950s but revived after the premiere of the jazz festival in 1979.

The city's other celebrated jazz pianist, Oliver Jones, was already in his 50s when he was discovered by the music world. Since the 1980s he has established himself as a major mainstream player with impressive technique and a hard-swinging style.

Singer and pianist Diana Krall has enjoyed mass appeal without sacrificing her bop and swing roots. In 1993 she launched her career on Montréal's Justin Time record label, and she remains a perennial local favorite during regular appearances at Montréal's jazz festival.

Originally from New York City, singer Ranee Lee is known for her virtuosity that spans silky ballads, swing standards and raw blues tunes. She has performed with many jazz notables and is a respected teacher on the McGill University music faculty.

The Scoop

Free festival programs can be found at kiosks around the Place des Arts. Some concerts are held indoors, others on outdoor stages; several downtown blocks are closed to traffic. The music starts around noon and lasts until late evening when the clubs take over.

Old Montréal

On the edge of the St Lawrence River, Old Montréal is the city's birthplace, composed of picturesque squares and grand old-world architecture.

Start Basilique Notre-Dame
Distance 2km
Duration 2 hours

2 Head along Rue St-Jacques, once known as Canada's Wall St. Stop at the grand **Royal Bank Tower**, Montréal's tallest building in 1928, to see its palatial interior.

3 Loop onto Rue Notre-Dame and down Rue St-Jean. On the corner of Rue de l'Hôpital, the **Lewis Building** has dragons and mischievous gargoyles on the facade. It was built for Cunard Shipping Lines, a steamship company founded in 1840.

Take a Break
Refuel at **Olive + Gourmando** (p107) with hearty breakfasts and lunches.

4 A few blocks further is **Place d'Youville**, one of Old Montréal's prettiest squares. Some of the first Europeans settled here in 1642. An obelisk commemorates the city's founding.

5 Nearby is the fascinating **Pointe-à-Callière Cité d'archéologie et d'histoire de Montréal** (p101). Inside see the city's ancient foundations, or go to the top floor for fine views over the Old Port.

9 Turn right on Rue St-Sulpice and return to Place d'Armes. Note the **New York Life Building**, Montréal's first skyscraper (1888), eight stories tall.

Classic Photo

Basilique Notre-Dame

1 Start with the city's most celebrated cathedral, the magnificent **Basilique Notre-Dame** (p100). Inside is a spectacularly carved pulpit and richly hued stained-glass windows relating key events from the city's founding.

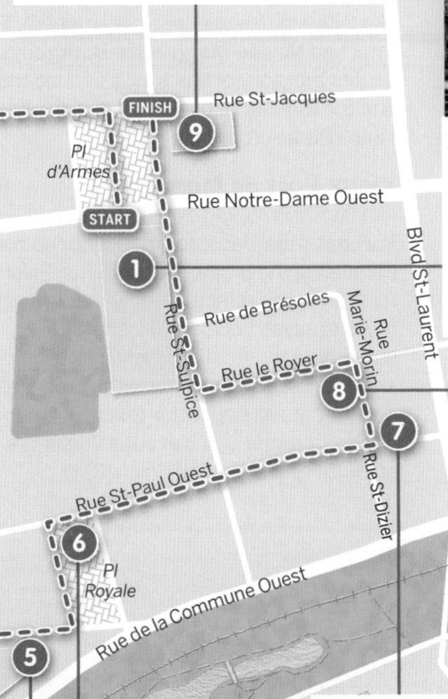

8 Head up Rue Marie-Morin and turn left onto lovely **Cours Le Royer**, a tranquil pedestrian mall with fountains. On the north-side passageway is a stained-glass window of Jérôme Le Royer, one of Montréal's founders.

7 Walk down Rue St-Paul to see the 2006 bronze sculpture **Les Chuchoteuses** (the Whisperers), tucked in a corner near Rue St-Dizier. This was one of many projects to revitalize the old quarter.

6 Across the road is the 1836 **Old Customs House**. It's in front of Place Royale, the early settlement's marketplace in the 17th and 18th centuries.

Bassin King Edward

0 200 m
0 0.1 miles

SIGHTS

Old Montréal

Basilique Notre-Dame — Church

(Map p102; 846-842-2925; www.basiliquenotredame.ca; 110 Rue Notre-Dame Ouest; adult/child $8/5; 8am-4:30pm Mon-Fri, to 4pm Sat, 12:30-4pm Sun; M Place-d'Armes) Montréal's famous landmark, Notre Dame Basilica, is a visually pleasing if slightly gaudy symphony of carved wood, paintings, gilded sculptures and stained-glass windows. Built in 1829 on the site of an older and smaller church, it also sports a famous Casavant Frères **organ** and the **Gros Bourdon**, said to be the biggest bell in North America. Admission includes an optional 20-minute guided tour in English.

Chapelle Notre-Dame-de-Bon-Secours — Church

(Map p102; 514-282-8670; https://margueritebourgeoys.org; 400 Rue St-Paul Est; chapel free, museum adult/student/child $12/9/7; 10am-6pm Tue-Sun May-Oct, 11am-4pm Tue-Sun Nov–mid-Jan & Mar-Apr; ; M Champ-de-Mars) Known as the Sailors' Church, this enchanting chapel derives its name from the sailors who left behind votive lamps in the shapes of ships in thanksgiving for safe passage. The restored interior has stained-glass windows and paintings depicting key moments in the life of the Virgin Mary (for whom Montréal – aka Ville-Marie – was originally named). The attached **Musée Marguerite-Bourgeoys** relates the story of Montréal's first teacher and the founder of the Congregation of Notre-Dame order of nuns.

Vieux-Port de Montréal — Park

(Old Port; Map p102;) Montréal's Vieux-Port has morphed into a park and fun zone paralleling the mighty St Lawrence River for 2.5km and punctuated by four grand *quais* (quays). Locals and visitors alike come here for strolling, cycling and in-line skating. Cruise boats, ferries, jet boats and speedboats all depart for tours from various docks. In winter you can cut a fine figure on an outdoor ice-skating rink (p104).

> *Locals and visitors alike come here for strolling*

Vieux-Port de Montréal

Place d'Armes — Historic Site

(Map p102; M Place-d'Armes) This open square is framed by some of the finest buildings in Old Montréal, including its oldest bank, first skyscraper and Basilique Notre-Dame. The square's name references the bloody battles that took place here as religious settlers and Indigenous groups clashed over control of what would become Montréal. At its center stands the **Monument Maisonneuve**, dedicated to city founder Paul de Chomedey, *sieur* de Maisonneuve.

Pointe-à-Callière Cité d'archéologie et d'histoire de Montréal — Museum

(Museum of Archaeology & History; Map p102; ☎514-872-9150; www.pacmuseum.qc.ca; 350 Pl Royale; adult/child $22/8; ⏰10am-5pm Tue-Fri, from 11am Sat & Sun; 👪; M Place-d'Armes) One of Montréal's most fascinating sites, this museum takes visitors on a historical journey through the centuries, beginning with the early days of Montréal. Visitors should start with *Yours Truly, Montréal,* an 18-minute multimedia show that covers the arrival of the Amerindians, the founding of Montréal and other key moments. Afterward, head to the **archaeological crypt** where you can explore the remains of the city's ancient sewage and river system, and the foundations of its first buildings and public square.

Place Jacques-Cartier — Square

(Map p102; M Champ-de-Mars) FREE The liveliest spot in Old Montréal, this gently inclined square hums with performance artists, street musicians and the animated chatter from terrace restaurants lining its borders. A public market was set up here after a château burned down in 1803. At its top end stands the **Colonne Nelson**, a monument erected to Admiral Lord Nelson after his defeat of Napoleon's fleet at Trafalgar.

Downtown

Musée des Beaux-Arts de Montréal — Museum

(Museum of Fine Arts; Map p102; www.mbam.qc.ca; 1380 Rue Sherbrooke Ouest; all exhibitions & pavilions adult over 30yr/21-30yr/under 20yr $24/16/free, after 5pm Wed special exhibition $12; ⏰10am-5pm Tue-Sun, to 9pm Wed special exhibitions only; M Guy-Concordia) A must for art-lovers, this museum has amassed centuries' worth of paintings, sculpture, decorative arts, furniture, prints, drawings and photographs. European heavyweights include Rembrandt, Picasso and Monet, but the museum really shines when it comes to Canadian art. Highlights include works by Prudence Heward and Paul Kane, landscapes by the Group of Seven and abstractions by Martha Townsend and Jean-Paul Riopelle. Temporary exhibits are often exceptional and have included a showcase on French fashion designer Thierry Mugler.

Musée McCord — Museum

(McCord Museum of Canadian History; Map p102; ☎514-861-6701; www.mccord-museum.qc.ca; 690 Rue Sherbrooke Ouest; adult/student/child $20/14/free, special exhibitions extra $5, after 5pm Wed free; ⏰10am-6pm Tue, Thu & Fri, to 9pm Wed, to 5pm Sat & Sun; M McGill) With hardly an inch to spare in its cramped but welcoming galleries, the McCord houses thousands of artifacts and documents illustrating Canada's social, cultural and archaeological history from the 18th century to the present day, with a small-but-excellent First Nations permanent collection displaying Indigenous dress and artifacts.

Place des Arts — Arts Center

(Map p102; ☎box office 514-842-2112; www.placedesarts.com; 175 Rue Ste-Catherine Ouest; M Place-des-Arts) Montréal's performing-arts center is the nexus for artistic and cultural events. Several renowned musical companies call Place des Arts home, including **Opéra de Montréal** (☎514-985-2258; www.operademontreal.com) and the Montréal Symphony Orchestra (p111), based in the acoustically brilliant 2100-seat **Maison Symphonique**. It's also center stage for **Festival International de Jazz de Montréal** (www.montrealjazzfest.com; ⏰late Jun-early Jul). A key part of the Quartier des Spectacles, the complex embraces an outdoor plaza with fountains and an ornamental pool and is attached to the Complexe Desjardins shopping center via an underground tunnel.

Downtown Montréal
0 500 m
0 0.25 miles
A
B
C
D
E
F
1
2
3
4
McGill University
Rue Sherbrooke Ouest
Ave du Président Kennedy
Blvd de Maisonneuve Ouest
Peel
McGill
Place-des-Arts
Pl des Arts
St-Laurent
Blvd de Maisonneuve Est
Berri-UQAM
Pl Émilie-Gamelin
Gare d'Autocars de Montréal
Rue St-Norbert
Rue Ontario Est
Ave Savoie
Kazu (400m)
Rue Ste-Catherine Ouest
Rue Ste-Catherine Est
Université du Québec à Montréal
Rue Bishop
Rue Crescent
Rue de la Montagne
Rue Drummond
Rue Stanley
Rue Peel
Sq Dorchester
Rue Mansfield
Ave McGill College
Rue University
Ave Union
Sq Phillips
Rue Mayor
Rue St-Alexandre
Rue de Bleury
Rue Anderson
Rue Jeanne-Mance
Rue St-Urbain
Rue Clark
Blvd St-Laurent
Rue Charlotte
Rue Berri
Rue St-Hubert
Rue St-André
Rue St-Timothée
Rue Amherst
Rue Wolfe
Blvd René-Lévesque Ouest
Blvd René-Lévesque Est
DOWNTOWN
Pl du Canada
Gare Centrale
VIA Rail
CHINATOWN
Rue de la Gauchetière Est
Champ-de-Mars
Rue St-Denis
Ave Viger Est
Sq Viger
Lucien-L'Allier
Bonaventure
Place Bonaventure
Square-Victoria
Ave Viger Ouest
Place-d'Armes
Rue St-Antoine Ouest
Rue St-Antoine Est
Rue Lucien-L'Allier
Rue de la Montagne
Rue St-Jacques
Sq Chaboillez
Sq Victoria
Pl Vauquelin
Rue Notre-Dame Est
Liverpool House (1.1km); Canal Lounge (1.8km); Satay Brothers (1.8km); Ma Bicyclette (2km)
Parc Labatt
Rue Notre-Dame Ouest
Rue St-François-Xavier
Rue St-Paul Est
OLD MONTRÉAL
Rue St-Maurice
Autoroute 10
Rue McGill
Rue de la Commune Est
Bassin de l'Horloge
Rue Barré
Rue Peel
Rue St-Paul Ouest
Rue St-Pierre
Pl Royale
Pl d'Youville
Rue de la Commune Ouest
Rue William
Parc du Bassin Bonsecours
Quai de l'Horloge
Quai Jacques-Cartier
Conveyor Pier
Quai King Edward
Quai Alexandra
St Lawrence River
Rue Ottawa

Downtown Montréal

Sights

1 Basilique Notre-Dame D3
2 Chapelle Notre-Dame-de-Bon-Secours E4
3 Musée des Beaux-Arts de Montréal A1
4 Musée McCord C1
5 Old Port E4
6 Place d'Armes D3
7 Place des Arts D1
8 Place Jacques-Cartier E4
9 Pointe-à-Callière Cité d'archéologie et d'histoire de Montréal D4
10 Rue St-Denis E1

Activities, Courses & Tours

11 La Patinoire Natrel du Vieux Port E4
12 Le Petit Navire E4
13 Les Fantômes du Vieux-Montréal D4
14 Montréal Canadiens A3

Shopping

15 Camellia Sinensis E1
16 Cheap Thrills B1

Eating

17 Barroco C4
18 Café Parvis C2
19 Olive + Gourmando C4
20 Orange Rouge D3

Drinking & Nightlife

21 Crew Café C3

Entertainment

Aura Basilica .... (see 1)
Bell Centre .... (see 14)
22 Cirque du Soleil E4
23 Foufounes Électriques E2
Opéra de Montréal .... (see 7)
24 Orchestre Symphonique de Montréal D1

Marché Atwater — Market

(514-937-7754; www.marchespublics-mtl.com; 138 Ave Atwater; 7am-6pm Mon-Wed, to 7pm Thu, to 8pm Fri, to 5pm Sat & Sun; M Atwater) Just off the Canal de Lachine (p115), this fantastic market has a mouthwatering assortment of fresh produce from local farms, excellent wines, crusty breads, fine cheeses and other delectable fare. The market's specialty shops operate year-round, while outdoor stalls open from March to October. The grassy banks overlooking the canal are great for a picnic.

Rue St-Denis & the Village

Rue St-Denis — Area

(Map p102; M Berri-UQAM) The backbone of Montréal's francophone shopping district, Rue St-Denis is lined with hat and garment shops, uberhip record stores and terrace cafes designed to keep people from getting any work done. Summer crowds flock to the inviting bistros and bars on both sides of the street.

Plateau Mont-Royal & the Northeast

Biodôme — Museum

(514-868-3000; www.espacepourlavie.ca; 4777 Ave du Pierre-De Coubertin; adult/child $20/10; 9am-6pm daily late Jun-Sep, 9am-5pm Tue-Sun rest of year; M Viau) At this captivating exhibit you can amble through a rainforest, explore Antarctic islands, view rolling woodlands, take in aquatic life in the Gulf of St Lawrence or wander along the raw Atlantic oceanfront – all without ever leaving the building. The five ecosystems house many thousands of animal and plant species; follow the self-guided circuit and you will see everything. Be sure to dress in layers for the temperature swings. You can borrow free strollers, and interactive exhibits are at small-child height.

Parc du Mont-Royal — Park

(514-843-8240; www.lemontroyal.qc.ca; 1260 Chemin Remembrance; M Mont-Royal, then bus 11) FREE Montréalers are proud of their 'mountain,' the work of New York Central Park designer Frederick Law Olmsted. It's a sprawling, leafy playground that's perfect for cycling, jogging, horseback riding, picnicking and, in winter, cross-country skiing and tobogganing (kid-sized rental equipment available). In fine weather, enjoy panoramic views from the **Belvédère Kondiaronk lookout** (514-872-3911; 1196 Voie Camillien-Houde; 6am-midnight) FREE fronting **Chalet du Mont-Royal** (10am-5pm

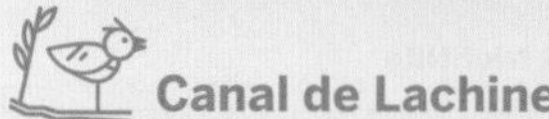

Canal de Lachine

To see a perfect marriage of urban infrastructure and green civic planning, visit this 14km-long cycling and pedestrian **pathway** (Rue Charles-Biddle;) FREE, with picnic areas and outdoor spaces. Since the canal was reopened for navigation in 2002, flotillas of pleasure and sightseeing boats glide along its calm waters. Old warehouses converted into luxury condos line the canal near Atwater market. The Lachine Canal was originally built in 1825 as a means of bypassing the treacherous Lachine Rapids on the St Lawrence River.

GLASS AND NATURE / SHUTTERSTOCK ©

Mon-Thu, to 8pm Fri-Sun) FREE, a grand old stone villa that hosts big-band concerts in summer, or from the **Observatoire de l'Est**, a favorite rendezvous for lovebirds.

Little Italy, Mile End & Outremont

Marché Jean-Talon Market

(514-937-7754; www.marchespublics-mtl.com; 7075 Ave Casgrain; 7am-6pm Mon-Wed & Sat, to 8pm Thu & Fri, to 5pm Sun; P; M Jean-Talon) The pride of Little Italy, this huge covered market is Montréal's most diverse. Many chefs buy ingredients for their menus here or in the specialty food shops nearby. Three long covered aisles are packed with merchants selling fruit, vegetables, flowers and baked goods, all flanked by delis and cafe-restaurants with tiny patios. Even in winter, the market is open under big tents.

ACTIVITIES

La Patinoire Natrel du Vieux Port Skating

(Map p102; Parc du Bassin Bonsecours; adult/child $6/4, skate rental $7; 10am-9pm Mon-Wed, to 10pm Thu-Sun; 14, M Champ-de-Mars) This is one of Montréal's most popular outdoor-skating rinks, located on the shore of the St Lawrence River next to the Pavilion du Bassin Bonsecours. DJs add to the festivities. At Christmas time there's a big nativity scene.

Ma Bicyclette Cycling

(514-317-6306; www.mybicyclette.com; 2985 Rue St-Patrick; bicycle per 2hr/day from $22/45; 10am-6pm; M Charlevoix) Located along the Canal de Lachine – just across the bridge from the Atwater market – this place rents bikes and other gear during the warmer months. It also sponsors city bike tours, and the repair shop next door is a good place to go if your bike conks out on the canal path.

TOURS

Le Petit Navire Boating

(Map p102; 514-602-1000; www.lepetitnavire.ca; Quai Jacques-Cartier; adult/child 45min tour $20/10, 90min tour $27/20; 10am-7pm mid-May–mid-Oct; M Champ-de-Mars) Aside from rowing a boat yourself, this outfit offers the most ecologically friendly boat tours in Montréal. The silent, electric-powered Le Petit Navire takes passengers on 45-minute tours departing hourly around the Old Port area. Equally intriguing are the 1½-hour cruises up the Canal de Lachine, departing Friday, Saturday and Sunday at 11:30am from Quai Jacques-Cartier and 2pm from Marché Atwater.

Les Fantômes du Vieux-Montréal Walking

(Map p102; 514-844-4021; www.fantommontreal.com; 360 Rue St-François-Xavier, ticket office; adult/youth $25/16; scheduled tours 8:30pm Sat May-Jun, daily Jul-Aug & late Oct-early Nov, Fri & Sat early Sep–mid-Oct) Gives 90-minute evening tours tracing historic

ANDRIY BLOKHIN / SHUTTERSTOCK ©

Marché Jean-Talon (p106)

crimes and legends, led by guides in period costume. You'll hear talk of hangings, sorcery, torture and other light bedtime tales on this good-time evening outing.

SHOPPING

Drawn & Quarterly Books

(Map p106; ☎514-279-2224; http://mtl.drawnandquarterly.com; 211 Rue Bernard Ouest; ⏰10am-8pm; Ⓜ Outremont) The flagship store of this cult independent comic-book and graphic-novel publisher has become something of a local literary haven. Cool book launches take place here, and the quaint little shop sells all sorts of reading matter, including children's books, vintage Tintin comics, recent fiction and art books.

Camellia Sinensis Food & Drinks

(Map p102; www.camellia-sinensis.com; 351 Rue Émery; ⏰10am-6pm Mon-Wed, Sat & Sun, to 9pm Thu & Fri; Ⓜ Berri-UQAM) Right in front of the Cinéma Quartier Latin, this welcoming tea shop has more than 200 varieties of tea from China, Japan, India and elsewhere in Asia, plus quality teapots, tea accessories, books, and workshops such as pairing tea with chocolate. You can taste exotic teas and carefully selected desserts in the salon next door, which features brews from recent staff travels.

Monastiraki Vintage

(Map p106; ☎514-278-4879; www.monastiraki.blogspot.ca; 5478 Blvd St-Laurent; ⏰noon-6pm Wed, to 8pm Thu & Fri, to 5pm Sat & Sun; Ⓜ Laurier) This unclassifiable store named after a flea-market neighborhood in Athens calls itself a 'hybrid curiosity shop/art space,' but that doesn't do justice to what illustrator Billy Mavreas sells: 1960s comic books, contemporary zines, silk-screen posters, and myriad antique and collectible knickknacks, as well as recent works mainly by local graphic artists.

Cheap Thrills Music

(Map p102; ☎514-844-8988; www.cheapthrills.ca; 2044 Rue Metcalfe; ⏰11am-6pm Mon-Wed & Sat, to 9pm Thu & Fri, noon-5pm Sun) It's easy to lose track of time as you browse through this big selection of used books

Outremont & Mile End
400 m
0.2 miles
Damas Restaurant (700m)
Marché Jean-Talon (1.5km)
Ave Lajoie
OUTREMONT
Rue Bernard Ouest
Parc St-Viateur
Viaduc Rosemont Van Horne
Rosemont
Ave Outremont
Ave Champagneur
Ave Bloomfield
Ave Querbes
Ave Durocher
Rue Hutchison
Rue St-Viateur Ouest
Ave Elmwood
Ave de l'Épée
Ave du Parc
Rue Jeanne-Mance
Ave de l'Esplanade
Rue Waverly
Rue St-Urbain
Rue Clark
Blvd St-Laurent
Rue St-Dominique
Ave Casgrain
Ave de Gaspé
Ave Henri-Julien
Rue St-Denis
Rue Maguire
MILE END
Rue Boucher
Rue Rivard
Ave Fairmount Ouest
Ave Fairmount Est
Parc AT Lépine
Parc St-Michel
Rue Drolet
Ave Laurier Ouest
Ave Laurier Est
Rue Edouard Charles
Parc Lahaie
Laurier
Blvd St-Joseph Ouest
Blvd St-Joseph Est
Ave Van Horne
Chemin de la Côte Ste-Catherine
Rue Villeneuve Ouest
Ave Coloniale
Rue de Bullion
Ave de l'Hôtel-de-Ville
Cimetière Notre-Dame-des-Neiges
Voie Camillien-Houde
Mont-Royal
Ave du Mont-Royal Ouest
Ave du Mont-Royal Est
Ave Laval
Rue Berri
Rue Marie-Anne Est
Parc du Portugal
Parc du Mont-Royal
Rue Rachel Ouest
Rue Rachel Est
Parc Jeanne-Mance
Ave Duluth Ouest
Ave Duluth Est
Rue Bagg
Rue Napoléon
McGill University
Rue Roy Est

Outremont & Mile End

Shopping
1 Drawn & Quarterly B1
2 Monastiraki C2

Eating
3 Fairmount Bagel C3
4 L'Express D6
5 St-Viateur Bagel B2

Drinking & Nightlife
6 Barfly C6
7 Big in Japan C5
8 La Buvette Chez Simone B3

and music (CDs and some vinyl), both with a mainstream and offbeat bent and sold at bargain prices.

EATING

St-Viateur Bagel Bakery $

(Map p106; 514-276-8044; www.stviateurbagel.com; 263 Rue St-Viateur Ouest; bagels 90¢; 24hr; M Place-des-Arts, then bus 80) Currently the bagel favorite of Montréal (or is it Fairmount?), St-Viateur Bagel was set up in 1957 and has a reputation stretching across Canada and beyond for its perfectly crusty, chewy and slightly sweet creations. The secret to their perfection seems to be boiling in honey water followed by baking in the wood-fired oven.

Kazu Japanese $

(514-937-2333; www.kazumontreal.com; 1862 Rue Ste-Catherine Ouest; mains $10-17; noon-3pm Sun, Mon, Thu & Fri, also 5:30-9:30pm Thu-Mon; M Guy-Concordia) Kazuo Akutsu's frenetic hole-in-the-wall in the Concordia Chinatown draws long lines of people waiting for *gyoza* (dumplings), ramen-noodle soup and awesome creations such as the 48-hour pork. Its popularity is well earned, but be warned: it gets cramped inside.

Satay Brothers Malaysian $

(514-933-3507; www.sataybrothers.com; 3721 Rue Notre-Dame Ouest; mains $9-15; 11am-11pm Wed-Sun; M Lionel-Groulx) Amid red walls, hanging lamps and mismatched thrift-store furnishings, this lively and Malaysia-chic bar-bistro serves some of the best 'street food' in Montréal. Crowds flock here to gorge on delicious chicken-satay sandwiches with peanut sauce served on grilled bread, tangy green papaya salad, braised pork (or tofu) buns, and *laksa lemak*, a rich and spicy coconut soup. It has great cocktails too.

Fairmount Bagel Bakery $

(Map p106; 514-272-0667; http://fairmountbagel.com; 74 Ave Fairmount Ouest; bagels $1; 24hr; M Laurier) One of Montréal's famed bagel bakeries – people flood in here around the clock to scoop them up the minute they come out of the oven. Classic sesame- or poppy-seed varieties are hits, though everything from cinnamon to all-dressed is here too. If you want an immediate fix of these honey-water boiled bagels, there is public seating outside.

Café Parvis Bistro $$

(Map p102; 514-764-3589; www.cafeparvis.com; 433 Rue Mayor; small plates $6-9; 7am-11pm Mon-Wed, to midnight Thu & Fri, 10am-midnight Sat, to 10pm Sun; ; M Place-des-Arts) Hidden on a quiet downtown lane, Café Parvis is set with oversized windows, hanging plants, old wooden floorboards and vintage fixtures. Once part of the fur district, this cleverly repurposed room serves up delicious pizzas ($10 at lunch; about $20 at night) in inventive combinations (such as duck, fennel and squid, ham and eggplant, or roasted vegetables with Gruyère).

Olive + Gourmando Cafe $$

(Map p102; 514-350-1083; www.oliveetgourmando.com; 351 Rue St-Paul Ouest; mains $11-18; 8am-5pm Wed-Sun; ; M Square-Victoria) Named after the owners' two cats, this bakery-cafe is legendary in town for its hot panini, generous salads and flaky baked goods. Excellent choices include the melted goat's-cheese panini with caramelized onions, decadent mac 'n' cheese, and 'the Cubain' (a ham, roast pork and Gruyère sandwich). Try to avoid the busy lunch rush (11:30am to 1:30pm).

Orange Rouge Asian $$

(Map p102; 514-861-1116; www.orangerouge.ca; 106 de la Gauchetière Ouest; mains $15-20; 11:30am-2:30pm Tue-Fri & 5:30-10:30pm Tue-Sat; Place-d'Armes) Hidden down a narrow lane of Chinatown, Orange Rouge has a quaint, low-lit interior that's rather nondescript save for the bright open kitchen at one end and a neon-lit crab sculpture on the wall. Grab a seat at the dark lacquered bar or on one of the banquettes for a feast of Asian fusion.

L'Express French $$

(Map p106; 514-845-5333; www.restaurantlexpress.com; 3927 Rue St-Denis; mains $19-29; 8am-2am Mon-Fri, from 10am Sat & Sun; Sherbrooke) L'Express has all the hallmarks of a Parisian bistro – black-and-white checkered floor, art-deco globe lights, papered tables and mirrored walls. High-end bistro fare completes the picture, with excellent dishes such as grilled salmon, bone marrow with sea salt, roast duck with salad, and beef tartare. The waiters can advise on the extensive wine list. Reservations are essential.

Barroco International $$$

(Map p102; 514-544-5800; www.barroco.ca; 312 Rue St-Paul Ouest; mains $27-41; 5-10:30pm Sun-Wed, to 11pm Thu, to midnight Fri & Sat; Square-Victoria) Small, cozy Barroco has stone walls, flickering candles and beautifully presented plates of roast guinea fowl, paella, braised short ribs and grilled fish. The selection is small (just six or so mains and an equal number of appetizers), but you can't go wrong here – particularly if you opt for the outstanding seafood and chorizo paella.

Damas Restaurant Syrian $$$

(514-439-5435; www.restaurant-damas.com; 1201 Ave Van Horne; mains $34-62; 5-10pm Mon-Thu, to 11pm Fri, 4-11pm Sat, 4-10pm Sun; ; Outremont) With unique Syrian-inspired cuisine just a few minutes from Mile End and Little Italy, Damas is consistently rated as one of the top restaurants in

From left: St-Viateur Bagel (p107); Olive + Gourmando (p107); Crew Café (p110)

JOANNA K DRAKOS / SHUTTERSTOCK ©

HEMIS / ALAMY STOCK PHOTO ©

the city. A warm and welcoming ambience, along with an eclectic menu of Syrian classics (Damascus marinated chicken, tahini seabass) and inspiring new flavors (herbed dumplings, sumac fries) all come together for a complete fine-dining experience.

Tuck Shop Québécois $$$

(☎514-439-7432; www.tuckshop.ca; 4662 Rue Notre-Dame Ouest; mains $30-36; ⏲5-11pm Tue-Sat; ✎; Ⓜ Place-St-Henri) Set in the heart of working-class St-Henri, Tuck Shop could have been plucked from London or New York if it weren't for its distinctly local menu, a delightful blend of market and terroir (locally sourced) offerings such as Kamouraska lamb shank, fish of the day with Jerusalem-artichoke puree and a Québec cheese plate, all prepared by able chef Theo Lerikos.

Liverpool House Québécois $$$

(☎514-313-6049; www.joebeef.ca; 2501 Rue Notre-Dame Ouest; mains $24-50; ⏲5-11pm Tue-Sat; ✎) Liverpool House sets the standard so many Québec restaurants are racing for: an ambience that feels laid-back, like a friend's dinner party, where the food is sent from angels on high. Expect oysters, smoked trout, braised rabbit, lobster spaghetti and various other iterations of regional excellence. There is usually a vegetarian main, but sometimes just one choice.

DRINKING & NIGHTLIFE

Canal Lounge Cocktail Bar

(☎514-451-2665; www.canallounge.com; 22 Ave Atwater; ⏲3-11pm Tue-Sat, to 10pm Sun late May-early Oct; Ⓜ Lionel Groulx) This permanently docked boat-bar nestles along the canal in front of a lovely pedestrian bridge. The over-45-year-old vessel has been converted into an upscale cocktail lounge. Sit on the rooftop for some fresh air or inside for maritime ambience. The friendly owners moonlight as bartenders and whip up finely crafted cocktails.

La Buvette Chez Simone Wine Bar

(Map p106; ☎514-750-6577; www.buvettechezsimone.com; 4869 Ave du Parc; ⏲4pm-3am; Ⓜ Laurier) An artsy-chic crowd of (mostly) Francophone bons vivants and

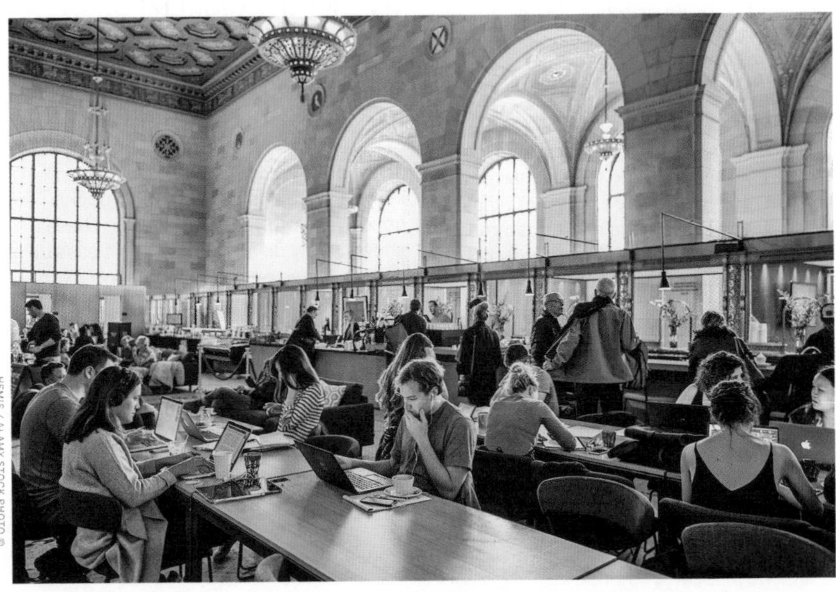

Hockey Heroes

The **Montréal Canadiens** (☎514-932-2582; www.canadiens.com; 1909 Ave des Canadiens-de-Montréal, Bell Centre; tickets $54-277; Ⓜ Bonaventure) of the National Hockey League have won the Stanley Cup 24 times. Although the team has struggled in recent years, Montréalers, especially Francophones, have a soft spot for the 'Habs' and matches at the **Bell Centre** (☎514-790-2525; www.centrebell.ca) sell out routinely. Scalpers hang around the entrance on game days, and you might snag a half-price ticket after the puck drops.

Bring your binoculars for the rafter seats. The center also hosts big-name concerts, boxing matches, Disney on Ice and visits by the Dalai Lama.

professionals loves this cozy wine bar. The staff know their vino and the extensive list is complemented by a gourmet tapas menu. On weekends, the place is jammed from *cinq à sept* (5pm to 7pm 'happy hour') into the wee hours.

Crew Café Cafe

(Map p102; http://crewcollectivecafe.com; 360 Rue St-Jacques; ⌚8am-8pm; 📶; Ⓜ Square-Victoria) Easily the most spectacular cafe in Montréal, Crew converted the old Royal Bank into a caffeine and laptop powerhouse. Order from a teller, then sip green tea and good lattes at a gilded deposit-slip counter (remember those?) and gaze way up at the ornate ceiling laden with chandeliers. It's worth popping in just to have a gander, especially for architecture and interior-design fans.

Barfly Bar

(Map p106; ☎514-284-6665; www.facebook.com/BarflyMtl; 4062 Blvd St-Laurent; ⌚4pm-3am; Ⓜ St-Laurent, then bus 55) Cheap, gritty, loud, fun and a little bit out of control – just the way we like our dive bars. Live bluegrass and rockabilly bands and bedraggled hipsters hold court alongside aging rockers at this St-Laurent hole-in-the-wall.

Big in Japan Cocktail Bar

(Map p106; ☎438-380-5658; 4175 Blvd St-Laurent; ⌚5pm-3am; Ⓜ St-Laurent, then bus 55) Completely concealed from the street, Big in Japan always amazes first-timers. There you are walking along bustling St-Laurent, you find the unmarked door (looking for its small window) by the address, walk down a rather unpromising corridor and emerge into a room lit with a thousand candles (or so it seems). Everything is Japanese-inspired – cocktails, whiskey, beer and bar food.

ENTERTAINMENT

Cirque du Soleil Theater

(Map p102; www.cirquedusoleil.com; Quai Jacques-Cartier; tickets from $67; Ⓜ Champ-de-Mars) Globally famous Cirque du Soleil, one of the city's most famous exports, puts on a new production of acrobats and music in this marvelous tent complex roughly once every two years in summer. These shows rarely disappoint, so don't pass up a chance to see one on its home turf.

Aura Basilica Arts Center

(Map p102; ☎866-842-2925; www.aurabasiliquemontreal.com; 110 Rue Notre-Dame Ouest; adult/child $26.50/15.50; ⌚shows 6pm Mon-Thu, 6pm & 8pm Fri, 7pm & 9pm Sat; Ⓜ Place-d'Armes) A unique immersive multimedia show where the interior of the Basilique Notre-Dame becomes the canvas for a light show set to surging orchestral music. The columns, ceiling and statues seem to pulse with life as video and lasers are projected all around you in a dazzling 20-minute show. You also receive another 20 minutes to take in the basilica in a calmer light show.

Foufounes Électriques Live Music
(Map p102; 514-844-5539; www.foufounes electriques.com; 87 Rue Ste-Catherine Est; cover $4-6; 4pm-3am; St-Laurent) A one-time bastion of the alternafreak, this cavernous quintessential punk venue still stages some wild music nights (retro Tuesdays, hip-hop Thursdays, rockabilly/metal/punk Saturdays), plus the odd one-off (a night of pro-wrestling or an indoor skateboarding contest). The graffiti-covered walls and industrial charm should tip you off that 'Electric Buttocks' isn't exactly a mainstream kinda place.

Orchestre Symphonique de Montréal Classical Music
(OSM; Map p102; 514-840-7400; www.osm.ca; 1600 Rue St-Urbain, Maison Symphonique, Pl des Arts; box office 9am-5pm Mon-Fri & 90mins before shows; Place-des-Arts) This internationally renowned orchestra plays to packed audiences in its Place des Arts base, the Maison Symphonique de Montréal, a venue with spectacular acoustics that was inaugurated in 2011. The OSM's Christmas performance of *The Nutcracker* is legendary.

INFORMATION

TOURIST INFORMATION

Centre Infotouriste Montréal (Map p102; 514-844-5400; www.mtl.org; 1255 Rue Peel; 9am-6pm May-Sep, to 5pm Oct-Apr; Peel) Provides maps, info about attractions and booking services (hotels, car hire, tours).

Tourisme Montréal (877-266-5687; www.mtl.org; 9am-noon & 1-5pm Mon-Fri, from 10am Wed) Has reams of information and a last-minute hotel search engine with guaranteed best price.

"Big in Japan always amazes first-timers"

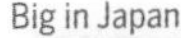

Big in Japan

 GETTING THERE & AWAY

AIR

Montréal is served by **Montréal-Pierre Elliott Trudeau International Airport** (Trudeau, YUL; www.admtl.com; Dorval), known in French as Aéroport Montréal-Trudeau, or simply as Trudeau Airport. It's about 21km west of downtown and is the hub of most domestic, US and overseas flights.

BUS

Most long-distance buses arrive at Montréal's **Gare d'Autocars** (Map p102; ☎514-842-2281; www.gamtl.com; 1717 Rue Berri; Ⓜ Berri-UQAM).

If buying tickets here for other destinations in the province, allow about 45 minutes before departure; most advance tickets don't guarantee a seat, so arrive early to line up at the counter.

Greyhound (www.greyhound.ca) operates long-distance routes to Ottawa, Toronto, Vancouver, Boston, New York City and other points throughout Canada and the United States.

TRAIN

Gare Centrale (Map p102; Central Train Station; ☎arrivals & departures 888-842-7245, info & reservations 514-989-2626; www.viarail.ca; 895 Rue de la Gauchetière Ouest; Ⓜ Bonaventure) is the local hub of **VIA Rail**, Canada's vast rail network, which links Montréal with cities all across the country.

Amtrak (www.amtrak.com) provides service between New York City and Montréal on its Adirondack line. The trip, though slow (11 hours), passes through lovely scenery along Lake Champlain and the Hudson River.

 GETTING AROUND

TO/FROM THE AIRPORT

Bus 747 (www.stm.info), the cheapest way to get into town, takes 25 to 60 minutes. Buses run round the clock, leaving from just outside the arrivals hall.

A taxi from the airport to the center takes at least 20 minutes; the fixed fare is $40.

BICYCLE

One of the best ways to see the city is by the public bike-rental service **Bixi** (☎514-789-2494; http://montreal.bixi.com; per 30min $2.95; ⏲24hr mid-Apr–Oct) 🍃. Short-term subscription fees allowing you to use the system for one day are very reasonably priced and allow unlimited free 30-minute rides (with fees rising steeply after 45 minutes).

There are also bike paths around the islands of Parc Jean-Drapeau, the Île de Soeurs and Parc du Mont-Royal.

PUBLIC TRANSPORTATION

STM (Société de Transport de Montréal; ☎514-786-4636; www.stm.info) is the city's bus and metro (subway) operator. Schedules vary depending on the line, but trains generally run from 5:30am to midnight from Sunday to Friday, slightly later on Saturday night (to 1:30am at the latest).

A single bus or metro ticket costs $3.25, and allows transfers between bus and metro for up to 120 minutes.

TAXI

Flag fall is a standard $3.50, plus another $1.70 per kilometer and 63¢ per minute spent waiting in traffic. Prices are posted on the windows inside taxis.

Taxi Champlain (☎514-271-1111; http://taxichamplain.com)

Taxi Co-Op (☎514-725-9885; www.taxi-coop.com)

Where to Stay

Hotels fill up fast in the summer, when warm weather and festivals galore bring hordes of tourists to Montréal, making reservations essential.

Neighborhood	Atmosphere
Old Montréal	Ultraconvenient for many sights, old-world charm, access to the Old Port; crowded with tourists at peak times, few inexpensive rooms, hard to find parking.
Downtown	Convenient for public transportation and sights throughout the city; can be congested, with few inexpensive options compared with other districts.
Rue St-Denis & the Village	Nightlife-charged area with excellent metro connections and walking access to both downtown and Old Montréal; expect noise from bars and clubs on weekend nights.
Plateau Mont-Royal & the Northeast	Staying in the most fashionable district of Montréal means being close to some of the best eateries and nightlife in town. Like the Village, the Plateau is packed with B&Bs; hotels are few and far between.

QUÉBEC CITY

In this Chapter

Québec City at a glance...

Québec City is the soul of the province, with a fierce grip on French Canadian identity. One of North America's oldest and most magnificent settlements, its picturesque old town is a Unesco World Heritage site – a living museum of narrow cobblestone streets, 17th- and 18th-century houses, and soaring church spires. The city also goes to great lengths to entertain visitors. All summer, musicians, acrobats and actors in period costume take to the streets, while festivals fill the air with fireworks and song. In January and February, Québec's Winter Carnival is arguably the biggest and most colorful winter celebration around.

One Day in Québec City

Wander through Old Québec, taking a gander inside the historic **Le Château Frontenac** (p122) and following our **walking tour** to see the top sights. Visit the spectacular **Musée de la Civilisation** (p122) and then dine on local specialties at **Chez Boulay** (p129). Wrap up the day with a ghostly night tour at **La Citadelle** (p118) or a night cap at **Le Sacrilège** (p130).

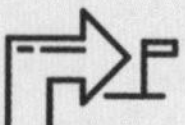

Two Days in Québec City

Begin the day at the absorbing **Musée National des Beaux-Arts du Québec** (p125). Pick up some picnic treats at **Le Croquembouche** (p127) and head to **Battlefields Park** (p123) to soak up some history. Return to Old Québec to burn off the croissants with a scenic trek around the **Fortifications** (p123). Finish the evening with live music at a local venue such as **Pape Georges** (p131) or **Fou-Bar** (p131).

Previous page: Le Château Frontenac (p122)

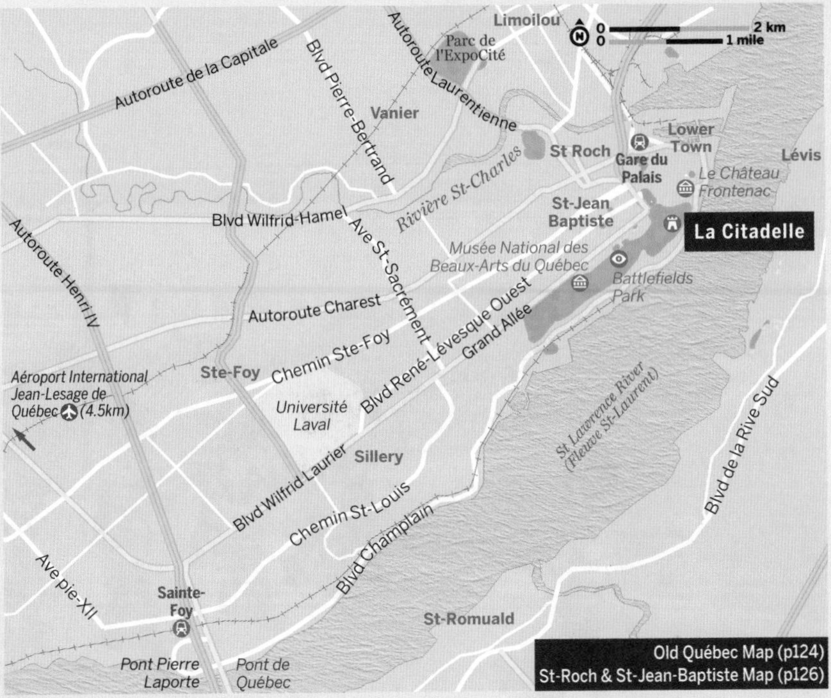

Old Québec Map (p124)
St-Roch & St-Jean-Baptiste Map (p126)

Arriving in Québec City

Aéroport International Jean-Lesage de Québec A taxi costs a flat fee of $35 into the city, or $15 if you're only going to the boroughs surrounding the airport.

Gare du Palais Conveniently located and served by daily VIA Rail trains from Montréal's Gare Centrale. There is also a major bus station adjacent to the train station, with regular bus service to Montréal.

Where to Stay

From old-fashioned B&Bs to stylish boutique hotels, Québec City has some fantastic overnight options. The best choices are the numerous small European-style hotels and Victorian B&Bs scattered around Old Québec. Make reservations well in advance, especially for weekends. Prices rise in the high-season summer months and during Winter Carnival. At other times of year, you can usually save 30% or so off the high-season prices.

Changing of the guard

La Citadelle

Towering above the St Lawrence River and covering 2.3 sq km, North America's largest fort was intended to defend against an American invasion that never came.

Great For...

☑ Don't Miss

Taking in the panoramic views from the northeastern ramparts.

History & Architecture

French forces started building a defensive structure here in the late 1750s, but the Citadelle we know today was built in the early to mid-1800s by the British, who feared two things: an American invasion of the colony and a possible revolt by the French-speaking population (that's why the cannons point not only at the river, but at Québec City itself).

By the time the Citadelle was completed, things were calming down. In 1871, the Treaty of Washington between the United States and the newly minted Dominion of Canada ended the threat of American invasion.

The giant fort, built atop the area's highest point, was designed to both intimidate and function as a stronghold; it was given

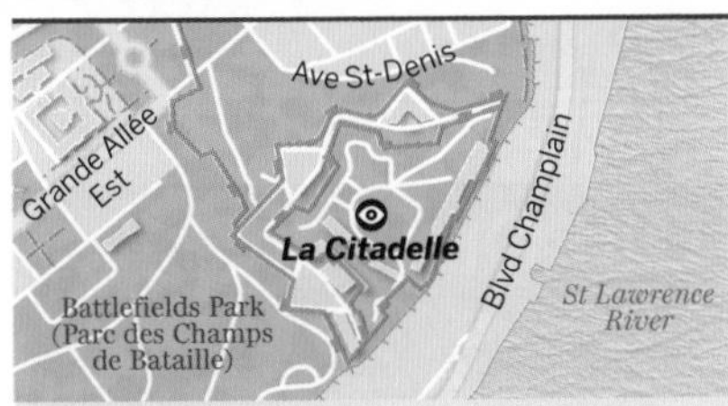

Need to Know

Map p124; ☎418-694-2815; www.lacitadelle.qc.ca; Côte de la Citadelle, Old Upper Town; adult/child $16/6; ⊙9am-5pm May-Oct, 10am-4pm Nov-Apr

Take a Break

A cafe on the grounds serves up drinks, snacks and, in winter, hot chocolate.

★ Top Tip

Hour-long guided tours of the Citadelle are excellent. In summertime don't miss the daily 10am changing of the guard.

a complex system of controlled access and the makings for a self-sufficient community inside. A polygonal star with a bastion at each of the four corners, its shape was inspired by the architecture of Vauban, France's foremost military engineer in the late 1600s.

The Noon-Day Gun

If you visit at noon, you may wonder if the fort is under siege. Each day at 12pm, a cannon is fired from the citadel, a tradition that dates back to 1871 when the Royal Canadian Artillery's garrison arrived. The purpose was to allow city residents to synchronize their watches. Some say it was also a call to lunch, while others argue it was meant to mark Angelus, the noon-day prayer.

Current Residents

The Citadelle now houses about 200 members of the Royal 22e Régiment. The Vandoos, a nickname taken from the French for 22 (vingt-deux), is the only entirely French-speaking battalion in the Canadian Forces. The second official residence of the governor general (the Queen of England's Canadian representative) has also been located here since 1872.

Guided Tours

Tours depart every 15 minutes to an hour depending on the season, with French- and English-language tours alternating throughout the day. From late June through October, lantern-lit evening tours (adult/child $20/18) are also offered. Summer-only events (late June through early September) include a changing of the guard at 10am daily and the beating of the retreat (6pm Saturday), which features soldiers banging on their drums at shift's end.

Old Québec

This historical walking tour encompasses a mix of well-known and lesser-known Vieux-Québec attractions. Set off early, before tour buses fill the streets.

Start Porte St-Louis
Distance 2km
Duration 1 to 2 hours

5 Descend **Côte de la Canoterie**, a longtime link between the Lower and Upper Towns. Hope Gate stood atop the côte until 1873 to keep the riffraff from entering the Upper Town. Turn right onto Rue St-Paul, the heart of Québec's antique district, then take a peek at Rue Sous-le-Cap, a former red-light district.

3 Left down Rue St-Anne is **Edifice Price**, one of Canada's first skyscrapers, built in 1929 for $1 million. Next door is the elegant 1870 Hotel Clarendon, the city's oldest hotel, currently undergoing renovations after a bad fire in 2019.

1 Begin at **Porte St-Louis**, an impressive gate first erected in 1693 (though this version dates from 1878). Follow Rue St-Louis to the corner of Rue du Corps-de-Garde, where a cannonball sits embedded in a tree (allegedly since 1759). Nearby, 47 Rue St-Louis is where French general Montcalm died, a day after being shot by the British during the destiny-changing Plains of Abraham Battle in September 1759.

4 Further up Rue des Jardins, Rue de Buade brings you face-to-face with the heavily restored Notre-Dame-de-Québec cathedral; just to the left is the entrance to the **Québec Seminary**, founded in 1663; American officers were imprisoned here after their unsuccessful siege of Québec in 1775–76. Detour down pretty Rue Garneau, then descend to Rue des Remparts for fine views over Québec City's waterfront factory district.

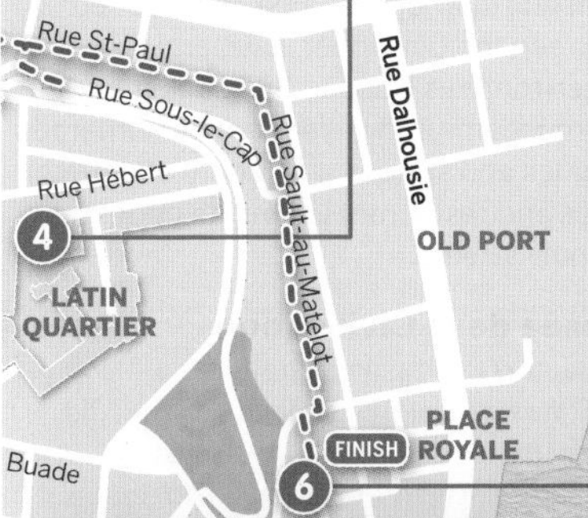

Classic Photo

Fresque des Québécois.

6 Turn right and follow Rue Sault-au-Matelot to the 420-sq-meter trompe-l'oeil **Fresque des Québécois**, where you can pose for the requisite tourist pic alongside historical figures such as Jacques Cartier and Samuel de Champlain.

Take a Break

Request the *menu du jour* at Aux Anciens Canadiens

2 At 34 Rue St-Louis, a 1676 home houses the Québécois restaurant **Aux Anciens Canadiens** (p129). Its steeply slanted roof was typical of 17th-century French architecture. Follow Rue des Jardins to the Ursuline Convent and Museum, where generations of nuns educated both French and Aboriginal girls starting in 1641.

St Lawrence River (Fleuve St-Laurent)

N 0 — 400 m
0 — 0.2 miles

SIGHTS

Most of Québec City's sights are found within the compact cluster of Old Québec walls, or just outside them, making this a dream destination for pedestrians.

Chapelle des Ursulines Chapel

(Ursulines Chapel; Map p124; www.museedesursulines.com; 12 Rue Donnacona, Old Upper Town; ⏱10:30am-noon & 1-4:30pm Tue-Sun May-Oct, 1-4:30pm Sat & Sun Nov-Apr) This glittering chapel just across from the **Musée des Ursulines** (Ursulines Museum; Map p124; ☎418-694-0694; www.polecultureldesursulines.ca; 10 Rue Donnacona; adult/youth/child $10/5/free; ⏱10am-5pm Tue-Sun May-Sep, 1-5pm Tue-Sun Oct-Apr) contains some of the finest wood carving in Québec and was gilded by the nuns themselves. French General Louis-Joseph Montcalm was buried here after he died in the decisive 1759 battle on the Plains of Abraham. However, in 2001 his remains were transferred to the cemetery at the Hôpital Général de Québec on Blvd Langelier to rest with those of his comrades-in-arms.

Le Château Frontenac Historic Building

(Map p124; ☎418-692-3861; www.fairmont.com/frontenac-quebec; 1 Rue des Carrières, Old Upper Town) Reputedly the world's most photographed hotel, this audaciously elegant structure was opened in 1893 by the Canadian Pacific Railway as part of its chain of luxury hotels. Its fabulous turrets, winding hallways and imposing wings graciously complement its dramatic location atop Cap Diamant, a cliff that cascades into the raging St Lawrence River. Over the years, it has lured a never-ending lineup of luminaries, including Alfred Hitchcock, who chose this setting for the opening scene of his 1953 mystery *I Confess*.

Le Monastère des Augustines Museum

(Map p124; ☎418-694-1639; https://monastere.ca; 77 Rue des Ramparts, Old Upper Town; adult/youth/child $10.50/4.50/free, guided tour $15/9/free; ⏱10am-5pm late Jun-Aug, Tue-Sun Sep-late Jun) On no account should you miss this museum, which traces the history of the order of Augustinian nuns who founded Québec's first hospital, the Hôtel-Dieu, in 1644 and ran it for over 300 years. OK, it may not sound like a crowd-pleaser, but the half-dozen rooms around a central cloister are filled with remarkable displays of religious items, crafts (artificial flowers were mandatory where flowers bloom only four months a year), an old apothecary and an 18th-century refectory.

Le Quartier Petit-Champlain Area

(Map p124) Arguably the city's most picturesque district, this area sandwiched between the Old Upper Town and the waterfront has Québec City's most intriguing museums and galleries, plus numerous plaques and statues and plenty of outdoor cafes and restaurants along its pedestrian-friendly streets.

Musée de la Civilisation Museum

(Museum of Civilization; Map p124; ☎418-643-2158; www.mcq.org/en; 85 Rue Dalhousie, Old Lower Town & Port; adult/teen/child $17/6/free, with temporary exhibitions $22/7/free; ⏱10am-5pm mid-Jun–early Sep, closed Mon early Sep–mid-Jun) This world-class museum wows even before you've clapped your eyes on the exhibits. It is a fascinating mix of modern design that incorporates preexisting buildings with contemporary architecture. The permanent exhibits – 'People of Québec: Then and Now' and 'This Is Our Story' on the province's Indigenous people today – are unique, sensitively curated and highly educational, with some clever interactive elements. At any given moment there's an outstanding variety of rotating shows.

Terrasse Dufferin Park

(Map p124; Rue des Carrières, Old Upper Town) Perched on a clifftop 60m above the St Lawrence River, this 425m-long boardwalk is a marvelous setting for a stroll, with spectacular, sweeping views. In summer it's peppered with street performers; in winter it hosts a dramatic **toboggan run** (Glissade de la Terrasse; Map p124; ☎418-528-1884; www.au1884.ca;

ANDRIY BLOKHIN / SHUTTERSTOCK ©

Rue du Petit-Champlain

per person 1/4 slides $3/10; ⏰10am-5pm Sun-Thu, to 6pm Fri & Sat mid-Dec–mid-Mar; 👪). Near the statue of Samuel de Champlain, stairways descend to the excavations of Champlain's **second fort** (Map p124; ☎418-648-7016; www.pc.gc.ca/eng/lhn-nhs/qc/saintlouisforts/index.aspx; adult/child $4/free, incl guided tour $15/10; ⏰9am-5:30pm mid-May–early Oct) 🍃, which stood here from 1620 to 1635. Nearby, you can take the **funicular** (Map p124; www.funiculaire-quebec.com; Rue du Petit-Champlain; one way $3.50; ⏰7:30am-10:30pm, to 11:30pm summer) to the Old Lower Town.

Battlefields Park Historic Site

(Parc des Champs-de-Bataille; ☎418-649-6157; www.theplainsofabraham.ca; Ave George VI, Montcalm & Colline Parlementaire; ⏰9am-5:30pm; 👪) 🍃 One of Québec City's must-sees, this verdant clifftop park contains the **Plains of Abraham**, site of the infamous 1759 battle between British General James Wolfe and French General Louis-Joseph Montcalm that determined the fate of the North American continent. Packed with old cannons, monuments and Martello towers, it's a favorite local spot for picnicking, running, skating, skiing and snowshoeing, along with Winter Carnival festivities and open-air summer concerts. For information and to learn more, visit the **Musée des Plaines d'Abraham** (Plains of Abraham Museum; Map p124; ☎418-649-6157; www.theplainsofabraham.ca; 835 Ave Wilfrid-Laurier, Montcalm & Colline Parlementaire; adult/youth/child $12.25/10.25/4, incl Abraham's bus tour & Martello Tower 1 Jul-early Sep $15.25/11.25/5; ⏰9am-5:30pm).

> *Arguably the city's most picturesque district*

Fortifications of Québec National Historic Site Historic Site

(Map p124; ☎418-648-7016; www.pc.gc.ca and search 'fortifications of Québec'; 2 Rue d'Auteuil, Old Upper Town; adult/child $4/free; ⏰10am-5pm mid-May–early Oct, to 6pm Jul & Aug) These largely restored old walls are protected as both a Canadian National Historic site and a Unesco World Heritage site. Walking the complete 4.6km circuit around the walls

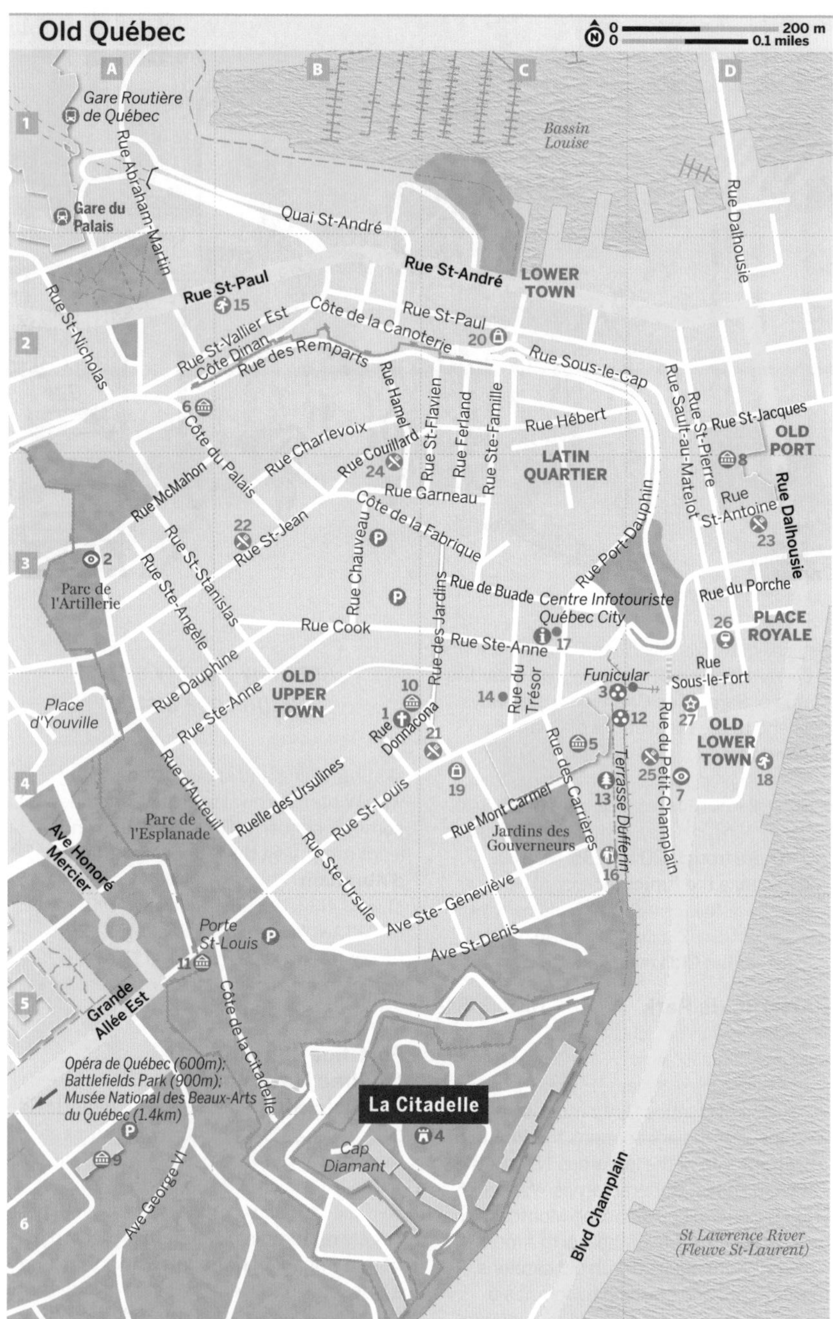
Old Québec
0 200 m
0 0.1 miles
Gare Routière de Québec
Gare du Palais
Rue Abraham-Martin
Quai St-André
Bassin Louise
Rue Dalhousie
Rue St-André
LOWER TOWN
Rue St-Paul
Rue St-Nicholas
Rue St-Vallier Est
Côte Dinan
Côte de la Canoterie
Rue des Remparts
Rue Sous-le-Cap
Rue Hamel
Rue St-Flavien
Rue Ferland
Rue Ste-Famille
Rue Hébert
Rue Sault-au-Matelot
Rue St-Pierre
Rue St-Jacques
OLD PORT
Côte du Palais
Rue Charlevoix
Rue Couillard
LATIN QUARTIER
Rue McMahon
Rue Garneau
Rue St-Antoine
Rue St-Jean
Côte de la Fabrique
Rue Port-Dauphin
Rue Chauveau
Parc de l'Artillerie
Rue St-Stanislas
Rue Ste-Angèle
Rue de Buade
Centre Infotouriste Québec City
Rue du Porche
PLACE ROYALE
Rue Cook
Rue des Jardins
Rue Ste-Anne
Rue Dauphine
OLD UPPER TOWN
Rue du Trésor
Funicular
Rue Sous-le-Fort
Place d'Youville
Rue Donnacona
Rue du Petit-Champlain
OLD LOWER TOWN
Rue des Carrières
Terrasse Dufferin
Rue d'Auteuil
Ruelle des Ursulines
Rue St-Louis
Rue Mont Carmel
Parc de l'Esplanade
Jardins des Gouverneurs
Ave Honoré Mercier
Rue Ste-Ursule
Ave Ste-Geneviève
Ave St-Denis
Porte St-Louis
Grande Allée Est
Côte de la Citadelle
Opéra de Québec (600m); Battlefields Park (900m); Musée National des Beaux-Arts du Québec (1.4km)
La Citadelle
Cap Diamant
Ave George VI
Blvd Champlain
St Lawrence River (Fleuve St-Laurent)

Old Québec

Sights

1 Chapelle des Ursulines ... B4
2 Fortifications of Québec National Historic Site ... A3
3 Frontenac Kiosk ... C4
4 La Citadelle ... C6
5 Le Château Frontenac ... C4
6 Le Monastère des Augustines ... A2
7 Le Quartier Petit-Champlain ... D4
8 Musée de la Civilisation ... D3
9 Musée des Plaines d'Abraham ... A6
10 Musée des Ursulines ... B4
11 Porte St-Louis – Fortifications of Québec ... A5
12 St-Louis Forts & Châteaux National Historic Site ... C4
13 Terrasse Dufferin ... C4

Activities, Courses & Tours

14 Calèches – Place d'Armes ... C4
15 Cyclo Services ... B2
16 Glissade de la Terrasse ... C4
17 Gourmet Food Tour ... C3
Les Tours Voir Québec ... (see 17)
18 Lévis Ferry ... D4

Shopping

19 Galerie d'Art Inuit Brousseau ... C4
20 Les Branchés Lunetterie ... C2

Eating

1608 ... (see 5)
21 Aux Anciens Canadiens ... C4
22 Chez Boulay ... B3
23 Chez Muffy ... D3
24 Chez Temporel ... B3
25 Le Lapin Sauté ... D4

Drinking & Nightlife

26 L'Oncle Antoine ... D3

Entertainment

27 Pape Georges ... D4

outside on your own is free of charge, and you'll enjoy fine vantage points on the city's historical buildings as you trace the perimeter of the old town. There are two other entrances: at **Porte St-Louis** (Map p124; 100 Rue St-Louis) and the **Frontenac Kiosk** (Map p124; off Rue St-Louis) on the Terrasse Dufferin.

Musée National des Beaux-Arts du Québec — Museum

(Québec National Museum of Fine Arts; 418-643-2150; www.mnbaq.org; 179 Grande Allée Ouest, Plains of Abraham; adult/youth/child $20/11/free; 10am-6pm Jun-Aug, to 5pm Tue-Sun Sep-May, to 9pm Wed year-round) Spare at least a half-day to visit this extraordinary art museum, one of the province's best. Permanent exhibitions range from art in the early French colonies to Québec's contemporary artists, with individual halls devoted entirely to 20th-century artistic giants such as Jean-Paul Lemieux, Fernand Leduc and Jean-Paul Riopelle. Arguably the museum's highlight is the **Brousseau Collection of Inuit Art**, a selection of 100 pieces by 60 artists located at the top of the **Pavillon Pierre Lassonde**.

ACTIVITIES

Corridor du Littoral & Promenade Samuel-de-Champlain — Cycling, Walking

Starting southwest of Québec City at Cap-Rouge and extending northeast via the Old Lower Town to Montmorency Falls, the Corridor du Littoral is a 48km multipurpose recreation path along the St Lawrence River, popular with cyclists, walkers and in-line skaters. The heart of the path is the Promenade Samuel-de-Champlain, an especially beautiful 2.5km section.

Lévis Ferry — Boating

(Map p124; 877-787-7483; www.traversiers.com; 10 Rue des Traversiers, Gare Fluviale de Québec, Old Lower Town & Port; car & driver/adult/child one way $8.65/3.65/2.45) For city views, you can't beat the 12-minute ferry ride to Lévis; boats operate from 6am to 2am, departing every 30 to 60 minutes depending on the time, day and season. If you purchase a round-trip ticket, you must disembark for security reasons. There's usually a 20-minute layover in Lévis.

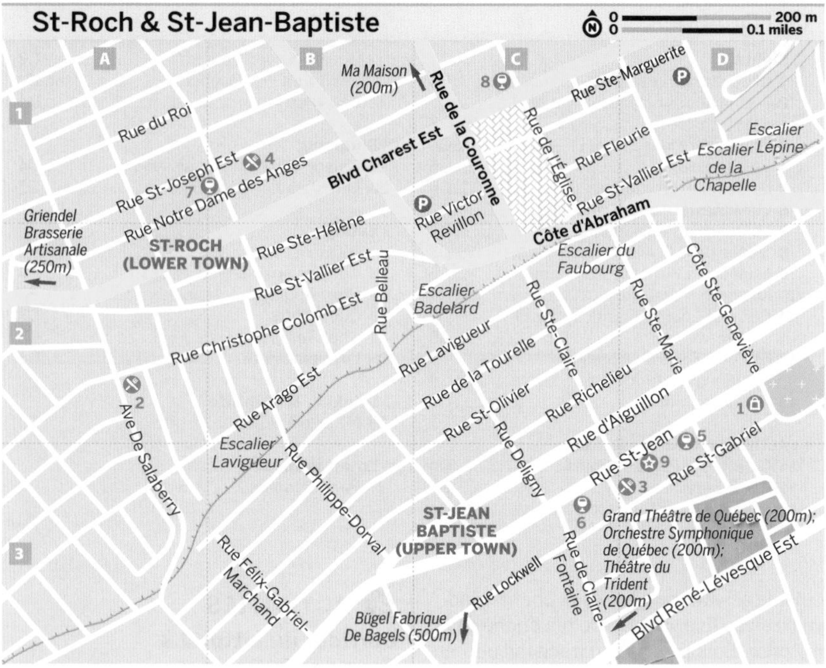

St-Roch & St-Jean-Baptiste

St-Roch & St-Jean-Baptiste

Shopping

1 JA Moisan Épicier D2

Eating

2 Battuto A2
3 Buvette Scott D3
4 Le Croquembouche B1

Drinking & Nightlife

5 Le Moine Échanson D2
6 Le Sacrilège C3
7 Macfly Bar Arcade B1
8 Noctem Artisans Brasseurs C1

Entertainment

9 Fou-Bar D3

TOURS

Les Tours Voir Québec Walking

(Map p124; ☎418-694-2001, 1-866-694-2001; www.toursvoirquebec.com; 12 Rue Ste-Anne, Old Upper Town; walking tour adult/student/child $23/19.50/11) This group offers excellent tours on the history, architecture and food of Québec City. The popular two-hour 'grand tour,' probably the city's best walking tour, takes in the Old City's highlights, while the food tour includes tastings of wines, cheeses, crepes and chocolate at a variety of shops and restaurants. Buy tickets at and depart from Centre Infotouriste Québec City (p132).

Gourmet Food Tour Food & Drink

(Map p124; ☎1-866-694-2001, 418-694-2001; www.toursvoirquebec.com; 12 Rue Ste-Anne, Old Upper Town; adult/child $46/25; ⏰tours 2pm May-Oct, Tue-Sat Nov-Apr) Wending through the St-Jean Baptiste neighborhood, this 2½-hour culinary tour offers tastings of wines, cheeses, crepes, chocolate and other Québécois specialties at a variety of shops and restaurants. From November through April, a two-person minimum is required. It's one of several city tours offered by Les Tours Voir Québec. Buy tickets at and depart from the Centre Infotouriste Québec City (p132).

SHOPPING

JA Moisan Épicier Food
(Map p124; ☎418-522-0685; www.jamoisan.com; 695 Rue St-Jean, St-Jean-Baptiste; 8:30am-7pm Mon-Wed & Sat, to 9pm Thu & Fri, 10am-7pm Sun, extended hours summer) Established in 1871, this charming store bills itself as North America's oldest grocery. It's a browser's dream come true, packed with beautifully displayed edibles and kitchen and household items alongside antique cash registers and wood shelving. You'll find items here you've never seen before, along with heaps of local goods and gift ideas.

Galerie d'Art Inuit Brousseau Art
(Map p124; ☎418-694-1828; www.artinuit.ca; 35 Rue St-Louis, Old Upper Town; 9:30am-5:30pm) Devoted to Inuit soapstone, serpentine and basalt carvings and sculptures from artists all over Arctic Canada, this place is gorgeously set up and elaborately lit, with well-trained staff who knowledgeably answer questions. Works range from the small to the large and intricate. Expect high quality and steep prices. International shipping is available.

Les Branchés Lunetterie Fashion & Accessories
(Map p124; ☎418-614-1697; www.lesbrancheslunetterie.ca; 155 Rue St-Paul, Old Lower Town & Port; 10am-6pm Mon-Wed, to 8pm Thu & Fri, to 5pm Sat) Displaying a fanciful, wildly colorful mix of designer eyewear from Québec, France and Spain, this is a fun place to browse, even if you're not necessarily in the market for new glasses frames. The collection's centerpiece is the room dedicated to frames from Montures Faniel (www.monturesfaniel.com), a Québécois business founded by opera-singer-turned-designer Anne-Marie Faniel, whose music also fills the store.

EATING

Chez Temporel Cafe $
(Map p124; ☎418-694-1813; www.facebook.com/cheztemporel; 25 Rue Couillard, Old Upper Town; mains $9-20; 11am-5pm Mon-Thu, to 8:30pm Fri & Sat, to 7:30pm Sun) Hidden away on a side street just off the beaten path, this charming little cafe serves tasty sandwiches, homemade soups and quiches, pizza plus prodigious salads, fresh-baked goods and excellent coffee. Being slightly off the track, it attracts a healthy mix of locals and travelers.

Bügel Fabrique de Bagels Canadian $
(☎418-523-7666; http://bugel-fabrique.ca; 164 Rue Crémazie Ouest, St Jean-Baptiste; bagel sandwiches $11-12.75, breakfast $7.50-15; 7am-7pm Sat-Wed, to 9pm Thu & Fri) Don't be fooled by the title: there's more than plain bagels ($3.60) at this cute neighborhood nook, in situ since 1987. More accurately, imagine bagels and then some: served with Brie or goat's cheese, or au gratin with ham and asparagus, or topped with smoked salmon or turkey. Ingredients are locally sourced, and the strong coffee kicks like a mule.

Le Croquembouche Bakery $
(Map p126; ☎418-523-9009; www.lecroquembouche.com; 225 Rue St-Joseph Est, St-Roch; pastries from $2, sandwiches from $5.25; 7am-6:30pm Tue-Sat, to 5pm Sun) Widely hailed as Québec City's finest bakery, Le Croquembouche draws devoted locals from dawn to dusk. Among its seductive offerings are fluffy-as-a-cloud croissants, tantalizing cakes and éclairs, brioches brimming with raspberries, and gourmet sandwiches on fresh-baked bread. There's also a stellar array of *danoises* (Danish pastries), including orange and anise, cranberry, pistachio and chocolate.

1608 Cheese $$

(Map p124; ☎418-692-3861; http://1608baravin.com; 1 Rue des Carrières, Fairmount Le Château Frontenac, Old Upper Town; mains $21-34; ⏲4pm-midnight Sun-Thu, 2pm-1am Fri & Sat) At this Frontenac-based wine-and-cheese bar you can either select some cheeses yourself or let the staff take you down a wine-and-cheese rabbit hole that's difficult to emerge from; platters of three/four/five cheeses are $21/26/30 (five types with charcuterie $34). Wine, *fromage* and an incomparable view of the St Lawrence all make for a very romantic setting.

Le Lapin Sauté French $$

(Map p124; ☎418-692-5325; www.lapinsaute.com; 52 Rue du Petit-Champlain, Old Lower Town & Port; mains $17-29; ⏲11am-10pm Mon-Fri, 9am-10pm Sat & Sun) Naturally, *lapin* (rabbit) plays a starring role at this cozy, rustic restaurant just south of the funicular's lower terminus, in such dishes as rabbit cassoulet or rabbit poutine. Other enticements include salads, French onion soup, charcuterie platters and an excellent-value lunch menu (from $16). In good weather, sit on the flowery patio overlooking tiny Parc Félix-Leclerc.

Battuto Italian $$

(Map p126; ☎418-614-4414; www.battuto.ca; 527 Blvd Langelier, St-Roch; mains $21-23; ⏲5:30-10pm Tue-Sat) Considered by many Québécois to be the best Italian restaurant in town, this wonderful place on the edge of St-Roch mixes traditional dishes like *vitello tonnato* (veal topped with a tuna sauce) with more inventive pasta ones such as Sicilian *casarecce* served with sweetbreads and sherry. It's a tiny place, with a mere 24 seats, so book well ahead.

Buvette Scott French $$

(Map p126; ☎581-741-4464; www.buvettescott.com; 821 Rue Scott, St-Jean-Baptiste; mains $12-18; ⏲4:30-11pm Mon-Sat) At this tiny wine bistro with just eight tables and seating at the bar, enlightened French classics like breaded calf's brains, bone marrow and *brandade de morue* (Provençal puree of cod mixed with milk,

Le Lapin Sauté

olive oil and garlic, and served with croutons) dominate the menu. The chalkboard wine list is exceptional, with six reds and six whites.

Ma Maison Québécois $$
(☎418-204-6323; www.restomamaison.com; 281 Rue de la Couronne, St-Roch; mains $21-24; ⊙10am-2pm Thu-Sat, 5-9pm Wed-Sat) A quiet little *bistro du quartier* (neighborhood bistro) well worth seeking out, 'My House' serves traditional Québécois dishes like *grand-maman* used to make: trout pie, maple ham and horse (yes, as in *cheval*) stroganoff. Try the cod sticks with *gribiche* (mayonnaise-style cold egg sauce) or the smelts as a starter, and don't miss the scrumptious shop-made desserts.

Chez Muffy French, Québécois $$$
(Map p124; ☎418-692-1022; www.saint-antoine.com/chez-muffy; 10 Rue St-Antoine, Old Lower Town & Port; lunch/dinner menu $22/50, mains $37-50; ⊙6:30-10:30am Mon-Fri, 7-11am Sat, 10am-1pm Sun, 6-10pm Wed-Sun) The celebrated restaurant of **Auberge St-Antoine** (☎888-692-2211, 418-692-2211; www.saint-antoine.com) receives top marks for its exquisite, imaginatively prepared Québécois cuisine and top-notch service. Dinners and attractively priced midday *tables d'hôte* feature locally sourced ingredients like sable fish *a la plancha* (grilled), Appalachian red deer with wild-berry sauce or St-Gervais suckling pig. It's set in a stone-walled 19th-century maritime warehouse, with rustic wood beams.

Chez Boulay Québécois $$$
(Map p124; ☎418-380-8166; www.chezboulay.com; 1110 Rue St-Jean, Old Upper Town; lunch menus $18-24, dinner mains $26-35; ⊙11:30am-10pm Mon-Fri, 10am-10pm Sat & Sun) Renowned chef Jean-Luc Boulay's flagship restaurant serves an ever-evolving menu inspired by seasonal Québécois staples such as venison, goose, blood pudding, wild mushrooms and Gaspé Peninsula seafood. Lunch specials and charcuterie platters for two (served 2pm to 5pm) offer an affordable afternoon pick-me-up, while the sleek, low-lit dining area with views of the open kitchen makes a romantic dinner setting.

The Québécois Table

French food is king in Québec City. The lack of a significant immigrant population means that there is not the kind of massive ethnic smorgasbord that you'll find in Montréal; even so, the quality of restaurants here is outstanding.

Québec City also boasts at least one drink that you won't find in Montréal. *Caribou* is a potent blend of fortified wine and grain alcohol, sometimes mixed with spices and sweetened with maple syrup. Served hot at outdoor bars and streetside stalls during the Carnaval de Québec, it's designed to warm body and soul in the coldest depths of winter.

Aux Anciens Canadiens Québécois $$$
(Map p124; ☎418-692-1627; www.auxancienscanadiens.qc.ca; 34 Rue St-Louis, Old Upper Town; mains $33-89, 3-course menu from $20; ⊙noon-9pm) Housed in the historic Jacquet House, which dates from 1675, this place is a well-worn tourist destination, specializing in robust country cooking and typical Québécois specialties served by waitstaff in historic garb. The *menu du jour*, offered from noon to 5.45pm, is by far the best deal at around $20 for three courses, including a glass of wine or beer.

Calèches

In Québec City, horse-drawn coaches called **calèches** (☎418-683-9222, 418-520-1555; www.calecheduvieuxquebec.com; Place d'Armes, Old Upper Town; 35/80/120min rides $90/180/270) cost $90 for a 35-minute tour for up to four passengers. You'll find them just inside the Porte St-Louis, in the Parc de l'Esplanade and, most frequently, in the Place d'Armes near the Château Frontenac.

CHARLES LEWIS / SHUTTERSTOCK ©

DRINKING & NIGHTLIFE

Griendel Brasserie Artisanale Microbrewery

(☎591-742-2884; www.facebook.com/Brasserie.artisanale.griendel; 195 Rue St-Vallier Ouest, St-Sauveur; ⏲3pm-1am Mon-Wed, to 3am Thu & Fri, 1pm-3am Sat, to 1am Sun) Anchor tenant on Rue St-Vallier Ouest in up-and-coming St-Sauveur, Griendel occupies a huge old corner shop with lots of windows and great light. Choose from among the two-dozen *broues* (brews) on the blackboard, most of which are brewed in-house. There are burgers and poutine, but it's generally agreed they serve the best fish-and-chips ($15) in town.

Le Sacrilège Bar

(Map p126; ☎418-649-1985; www.lesacrilege.com; 447 Rue St-Jean, St-Jean-Baptiste; ⏲noon-3am) With its unmistakable sign of a laughing, dancing monk saucily lifting his robes, this bar has long been the watering hole of choice for Québec's night owls. Even on Monday, it's standing-room only. There's a quite good selection of beers (including many craft varieties), live music most nights at 8pm and seating on a lovely garden terrace out back.

Noctem Artisans Brasseurs Microbrewery

(Map p126; ☎581-742-7979; www.noctem.ca; 438 Rue du Parvis, St-Roch; ⏲11am-3am) One of the most interesting microbreweries in town, Noctem goes beyond the *blonde* (lager), *blanche* (white), *rousse* (red) and IPA tick list to offer a blackboard of up to 18 different beers and ales that change daily. If peckish, eschew the pizza/burger/taco choices in favor of a platter of charcuterie to share.

Le Moine Échanson Wine Bar

(Map p126; ☎418-524-7832; www.lemoineechanson.com; 585 Rue St-Jean, St-Jean-Baptiste; ⏲4-10pm Sun-Wed, to 11pm Thu-Sat) A darling of the city's wine connoisseurs, this convivial brick-walled wine bar and bistro pours an enticing and ever-changing array of wines from all over the Mediterranean, by the glass and by the bottle, accompanied by hearty and homespun snacks and main dishes such as blood sausage, cheese fondue or lentil soup. Three-/four-course set menus are $40/45.

Macfly Bar Arcade Bar

(Map p126; ☎418-528-7000; www.macflybararcade.com; 422 Rue Caron, St-Roch; ⏲3pm-3am) This bar's *Back to the Future*-ish name is no accident: the entire interior evokes the 1980s, or at least an idea of what the '80s were about – old-school arcade consoles, bright countertops, TV set stuck on a test pattern and pinball machines awaiting your wizardry. Not that it's easy to top your highest score after a couple of well-pulled beers…

L'Oncle Antoine Pub

(Map p124; ☎418-694-9176; 29 Rue St-Pierre, Old Lower Town & Port; ⏲11am-1am) Set clandestinely in the vaulted brick cellar of one of the city's oldest surviving houses (dating from 1754), this great tavern pours excellent Québec microbrews (try the Barberie Noir stout), several drafts and various European beers. Its in-house brews include #1 Blonde (lager), #21 Rousse (red) and #29 IPA. Try its famous onion soup on a cold Sunday afternoon.

ENTERTAINMENT

Pape Georges Live Music

(Map p124; ☎418-692-1320; www.facebook.com/papegeorges; 8 Rue de Cul-de-Sac, Old Lower Town & Port; ⏰11am-3pm) With live music from 10pm on Friday and Saturday night at the very minimum (more in the summer), this charming bar located in a 400-year-old house also serves cheeses, meats and baguettes with a healthy dollop of Québécois culture. It always attracts a lively crowd.

Fou-Bar Live Music

(Map p126; ☎418-522-1987; www.foubar.ca; 525 Rue St-Jean, St-Jean-Baptiste; ⏰2:30pm-1am Sun & Mon, to 2am Tue & Wed, to 3am Thu-Sat) Laid-back and offering an eclectic mix of bands, this bar is one of the town's classics for good live music. It's also popular for its reasonably priced food menu and its free *pique-assiettes* (literally 'freeloaders' aka appetizers) on Thursday and Friday evenings. There can be a cover charge of up to $20 depending on the band.

Grand Théâtre de Québec Performing Arts

(☎877-643-8131, 418-643-8131; www.grandtheatre.qc.ca; 269 Blvd René-Lévesque Est, Montcalm & Colline Parlementaire; ⏰box office noon-5pm Mon-Sat & 30min before performances) Designed by the Polish-Canadian architect Victor Prus in 1971, the 'Great Theater' is Québec City's main performing-arts center, with a steady diet of top-quality classical concerts, opera, dance and theater. Major companies that are based or perform here regularly include the Opéra de Québec (p132), the **Orchestre**

> *the watering hole of choice for Québec's night owls*

Le Sacrilège

LEONID ANDRONOV / SHUTTERSTOCK ©

Gare du Palais

Symphonique de Québec (☎418-643-8131; www.osq.org; ⏰box office noon-5pm Mon-Sat & 30min before performances) and the **Théâtre du Trident** (☎418-643-5873; www.letrident.com; ⏰box office 9am-noon & 1:30-4:30pm Mon-Thu).

Opéra de Québec Classical Music
(☎418-529-0688; www.operadequebec.com; 1220 Ave Taché, Montcalm & Colline Parlementaire; ⏰9am-noon & 1:30-5pm Mon-Fri) Under the artistic direction of Grégoire Legendre, this world-class company presents classics such as *Aida, Pagliacci, Madame Butterfly, La Traviata, Carmen, Nabucco* and more. Performances take place in the majestic Grand Théâtre de Québec (p131), where you can also buy tickets.

ℹ INFORMATION

Centre Infotouriste Québec City (Québec Original; Map p124; ☎418-641-6290, 877-266-5687; www.quebecoriginal.com; 12 Rue Ste-Anne, Old Upper Town; ⏰9am-5pm Nov-Jun, to 6pm Jul-Oct) The main tourist office, in the heart of Old Québec. It has scads of brochures and maps, and helpful staff.

ℹ GETTING THERE & AWAY

AIR

Québec City's petite **Aéroport International Jean-Lesage de Québec** (YQB; ☎877-769-2700, 418-640-3300; www.aeroportdequebec.com; 505 Rue Principal, Ste-Foy) lies about 15km west of Old Québec. It mostly has connections to Montréal, but there are also flights to Toronto, Ottawa, Chicago, Newark, New York City (JFK) and resorts in the Caribbean (including Cuba) and Mexico. Check the website for additional destinations.

Regularly scheduled flights (45 minutes) on Air Canada and several other budget airlines, including Air Transat, PAL Airlines and Pascan, run between Montréal and Québec City's airport.

BUS

Gare d'Autocars de Ste-Foy (Ste-Foy Bus Station; ☎418-650-0087; 3001 Chemin des Quatre Bourgeois, Ste-Foy) If you're coming from

Montréal, your bus may first stop at this station 12km southwest of the center, so ask before you get off.

Orléans Express (833-449-6444, 418-525-3000; www.orleansexpress.com) runs services from Montréal's main bus station, Gare d'Autocars, to Québec City's **bus station** (Québec Bus Station; Map p124; 418-525-3000; 320 Rue Abraham-Martin) at the Gare du Palais on the hour between 6am and 11pm daily. From Québec City they run on the half-hour between 6:30am and 10:30pm daily. Prices for the journey (2¾ to 3¼ hours) start at $55/89 for a one-way/return ticket.

TRAIN

VIA Rail (www.viarail.ca) has between four and six daily trains between Montréal's Gare Centrale and Québec City's **Gare du Palais** (Palace Station; 888-842-7245; www.viarail.ca; 450 Rue de la Gare du Palais, Old Lower Town & Port). Normal prices for the 3¼-hour journey start at $42/87 for a one-way/return ticket. Some trains stop at the suburban **Gare de Ste-Foy** (Ste-Foy Train Station; 888-842-7245; www.viarail.ca; 3255 Chemin de la Gare, Ste-Foy) as well.

Service is also good along the so-called Québec City–Windsor corridor that connects Québec City with Montréal, Ottawa, Kingston, Toronto and Niagara Falls.

GETTING AROUND

TO/FROM THE AIRPORT

RTC (www.rtcquebec.ca) has launched a bus service linking Jean-Lesage Airport with the train and bus stations in Ste-Foy, from where you can catch city bus 11 to Old Québec or Métrobus 800 or 801 to Colline Parlementaire. Bus 76 leaves the airport about every 15 minutes from 5:30am to 11pm daily; the trip takes about 30 minutes.

A taxi costs a flat fee of just over $35 to go into the city.

BICYCLE

Québec City has an extensive network of bike paths (more than 70km in all), including a route along the St Lawrence that connects to paths along the Rivière St-Charles. Pick up the free *Carte Vélo Officielle/Official Cycling Map* at local tourist offices or bike shops.

Just across from Québec City's train station, **Cyclo Services** (Map p124; 418-692-4052, 877-692-4050; www.cycloservices.net; 289 Rue St-Paul, Old Lower Town & Port; rental per 2/24hr city bike $17/38, electric bike $34/76; 9am-5:30pm Mon-Fri, 10am-5pm Sat & Sun, variable hours Nov-Apr;) rents a wide variety of bikes, including city, tandem, road, electric and kids' models. It also organizes cycling tours in the Québec City region.

BUS

RTC's bus network (www.rtcquebec.ca) is largely designed to get workers and other employees into and out of the city from/to the sprawling suburbs and nearby towns and villages. As a result, most of its 145 or so lines will be of little use to travelers. Still, there are a few lines that will come in handy, and RTC lines link a couple of places of interest around Québec City with downtown.

TAXI

Flag fall is a standard $3.50 plus another $1.75 per kilometer and 65¢ per minute spent waiting in traffic. Prices are posted on the windows inside taxis.

Taxis Coop (418-525-5191; www.taxiscoop-quebec.com)

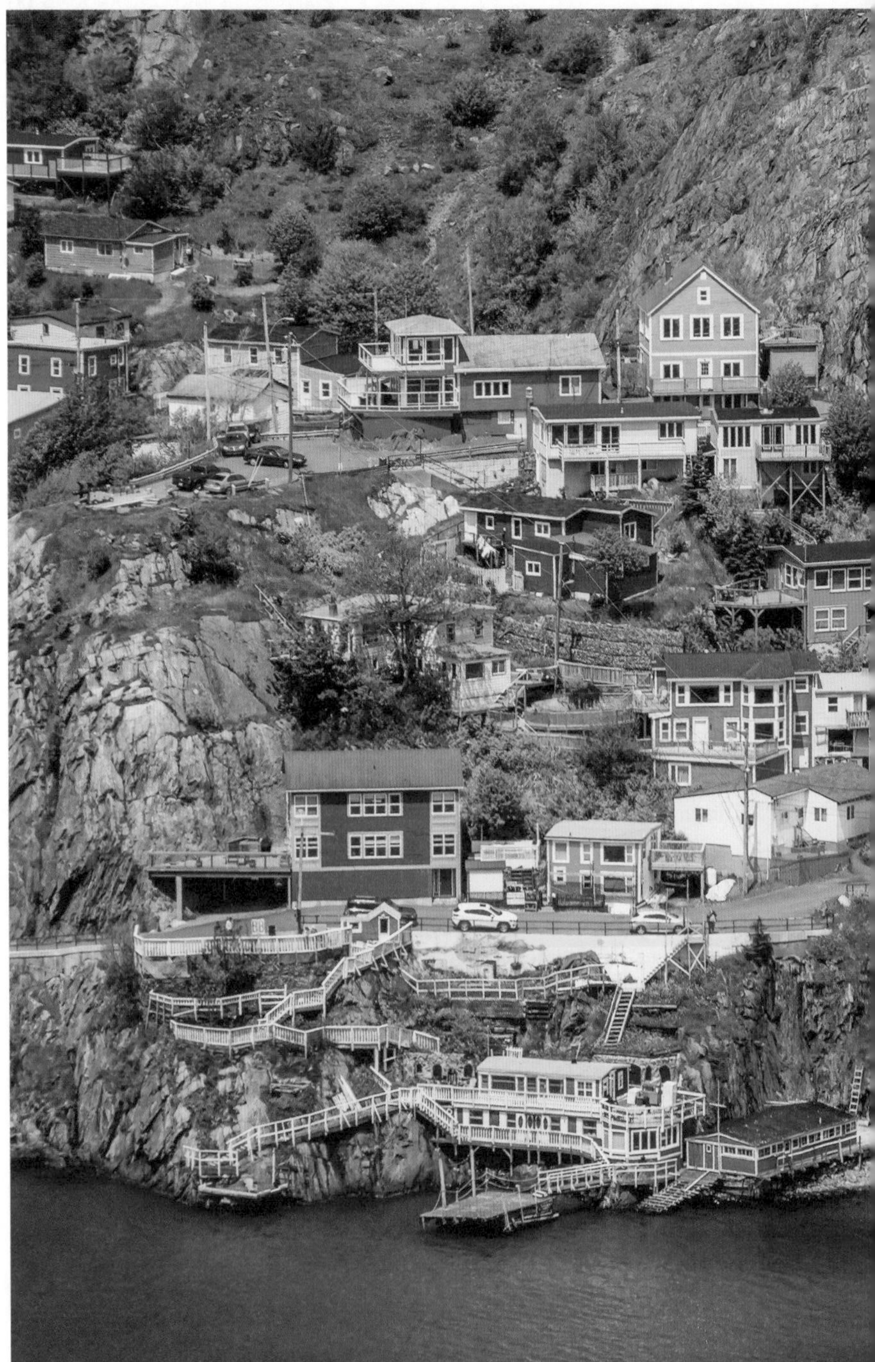

THE ATLANTIC PROVINCES

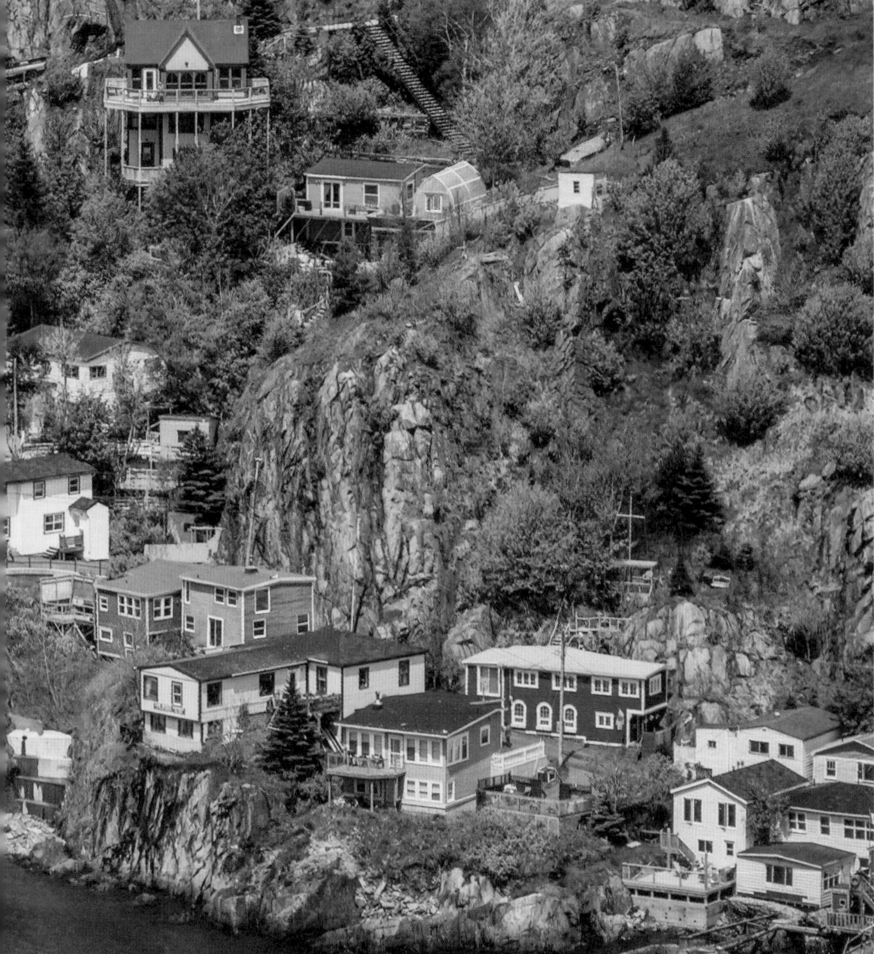

In this Chapter

The Atlantic Provinces at a glance...

If the Atlantic Provinces were a film, its protagonists would be rugged yet kind-hearted, burnt by the wind and at one with the sea. It would be shot against a backdrop of rolling green fields and high sea cliffs; its soundtrack would feature fiddles, drums and evocative piano scores; and its plot would be a spirited romp around themes of history, community and family. Comprising a group of Canadian provinces – Nova Scotia, New Brunswick, Prince Edward Island, Newfoundland and Labrador – this region is an adventure waiting to happen.

Two Days in the Atlantic Provinces

Enjoy Halifax (p144) for a day, swinging down to snap a few photos at **Peggy's Cove** and feasting in the city's top restaurants – perhaps try **Chives Canadian Bistro** (p148) for formal fine dining. Round out the day with a cocktail at **Lot Six** (p148). The following morning, head north to explore the **Cabot Trail**, taking in amazing views and Acadian culture in **Chéticamp**.

Four Days in the Atlantic Provinces

On day three, drive across the Confederation Bridge to Prince Edward Island (PEI) to visit Charlottetown's **Point Prim Lighthouse** (p153). Swing by Cavendish (p154) to meet Anne of Green Gables, and stop for seafood fresh from Malpeque Bay at **Carr's Oyster Bar** (p156). Return to Halifax and hop a flight to hip St John's (p156), North America's oldest city and home to **Signal Hill** (p156) and the stunning **North Head Trail** (p157).

Previous page: St John's (p156)

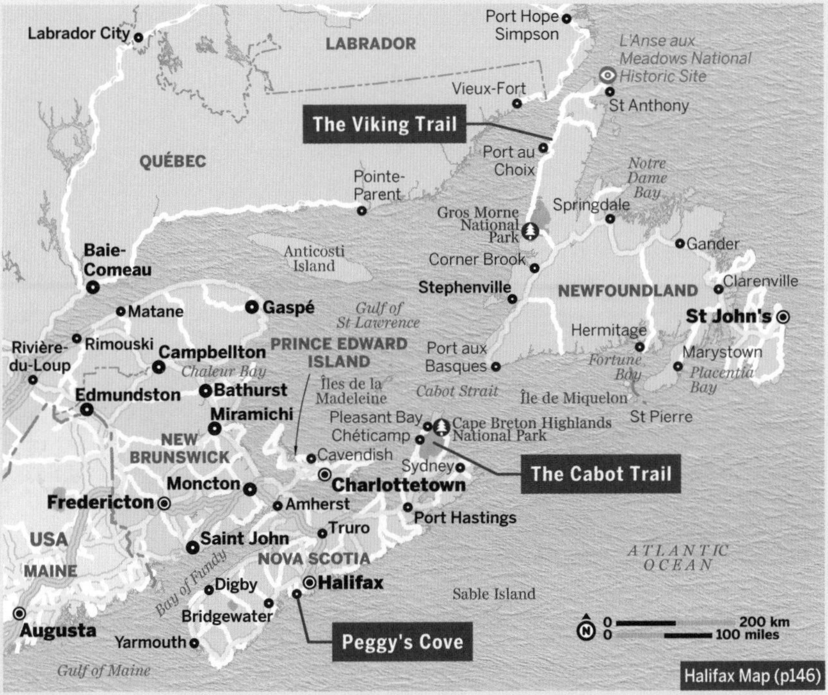

Halifax Map (p146)

Arriving in the Atlantic Provinces

Halifax Stanfield International Airport MetroX bus 320 runs frequently from 5:45am to 12:15am, or grab a taxi ($56, 30 minutes).

St John's International Airport Taxis to downtown (10 minutes) cost $25 plus $3 for each additional passenger.

Land Border Crossings The Canadian Border Services Agency posts updated wait times hourly; it's usually less than 30 minutes.

Where to Stay

In this part of the world, historic B&Bs rule the roost, ranging from boringly bland to ridiculously sublime. Road-trip lovers will be in motel heaven. Halifax has a wide range of accommodations, with an excellent selection of quality hostels and mid-priced hotels. Charlottetown's old town is a charming place to stay, while St John's has scores of good-value B&Bs. Remember to book in advance during Atlantic Canada's short-lived tourist season.

Peggy's Point Lighthouse

Peggy's Cove

This fishing village, with its rolling granite cove and perfect red-and-white lighthouse, exudes a dreamy seaside calm, even through the parading tour buses.

Great For...

☑ Don't Miss

Joining a free 45-minute walking tour from the tourist office, daily from mid-June through August.

Who Was Peggy?

The cove was first recorded as Pegg's Harbour in 1766. While many pragmatists claim this is simply a shortened version of Margaret (the harbor marks the eastern point of St Margaret's Bay), others prefer the more charming story of a young lass who was the sole survivor of a nearby shipwreck. Brought ashore, she was adopted and named Peggy. Her story spread and people came to see Peggy of the Cove – or Peggy's Cove.

Peggy's Point Lighthouse

The highlight of the cove is this picture-perfect **lighthouse** (185 Peggys Point Rd; ⌚9:30am-5:30pm May-Oct), which for many years was a working post office. Meander around the granite landscape that undulates much like the icy sea beyond.

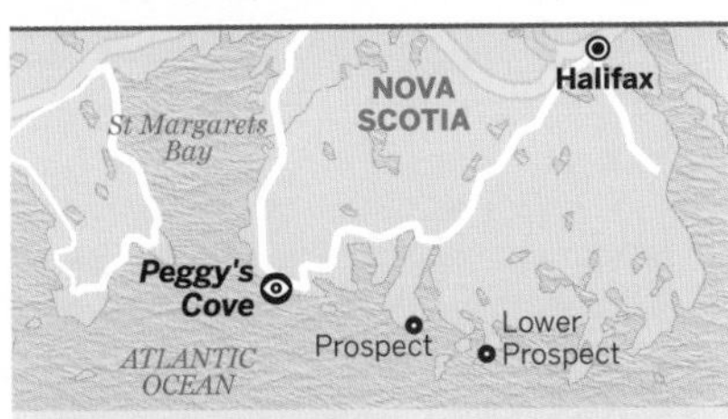

Need to Know

Peggy's Cove is 43km southwest of Halifax on Hwy 333. The **Visitor Information Centre** (VIC; 902-823-2253; 109 Peggy's Point Rd; 9am-7pm Jul & Aug, to 5pm mid-May–Jun & Sep–mid-Oct) has free parking.

Take a Break

Cool off with a delicious homemade ice cream from **Dee Dee's** (www.deedees.ca; 110 Peggy's Point Rd; cones from $3.50; noon-6pm May-Sep).

★ Top Tip

Visit before 10am, after 6pm or in the off-season to avoid the crowds.

William E deGarthe Gallery & Monument

Finnish-born local artist William deGarthe (1907–83) sculpted the magnificent *Lasting Monument to Nova Scotian Fishermen* into a 30m granite outcropping behind his home. The sculpture depicts 32 fishers, their wives and children, St Elmo with wings spread, and the legendary Peggy of her eponymous Cove. The homestead is now a **gallery** (902-823-2256; 109 Peggy's Point Rd; $2; gallery 10am-4pm May-Oct) showcasing 65 of deGarthe's other works.

Swissair 111 Memorial

This moving **memorial** (8250 Hwy 333) commemorates the 229 people who lost their lives on September 2, 1998, when Swissair Flight 111 plunged into the ocean 8km off the coast of Peggy's Cove, not long after taking off from New York's JFK airport, bound for Geneva, Switzerland.

Peggy's Cove Boat Tours

Get a different perspective on the cove and the lighthouse with this experienced **local guide** (902-541-9177; www.peggyscoveboattours.com; Government Wharf; tours adult/child from $35/21.50). The standard sightseeing tour runs several times daily in summer; there are also seal- and puffin-watching trips, lobster dinner cruises, and special sunset trips on Tuesday, Thursday and Friday.

What's Nearby?

If you're looking for the same kind of vibe without the mass of visitors, albeit without the iconic lighthouse as well, cute-as-a-button **Lower Prospect** is 30km to the east via Terrence Bay.

Gros Morne National Park

The Viking Trail

The Viking Trail links Newfoundland's west coast to Southern Labrador, with two of the province's not-to-be-missed World Heritage–listed sites en route.

The Viking Trail follows the Northern Peninsula upward from the body of Newfoundland like an extended index finger. The region continues to gain in tourism, yet what's considered a crowd in Newfoundland might be considered a small gathering elsewhere.

Gros Morne National Park

A highlight of a visit to Newfoundland, this 1800-sq-km coastal **park** (☎709-458-2417; www.pc.gc.ca/grosmorne; per day adult/child/family $9.80/free/19.60) and Unesco World Heritage site features dramatic mountains, fjords, beaches, bogs and barren cliffs, and is popular for hiking, sea kayaking and sightseeing cruises. The bronze-colored Tablelands feature rock from deep within the earth's crust, supplying evidence for plate-tectonic theories. West of the

Great For...

☑ Don't Miss

The stunning view of the Tablelands from a distance at the lookout above Norris Point.

L'Anse aux Meadows National Historic Site

ALL CANADA PHOTOS / ALAMY STOCK PHOTO ©

QUÉBEC
LABRADOR
ATLANTIC OCEAN
Bird Cove
Port au Choix
The Viking Trail
Parc National du Canada Gros-Morne
Rocky Harbour
Gulf of St Lawrence
Deer Lake
NEWFOUNDLAND

Need to Know

For the nitty-gritty, including where to see whales and stay along the trail, check out www.vikingtrail.org.

Take a Break

In L'Anse aux Meadows, **Norseman Restaurant & Art Gallery** (☎709-754-3105; www.valhalla-lodge.com; Rte 436; mains $20-38; ⊙noon-9pm May-Sep; P) ranks among Newfoundland's best.

★ Top Tip

On the road, towns and amenities are few and far between – make sure to fuel up when you can.

Tablelands, dramatic volcanic sea stacks and caves mark the coast at Green Gardens.

Several small fishing villages dot the shoreline and provide amenities. Centrally located Rocky Harbour is the largest village and most popular place to stay.

Port Au Choix

These **ancient burial grounds** (☎709-861-3522; www.pc.gc.ca/portauchoix; Point Riche Rd; adult/child $3.90/1.90; ⊙9am-6pm Jun-Sep; P) of three different Indigenous groups date back 5500 years. The modern visitor center tells of these groups' creative survival in the area and of one group's unexplained disappearance 3200 years ago.

L'Anse aux Meadows

Lying in a forlorn sweep of land, **L'Anse aux Meadows National Historic Site** (☎709-623-2608; www.pc.gc.ca/lanseauxmeadows; Rte 436; adult/child $11.70/free; ⊙9am-6pm Jun-Sep; P) is one of Newfoundland's most stirring attractions. Leif Erikson and his Viking friends lived here circa 1000 CE. Visitors can see the remains of their waterside settlement, now just vague outlines left in the spongy ground, plus three replica buildings inhabited by costumed docents.

Be sure to browse the interpretive center and take in the 3km trail that winds through the barren terrain and along the coast.

Can't get enough of the long-bearded Viking lifestyle? Stop by **Norstead** (☎709-623-2828; www.norstead.com; Rte 436; adult/child/family $10/6.50/30; ⊙9:30am-5:30pm Jun-Sep), just beyond the turnoff to the National Historic Site. This recreated Viking village features costumed interpreters smelting, weaving, baking and telling stories around real fires throughout four buildings. Sounds cheesy, but they pull it off with class. There's also a large-scale replica of a Viking ship on hand.

Cape Breton Highlands

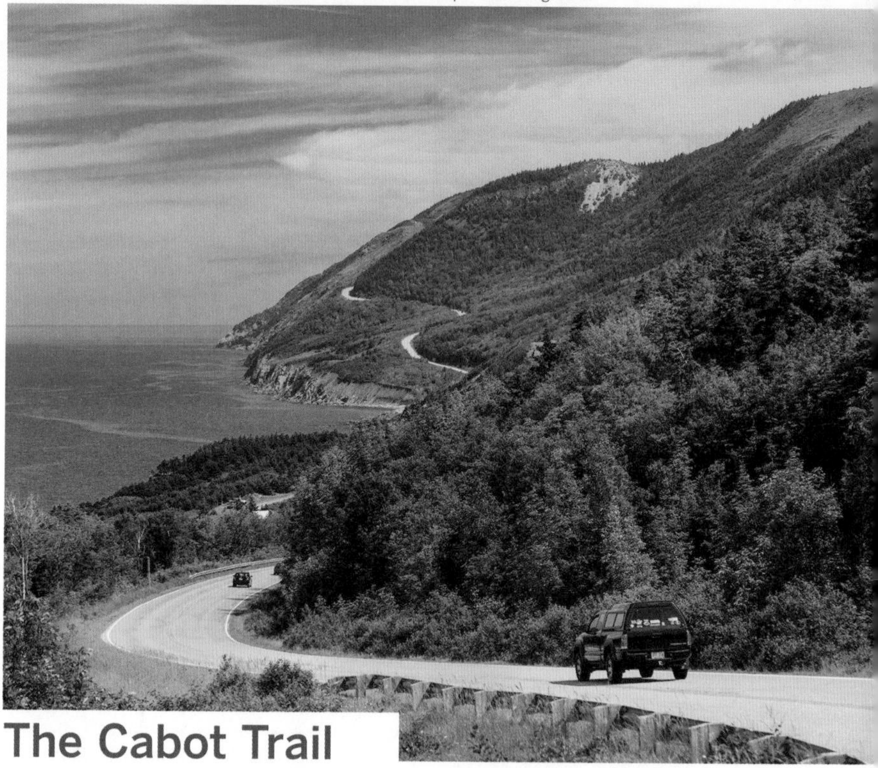

The Cabot Trail

Driving the Cabot Trail – the looping, diving, dipping roller-coaster of a road that snakes its way around the northern tip of Cape Breton – is Nova Scotia's most famous recreational activity.

Great For...

☑ Don't Miss

Hopping on a whale-watching tour in Chéticamp or Pleasant Bay.

Dotting the southeastern flank of the trail like Easter eggs, artists' workshops can be found from Englishtown to Saint Ann's Bay; drop in to a studio or two to meet an interesting mishmash of characters and to discover living remnants of Mi'kmaw and Acadian culture.

For the most breathtaking scenery, head to the island's northwestern shore where the trail slopes down to Pleasant Bay and Chéticamp. Keep your eyes on the circuitous road, as tempting as the views become; there are plenty of places to stop, look, and hike through a tapestry of terrain for vistas over the endless, icy ocean.

Cape Breton Highlands

This **national park** (☎902-224-2306; www.pc.gc.ca/en/pn-np/ns/cbreton; adult/child day pass $7.80/free, summer season pass adult/

Chéticamp

FENG YANG / EYEEM / GETTY IMAGES ©

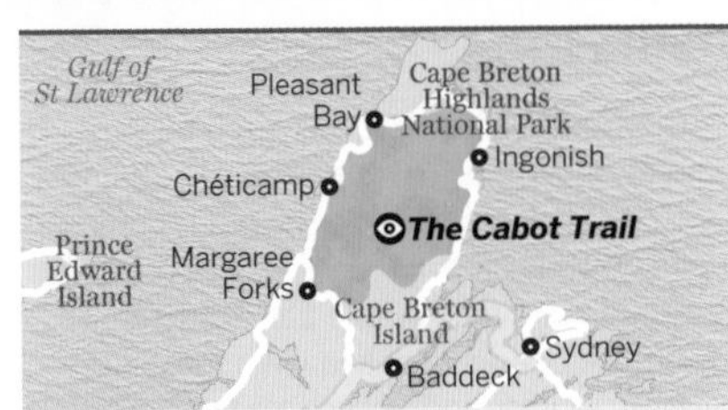

Need to Know

You'll find tourist information centers in Cape Breton Highlands National Park and Chéticamp.

Take a Break

Stop by the **Dancing Goat** (902-248-2727; www.facebook.com/DancingGoatCafe; 6289 Cabot Trail, Margaree Valley; items $5-13; 8am-5pm Sat-Thu, to 8pm Fri;), open year-round, for a hearty breakfast or huge sandwich.

★ Top Tip

The best way to enjoy the trail, with the freedom of starting and stopping as you choose, is by self-driving.

family $39.20/78.50) offers visitors some of Eastern Canada's most dramatic scenery. One-third of the Cabot Trail runs through the park. You'll find expanses of woodland, tundra and bog, and startling sea views. Established in 1936 and encompassing 20% of Cape Breton's landmass, it's the fancy feather in Nova Scotia's island cap.

There are two park entrances, one at Chéticamp and one at Ingonish Beach. Purchase an entry permit at either park entrance. A one-day pass is good until noon the next day. Wheelchair-accessible trails are indicated on the free park map available at either entrance.

Chéticamp

Chéticamp is Nova Scotia's most vibrant and thriving Acadian community, owing much of its cultural preservation to its geographical isolation; the road didn't make it this far until 1949. Upon entering the town from either direction you'll immediately feel like you've arrived in a little French village, although the landscape is decidedly reminiscent of the rugged Scottish highlands.

In the warmer months, there's always something going on, with plenty of opportunities to observe and experience Acadian culture, from interesting museums to sampling folk-crafts (Chéticamp is famed for its hooked rugs) and toe-tapping live-music performances.

Pleasant Bay

Pleasant Bay is a carved-out bit of civilization hemmed in on all sides by wilderness. It's also an active fishing harbor known for its whale-watching tours and its Tibetan monastery.

Halifax

Compared to conurbations such as Vancouver and Toronto, Halifax barely qualifies as a city, but this seaside town punches well above its size: it's dotted with red-brick heritage buildings, public parks and a landmark citadel, blessed with some first-rate museums, and home to a truly epic 4km seafront boardwalk. True, relentless downtown redevelopment has done little to enhance the city's charm: boxy office blocks and uninspiring concrete carbuncles are rising where handsome ironstones and Victorian townhouses once stood, although some exceptions (notably the new Central Library) show what can be achieved when planners exercise a little more quality control.

SIGHTS

Canadian Museum of Immigration at Pier 21 Museum

(☎902-425-7770; www.pier21.ca; 1055 Marginal Rd; adult/child $12/8; ⏰9:30am-5:30pm May-Nov, reduced hours Dec-Apr) There's an argument that this dockside museum is Canada's most important institution. Between 1928 and 1971, Pier 21 was the Canadian version of the USA's Ellis Island, where all prospective immigrants arrived. More than a million people passed through these redbrick halls, and it's an emotional experience to walk through the very same doorways where refugees from across the globe began new lives. A mix of audiovisual exhibits, poignant artifacts and personal testimonies make for a powerful and moving museum.

Citadel Hill National Historic Site Historic Site

(☎902-426-5080; www.pc.gc.ca/en/lhn-nhs/ns/halifax; 5425 Sackville St; adult/child Jun–mid-Sep $11.70/free, May & mid-Sep–Oct $7.80/free, other times free; ⏰9am-6pm Jul & Aug, to 5pm rest of year) Perched atop the grassy hillock looming over town, this star-shaped fort played a key role in Halifax's founding. Construction began in 1749; the current citadel is the fourth, built from 1818 to 1861. The grounds and battlements inside the fort are open year-round, with free

Canadian Museum of Immigration at Pier 21

FQROY / SHUTTERSTOCK ©

admission when the exhibits are closed, but it's better to come between May and October, when you can visit the barracks, the guards' room, the signal post, the engineer's store and the gunpowder magazines.

Halifax Central Library Library

(902-490-5700; www.halifaxpubliclibraries.ca; 5440 Spring Garden Rd; 9am-9pm Mon-Thu, to 6pm Fri & Sat, noon-6pm Sun) FREE Built on a former parking lot, this stunning modern library, composed of glass boxes stacked artfully on top of each other, was opened in 2014 and has become a much-loved meeting spot for Haligonians. Inside, concrete staircases ascend Escher-like through the central atrium, leading toward a rooftop where there's an excellent cafe and viewing garden.

Art Gallery of Nova Scotia Gallery

(902-424-5280; www.artgalleryofnovascotia.ca; 1723 Hollis St; adult/child $12/5, 5-9pm Thu free; 10am-5pm Sat-Wed, to 9pm Thu & Fri) The province's premier art institution is a must-see. It has a strong collection of local art, particularly the work of folk artist Maud Lewis, including the original tiny house (measuring 3m by 4m) where she lived most of her life, and which she turned into a living canvas. The main exhibit in the lower hall changes regularly and features anything from ancient art to the avant-garde.

Halifax Public Gardens Gardens

(www.halifaxpublicgardens.ca; 5665 Spring Garden Rd; sunrise-sunset) FREE Established in 1867 to mark Confederation, but formally opened to the public in 1875, Halifax's delightful 6.5-hectare public gardens are a fine example of Victorian horticultural planning. Stocked with lakes, statues, fountains, bridges, ponds and a huge variety of trees and formal flower beds, the gardens also have a bandstand where old-time tunes parp away on Sunday afternoons.

ACTIVITIES

Cycling is a great way to see sights on the outskirts of Halifax. You can take bikes on the ferries to Dartmouth or cycle over the MacDonald Bridge. In summer there are usually a few outfitters renting out bikes along the waterfront around Bishop's Landing (at the end of Bishop St), including **I Heart Bikes** (902-406-7774; www.iheartbikeshfx.com; 1507 Lower Water St; rentals per hour from $12; 10am-6pm May, 9am-8pm Jun-Aug).

Sable Island

The ever-shifting, 44km-long spit of sand that makes up Sable Island lies some 300km southeast of Halifax and has caused more than 350 documented shipwrecks. But what makes the island most famous is that it's home to one of the world's few truly wild horse populations, as well as the planet's largest breeding colony of gray seals.

Today the island works as a research center: scientists come every year to study the horses and other wildlife, and to keep an eye on any impact from their neighbor, the ExxonMobil Sable Offshore Energy Project. Just 10km away, this site has been harvesting natural gas since 1999, although decommissioning plans are currently underway.

It's complicated and expensive – but not impossible – to reach Sable Island as a visitor: 50 to 100 adventurous souls make it there each year. Contact **Sable Island Station** (902-426-1993; sable@pc.gc.ca), in conjunction with Environment Canada, for information about how to get the necessary permissions and independently arrange transport.

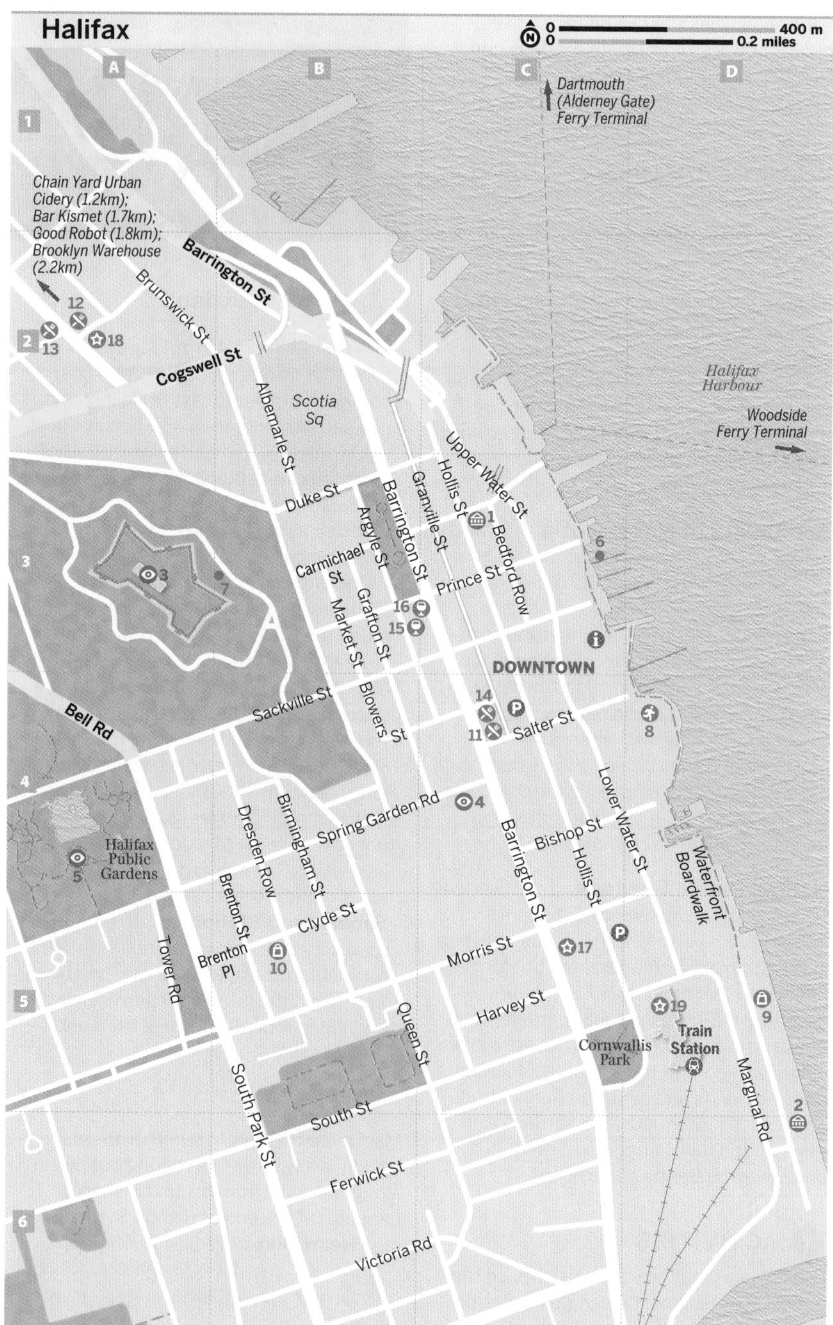
Halifax
0 400 m
0 0.2 miles
A
B
C
D
1
2
3
4
5
6
Dartmouth (Alderney Gate) Ferry Terminal
Chain Yard Urban Cidery (1.2km); Bar Kismet (1.7km); Good Robot (1.8km); Brooklyn Warehouse (2.2km)
Barrington St
Brunswick St
Cogswell St
Albemarle St
Scotia Sq
Halifax Harbour
Woodside Ferry Terminal
Upper Water St
Hollis St
Granville St
Barrington St
Argyle St
Duke St
Carmichael St
Bedford Row
Prince St
Grafton St
Market St
Blowers St
DOWNTOWN
Sackville St
Bell Rd
Salter St
Lower Water St
Spring Garden Rd
Birmingham St
Dresden Row
Brenton St
Brenton Pl
Bishop St
Hollis St
Barrington St
Waterfront Boardwalk
Halifax Public Gardens
Clyde St
Tower Rd
Morris St
Harvey St
Queen St
Cornwallis Park
Train Station
Marginal Rd
South Park St
South St
Ferwick St
Victoria Rd
1
2
3
4
5
6
7
8
9
10
11
12
13
14
15
16
17
18
19

Halifax

Sights
1 Art Gallery of Nova Scotia........................C3
2 Canadian Museum of Immigration at Pier 21........................D6
3 Citadel Hill National Historic Site........................A3
4 Halifax Central Library........................C4
5 Halifax Public Gardens........................A4

Activities, Courses & Tours
6 Bluenose II........................C3
7 Halifax Free Tours........................B3
8 I Heart Bikes........................D4

Shopping
9 Halifax Seaport Farmers Market........................D5
10 NSLC Clyde St........................B5

Eating
11 Chives Canadian Bistro........................C4
12 Edna........................A2
13 Field Guide........................A2
14 Old Apothecary........................C4

Drinking & Nightlife
15 Lot Six........................B3
16 Stilwell........................C3

Entertainment
17 Bearly's House of Blues & Ribs........................C5
18 Seahorse Tavern........................A2
19 Yuk Yuks........................D5

McNabs Island Hiking

(https://mcnabsisland.ca) Fine sand and cobblestone shorelines, salt marshes, forests and abandoned military fortifications paint the landscape of this 400-hectare island in Halifax Harbour. The website has a list of local boat operators who can shuttle you over (from $20 per person). It's a popular hiking and bird-spotting location, and in summer there are guided tours once a week.

TOURS

Halifax Free Tours Walking

(www.halifaxfreetours.wixsite.com/halifaxfreetours; 10am & 3pm Jun-Sep) FREE You can't beat the price of these free 1½-hour walking tours of downtown Halifax, led by friendly local guides. Send an email to reserve a spot, and please remember to tip! All tours leave from the viewing platform next to Halifax Citadel.

Bluenose II Boating

(800-763-1963; https://bluenose.novascotia.ca; Lower Water St; 2hr cruises adult/child $65/36) This classic replica of the famous *Bluenose* racing schooner (as seen on the Canadian dime) is sometimes in Halifax and sometimes in Lunenburg. Check the website for details. Cruises last two hours, and in season there are usually two a day, at 9:30am and 1:30pm.

SHOPPING

Halifax Seaport Farmers Market Market

(902-492-4043; www.halifaxfarmersmarket.com; 1209 Marginal Rd; 10am-5pm Mon-Fri, 7am-3pm Sat, 9am-3pm Sun) Although it has operated in several locations since its inception in 1750, what's now known as the Halifax Seaport Farmers Market (in its present location since 2010) is North America's longest continuously operating market. With more than 250 local vendors from a province that prides itself on strong farm-to-table and maritime traditions, it's well worth a visit.

NSLC Clyde St Dispensary

(902-423-6716; www.mynslc.com; 5540 Clyde St; 10am-10pm Mon-Sat, noon-5pm Sun) This is the flagship NSLC cannabis store in Halifax; the staff are well informed, so head here if you're after advice, equipment or supplies.

EATING

Old Apothecary Bakery $

(902-423-1500; www.theoldapothecary.com; 1549 Barrington St; cakes & pastries $2-5; 8am-5pm Mon-Sat) For a sweet fix, a superb croissant and probably the best baguettes in the city, this downtown bakery is the place. It's decked out like a junk shop, with a jumble of mismatched antiques in the salon upstairs, but the baking is patisserie precise.

Bar Kismet Bistro **$$**

(☎902-487-4319; www.barkismet.com; 2733 Agricola St; small plates $12-15, large plates $25-27; ⏰5pm-midnight Tue-Sun) Impeccable small plates of seafood have made this tiny bar-bistro a favorite among foodie North Enders, and deservedly so: dishes zing with surprising combinations and flavors, such as bass with morel mushrooms and artichokes, or raw scallop with lemongrass and turnip. The decor's stripped right back – bare wood, mirrors, pendant lights – putting the focus firmly on the food.

Brooklyn Warehouse Canadian **$$**

(☎902-446-8181; www.brooklynwarehouse.ca; 2795 Windsor St; mains lunch $12-18, dinner $23-30; ⏰11:30am-10pm Mon-Sat; 🖉) It's aptly named: there's definitely a New York flavor to this neighborhood eatery, with its worn wood, tobacco-yellow walls and chalkboard menus. The food selection changes fast, but it's strong on rich, hearty bistro fare; hopefully the Dragon's Breath (a take on the classic Caesar salad) will be on when you visit.

Edna Canadian **$$**

(☎902-431-5683; www.ednarestaurant.com; 2053 Gottingen St; brunch $12-20, mains $24-36; ⏰5-11pm Fri & Sat, 5-10pm Tue-Thu & Sun) At the edge of the North End, this hipster diner has strong competition but is still many people's first choice. It's bare bones as far as decor goes: a long wooden table for communal dining, a tiled bar, metal stools and tables for two. Food is modern bistro: risotto, seared scallops, classic steaks, all lovingly prepared. Edna equals excellence.

Field Guide Bistro **$$**

(☎902-405-4506; www.fieldguidehfx.com; 2076 Gottingen St; mains $12-24; ⏰5pm-midnight Tue-Sat, 10am-2pm & 5pm-midnight Sun) At Field Guide you order according to hunger level (from 'Sorta Hungry' starters to 'Still Hungry' desserts). It's a gimmick, but the food is first rate: fresh, surprising and modern, from cured salmon on seed bread with ricotta to fried chicken on a biscuit. The decor is minimal: brushed-concrete floors, a long bar, and big windows onto the street.

Chives Canadian Bistro Canadian **$$$**

(☎902-420-9626; www.chives.ca; 1537 Barrington St; mains $25-35; ⏰5-9:30pm) Proper, formal Canadian fine dining in the heart of downtown is on offer at Chives, one of the city's longest-running restaurants. Seasonally driven, artfully presented dishes are the stock-in-trade of chef Craig Flinn, and the food tastes as lovely as it looks. Freshened up by a 2018 refit, it features dark wood, blue-velour benches and antique-mirrored walls.

DRINKING & NIGHTLIFE

Good Robot Craft Beer

(☎902-446-1692; www.goodrobotbrewing.ca; 2736 Robie St; ⏰noon-2am Mon-Fri, 10am-2am Sat & Sun) This new North End microbrewery has become known for its wild beers: you might taste a watermelon-and-kiwifruit Pink Flamingo, a coffee-and-cherry-pie pale ale or a jalapeño-spiked lager (the names are equally wild). It's in a warehouse-style space with a pleasant beer garden; the pub snacks are delicious, too.

Lot Six Cocktail Bar

(☎902-428-7428; www.lotsix.ca; 1685 Argyle St; cocktails $12-15; ⏰4pm-2am, plus brunch 11am-2pm Sat & Sun) The soaring glass atrium that floods the room with light adds an extra touch of class to this slinky cocktail joint, which mostly crafts its own mixes but also offers a few shaken-up classics. Try the Springtime Smash, with tequila, Aperol, lemon, grapefruit and mint. It also serves fantastic food (mains $14 to $24).

Stilwell Craft Beer

(☎902-421-1672; www.barstillwell.com; 1672 Barrington St; ⏰noon-2am Thu-Sat, 4pm-2am Sun-Wed) A massive, wall-size chalkboard

Seared scallops at Edna

Maritimes Music

If Atlantic Canada were a bowl of chowder, music would be the stock in which everything floats. As a visitor you'll run into live performances everywhere, be they called ceilidhs (*kay*-lees), shindigs or kitchen parties. Even if you never gave fiddle music a second thought, the festive ambience will make you want to join in, sing along or tap your feet surreptitiously in time.

This playlist will get you in the mood for highland hills, long stretches of Atlantic coastline and perhaps a stop for some step dancing on the way. These old and new favorites are a little bit folk and a little bit country:

- 'Guysborough Train', Stan Rogers
- 'Silver Spear', Natalie MacMaster
- 'Gypsy Dancer', Irish Mythen
- 'Rant and Roar', Great Big Sea
- 'Home I'll Be', Rita MacNeil
- 'My Nova Scotia Home', Hank Snow
- 'Wrong Side of the Country', Old Man Luedecke
- 'Snowbird', Anne Murray
- 'Sail Away to the Sea', The Once

of brews from across Canada and beyond (all with a handwritten description and each delivered through a brass tap) gives this downtown bar probably the best beer selection in the city. Staff are incredibly knowledgeable and will help guide your choice. There's a menu of delicious small plates for late-night snacking.

Chain Yard Urban Cidery Pub
(902-407-2244; www.chainyardcider.com; 2606 Agricola St; 11:30am-11pm or 11:30pm) Craving a change from the craft-beer tsunami in Halifax? No sweat: head for the city's only craft cidery, with wares made from 100% Nova Scotia apples. Try a dry Pippin Russet, a super-tart Farmhouse Sour or a Polar Perry (made with pears), or really offbeat brews laced with kombucha, grape skins and rose petals. There's a patio for outdoor drinking.

ENTERTAINMENT

Bearly's House of Blues & Ribs Live Music
(902-423-2526; www.bearlys.ca; 1269 Barrington St; 5pm-midnight) Some of the best blues musicians in Atlantic Canada play here, often at very low cover charges.

Seahorse Tavern Live Music
(902-423-7200; www.theseahorsetavern.ca; 2037 Gottingen St) Indie acts and local bands are the mainstay at the rough-and-ready Seahorse. It also hosts a monthly dance party, plus retro nights devoted to the '80s and '90s. It's worth a visit just to see the giant seahorses on the bar.

Shakespeare by the Sea Theater
(902-422-0295; www.shakespearebythesea.ca; Point Pleasant Park; Jun-Sep) Performances of the Bard's works take place at the Cambridge Battery, an old fortification in the middle of Point Pleasant Park. When the weather's bad, the show moves to the Park Place Theatre nearby.

Yuk Yuks Comedy
(902-429-9857; www.yukyuks.com/halifax; 1181 Hollis St) This is the place to go for local and international stand-up and improv gigs; check the website for what's on when.

INFORMATION

Halifax Waterfront Visitor Information Centre (VIC; 902-424-4248; www.novascotia.com; 1655 Lower Water St; 9am-7pm Jul & Aug, to 5pm mid-May–Jun, Sep & Oct) A great place to start your wanderings of downtown Halifax; it'll load you up with maps and friendly advice. There's also a VIC welcome center at the **airport** (VIC; 902-873-1223; 10am-9pm Jun-Oct, 9am-4:30pm Mon-Fri Nov-May).

Halifax waterfront

Tourism Nova Scotia (☎902-425-5781, 800-565-0000; www.novascotia.com) Operates visitor centers in Halifax and other locations within Nova Scotia province, plus a free accommodation-booking service, which is useful when rooms are scarce in midsummer. It publishes the *Doers & Dreamers Guide*, which lists places to stay, attractions and tour operators.

GETTING THERE & AWAY

AIR

Halifax Stanfield International Airport (YHZ; ☎902-873-4422; www.hiaa.ca; 1 Bell Blvd) is 32km northeast of town on Hwy 102, toward Truro.

BUS

Maritime Bus (☎800-575-1807; www.maritimebus.com) runs services from Halifax to various points around Nova Scotia, as well as Prince Edward Island (PEI) and New Brunswick. Some services require you to book at least three hours ahead.

For journeys along the South Shore, **Cloud Nine Shuttle** (☎902-742-3992; www.thecloudnineshuttle.com) can drop you at any point as far as Yarmouth for a flat $75 fare. It also offers airport transfers for $80.

> *this seaside town punches well above its size*

TRAIN

One of the few examples of monumental Canadian train-station architecture left in the Maritimes is found at 1161 Hollis St. VIA Rail (www.viarail.ca) operates an overnight service to Montréal (from $223, 21 hours, daily except Tuesday).

GETTING AROUND

Halifax Transit (☎902-480-8000; www.halifax.ca/transit; single ride $2.50-3.50) runs the city bus system and the ferries to Dartmouth. Maps and schedules are available at the ferry terminals and at the information booth in Scotia Sq mall.

Bus 7 cuts through downtown Halifax and the North End via Robie and Gottingen Sts, passing both of Halifax's hostels. Bus 1 travels along Spring Garden Rd, Barrington St and the southern part of Gottingen St before crossing the bridge to Dartmouth.

Charlottetown

If there's a prettier provincial capital in Canada than Charlottetown, the largest city on Prince Edward Island (PEI), we're yet to find it. Eschewing the headlong rush for concrete and glass that characterizes many big Canadian cities, Charlottetown has stayed true to its small-town roots, with a low-rise downtown that retains many of the redbrick facades and Victorian buildings of its late-19th-century heyday. Covering just a few blocks inland from the harbor, the old part of town was designed to be walkable, and it pays to wander and soak up the sights – including its impressive mock-Gothic cathedral and a surfeit of heritage homes, browsable shops and colorful clapboard buildings.

SIGHTS

Victoria Park Park

(www.discovercharlottetown.com/listings/victoria-park) Dedicated in 1873, Charlottetown's most popular and beautiful waterfront green space has 16 hectares of lush loveliness for you to enjoy on a fine day. A boardwalk runs along the park's southern edge.

St Dunstan's Basilica Notable Building

(902-894-3486; www.stdunstanspei.com; 45 Great George St; 9am-5pm) FREE Rising from the ashes of a 1913 fire, the three towering stone spires of this Catholic, neo-Gothic basilica are now a Charlottetown landmark. The marble floors, Italianate carvings and decoratively embossed ribbed ceiling are surprisingly ornate.

TOURS

Confederation Players Walking Tours Walking

(800-565-0278; www.confederationcentre.com/heritage/confederation-players; 6 Prince St; adult/child $17/12; Jul & Aug) There is no better way to tour Charlottetown. Playing the fathers and ladies of Confederation, actors garbed in 19th-century dress educate and entertain visitors as they walk through the town's historic streets. Tours leave from the Visitor Information Centre (p154) at Founders' Hall, with a variety of themes and itineraries to choose from.

EATING

Receiver Coffee Diner $

(www.receivercoffee.com; 128 Richmond St; coffee $2-5; 7am-7pm Sun-Thu, to 8pm Fri & Sat) Receiver is the coffee connoisseurs' choice in Charlottetown. Come here for the perfect flat white made with ethically sourced Ethiopian single-origin beans. And don't miss the muffins. It's on the attractive pedestrianized part of Richmond St known as Victoria Row (look out for the wrought-iron sign).

Terre Rouge Canadian $$

(902-892-4032; www.terrerougepei.ca; 72 Queen St; mains $15-28; 11am-10pm) For our money, the top table in Charlottetown, known for its creative use of island ingredients: a seasonal island veggie platter, brined local lamb chops, a PEI beef burger infused with pork belly, or a deconstructed lobster picnic for two. The space is lovely, with potted plants, colorful furniture, big windows onto the street and a showpiece bar.

Water Prince Corner Shop & Lobster Pound Seafood $$

(902-368-3212; http://waterprincelobster.ca; 141 Water St; mains $12-36; 9:30am-8pm) When locals want seafood they head to this inconspicuous, sea-blue eatery near the wharf. It is deservedly famous for its scallop burgers, but it's also the best place in town for fresh lobster. You'll probably have to line up for a seat; otherwise order take-out lobster, which gets you a significant discount.

Brickhouse Kitchen & Bar Canadian $$

(902-566-4620; http://brickhousepei.com; 125 Sydney St; mains $16-30; 11am-10pm) An upscale-grub pub that's crammed with rough-bricked, industrial chic, from the trendy booth seats and open-view kitchen to the pop-art prints on the walls. Dishes take their cue from PEI ingredients – chef Seth's seafood chowder is a favorite, as is the tandoori-spiced roasted hen.

Pilot House Canadian **$$$**

(☎902-894-4800; www.thepilothouse.ca; 70 Grafton St; mains $25-33; ⏲11am-10pm Mon-Sat) The old Roger's Hardware building has now become this smart gastropub, but the old wood beams, brick columns and etched windows have been left in situ for character. There's a choice of pub classics or upscale dining, washed down with a generous supply of beers, wines and whiskies.

DRINKING & NIGHTLIFE

Hopyard Bar

(☎902-367-2599; 131 Kent St; ⏲11am-midnight) It's almost too-cool-for-school, this place – with craft beer on tap, racks of vinyl to browse and a regularly changing menu of small plates to snack on. It's a big hit locally, and has since spawned a sister establishment over in Halifax.

Charlottetown Beer Garden Beer Garden

(☎902-367-6070; www.beergardenpei.com; 190-192 Kent St; ⏲4pm-1am or 1:30am Mon-Fri, from 2pm Sat & Sun) This building on Hunter's Corner has been many things – house, tearoom, bike shop, tattoo parlor – but its current incarnation as a beer garden seems to be the most popular. Pan-Canadian brews on tap, with a special focus on beers from Nova Scotia, New Brunswick and PEI.

Craft Beer Corner Brewery

(Upstreet Craft Brewing; ☎902-894-0543; www.upstreetcraftbrewing.com; 156 Great George St; ⏲noon-midnight) Charlottetown's premier craft brewer now has a downtown location for its hip taproom, where you can sip brews like the Commons Pilsner, White Noize IPA and unusual strawberry-rhubarb Rhuby Social. The brewery serves sharing plates too.

Orwell Corner & Point Prim

If you're looking for a sweet, kid-friendly, half-day trip from Charlottetown and have had your fill of *Anne of Green Gables* action, head east on Rte 1. After about 30km, you'll come to **Orwell Corner Historic Village** (☎902-651-8510; www.orwellcornervillage.ca; Resource Rd 2, Vernon Bridge; adult/child $10.30/5.18; ⏲8:30am-4:30pm daily Jul & Aug, Mon-Fri Jun), a recreation of a rustic 19th-century farming community with animals, antiques and costumed locals. Further down the road, the **Sir Andrew MacPhail Homestead** (☎902-651-2789; www.macphailhomestead.ca; 271 MacPhail Park Rd, Vernon Bridge; ⏲9:30am-4:30pm Tue-Fri Jun-Sep) is open for tea on summer afternoons.

The real delight of the excursion is found continuing south on Rte 1 for a further 11km, where you'll come to signs for Point Prim. This skinny spit of land is covered in wild rose, Queen Anne's lace and wheat fields through summer and has views of red-sand shores on either side. At the tip is the **Point Prim Lighthouse** (☎902-659-2768; www.pointprimlighthouse.com; 2147 Point Prim Rd, Belfast; adult/child $5/3.50; ⏲10am-6pm mid-Jun–mid-Sep): the province's oldest and, we think, prettiest.

Round out your day with a cup of chowder by the ocean at **Point Prim Chowder House** (☎902-659-2187; www.chowderhousepei.com; 2150 Point Prim Rd, Belfast; mains $9-46; ⏲11am-3pm & 4:30-8pm mid-Jun–Sep), then head back to Charlottetown.

Point Prim Lighthouse
LISA-BLUE / GETTY IMAGES ©

Prince Edward Island National Park

Running along the island's north coast for 42 sandy kilometers, this **national park** (☎902-672-6350; www.pc.gc.ca/eng/pn-np/pe/pei-ipe/visit.aspx; day pass adult/child $7.80/free) encompasses some of the island's finest beaches, alongside a diverse range of habitats including undulating dunes, sandstone bluffs and important wetlands. Although the park is open year-round, most facilities and services are seasonal, only operating between mid-May and mid-October, with full services operational for the months of July and August. There are entry gates at various points along the park.

Entrance fees (charged when the picnic grounds and beaches are open, from mid-June to mid-September) admit you to all park sites, except Green Gables Heritage Place. If you're planning to stay longer than five days, look into a seasonal pass. The park maintains an information desk at the Cavendish Visitor Information Centre (p151).

ENTERTAINMENT

Confederation Centre of the Arts Theater

(☎902-566-1267; www.confederationcentre.com; 145 Richmond St) This modern complex's large theater and outdoor amphitheater host concerts, comedic performances and elaborate musicals. *Anne of Green Gables – The Musical* has been entertaining audiences here as part of the Charlottetown Festival since 1964, making it Canada's longest-running musical.

Olde Dublin Pub Live Music

(☎902-892-6992; 131 Sydney St; $8) A traditional Irish pub with a jovial spirit and live entertainment nightly during the summer months.

INFORMATION

Charlottetown Visitor Information Centre

(☎902-368-4444; viccharlottetown@gov.pe.ca; 6 Prince St; ⏰9am-5pm) The island's main tourist office at Founder's Hall has all the lowdown you need on Charlottetown and the wider island, plus a plethora of brochures and maps, and free wi-fi.

GETTING THERE & AWAY

AIR

Charlottetown Airport (YYG; ☎902-566-7997; www.flypei.com; 250 Maple Hills Ave) is 8km north of the city center. A taxi to/from town costs $16, plus $5 for each additional person.

BUS

T3 Transit County Line Express (T3 Transit; ☎902-566-9962; www.t3transit.ca; 7 Mt Edward Rd) runs between Charlottetown and Summerside ($9, 1½ hours, Monday to Friday only).

Maritime Bus (p151) also runs a bus service to/from Halifax ($58.25 one way, 4½ hours, two daily).

GETTING AROUND

Limited public transportation is provided by T3 Transit (www.t3transit.ca), but walking or renting a bike are both great ways to get around this compact city.

Cavendish

Cavendish is famous across Canada as the hometown of Lucy Maud Montgomery (1874–1942), author of the beloved *Anne of Green Gables* stories ('round here she's known simply as Lucy Maud or LM). While it provided the model for the fictional town of Avonlea, fans of the stories might be in for a bit of a shock on arrival in Cavendish. Far from a quaint country village filled with clapboard houses and clip-clopping horses, these days the town has become a full-on tourist mecca, crisscrossed by busy roads, swallowed up by parking lots and populated with a mishmash of attractions of questionable value.

SIGHTS

Green Gables Heritage Place Historic Site

(☎902-672-7874; www.pc.gc.ca/en/lhn-nhs/pe/greengables; 8619 Hwy 6; adult/child $7.80/free; ⏲10am-5pm May-Oct) Owned by author LM Montgomery's grandfather's cousins, the now-famous House of Green Gables and its Victorian surrounds inspired the setting for *Anne of Green Gables* and other stories. Now a National Historic Site, the house has been carefully restored to reflect how it would have appeared in Anne's day, including the furniture, furnishings and decor. Tour guides and audiovisual displays are on hand to provide context – you might even spy Anne herself wandering about (look out for the red braids).

Lucy Maud Montgomery's Cavendish Homestead Historic Site

(☎902-963-2231; www.lmmontgomerycavendishhome.com; 8523 Cavendish Rd; adult/child $6/free; ⏲9:30am-5:30pm Jul & Aug, 10am-5pm May, Jun & Oct) This restored homestead arguably offers a more authentic picture of author Lucy Maud Montgomery's life and times than the more heavily marketed Green Gables Heritage Place. Lucy Maud lived here from 1876 to 1911 with her maternal grandparents Alexander and Lucy Macneill, after her mother Clara died of tuberculosis. It's here that she wrote books including *Anne of Green Gables* and *Anne of Avonlea*. There's a small museum and an Anne-themed bookstore.

Cavendish Beach Beach

(www.cavendishbeachpei.com) Beautiful Cavendish Beach gets crowded during summer months, but with perfect sand and a warm (ish) ocean in front, you won't really care.

Cavendish Beach

Fundy National Park

New Brunswick's **Fundy National Park** (www.pc.gc.ca/eng/pn-np/nb/fundy; daily permit adult/under 17yr/family $7.80/free/15.70; May-Oct) is understandably the region's most popular sight. Highlights include the world's highest tides, the irregularly eroded sandstone cliffs and the wide beach at low tide that makes exploring the shore for small marine life and debris such a treat. The park is delightfully wooded and lush and features an extensive network of impressive hiking trails and lakes. Unusually for a national park, you'll also find a motel, a golf course and an outdoor saltwater swimming pool.

Headquarters Visitors Centre (506-887-6000; Rte 114 & Wolfe Point Rd; 10am-6pm May & Aug-Oct, to 8pm Jun & Jul), just inside the park's southern entrance, has information on trail conditions, doles out maps and info, and can take reservations for campsites.

The park is best accessed from the fishing village of Alma; unless you join a tour from Moncton, you'll need your own wheels. To reach the park entrance, simply walk across the bridge on the western edge of town.

EATING

Carr's Oyster Bar Seafood $$

(902-886-3355; www.carrspei.ca; 32 Campbellton Rd, Stanley Bridge; mains $16-40; 11am-8pm) Dine on oysters straight from Malpeque Bay, or lobster, mussels and seafood you've never even heard of, like quahogs from Carr's own saltwater tanks (the menu helpfully divides dishes up into raw, steamed, fried or baked).

Lost Anchor Pub Pub $$

(902-388-0118; www.lostanchorpei.com; 8572 Cavendish Rd; mains $14-29; noon-9pm) If all the talk of Cavendish's favorite fictional orphan is driving you to drink, here's where to come. Simple but hearty pub meals are available: lobster mac 'n' cheese, fish-and-chips and pork-belly tacos.

INFORMATION

Cavendish Visitor Information Centre (902-963-7830; cnr Rte 6 & Hwy 13; 9am-5pm) The staff here can help you with any *Anne of Green Gables* info you could wish for, as well as background on Lucy Maud Montgomery.

St John's

Newfoundland is an island of austere, washed-out beauty and vast unpopulated wilderness. Yet here, in its capital and largest city, one finds scads of homes colored like tropical fruit, plus bustling street life and a dim urban (yet small-town friendly) buzz. For all that, North America's oldest city doesn't just contrast the province it dominates. St John's exudes wry wit, stoicism and lust for life, and to this end embodies some of Newfoundland's best values.

SIGHTS

Signal Hill National Historic Site Historic Site

(709-772-5367; www.pc.gc.ca/signalhill; 230 Signal Hill Rd; grounds 24hr, visitor center 10am-6pm; P) The city's most famous landmark is worth it for the glorious view alone, though there's much more to see. The tiny castle atop the hill is **Cabot Tower** (8:30am-5pm Apr-Nov) FREE, built in 1898 to honor both John Cabot's arrival in 1497 and Queen Victoria's Diamond Jubilee. In midsummer, soldiers dressed as the 19th-century Royal Newfoundland Company perform a **tattoo** (☎709-772-5367; www.signalhilltattoo.org; $10; ⏰11am & 3pm Wed & Thu, Sat & Sun Jul & Aug) and fire cannons.

The Rooms Museum

(☎709-757-8000; www.therooms.ca; 9 Bonaventure Ave; adult/child $10/5, 6-9pm Wed free; ⏰10am-5pm Mon, Tue, Thu & Sat, to 9pm Wed, to 10pm Fri, noon-5pm Sun, closed Mon Oct-Apr; 👪) Not many museums offer the chance to see a giant squid, hear avant-garde sound sculptures and peruse ancient weaponry all under one roof. But that's the Rooms, the province's all-in-one historical museum, art gallery and archives. The building itself, a massive stone-and-glass complex, is impressive to look at, with views that lord it over the city. Has an on-site cafe and excellent restaurant.

CA Pippy Park Park

(www.pippypark.com; 👪🐾) The feature-filled 13-sq-km CA Pippy Park coats downtown's northwestern edge. Recreational facilities include walking trails, picnic areas, playgrounds, a golf course and a campground. **Memorial University**, the province's only university, is here too. The university's **botanical garden** (☎709-737-8590; www.mun.ca/botgarden; 306 Mt Scio Rd; adult/child $9/6; ⏰10am-5pm May-Aug, reduced hours Sep-Apr) is at Oxen Pond, at the park's western edge.

Quidi Vidi Village

Over Signal Hill, away from town, is the tiny picturesque village of Quidi Vidi. Check out the 18th-century battery and the lakeside regatta museum, but make your first stop **Quidi Vidi Brewery** (☎709-738-4040; www.quidividibrewery.ca; 35 Barrows Rd; tasting or tour $10; ⏰tastings 11am, taproom noon-10pm Sun-Wed, to midnight Thu-Sat), which whips up Newfoundland's most popular microbrews.

ACTIVITIES

North Head Trail Walking

You only have to go to Signal Hill to get a taste of Newfoundland's majestic, rugged beauty. The North Head Trail (1.7km) connects Cabot Tower with the harborfront Battery neighborhood, and is a beloved local gem. The walk departs from the tower's parking lot and traces the cliffs, imparting tremendous sea views and sometimes whale spouts.

Rennie's River Trail Walking

(access at Carpasian Rd) It takes a city as understated as St John's to not make a big deal about this trail, which must be one of the most pleasant urban walks anywhere. In the middle of the city is a 5km trail, much of which runs alongside the rushing Rennie's River, which forms natural waterfalls and is flanked by grassy banks.

TOURS

Iceberg Quest Boating

(☎709-722-1888; www.icebergquest.com; Pier 6; 2hr tour adult/child $70/30) Departs from St John's Harbour and makes a run down to Cape Spear in search of icebergs in June and whales in July and August. There are multiple departures daily.

EATING

Adelaide Oyster House International $

(☎709-722-7222; www.facebook.com/theadelaideoysterhouse; 334 Water St; small plates $8-17; ⏰5-11pm Mon-Wed, to midnight Thu, to 1am Fri, 11am-3pm & 5pm-1am Sat, 11am-3pm & 5pm-midnight Sun) The Adelaide is a stylish sliver of a bar and restaurant where the specialty is small plates such as fish tacos, Kobe beef lettuce wraps topped with spicy kimchi, and, of course, fresh oysters from both coasts, plus some brick-strong cocktails to get the party started.

Georgestown Cafe and Bookshelf Cafe $

(☎709-579-7134; https://georgestowncafe.wordpress.com; 73 Hayward Ave; mains $5-10; ⏰8am-5pm Mon-Sat, from 10am Sun; 👪) If you've got younger kids and you need to kill time before heading to the Rooms, Georgestown Cafe is here to answer your every prayer.

It's a cafe, sure, serving fair-trade coffee and yummy treats such as granola, bagels, scones and muffins, but there's also a bookstore on-site, and a play area stacked with kids' books and toys.

Piatto Pizza $$
(☎709-726-0709; www.piattopizzeria.com; 377 Duckworth St; mains $12-19; ⌚11:30am-10pm Mon-Thu, to 11pm Fri & Sat, to 9pm Sun; 👪) Offering a great night out without breaking the bank, cozy brick Piatto wood-fires pizza like nobody's business. Go trad or try a thin-crust pie topped with prosciutto, figs and balsamic. It's all good. There are fresh salads, wine and Italian cocktails. Children's books plus pizza and ice-cream specials for kids make this a good option for families.

Merchant Tavern Canadian $$$
(☎709-722-5050; http://themerchanttavern.ca; 291 Water St; mains $21-40; ⌚11:30am-10pm Tue-Fri, from 10:30am Sat, 10:30am-2:30pm Sun) An elegant tavern housed in a former bank building, this restaurant is a fine choice for a splurge. Gorgeous seafood stews, duck and lentils, and cod with parsnip make for near culinary perfection – just bear in mind this is a seasonal, changing menu (but always solid). Some seating faces the open-view kitchen – good for chatting with the cooks.

Mallard Cottage Canadian $$$
(☎709-237-7314; www.mallardcottage.ca; 2 Barrows Rd; mains $19-35; ⌚10am-9pm Wed-Sat, to 6:30pm Sun, to 5pm Mon & Tue) A lot of restaurants give lip service to 'local and sustainable,' but this one is spot-on and devilishly good. The blackboard menu changes daily. Think turnips with yogurt and crispy shallots or brined duck with spaetzle and fried rosemary. The adorable Mallard Cottage, which dates from the 1750s, is a historical site in and of itself.

DRINKING & NIGHTLIFE

Duke of Duckworth Pub
(☎709-739-6344; www.dukeofduckworth.com; McMurdo's Lane, 325 Duckworth St; ⌚noon-2am; 📶) 'The Duke,' as it's known, is an unpretentious English-style pub that represents all that's great about Newfoundland. Stop in on a Friday night and you'll see a mix of

Cabot Tower (p156)

MMAC72 / GETTY IMAGES ©

blue-collar and white-collar workers, young and old, and perhaps even band members from Canadian folk-rockers Great Big Sea plunked down on the well-worn red-velour bar stools.

Geeks Public House Bar
(709-746-8469; www.facebook.com/geekspublichouse; 288 Duckworth St; 6pm-midnight Wed, Thu, Sun & Mon, to 1am Fri & Sat;) This bar serves its own butterbeer and scores a +5 bonus for getting customers happily buzzed while they peruse all five editions of the *Dungeons & Dragons Player's Handbook*. If that last sentence got you excited, you'll love this place. If it made you scratch your head, you'll likely still love this spot, dedicated to nerdy pursuits and affectations.

Inn of Olde Pub Bar
(709-576-2223; 67 Quidi Vidi Village Rd; noon-2am) Step inside the Inn of Olde and you'll feel like you've walked into the collective attic of the city, with a jumble of laminate tables, dusty hockey gear, black-and-white photos, framed newspaper clippings and faded NHL jerseys. Presiding over everything is Linda, who has been tending bar and bending ears for as long as anyone can remember.

ENTERTAINMENT

Ship Pub Live Music
(709-753-3870; www.facebook.com/TheShipPubKitchen; 265 Duckworth St; noon-late) Attitudes and ages are checked at the door of this little pub, tucked down Solomon's Lane. You'll hear everything from jazz to indie, and even the odd poetry reading. The pub closes when things slow down, but tends to stay open until 3am on weekends.

Rose & Thistle Live Music
(709-579-6662; 208 Water St; 9am-2am) Local musicians and visiting bands take the stage on the regular at this little pub.

Shamrock City Live Music
(709-758-5483; www.shamrockcity.ca; 340 Water St; noon-2am) Bands playing everything from Newfoundland folk to '80s hair ballads take the stage nightly at this all-ages pub.

INFORMATION

Visitors Centre (709-576-8106; www.stjohns.ca; 348 Water St; 9am-4:30pm Mon-Fri May-early Oct) Excellent resource with free provincial and city road maps, and staff to answer questions and help with bookings. There's another outlet at the **Quidi Vidi Village Plantation** (709-570-2038; http://qvvplantation.com; 10 Maple View Pl; 10am-4pm Wed-Sat, 11am-4pm Sun). The **Airport Visitors Centre** (709-758-8515; St John's International Airport; 10am-5pm) is the only St John's visitor center that's open year round.

GETTING THERE & AWAY

AIR

St John's International Airport (YYT; 709-758-8500; www.stjohnsairport.com; 100 World Pkwy;) is 7km north of the city on Portugal Cove Rd (Rte 40). Air Canada offers a daily direct flight to and from London, WestJet goes direct to Dublin and Gatwick. **United Airlines** (800-864-8331; www.united.com) flies to the USA.

BUS

DRL (709-263-2171; www.drl-lr.com) sends one bus daily each way between St John's and Port aux Basques ($126, cash only, 13½ hours) via the 905km-long Hwy 1, making 25 stops en route. It leaves at 7:30am from Memorial University's Student Centre, in CA Pippy Park (p157).

GETTING AROUND

The **Metrobus** (709-570-2020; www.metrobus.com) system covers most of the city (fare $2.50). Maps and schedules are online and in the Visitors Center. Bus 3 is useful; it circles town via Military Rd and Water St before heading to the university. **The Link** loops around the main tourist sights, including Signal Hill, between 10am and 5:30pm Wednesday to Sunday from late June to September. Hop-on/hop-off fare is $10.

THE PRAIRIES

In this Chapter

The Prairies at a glance...

Comprising the wide-open provinces of Alberta, Saskatchewan and Manitoba, the magnitude of this land is only fully appreciated while standing on the edge of a vivid-yellow canola field counting three different storms on the horizon. Travel the Prairies' byways and expect surprises, whether it's a moose looming up on an otherwise empty road or the dinosaur-encrusted badlands around Drumheller. Calgary has become unexpectedly cool; Winnipeg will stun with its arts scene; while Saskatoon will wow you with its music. There aren't so many people on the prairies – but those that are here will go out of their way to make your visit memorable.

Three Days in the Prairies

Spend the day in Calgary exploring the **Glenbow Museum** (p170) and the **National Music Centre** (p166), then grab a meal from **Market** (p173) on trendy 17th Ave. The next day, get into dino mode by taking a day trip to **Drumheller** and visiting the **Royal Tyrrell Museum of Palaeontology** (p164). Back in Calgary, head east to step back in time at the authentic **Ukrainian Cultural Heritage Village** (p169).

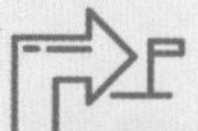

One Week in the Prairies

Head east to Saskatoon (p174) to enjoy the urban pleasures – especially the food and drink – of the Paris of the Prairies. Carry on across those endless golden fields to Winnipeg (p177). Take in the **Canadian Museum for Human Rights** (p177) and the eclectic **St-Boniface Museum** (p178). End your prairie sojourn with live music at **Times Chang(d) High & Lonesome Club** (p181) and a micro-brewed beer with the locals at **Torque Brewing** (p180).

Previous page: Shale gas well in a canola field, Alberta

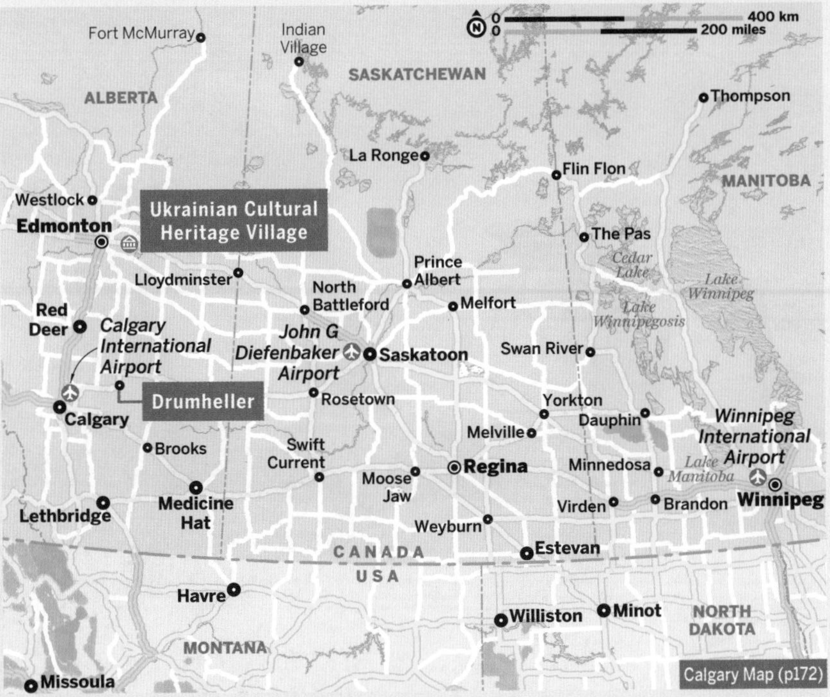

Calgary Map (p172)

Arriving in the Prairies

Calgary International Airport Take bus 300 ($3.40, 45 minutes) or a taxi ($40 to $55) to the center.

John G Diefenbaker Airport A taxi into central Saskatoon costs around $20.

Winnipeg International Airport Take bus 15 ($2.95) or grab a cab ($25 to $30).

Bus Bus transport in Western Canada is limited following the termination of Greyhound services.

Train VIA Rail scoots across the Prairies, stopping in Winnipeg and Saskatoon.

Where to Stay

Calgary has recently found its independent spirit and established a range of boutique hotels across different price ranges. Hotels downtown in both Calgary and Winnipeg can be expensive, although many run frequent specials; Saskatoon offers better deals. All three have chain motels on the outskirts. During events such as the Calgary Stampede or music festivals, rates rise and availability plummets; book ahead.

Hoodoos

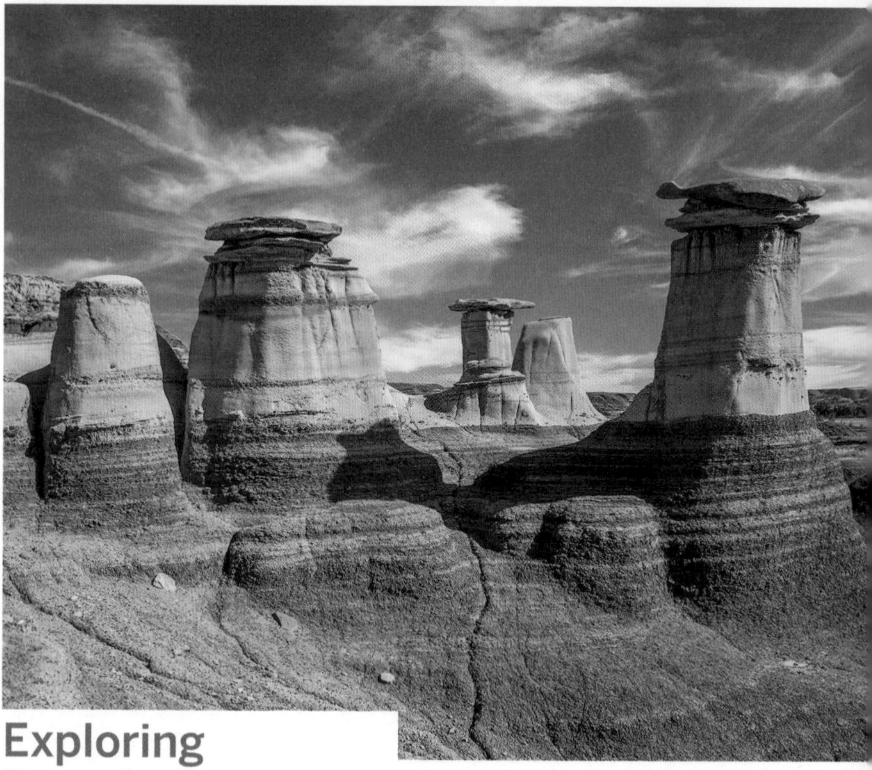

Exploring Drumheller

This community in the Red Deer River Valley was founded on coal but now thrives on another subterranean resource – dinosaur bones.

A small town set amid Alberta's enigmatic badlands, Drumheller is serious about its paleontology. Add in the museums in nearby East Coulee and the ghosts of Wayne, and you've got a full itinerary.

Great For...

☑ Don't Miss

Discovering your own dino treasures on a summertime dinosaur dig ($15) at the Royal Tyrrell Museum.

Palaeontology Museum

The fantastic **Royal Tyrrell Museum of Palaeontology** (403-823-7707; www.tyrrellmuseum.com; 1500 North Dinosaur Trail, Midlands Provincial Park; adult/child/family $19/10/48; 9am-9pm mid-May–Aug, 10am-5pm Sep, 10am-5pm Tue-Sun Oct–mid-May;) is one of the preeminent dinosaur museums on the planet, made even better by a $5.9 million expansion project completed in 2019. Look for the skeleton of 'Hell-Boy,' a new dinosaur discovered in 2005, and 'Black Beauty,' a 67-million-year-old T rex rearing its head into the sky. Unlike some other dinosaur

World's Largest Dinosaur

RONNIE CHUA / SHUTTERSTOCK ©

Need to Know

Tourist Information Center (☎403-823-1331; https://traveldrumheller.com; 60 1st Ave W; ⌚9am-9pm mid-May–Sep, 10am-5:30pm Oct–mid-May) The entrance to the T rex is in the same building.

Take a Break

Stop by **Café Olé** (☎403-800-2090; www.facebook.com/cafeoledrum; 11 Railway Ave; sandwiches $8-13; ⌚8am-5pm Sun-Thu, to 7pm Fri & Sat;) for soups, sandwiches, coffees and desserts.

★ Top Tip

Go on a dinosaur hunt – there are over 30 colorful dino sculptures around town.

exhibits, there's nothing dusty or musty about this super-modern place.

World's Largest Dinosaur

In a town filled with dinosaurs, this **T rex** (60 1st Ave W; adult/family $4/10.50; ⌚10am-5:30pm;) is the king of them all. Standing 26m high above a parking lot, it dominates the Drumheller skyline. You can climb the 106 steps to the top for great views.

Dinosaur Trail & Hoodoo Drive

The scenic 48km Dinosaur Trail loop runs northwest from Drumheller and includes Hwys 837 and 838.

The loop takes you past **Midland Provincial Park**, where you can take a self-guided hike, and past the vast **Horsethief Canyon** and its picturesque views. Glide peacefully across the Red Deer River on the free, cable-operated **Bleriot Ferry**, which has been running since 1913. On the west side of the valley, pause at **Orkney Viewpoint**, which overlooks the area's impressive canyons.

The 25km Hoodoo Drive starts about 18km southeast of Drumheller on Hwy 10. Along this drive you'll find the best examples of hoodoos – weird, eroded, mushroom-like columns of sandstone rock – between Rosedale and Lehigh; there's also an interpretive trail.

This area was once the site of a prosperous coal-mining community; the historic **Atlas Coal Mine** (☎403-822-2220; https://atlascoalmine.ab.ca; East Coulee; adult/family $12/35, tours $14-27; ⌚9:45am-5pm Sep-Jun, to 6:30pm Jul & Aug) and **East Coulee School Museum** (☎403-822-3970; http://ecsmuseum.ca; 359 2nd Ave, East Coulee; $7; ⌚10am-5pm May-Sep) are both worth a stop. Take the side trip on Hwy 10X from Rosedale to the small community of **Wayne** (population 27) with its famous and supposedly haunted saloon.

MICHAEL WHEATLEY / ALAMY STOCK PHOTO ©

National Music Centre

Looking like a whimsical copper castle, this fabulous new museum in Calgary will take you on a ride through Canada's musical history.

Great For...

☑ Don't Miss

The guitar that the Guess Who used to record 'American Woman.'

With studio space and numerous theaters, the National Music Centre is all about getting Canadian artists heard. Check the website for who's playing.

Get Musical

Who wouldn't want to try out a drum kit, strum an electric guitar or step into a sound-recording room to sing your heart out? You can also create your own instruments here with rubber bands, string, pegs, and other unlikely objects. And be sure to find your groove in the Body Phonic Room, where your moves control the tunes.

The Collection

With over 2000 musical artifacts, you're certain to find something to wow you. You'll find everything from Elton John's 'songwriting' piano to Shania Twain's dresses

Need to Know

☎403-543-5115; http://nmc.ca; 850 4th St SE; adult/child $18/11; ⊙10am-5pm May-Aug, Wed-Sun Sep-Apr

Take a Break

You probably won't want to take a breather – but if you do, there's an excellent cafe on-site.

★ Top Tip

If you're looking for cool and very-Canadian souvenirs, be sure to stop in at the gift shop.

and the Rolling Stones' mobile recording studio. Keep your eyes peeled for the Electronic Sackbut, a Canadian forerunner to 1970s synthesizers that is being restored and cloned for visitors to test out.

The Canadian Hall of Fame is especially impressive. From Leonard Cohen to Justin Bieber, Neil Young, Drake, Gordon Lightfoot, Diana Krall and Sarah McLachlan, Canadian's sure know how to hold a tune.

Sound Sculpture

As you wander into the Skywalk between the museum and the neighboring King Eddie building, you may wonder where the whistling and humming is coming from. Look up and you'll see 16 piano pieces hanging from the ceiling. These are instruments that were destroyed in Calgary's 2013 flood, repurposed and solar powered to fill the air with music once again.

The Tragically Hip

If you're not Canadian, you're forgiven for not knowing the Tragically Hip – almost. Formed in the '80s in Kingston, Ontario, they sold out stadiums across the country. Their lyrics tell stories linked to Canada's geography and history, and their unique sound is often quoted as being 'distinctly Canadian.' With 14 studio albums, two live albums and 54 singles under their belt, along with 14 Juno Awards and nine number-one albums, it's not surprising that they figure prominently in the National Music Centre.

When Gord Downie, the Hip's singer and songwriter, was diagnosed with brain cancer in 2016, the country went into mourning. One final tour across the country included a Canada Day performance at the then-brand-new Centre.

JOSEPH HOLOIEN / SHUTTERSTOCK ©

Ukrainian Cultural Heritage Village

With original buildings and authentic characters, experience firsthand what life was like for Ukrainian immigrants on the prairies.

Great For...

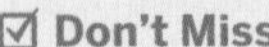

☑ Don't Miss

Hopping on a free horse-drawn-wagon ride from Thursday to Monday during summer.

The People

By visiting the Heritage Village, you are paying homage to the 250,000 Ukrainian immigrants who came to Canada between 1892 and 1930. Many settled in central Alberta, where the landscape reminded them of the snowy steppes of home.

The interpreters you encounter here aren't just staff in costume; they perform in roles of real-life immigrants from Ukraine and go about their day as if they really are the hotelier, the farmer, the school-teacher or the blacksmith. Some speak only Ukrainian; others speak English with heavy accents. They know the history and family tree of the person they've assumed and won't – at any cost – break character. Expect to be asked if you'd like a hotel room or if your horse needs shoes. Be sure to visit the very new immigrants in their *burdei*

Need to Know

780-662-3640; https://ukrainianvillage.ca; adult/child/family $15/10/40; 10am-5pm May-Sep

Take a Break

Before you leave, visit the kiosk for some of the best pierogi and cabbage rolls this side of Lviv.

★ Top Tip

Wear good walking shoes – these are turn-of-the-century dirt roads.

(sod house) to see what they've brought with them and how they're beginning to farm the land. If you don't speak Ukrainian, be prepared for lots of charades!

The Buildings

The buildings are all original, moved here from various towns in Alberta, refurbished to their original state and filled with authentic original furnishings. Around 35 are set out like a genuine village, with more added each year. Highlights include a sod house, three Byzantine churches, a hotel, a grain elevator and a schoolhouse.

When the 1920s school was first renovated, students who had once attended were invited to visit. Now in their 80s, these students sat in their original seats and felt the time-warp effect of the painstakingly accurate renovation.

What's Nearby?

Virtually across the road, **Elk Island National Park** (780-922-5790; www.parkscanada.gc.ca/elkisland; adult/child/senior $7.80/free/6.80, campsites & RV sites $25.50, campfire permits $8.80; visitor center 8:30am-5:30pm, gates 24hr) contains the highest density of wild hoofed animals in the world after the Serengeti; many come here to see the resident wild bison. The wood bison live entirely in the quieter southern portion of the park (which is cut in two by Hwy 16), while the plains bison inhabit the north. Most of the infrastructure lies in the north, too, around Astotin Lake. Here you'll find a campground, a nine-hole golf course (its clubhouse has a restaurant), a beach and a boat launch. Four of the park's 11 hiking trails lead away from the lakeshore through trademark northern Albertan aspen parkland – a kind of natural intermingling of the prairies and boreal forests.

Calgary

Calgary will surprise you with its beauty, cool eateries, nightlife beyond honky-tonk, and long, worthwhile to-do list. Calgarians aren't known for their modesty; it's their self-love and can-do attitude that got them through disastrous flooding in 2013 and, in 2016, saw them helping residents of wildfire-stricken Fort McMurray with unquestioning generosity. We mustn't forget – Calgary also hosted the highly successful 1988 Winter Olympics, elected North America's first Muslim mayor, and throws one of Canada's biggest festivals, the Calgary Stampede.

◉ SIGHTS

Glenbow Museum Museum

(☎403-777-5506; www.glenbow.org; 130 9th Ave SE; adult/child/family $18/11/45; ⊙9am-5pm Mon-Sat, noon-5pm Sun, closed Mon Oct-Jun) With an extensive permanent collection and an ever-changing array of traveling exhibitions, the impressive Glenbow has plenty for the history buff, art lover and pop-culture fiend to ponder. Temporary exhibits are often daring, covering contemporary art and culture. Permanent exhibits bring the past to life with strong historic personalities and lots of voice recordings. Hang out in a tipi, visit a trading post and walk through the railcar of a train.

Calgary Tower Notable Building

(☎403-266-7171; www.calgarytower.com; 101 9th Ave SW; adult/youth $18/9; ⊙observation gallery 9am-9pm Sep-Jun, to 10pm Jul & Aug) This 1968 landmark tower is an iconic feature of the Calgary skyline, though it has now been usurped by numerous taller buildings and is in danger of being lost in a forest of skyscrapers. There is little doubt that the aesthetics of this once-proud concrete structure have passed into the realm of kitsch, but, love it or hate it, the slightly phallic 191m structure is a fixture of the downtown area.

Heritage Park Historical Village Historic Site

(☎403-268-8500; www.heritagepark.ca; 1900 Heritage Dr SW, at 14th St SW; adult/child

Heritage Park Historical Village

SVETLANA123 / GETTY IMAGES ©

$26.25/13.65; ⏲10am-5pm daily May-Aug, Sat & Sun Sep & Oct; 👪) Want to see what Calgary used to look like? Head down to this historical park (the largest in Canada!) where all the buildings are from 1915 or earlier. There are 10 hectares of recreated town to explore, with a fort, grain mill, church and school. Go for a hay ride, visit the antique midway or hop on a train. Costumed interpreters are on hand to answer any questions.

ACTIVITIES

Eau Claire Rapid Rent Cycling

(☎403-444-5845; Barclay Pde SW; bikes/rollerblades/helmet per day from $40/25/7; ⏲10am-6pm May-Sep) Rents out bikes, junior bikes, tandem bikes, child trailers and rollerblades. And rafts, if you happen to have a car and trailer.

Olympic Oval Ice Skating

(☎403-220-7954; www.ucalgary.ca/oval; 288 Collegiate Blvd NW, University of Calgary; adult/child/family $7/5/18.50; ⏲Aug–mid-Mar) Get the Olympic spirit at the University of Calgary, where you can go for a skate on Olympic Oval. Used for the speed-skating events at the Olympics, it offers public skating on the long track and has skates available to rent, as well as mandatory helmets. See the website for current schedules.

TOURS

Hammerhead Tours Cultural

(www.hammerheadtours.com; half-day city tours $65) Join a half-day tour of the city or a very full day tour to destinations like Drumheller, Head-Smashed-In Buffalo Jump or Lake Louise. Multiday and 'create-your-own' tours are also available.

EATING

1886 Buffalo Cafe Breakfast $

(☎403-269-9255; www.1886buffalocafe.com; 187 Barclay Pde SW; breakfast mains $9-19; ⏲6am-3pm Mon-Fri, from 7am Sat & Sun) This is a true salt-of-the-earth diner in the high-rise-dominated city center. Built in 1911 and the only surviving building from the lumber yard once here, the exterior's peeling clapboards sure make it look authentic. This is a ketchup on the table, unlimited coffee refills kind of place famous for its brunches, especially its huevos rancheros.

Alforno Cafe & Bakery Cafe $

(☎403-454-0308; www.alforno.ca; 222 7th St SW; mains $9-21; ⏲7am-9pm Mon-Fri, 8am-9pm Sat, 8am-5pm Sun) This ultra-modern, super-comfortable cafe is the kind of place you'll want to hang out all day. Bellinis, beer on tap, carafes of wine and excellent coffee won't discourage you from lingering, nor will magazines, comfy sofas or window seats. With pastas, flatbreads, salads, soups and panini, all homemade, it's difficult to leave room for the amazing cakes, tarts and biscuits.

Una Pizza $$

(☎403-453-1183; www.unapizzeria.com; 618 17th Ave SW; pizzas $17-24; ⏲11:30am-1am) There's often a line out the door but nobody seems to mind waiting – that's how good these thin-crust pizzas are. There's plenty of good house wine, too.

Pulcinella Italian $$

(☎403-283-1166; www.pulcinella.ca; 1147 Kensington Cres NW; pizzas $16-30; ⏲11:30am-10pm Sun-Wed, to 11pm Thu, to midnight Fri & Sat) With an authentic pizza oven, Pulcinella specializes in amazing, thin, crispy Neapolitan pizzas with purposefully simple toppings. Don't leave without trying the homemade gelato with flavors like black cherry and pistachio.

Teatro Italian $$$

(☎403-290-1012; www.teatro.ca; 200 8th Ave SE; mains lunch $19-40, dinner $30-60; ⏲11:30am-3pm Mon-Fri, 5-10pm Sun-Thu, to 11pm Fri & Sat) In a regal bank building next to the Epcor Centre for the Performing Arts, Teatro has an art nouveau touch with its marble bar top, swirling metalwork and high-backed curved sofas. Dishes are works of art and fuse Italian influences, French nouvelle

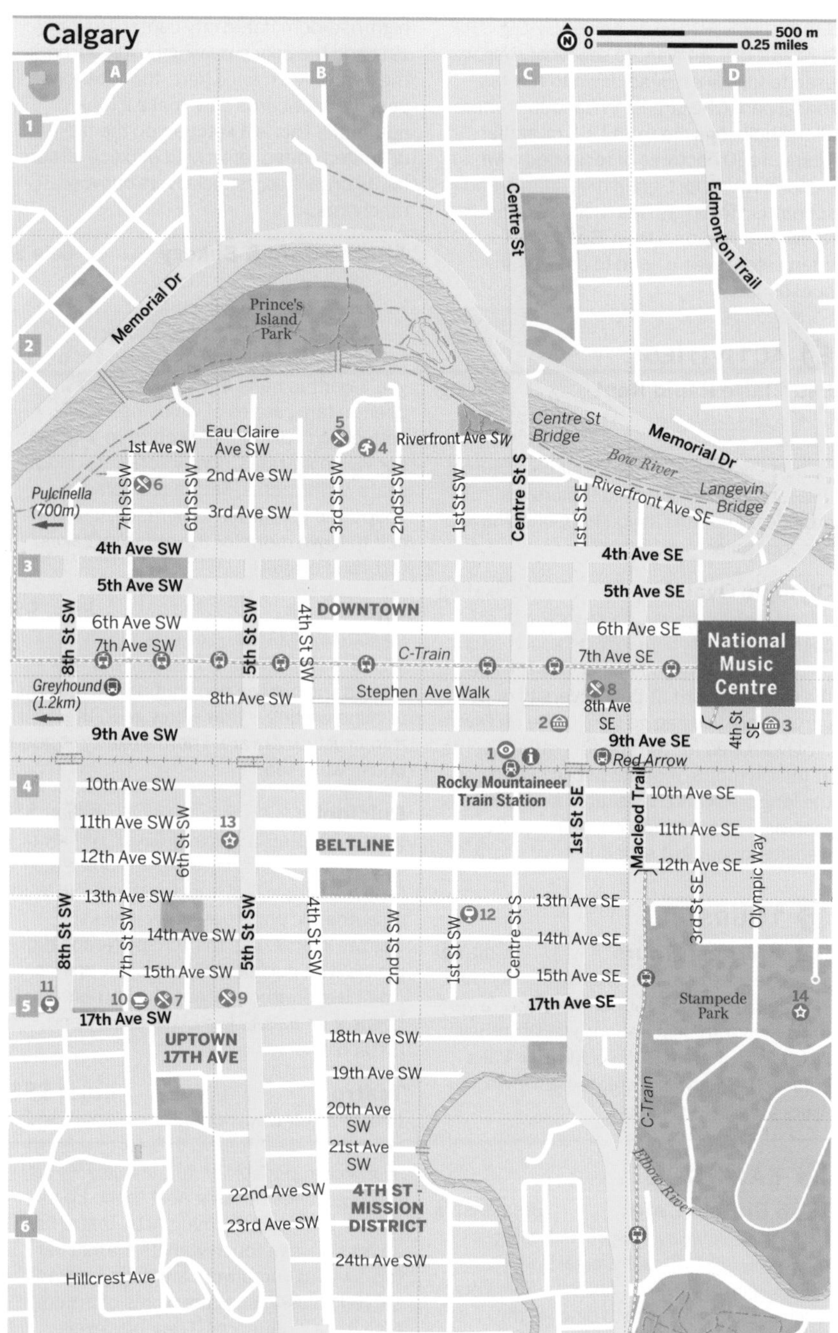
Calgary
0 500 m
0 0.25 miles
A
B
C
D
1
2
3
4
5
6
Memorial Dr
Prince's Island Park
Centre St
Edmonton Trail
Eau Claire Ave SW
1st Ave SW
2nd Ave SW
3rd Ave SW
4th Ave SW
5th Ave SW
6th Ave SW
7th Ave SW
8th Ave SW
9th Ave SW
Riverfront Ave SW
Centre St Bridge
Memorial Dr
Bow River
Riverfront Ave SE
Langevin Bridge
Pulcinella (700m)
Greyhound (1.2km)
7th St SW
6th St SW
3rd St SW
2nd St SW
1st St SW
Centre St S
1st St SE
4th Ave SE
5th Ave SE
6th Ave SE
7th Ave SE
8th Ave SE
9th Ave SE
8th St SW
5th St SW
4th St SW
DOWNTOWN
C-Train
Stephen Ave Walk
National Music Centre
4th St SE
Red Arrow
Rocky Mountaineer Train Station
10th Ave SW
11th Ave SW
12th Ave SW
13th Ave SW
14th Ave SW
15th Ave SW
17th Ave SW
BELTLINE
10th Ave SE
11th Ave SE
12th Ave SE
13th Ave SE
14th Ave SE
15th Ave SE
17th Ave SE
Macleod Trail
3rd St SE
Olympic Way
Stampede Park
UPTOWN 17TH AVE
18th Ave SW
19th Ave SW
20th Ave SW
21st Ave SW
22nd Ave SW
23rd Ave SW
24th Ave SW
4TH ST - MISSION DISTRICT
Hillcrest Ave
C-Train
Elbow River
1
2
3
4
5
6
7
8
9
10
11
12
13
14

Calgary

Sights

1 Calgary Tower C4
2 Glenbow Museum C4
3 National Music Centre D4

Activities, Courses & Tours

4 Eau Claire Rapid Rent B2

Eating

5 1886 Buffalo Cafe B2
6 Alforno Cafe & Bakery A3
7 Market A5
8 Teatro C4
9 Una B5

Drinking & Nightlife

10 Analog Coffee A5
11 Betty Lou's Library A5
12 Pr%f C5

Entertainment

13 Broken City Social Club B4
14 Saddledome D5

cuisine and a bit of traditional Alberta. Service is friendly and impeccable.

Market Canadian $$$

(☎403-474-4414; www.marketcalgary.ca; 718 17th Ave SW; mains lunch $19-26, dinner $18-42; ⊙11:30am-11pm) With an earthy yet futuristic feel, award-winning Market has gone a step further in the fresh-local trend. Not only does it bake its own bread, but it also butchers and cures meat, makes cheese and grows 16 varieties of heirloom seeds year-round. As if that weren't enough, it's then all whipped into meals that are scrumptious and entirely satisfying.

DRINKING & NIGHTLIFE

Pr%f Cocktail Bar

(☎403-246-2414; www.proofyyc.com; 1302 1st St SW; ⊙4pm-midnight Sun & Mon, to 1am Tue-Sat) No, that isn't a typo. Pr%f might be small but the bar is big enough to require a library ladder, and the drinks menu not only requires time, but also imagination. The menu itself is a beautiful thing to behold and the drinks look so stunning, you almost don't want to drink them. But you do. Trust us, you do.

Betty Lou's Library Cocktail Bar

(☎403-454-4774; www.bettylouslibrary.com; 908 17th Ave SW; ⊙5pm-12:30am Tue-Thu, to 2am Fri & Sat) Betty Lou's Library won't be for everyone, but if you like feeling like you've stepped back in time to Prohibition 1920s, then you'll get a kick out of coming here. The cocktails are superb; if you can't decide just ask one of the bartenders for a custom-crafted cup of yum. You'll need a password to enter, so call first.

Analog Coffee Coffee

(☎403-910-5959; www.analogcoffee.ca; 740 17th Ave SW; coffees $3-6; ⊙7am-10pm, to midnight Jul & Aug) The third-wave coffee scene is stirring in Calgary, led by companies like Fratello, which runs this narrow, overflowing hipster-ish 17th Ave cafe. Beans of the day are displayed on a clipboard and there are rows of retro vinyl along the back wall. Teas are here, too, as are tasty desserts aplenty.

ENTERTAINMENT

Broken City Social Club Live Music

(☎403-262-9976; www.brokencity.ca; 613 11th Ave SW; ⊙11am-2am) There's something on stage here most nights – everything from jazz jams to hip-hop, along with comedy and quiz nights. The rooftop patio is ace in the summer, and the small but well-curated menu keeps you happy whether you're after a steak sandwich or vegan cauliflower wings.

Calgary Flames Spectator Sport

(☎403-777-2177; http://flames.nhl.com) Archrival of the Edmonton Oilers, the Calgary Flames play ice hockey from October to April at the **Saddledome** (☎403-777-4646; Stampede Park). Make sure you wear red to the game and head down to 17th Ave afterward, or the 'Red Mile,' as they call it during play-offs.

Loose Moose Theatre Company Theater
(☎403-265-5682; www.loosemoose.com; 1235 26th Ave SE) Guaranteed to be a fun night out, Loose Moose has digs near the Inglewood neighborhood. It specializes in improv comedy and, at times, audience participation (you've been warned). You'll also find kids' theater.

INFORMATION

Visit Calgary (www.visitcalgary.com; 101 9th Ave SW; 8am-5pm) Operates a visitor center in the base of the Calgary Tower. The staff can help you find accommodations. Information booths are also available at both the arrivals and departures levels of the airport.

GETTING THERE & AWAY

AIR

Calgary International Airport (YYC; ☎403-735-1200; www.yyc.com; 2000 Airport Rd NE) is about 15km northeast of the center off Barlow Trail, a 25-minute drive away.

BUS

Luxurious **Red Arrow** (https://redarrow.ca; 205 9th Ave SE) buses run to Edmonton ($76, 3½ hours, six daily) and Lethbridge ($53, three hours, two daily).

Canmore and Banff ($72, 2¼ hours, eight daily) and Lake Louise ($99, 2½ hours, eight daily) are served by **Brewster Express** (☎403-762-6700; www.banffjaspercollection.com/brewster-express).

Red Arrow picks up downtown on the corner of 9th Ave SE and 1st Ave SE. Brewster Express buses pick up at various downtown hotels. Inquire when booking.

GETTING AROUND

TO/FROM THE AIRPORT

You can go between the airport and downtown on public transportation. From the airport, take bus 57 to the Whitehorn stop (northeast of the city center) and transfer to the C-Train; reverse that process coming from downtown. You can also take bus 300 from the city center all the way to the airport. Either way, the trip costs only $3.40, and takes between 45 minutes and an hour.

For transport to Banff or other places outside Calgary, the **Airporter Shuttle Express** (☎403-509-4799; www.airportshuttleexpress.com; from $85) and **Banff Airport Taxi** (☎403-720-5788; www.banffairporttaxi.com) are useful options. The Airporter Shuttle Express can also drop you in Calgary for around $85.

A taxi to the airport costs between about $40 and $55 from downtown.

CALGARY TRANSIT

Calgary Transit (www.calgarytransit.com) is efficient and clean. Use the website's handy plan-your-trip section to find out how to get where you're going. You can choose from the Light Rapid Transit (LRT) rail system, aka the C-Train, and ordinary buses. One fare ($3.40) entitles you to transfer to other buses or C-Trains. The C-Train is free in the downtown area along 7th Ave between 10th St SW and 3rd St SE. If you're going further or need a transfer, buy your ticket from a machine on the C-Train platform. Most buses run at 15- to 30-minute intervals daily. There is no late-night service.

Saskatoon

Saskatoon is full of hidden treasures. Head into the downtown core and inner neighborhoods to get a sense of this vibrant city. The majestic South Saskatchewan River winds through downtown, offering beautiful, natural diversions. Leafy parks and rambling riverside walks help you make the most out of long, sunny summer days, and there are plenty of great spots to stop for a refreshing drink and a chat with the locals.

SIGHTS

Meewasin Valley Nature Reserve
(www.meewasin.com) The Meewasin Valley, formed by the South Saskatchewan's wide swath through the center of town, is named for the Cree word for 'beautiful'. Mature trees populate the riverbanks, while sections of the 60km **Meewasin Trail** extend from downtown paths, winding through forests and along the riverbank. It is popular

Saskatoon

with walkers, cyclists and wandering travelers, and picnic areas line the trails. Further north, **Mendel Island** is home to abundant wildlife. The website has downloadable maps and info.

Remai Modern Gallery

(306-975-7610; www.remaimodern.org; 102 Spadina Cres E; adult/child $12/10; 10am-5pm Tue-Sun) A huge new attraction that anchors River Landing, Remai Modern is a museum of modern and contemporary art for Saskatoon. It has 11 gallery spaces over three floors, learning studios, a theater, restaurant, store, lounges and play areas. There are changing exhibitions, so check the website for what's coming up.

Western Development Museum Museum

(WDM; 306-931-1910; www.wdm.ca/saskatoon; 2610 Lorne Ave S; adult/child $12/5; 9am-5pm; P) The flagship Saskatoon branch of the province's Western Development Museum is a faithful re-creation of Saskatoon the boom town, c 1910. Inside Canada's longest indoor street, you can roam through the town's many buildings, from a dentist's office straight out of a horror film to the pharmacy, the walls of which are lined with hundreds of vintage concoctions. There are trains, tractors, buggies, sleighs and a jail. It's about 4km south of downtown.

TOURS

Prairie Lily Cruise

(306-955-5459; www.theprairielily.com; 950 Spadina Cres E; adult/child from $25/16; hours vary) The Prairie Lily riverboat runs popular sightseeing, dinner and specialty cruises, such as Sunday brunch cruises, on the South Saskatchewan River from its dock beside the Children's Discovery Museum. Check the website for weekly schedules.

EATING

Drift Sidewalk Cafe & Vista Lounge Cafe $

(306-653-2256; www.driftcafe.ca; 339 Ave A S; lunch mains from $8; 8am-10pm Mon-Thu, 8am-11pm Fri & Sat, 10am-3pm Sun) Split personalities mark this hip Riversdale spot.

The cafe serves crepes, sandwiches and a long list of varied snacks through the day; enjoy a coffee at a table outside. The lounge is sleeker and has a fun cocktail list, many with housemade libations. It also serves mid-priced international dishes.

Cathedral Social Hall Pub Food $$
(306-668-1011; www.cathedralsocialhall.com; 608 Spadina Cres E; mains from $14; 11am-midnight) CSH focuses on local Saskatchewan fare and beer, including gluten-free and vegetarian options. Try the Beer Soup ($8) or the Social Hall Burger ($15) out on the front terrace, along with your choice from the 30 taps.

Calories Restaurant Canadian $$
(306-665-7991; www.caloriesrestaurant.ca; 721 Broadway Ave; lunch mains from $12; 11am-10pm Mon-Thu, to 11pm Fri & Sat) Menus change regularly at this classy yet casual affair on Broadway that is proud of its commitment to using local, organic ingredients in its creative cuisine. With an extensive wine list, a Sunday brunch menu to look forward to, and a dessert counter that will make you drool, you can't go wrong. Outside tables, too.

Ayden Kitchen and Bar Canadian $$$
(306-954-2590; www.aydenkitchenandbar.com; 265 3rd Ave S; mains from $22; 5:30-9pm Mon-Sat) Saskatoon's restaurant-of-the-moment works magic with local produce and other seasonal specialties. Chef Dale MacKay is a star on the Canadian food scene. You never know what surprises he has in store at this unpretentious downtown bistro. Book ahead.

DRINKING & NIGHTLIFE

Hose & Hydrant Brew Pub Pub
(306-477-3473; www.hoseandhydrant.com; 612 11th St E; 11am-late) A fun pub in the Broadway area in what was Firehall No 3, built in 1911 and now a heritage-listed building. Enjoy tables on a patio and deck with mellow side-street outlooks.

Shelter Brewing Co Microbrewery
(306-979-9249; www.shelterbrewing.ca; 255 2nd Ave S; 4-11pm Tue-Thu, from 3pm Fri & Sat) New kid on the block Shelter Brewing is going off with locals, with some extremely tasty brews and tacos options. The core brews are solid with a great New England IPA and a classic Brown Ale.

ENTERTAINMENT

Persephone Theatre Theater
(306-384-7727; www.persephonetheatre.org; 100 Spadina Cres E) This perennial theatrical standout has excellent new quarters in the Remai Arts Centre at River Landing. Comedy, drama and musicals are all regulars.

Buds on Broadway Live Music
(306-244-4155; http://buds.dudaone.com; 817 Broadway Ave; 4pm-late) Classic blues and old-time rock and roll are the standards here in this beer-swilling joint. Check the website for upcoming live music and jam nights.

INFORMATION

Planet S (www.planetsmag.com) Irreverent and free biweekly newspaper with good entertainment listings.

Tourism Saskatoon (306-242-1206, 800-567-2444; www.tourismsaskatoon.com; 202 4th Ave N; 8:30am-5pm Mon-Fri) Has local and regional info.

GETTING THERE & AWAY

AIR

John G Diefenbaker International Airport (YXE; 306-975-8900; www.skyxe.ca; 2625 Airport Dr) is 5km northeast of the city, off Idylwyld Dr and Hwy 16. WestJet and Air Canada have services to major Canadian cities.

TRAIN

Saskatoon's **train station** (Chappell Dr) is 8km southwest from downtown; the thrice-weekly VIA Rail *Canadian* stops here on its Vancouver–Toronto run.

GETTING AROUND

A taxi to the airport or train station costs about $20. **Blueline Taxi** (0191-262-6666; www.unitedgroup.ca) is easily reached.

Bike Doctor (306-664-8555; www.bikedoctor.ca; 623 Main St; per day from $60) rents bikes.

Saskatoon Transit (360-975-7500; www.transit.saskatoon.ca; 226 23 St E; adult/child $3/2.25) runs city buses, which converge on the transit hub of 23rd St E (between 2nd and 3rd Aves N).

Winnipeg

Winnipeg surprises. Rising above the prairie, it's a metropolis where you least expect it. Cultured, confident and captivating, it's more than just a pit stop on the Trans-Canada haul, but rather a destination in its own right, with a couple of world-class museums and a wonderfully diverse dining scene. Explore its boom of craft-beer breweries and specialty coffee shops, wander its historic neighborhoods and lap up a vibe that both enjoys being the butt of a *Simpsons* joke ('That's it! Back to Winnipeg!') and revels in one of the world's best **fringe theater festivals** (204-943-7464; www.winnipegfringe.com; 174 Market Ave; mid-Jul).

SIGHTS

Canadian Museum for Human Rights Museum

(204-289-2000; www.humanrights.ca; Waterfront Dr & Provencher Blvd; adult/student/7-17yr/$18/14/9; 10am-5pm Thu-Tue, to 9pm Wed; P) Housed in a stunning contemporary building designed by American architect Antoine Predock, this terrific museum explores human rights issues through striking interactive displays, videos, art and more. Exhibits don't shy away from sensitive subjects, such as the internment of Canadian-Japanese people during WWII and Indigenous children forced into residential schools as recently as the 1990s, and the Holocaust and Holodomor (Ukrainian famine of 1932–33) are treated sensitively.

“striking interactive displays, videos, art and more”

Canadian Museum for Human Rights

SALVADOR MANIQUIZ / SHUTTERSTOCK ©

Polar Bears in Churchill

The 'Polar Bear Capital of the World,' Churchill lures people to the shores of Hudson Bay for its great bears, beluga whales, a huge old stone **fort** (www.pc.gc.ca/en/lhn-nhs/mb/prince) and endless subarctic majesty. But while the highly accessible wildlife is enough for Churchill to be on any itinerary, there's something less tangible that makes people stay longer and keeps them coming back: a hearty seductive spirit that makes the rest of the world seem – thankfully – even further away than it really is.

Lazy Bear Lodge Tours (☎204-663-9377; www.lazybearlodge.com; 313 Kelsey Blvd; 2-night summer tour from $595) has liveaboard tundra coaches and also runs multiday beluga- and polar-bear-spotting adventures in the summer, based out of its lodge.

There is no road to Churchill; access is by plane or train only. Calm Air and First Air both fly from Winnipeg (one to two daily), while Via Rail's Churchill train from Winnipeg is back in operation after the rails were washed out in May 2017 and Churchill was cut off from the rest of Manitoba for a year and a half.

SERGEY URYADNIKOV / SHUTTERSTOCK ©

Winnipeg Art Gallery Gallery

(WAG; ☎204-786-6641; www.wag.ca; 300 Memorial Blvd; adult/child $12/6; ⏰11am-5pm Tue, Wed & Fri-Sun, to 9pm Thu) This ship-shaped gallery displays contemporary Manitoban and Canadian artists, and has the world's largest collection of Inuit carvings (at the time of research there were plans to house these in a custom-built Inuit Art Centre, scheduled to open in 2020), alongside a permanent collection of European Renaissance art. Temporary exhibits have included artworks by Eugène Boudin, Canadian artist and potter Robert W Archambeau, and printmaker and painter David Blackwood. There's also a rooftop sculpture garden and a terrific gift shop.

Manitoba Museum Museum

(☎204-956-2830; www.manitobamuseum.ca; 190 Rupert Ave; adult/3-12yr from $19.50/11.50; ⏰10am-5pm Fri-Wed, to 9pm Thu; 👪) Nature trips through the subarctic, history trips into 1920s Winnipeg, cultural journeys covering the past 12,000 years – if it happened in Manitoba, it's here. Amid the superb displays are a planetarium and an engaging science gallery. One exhibit shows what Churchill was like as a tropical jungle, a mere 450 million years ago, while a replica of the *Nonsuch*, the 17th-century ship that opened up the Canadian west to trade, is another highlight.

St-Boniface Museum Museum

(☎204-237-4500; www.msbm.mb.ca; 494 Ave Taché; adult/under 12yr $7/free; ⏰10am-4pm Mon-Wed, Fri & Sat, 9am-9pm Thu) A mid-19th-century convent is Winnipeg's oldest building and the largest oak-log construction on the continent. The museum inside focuses on the establishment of St Boniface, the birth of the Métis nation, and the 3000km journey of the first Grey Nuns, who arrived here by canoe from Montréal. Artifacts include pioneer furniture and tools, First Nations beadwork and weaponry, Louis Riel's execution hood and the coffin used to transport his body afterward.

Assiniboine Park Park

(www.assiniboinepark.ca; Corydon Ave; ⏰24hr; P👪) Winnipeg's emerald jewel, this 4.5-sq-km urban park is easily worth at least a half-day's frolic. Besides the top-notch **zoo** (☎204-927-6000; www.assiniboineparkzoo.ca;

ABDUL KOROMA / SHUTTERSTOCK ©

Assiniboine Park

460 Assiniboine Park Dr; adult/child $20/11; 9am-6pm; P), there are playgrounds, gardens, a conservatory and the Leo Mol sculpture garden full of bronzes.

TOURS

Winnipeg Trolley Company Cultural
(204-226-8687; www.winnipeg.tours; 1 Forks Market Rd) Entertaining, engaging tours departing from just outside the Forks Market. The Ale Trail on Wednesdays and Fridays ($40 to $80) takes in three of Winnipeg's finest craft-beer breweries, while the Trolley of Terror ($40 to $50, Thursdays from August to October) introduces you to Winnipeg's ghosts, UFO sightings and a Nazi invasion. Class tours of the city, as well (daily except Monday from mid-June to September).

Historic Exchange District Walking Tours Walking
(204-942-6716; www.exchangedistrict.org/tours/historic-walking-tours; Old Market Sq; adult/child $10/free; 9am-4:30pm Mon-Sat May-Sep) Entertaining themed and history tours departing from Old Market Sq. Book in advance.

EATING

King + Bannatyne Sandwiches $
(204-691-9757; www.kingandbannatyne.com; 100 King St; sandwiches $10-15; 7:30-10am & 11am-8pm Mon-Sat;) The hand-cut meat sandwiches at this brisk, casual spot verge on the sublime. There are only five to choose from: brisket, smoked chicken, BLT, braised beef and one sole delicious concession to the noncarnivorous: the jalapeño pineapple barbecue jackfruit. They've branched out into heaped breakfast specials, too.

Close Company Fusion $$
(204-691-7788; www.close.company; 256 Stafford St; dishes $16-20; 5-11pm Sun-Thu, to midnight Fri & Sat;) With only 12 seats, this on-trend little restaurant is aptly named. The 10 small-plate dishes change at the chef's whim, but you might be treated to tuna with black garlic or scallop ceviche singing with the high notes of passion fruit.

The short and sweet cocktail menu also mostly changes with the seasons, though Oui Chef is a keeper.

Segovia Mediterranean $$
(204-477-6500; www.segoviatapasbar.com; 484 Stradbrook Ave; tapas $6-25; 5-11pm Wed-Mon;) Set in a stylishly renovated old home in a quiet spot just off noisy Osborne St, Segovia has an established reputation as one of Winnipeg's best places to eat. There's a long list of wines and cocktails you can savor on the patio while enjoying – and sharing – tapas such as seared scallops with gremolata and tuna tostadas with chipotle aioli.

529 Wellington Steakhouse Steak $$$
(204-487-8325; www.529wellington.ca; 529 Wellington Cr; steak $38-62; 11:30am-2pm & 5-11pm Mon-Fri, 5-11pm Sat, 5-9pm Sun;) A historic 1920s mansion provides a refined setting for some of Winnipeg's best steak, smoky and seared in all the right places – perfect for wooing your carnivorously inclined sweetie. The wine list is as thick as an Old Testament Bible and one of the best in town. Service is exemplary.

Home to the ... highly acclaimed Manitoba Opera

DRINKING & NIGHTLIFE

Torque Brewing Microbrewery
(204-410-2124; www.torquebrewing.beer; 330-830 King Edward St; noon-9pm Tue & Wed, to 11pm Thu-Sat;) The winner of the 2019 Canadian Brewing Awards, Torque is an offbeat brewery decked out with a vintage motorbike, foosball and sports on TV. Their four core beers are equally no-nonsense – the most popular being Witty Belgian – and they keep experimenting with tea beers and more. Live music Fridays 4pm to 7pm, and a great food truck parked outside.

Common Craft Beer
(204-942-6216; www.facebook.com/thecommonwpg; 1 Forks Market Rd; 11:30am-9pm Sun-Thu, to 11pm Fri & Sat) There's 16 rotating

Centennial Concert Hall

JOE FOX / AGE FOTOSTOCK ©

craft beers on tap from all over Canada and beyond, plus carefully selected wines, courtesy of Véronique Rivest, one of the world's best sommeliers with awards to prove it.

Forth Coffee
(☎204-505-7073; www.forth.ca; 171 McDermot Ave; ⏰7am-9pm Mon-Fri, 9am-5pm Sat & Sun) This is the epitome of a 21st-century hipster specialty coffee joint. It roasts its own beans (Dogwood) on-site, serves epic breakfasts, sells a range of fun merchandise, skater wear and grooming cream for men with beards, has a Bitcoin ATM and is spread across a split-level, industrial-chic space, with upstairs for socialising and a quieter nook downstairs.

ENTERTAINMENT

Times Change(d) High & Lonesome Club Live Music
(☎204-957-0982; www.highandlonesomeclub.ca; 234 Main St; ⏰8pm-late) Honky-tonk/country/rock/blues weekend bands jam while beer and whiskey flows at this small, rough, raunchy and real throwback. Don't miss the Sunday-night jam, led by the legendary bluesman Big Dave McLean, recent recipient of the Order of Canada.

Winnipeg Jets Ice Hockey
(www.nhl.com/jets; ⏰Sep-May) There's Manitoba mania for the Jets who play at the **Bell MTS Place** (☎204-987-7825; www.bellmtsplace.ca; 260 Hargrave St). The ice-hockey games are raucous and often sold out; ask around for tickets.

Centennial Concert Hall Concert Venue
(☎204-956-1360; www.centennialconcerthall.com; 555 Main St) Home to the **Winnipeg Symphony Orchestra** (☎204-949-3999; www.wso.ca; tickets $30-105; ⏰Sep-May), the **Royal Winnipeg Ballet** (☎204-956-0183; www.rwb.org) and the highly acclaimed **Manitoba Opera** (☎204-942-7479; www.mbopera.ca; tickets $35-115; ⏰Nov-Apr), complete with subtitles.

INFORMATION

Travel Manitoba (☎204-945-3777; www.travelmanitoba.com; 25 Forks Market Rd; ⏰9am-5pm) Provincial information center at the Forks; has plenty of info on Winnipeg and surrounds.

GETTING THERE & AWAY

AIR

Winnipeg International Airport (YWG; www.waa.ca; 2000 Wellington Ave) has a flash terminal a convenient 10km west of downtown. It has service to cities across Canada, such as Toronto, Montréal, Calgary and Vancouver, and to major hubs in the USA. Regional carriers handle remote destinations, including Churchill.

BUS

Greyhound bus services have been discontinued in Manitoba, but there were six weekly buses up to Thompson, Manitoba ($100, 9¼ hours) at the time of writing with **Thompson Bus** (☎204-939-3991; www.thompsonbus.com; 2015 Wellington Ave).

TRAIN

VIA Rail's transcontinental *Canadian* departs **Union Station** (☎204-691-7611; 123 Main St) three times weekly in each direction. The painfully slow *Hudson Bay* service to Churchill runs twice a week via Thompson; it was even slower than usual at the time of writing due to renovations on the track, so check for delays before you go.

GETTING AROUND

TO/FROM AIRPORT

A downtown taxi costs $25 to $30; some hotels have free shuttles. **Winnipeg Transit** (☎204-986-5700; www.winnipegtransit.com; adult/child $2.95/2.45) bus 15 runs between the airport and downtown every 20 minutes between 5:50am and 12:50am and takes 30 minutes.

BUS

Winnipeg Transit runs extensive bus routes around the area, most converging on Fort St. Get a transfer and use exact change. Alternatively, buy a reloadable Peggo card if you're in Winnipeg for a while. Free *Downtown Spirit* buses run on three daily routes, connecting the Forks with Portage Ave, the Exchange District and Chinatown.

THE ROCKIES

In this Chapter

The Rockies at a glance...

With the Rocky Mountains stretched across them, Banff and Jasper national parks are filled with dramatic, untamed wilderness. Mountaintops scrape the skyline while enormous glaciers cling to their precipices. Glassy lakes flash emerald and sapphire and deep forests blanket wide valleys. Through it all wander bears, elk, moose, wolves and bighorn sheep. However you choose to experience the Rockies, be it through hiking, backcountry skiing, paddling or simply relaxing at a lake's edge, the intensity and scale of the region will bowl over even the most seasoned traveler.

Two Days in the Rockies

Spend a day exploring Banff Town, taking in the **Whyte Museum** (p191) and getting out on the river with **Banff Canoe Club** (p191), before warming up in the **hot springs** (p191). Join the locals at **Bear St Tavern** (p193) for dinner. The next day visit **Lake Louise**, hiking to **Lake Agnes Teahouse** (p186), and then riding the **gondola** (p187) and counting grizzly bears meandering beneath you.

Four Days in the Rockies

Spend day three driving the **Icefields Parkway** (p188), taking in the gorgeous lakes and getting out onto **Athabasca Glacier** (p189). Spend your final day in Jasper. Grab snacks from **Other Paw Bakery** (p196), join a boat tour on **Maligne Lake** (p195) to set eyes on Spirit Island, soak away any aches at **Miette Hot Springs** (p194), then toast the adventure with the folks at **Jasper Brewing Co** (p197).

Previous page: Vermilion Lakes in Banff

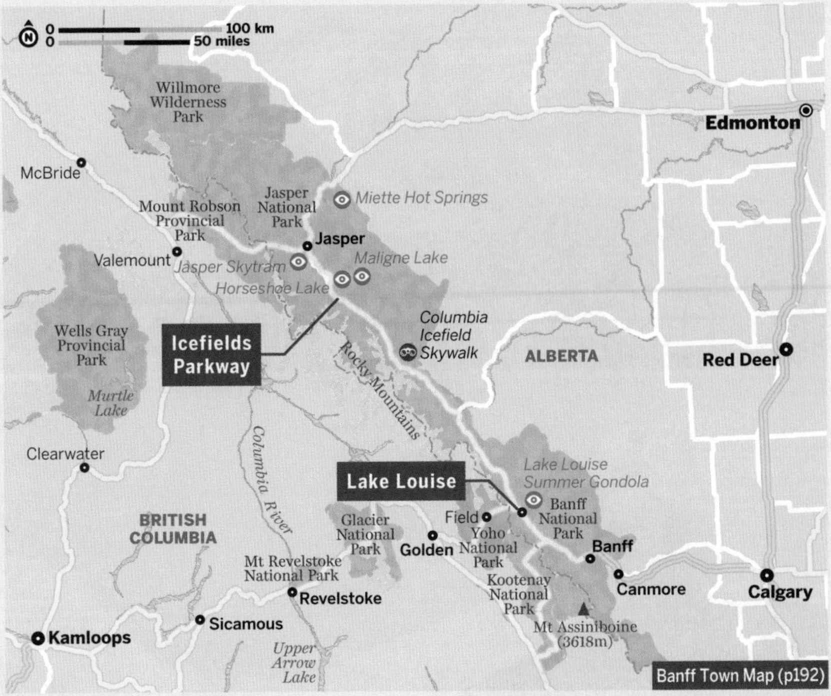

0 100 km
0 50 miles
Willmore Wilderness Park
McBride
Jasper National Park
Miette Hot Springs
Mount Robson Provincial Park
Jasper
Valemount
Jasper Skytram
Maligne Lake
Horseshoe Lake
Wells Gray Provincial Park
Icefields Parkway
Columbia Icefield Skywalk
Rocky Mountains
ALBERTA
Edmonton
Red Deer
Murtle Lake
Clearwater
Columbia River
Lake Louise
Lake Louise Summer Gondola
Banff National Park
BRITISH COLUMBIA
Glacier National Park
Field
Yoho National Park
Golden
Banff
Mt Revelstoke National Park
Canmore
Calgary
Revelstoke
Kootenay National Park
Mt Assiniboine (3618m)
Sicamous
Kamloops
Upper Arrow Lake
Banff Town Map (p192)

Arriving in the Rockies

Bus There are a number of shuttles from Calgary International Airport to Banff, including Brewster Express. Sundog Tour Company offers a similar service from Edmonton's airport to Jasper Town.

Car Major car rental companies have branches in both Banff Town and Jasper.

Train VIA Rail has thrice-weekly services between Jasper and Vancouver or east to Toronto.

Where to Stay

Staying in Banff and Jasper can be a pricey affair. There are plenty of upmarket cabins and lodges, along with plenty of mediocre ones charging top prices; shop around and book well in advance. If you're willing to rough it a little, many campgrounds and hostels have million-dollar locations and let you experience the true magic of the parks.

Lake Louise

Phenomenal Lake Louise – one of the most spectacular sights in the Rockies – is impossible to describe without resorting to shameless clichés.

Great For...

☑ **Don't Miss**

Hiring a canoe from the Lake Louise Boathouse to paddle across the icy waters.

Serene and implausibly turquoise Lake Louise is surrounded by an amphitheater of finely chiseled mountains that hoist Victoria Glacier up for all to see. Famous for its teahouses, grizzly bears and hiking trails, the Lake Louise area is also well known for its much-commented-on crowds. But, frankly, who cares? You don't come to Lake Louise to dodge other tourists. You come to share in a sight that has captured the imaginations of mountaineers, artists and visitors for more than a century.

Hiking & Skiing

From the towering concrete lump of Chateau Lake Louise, set out on the 3.4km grunt past Mirror Lake, up to the **Lake Agnes Teahouse** (www.lakeagnesteahouse.com; lunch $7.50-15; ⌚8am-5pm early Jun-early Oct) on its eponymous body of water. After tea made

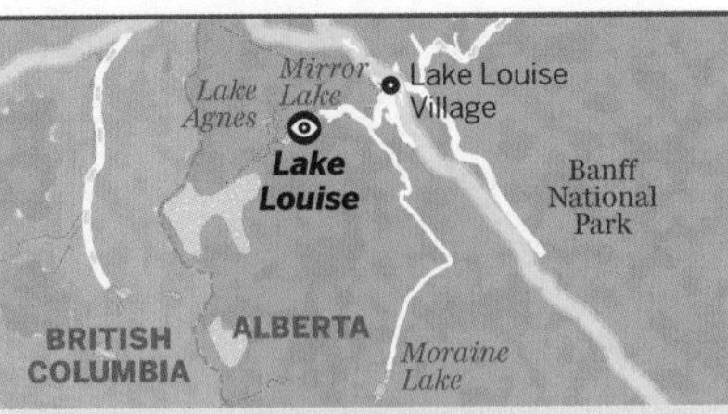

Need to Know

Lake Louise Visitors Centre (☎403-522-3833; www.pc.gc.ca/en/pn-np/ab/banff; Samson Mall, Lake Louise village; ⏰8:30am-7pm Jun-Sep, 9am-5pm Oct-May)

Take a Break

Stop in at the **Trailhead Café** (☎403-522-2006; www.facebook.com/lakelouiseAB; Samson Mall, Lake Louise village; sandwiches $6-10; ⏰7am-6pm) for a hearty, homemade packed lunch.

★ Top Tip

Get here via Bow Valley Pkwy rather than Hwy 1; Bow Valley isn't fenced, so it's great for wildlife sightings.

from glacier water and soup or thick-cut sandwiches (cash only), you can trek 1.6km further and higher to the view-embellished Big Beehive lookout and Canada's most unexpectedly sited gazebo. Be sure to bring along bug spray and a bear bell.

The **Lake Louise Ski Area** (☎403-522-3555; www.skilouise.com; 1 Whitehorn Rd; day pass adult/youth $114/98; 👪) has plenty of beginner and intermediate terrain on four separate mountains. The front side is a good place to get your ski legs back, while the far side offers some great challenges, from the knee-pulverizing moguls of Paradise Bowl to the high-speed cruising of the Larch area.

Lake Louise Gondola

For a bird's-eye view of the Lake Louise area – and a good chance of spotting grizzly bears on the avalanche slopes – climb aboard the **Lake Louise Gondola** (☎403-522-3555; www.lakelouisegondola.com; 1 Whitehorn Rd; adult/child $38/17; ⏰9am-4pm mid-May–mid-Jun, 8am-5:30pm mid-Jun–Jul, to 6pm Aug, to 5pm Sep–mid-Oct; 👪), which crawls up the side of Whitehorn Mountain to a dizzying viewpoint 2088m above the valley floor. Look out for the imposing fang of 3544m-high Mt Temple piercing the skyline on the opposite side of the valley. Take the gondola up for 360-degree views, and the chairlift down for an open-air thrill.

Moraine Lake

Thirteen kilometers to the southeast along a winding seasonal road is Moraine Lake, another spectacularly located body of water; it may not have the dazzling color of its famous sibling, but it has an equally beguiling backdrop in the Valley of Ten Peaks and the jaw-dropping Tower of Babel, which ascends solidly skyward.

Cave in Athabasca Glacier

Icefields Parkway

As the highest and most spectacular road in North America, the Icefields Parkway takes you about as close as you're going to get to the Rockies' craggy summits in your vehicle.

Much of the route followed by the parkway was established in the 1800s by Indigenous people and fur traders. An early road was built during the 1930s as part of a work project for the unemployed, and the present highway was opened in the early 1960s.

While you can cover the 230km route between Lake Louise and Jasper within a few hours, it's worth spending at least a day exploring the region to discover the parkway's brilliant glacial lakes, gushing waterfalls and exquisite viewpoints.

Great For...

☑ Don't Miss

The Icefield Skywalk – a breathtaking open-air glass-floored and glass-sided walkway and lookout.

Athabasca Glacier

The tongue of the Athabasca Glacier has retreated about 2km since 1844. To reach its bottom edge, walk from the **Columbia Icefields Glacier Discovery Centre** along the 1.8km Forefield Trail, then join the 1km Toe of the Athabasca Glacier Trail. While it is permitted to stand on a small roped section

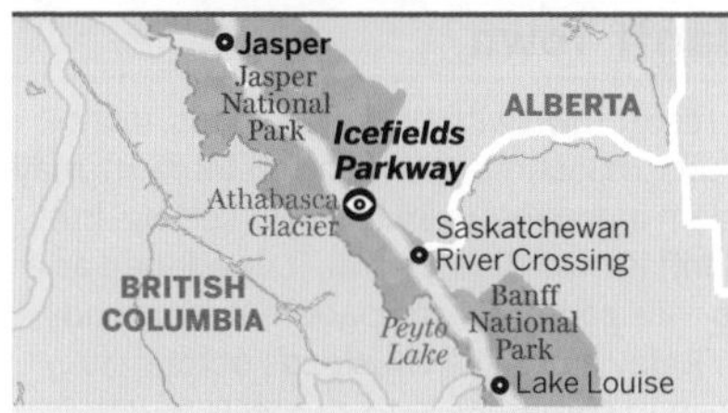

Need to Know

Parks Canada has a desk at the Discovery Centre. At the Parkway entrances, you can purchase your park pass and pick up a map.

Take a Break

Stop by rustic **Num-Ti-Jah Lodge** (403-522-2167; www.num-ti-jah.com; breakfast buffet cold/hot $14/22, dinner mains $30-50; 8-10am & 6:30-9pm mid-May–mid-Oct) for a 1940s-hunting-lodge vibe.

★ Top Tip

It's possible to tackle the parkway by bike – the road is wide and there are plenty of strategically spaced campgrounds, hostels and hotels.

of the ice, do not attempt to cross the warning tape – many do, but the glacier is riddled with crevasses and there have been fatalities. If you have time, pre-arranged tours can take you on ice hikes or perhaps even into ice caves at the right time of year.

The most popular way to get on the glacier is via an **Ice Explorer tour** (www.banffjaspercollection.com/attractions/columbia-icefield; adult/child $114/57; 9am-6pm Apr-Oct). The large hybrid bus-truck grinds a track onto the ice and gives you a 25-minute wander on the glacier. Dress warmly, wear good shoes and bring a water bottle to try some freshly melted glacial water.

Afterwards, the bus takes you to the architecturally award-winning **Columbia Icefield Skywalk** (adult/child skywalk only $37/19; 10am-5pm mid-Apr–May & Oct, to 6pm Jun–mid-Jul & Sep, to 7pm mid-Jul–Aug) for dramatic views of the Sunwapta River Valley.

Peyto Lake

You'll have already seen the indescribable blue of Peyto Lake in a thousand publicity shots, but there's nothing like gazing at the real thing – especially since the outlook for this lake is from a lofty vantage point 80m above the water. From the bottom of the lake parking lot, follow a paved trail for 15 minutes up a steady gradual incline to the wooden lookout platform.

Athabasca Falls

Despite being only 23m high, Athabasca is Jasper's most voluminous waterfall, a dramatic combination of sound, spray and water. The thunderous Athabasca River has cut into the soft limestone rock, carving potholes, canyons and water channels. Visitors crowd the large parking lot and short access trail. It's just west of the Icefields Parkway, 30km south of Jasper Town, and at its most ferocious during summer.

Banff Town

A resort town with boutique shops, nightclubs, museums and fancy restaurants may seem incongruous in this wild setting, but Banff is no ordinary town. It developed as a service center for the park that surrounds it. Today it brings in busloads of tourists keen to commune with shops as much as nature, alongside artists and writers drawn to the Rockies' unparalleled majesty. Whether you love or loathe Banff's cosmopolitan edge, wander 15 minutes in any direction and you're back in wild country, a primeval world of bears, elk and wolves.

SIGHTS

Cave & Basin National Historic Site Historic Site

(☎403-762-1566; www.pc.gc.ca/en/lhn-nhs/ab/caveandbasin; 311 Cave Ave; adult/child $3.90/free; ⏰9:30am-5pm mid-May–mid-Oct, 11am-5pm Wed-Sun rest of year) The Canadian National Park system was effectively born at these hot springs, discovered accidentally by three Canadian Pacific Railway employees on their day off in 1883 (though known to Indigenous peoples for 10,000 years). The springs quickly spurred a flurry of private businesses offering facilities for bathers to enjoy the then-trendy thermal treatments. To avert an environmental catastrophe, the government stepped in, declaring Banff Canada's first national park in order to preserve the springs.

Fairmont Banff Springs Historic Building

(www.fairmont.com/banffsprings; 405 Spray Ave) Looming up beside the Bow River, the Banff Springs is a local landmark in more ways than one. Originally built in 1888, and remodeled in 1928 to resemble a cross between a Scottish baronial castle and a European château, the turret-topped exterior conceals an eye-poppingly extravagant selection of ballrooms, lounges, dining rooms and balustraded staircases that would make William Randolph Hearst green with envy.

Fairmont Banff Springs

Upper Hot Springs Pool Hot Springs
(www.hotsprings.ca; Mountain Ave; adult/child/family $8.30/6.30/24.50; ⏲9am-11pm mid-May–mid-Oct, 10am-10pm Sun-Thu, to 11pm Fri & Sat rest of year) Banff quite literally wouldn't be Banff if it weren't for its hot springs, which gush out from 2.5km beneath **Sulphur Mountain** at a constant temperature of between 32°C (90°F) and 46°C (116°F) – it was the springs that drew the first tourists to Banff. You can still sample the soothing mineral waters at the Upper Hot Springs Pool, near the Banff Gondola.

Whyte Museum of the Canadian Rockies Museum
(☎403-762-2291; www.whyte.org; 111 Bear St; adult/student/child $10/5/free; ⏲10am-5pm) Founded by local artists Catharine and Peter Whyte, the century-old Whyte Museum is more than just a rainy-day option. It boasts a beautiful, ever-changing gallery displaying art from 1800 to the present, by regional, Canadian and international artists, many with a focus on the Rockies. Watch for work by the Group of Seven (aka the Algonquin School). There's also a permanent collection telling the story of Banff and the hardy men and women who forged a home among the mountains.

ACTIVITIES

Banff Canoe Club Canoeing, Kayaking
(☎403-762-5005; www.banffcanoeclub.com; cnr Wolf St & Bow Ave; canoe & kayak rental per 1st/additional hour $45/25, SUP/bike rental per hour $30/12; ⏲9am-9pm mid-Jun–Aug, reduced hours mid-May–mid-Jun & Sep) Rent a canoe or kayak and slide up the Bow River or the narrower, lazier Forty Mile Creek to Vermilion Lakes. Both routes will take you past gorgeous scenery with lots of opportunities for spotting wildlife such as beavers. Stand-up paddleboards and cruiser bikes are also available for rent. Note that you cannot leave your belongings in the office cabin.

Bow Falls & the Hoodoos Hiking
For a delightful jaunt from Banff's town center, explore the banks of the Bow River on this easy 10.2km out-and-back hike. Starting along the river's northern bank, the trail heads east to **Surprise Corner viewpoint** (Buffalo St), where you'll get dramatic views of **Bow Falls** and the Banff Springs Hotel, then continues to the whimsical wind-and-rain-sculpted rock formations known as the Hoodoos.

Sunshine Village Skiing
(www.skibanff.com; day ski pass adult/youth $114/89) If restricted time or funds mean that you can only ski one resort in Banff, choose Sunshine. Its 13.6-sq-km ski area is divided between 137 runs and the 6-hectare **Rogers Terrain Park**. With such a huge area, the resort can comfortably handle several thousand skiers and still feel relatively uncrowded. It boasts the country's first heated chairlifts, too.

TOURS

Hydra River Guides Rafting
(☎403-762-4554; www.raftbanff.com; 211 Bear St; ⏲7:30am-9pm) This well-regarded company has been running rafting trips for over three decades. The most popular is the 20km Kicking Horse Classic ($149), with varied rapids (up to class IV) and a BBQ lunch; novices and families will appreciate the sedate Mild float trip (adult/child $79/59); for late risers there's the Last Waltz ($115), which doesn't get going until midafternoon.

EATING

Wild Flour Cafe $
(☎403-760-5074; www.wildflourbakery.ca; 211 Bear St; mains $5-10; ⏲7am-4pm; 📶☎) If you're searching for an inexpensive snack or a relatively guilt-free sugary treat, make a beeline for Banff's best bakery, where you'll find cheesecake, dark-chocolate torte and macaroons – along with breakfasts, delicious fresh-baked focaccia, well-stuffed sandwiches on homemade bread, and soups, all of it organic. Not surprisingly, the place gets busy – but outdoor courtyard seating helps alleviate the crush.

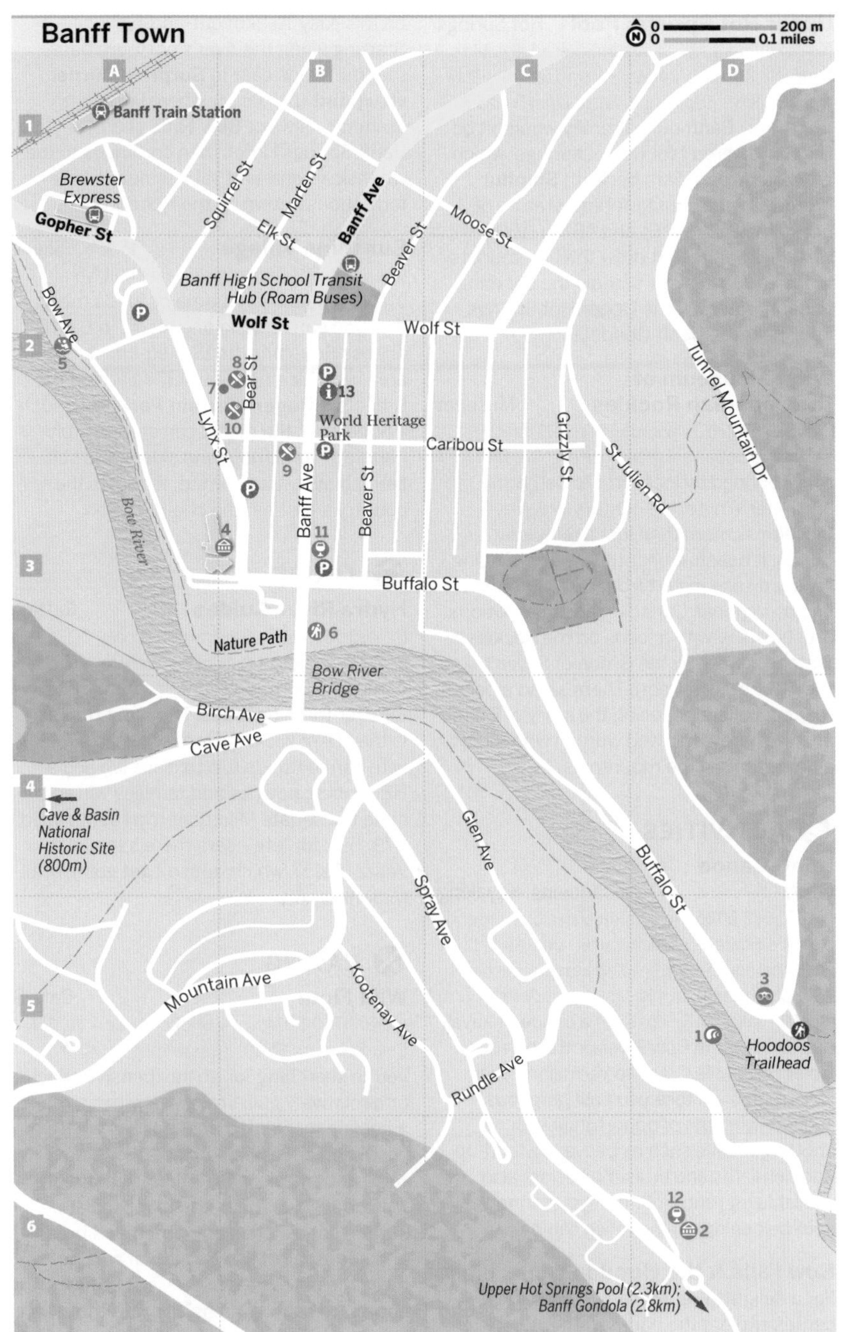

Banff Town
0 200 m
0 0.1 miles
A
B
C
D
1
2
3
4
5
6
Banff Train Station
Brewster Express
Gopher St
Squirrel St
Marten St
Banff Ave
Elk St
Beaver St
Moose St
Banff High School Transit Hub (Roam Buses)
Bow Ave
Wolf St
Wolf St
Bear St
Lynx St
World Heritage Park
Caribou St
Grizzly St
St Julien Rd
Tunnel Mountain Dr
Banff Ave
Beaver St
Bow River
Buffalo St
Nature Path
Bow River Bridge
Birch Ave
Cave Ave
Cave & Basin National Historic Site (800m)
Glen Ave
Buffalo St
Spray Ave
Mountain Ave
Kootenay Ave
Rundle Ave
Hoodoos Trailhead
Upper Hot Springs Pool (2.3km); Banff Gondola (2.8km)

Banff Town

Sights
1 Bow Falls D5
2 Fairmont Banff Springs D6
3 Surprise Corner Viewpoint D5
4 Whyte Museum of the Canadian Rockies B3

Activities, Courses & Tours
5 Banff Canoe Club A2
6 Bow Falls & the Hoodoos B3
7 Hydra River Guides B2

Eating
8 Bear Street Tavern B2
9 Eddie Burger Bar B2
Nourish .... (see 8)
10 Wild Flour B2

Drinking & Nightlife
11 Banff Ave Brewing Co B3
12 Grapes D6

Information
Banff Tourism Bureau .... (see 13)
13 Parks Canada Banff Visitor Centre B2

Bear Street Tavern Pub Food $$
(☎403-762-2021; www.bearstreettavern.ca; 211 Bear St; mains $15-25; ⏰11:30am-late) This gastropub hits a double whammy: ingeniously flavored pizzas washed down with locally brewed pints. Banffites head here in droves for a plate of pulled-pork nachos or a bison-and-onion pizza, accompanied by pitchers of hoppy ale. The patio overlooking Bison Courtyard is the best place to linger if the weather cooperates.

Eddie Burger Bar Burgers $$
(☎403-762-2230; www.eddieburgerbar.ca; 6/137 Banff Ave; burgers $17-23; ⏰11am-2am, from 11:30am Oct-May) Not your average fast-food joint, Eddie's is devoted to building large, custom-made and crave-worthy burgers, from the usual classics to specialties like the elk burger with blueberry chutney. Add to this a hearty helping of poutine and an Oreo milkshake or a shaken Caesar (cocktail, not salad!) garnished with a chicken wing, and you're set – for the next week.

Nourish Vegetarian $$
(☎403-760-3933; www.nourishbistro.com; 211 Bear St; mains $18-26; ⏰11:30am-10:30pm Mon-Thu, 7:30-10:30am & 11:30am-10:30pm Fri-Sun; 🌱) Confronted by a strangely beautiful papier-mâché tree when you walk in the door, you instantly know this vegetarian bistro is not average. With locally sourced dishes like wild-mushroom ravioli, Moroccan cauliflower bites or 27-ingredient nachos with Canadian cheddar or vegan queso, Nourish has carved out a gourmet following in Banff. Dinner is served as shareable tapas and larger plates.

Juniper Bistro Bistro $$$
(☎403-763-6219; www.thejuniper.com/dining; 1 Juniper Way; breakfast & small plates from $14, mains $28-34; ⏰7am-11pm; 🌱) Spectacular mountain views combine with an innovative, locally sourced menu at Juniper's, a surprisingly good hotel restaurant on Banff's northern outskirts. Beyond breakfasts and dinners, the midafternoon 'Graze' menu is also enticing – think small plates of orange and cardamom-poached beets or bison carpaccio with juniper berry and pink peppercorn, all accompanied by fab cocktails and mocktails. Vegetarian, vegan and gluten-free options abound.

DRINKING & NIGHTLIFE

Banff Ave Brewing Co Microbrewery
(☎403-762-1003; www.banffavebrewingco.ca; 110 Banff Ave; ⏰11am-2am) Banff Ave's sprawling 2nd-floor beer hall bustles day and night, slinging a dozen craft brews created on the premises alongside a wide range of nibbles: buttered soft pretzels, bratwurst, burgers and the like. Late-night half-price pizza specials offer welcome relief to late-returning hikers and help keep things hopping into the wee hours.

Grapes Wine Bar
(☎403-762-6860; www.fairmont.com/banff-springs/dining/grapeswinebar; Fairmont Banff Springs, 405 Spray Ave; 5-9:30pm Sun-Thu, from 3pm Fri & Sat) Sporting original crown molding and dark wood paneling from its early days as a ladies' writing salon, this intimate wine bar in Banff's Fairmont makes an elegant spot for afternoon aperitifs. British Columbian Meritage and Ontario Riesling share the menu with international vintages, while tapas of house-cured meats, cheeses, pickled veggies and candied steelhead will tempt you to linger for dinner.

INFORMATION

Banff Tourism Bureau (☎403-762-8421; www.banfflakelouise.com; 224 Banff Ave; 8am-8pm mid-May–Sep, 9am-5pm rest of year) Opposite the Parks Canada desks in the Banff Visitor Centre, this info desk provides advice on accommodations, activities and attractions.

Parks Canada Banff Visitor Centre (☎403-762-1550; www.pc.gc.ca/banff; 224 Banff Ave; 8am-8pm mid-May–Sep, 9am-5pm rest of year) Provides park info and maps. This is where you can find current trail conditions and weather forecasts, and register for backcountry hiking and camping.

GETTING THERE & AWAY

Brewster Express (☎403-221-8242; www.banffjaspercollection.com/brewster-express; 100 Gopher St; adult/child Banff to Calgary Airport $72/36, to Jasper $120/60, to Lake Louise $37/19) offers bus service from most Banff hotels to downtown Calgary ($72, 2½ hours), Jasper ($120, 4¾ hours) and Lake Louise ($37, one hour).

From late October through April, Jasper-based SunDog Tour Company (p196) also runs buses from Banff to Jasper ($79, four hours).

GETTING AROUND

Roam (☎403-762-0606; www.roamtransit.com; adult/child local routes $2/1, regional routes $6/3) runs Banff's excellent network of public buses. Five local routes serve Banff Town and its immediate surroundings. All routes pass through Roam's main downtown transit hub at **Banff High School** (Banff Ave). A day pass costs $5 for local buses or $15 for regional buses.

Taxis (which are metered) can easily be hailed on the street, especially on Banff Ave. Otherwise call **Banff Taxi** (☎403-762-0000; www.banfftransportation.com/banff-taxi-service.html).

Jasper

Filled with the kind of immense scenery that could turn the most monosyllabic hermit into a romantic poet, Jasper is a rugged beauty; more raw and less tourist-pampering than its southern cousin Banff, and hence host to a more ambitious, adventurous visitor. Its tour de force is its extensive multipurpose trail network, much of it instantly accessible from the park's compact townsite. Backing it up are abundant wildlife, colossal icefields and – for the brave – the kind of desolate backcountry that makes you feel as though you're a good few kilometers (and centuries) from anything resembling civilization.

SIGHTS

Miette Hot Springs Hot Springs
(www.pc.gc.ca/hotsprings; Miette Rd; adult/child/family $7.05/5.15/20.35; 9am-11pm mid-Jun–Aug, 10:30am-9pm May–mid-Jun & Sep–mid-Oct) More remote than Banff's historic springs, Miette Hot Springs ('discovered' in 1909) are 61km northeast of Jasper off Hwy 16, near the park's eastern boundary. The soothing waters, kept at a pleasant 37°C (98°F) to 40°C (104°F), are surrounded by peaks and are especially enjoyable when the fall snow is drifting down and steam envelops the crowd. Raining summer evenings also make for stunning, misty conditions.

Jasper Skytram Cable Car
(☎780-852-3093; www.jaspertramway.com; Whistlers Mountain Rd; adult/child/family $50/27/125; 8am-9pm late Jun-Aug, 9am-8pm mid-May–late Jun, 10am-5pm late Mar–mid-May, Sep & Oct) If the average, boring views from

TATSUO115 / GETTY IMAGES ©

Miette Hot Springs

Jasper just aren't blowing your hair back, go for a ride on this sightseeing gondola. The seven-minute journey (departures every nine minutes) zips up through various mountain life zones to the high, barren slopes of the Whistlers. From the gondola's upper station a steep 1.25km hike leads to the mountain's true summit, where views stretch for 75km. Arrive early or late to avoid midday lines. There's a small restaurant and gift shop up top.

Maligne Lake Lake

Almost 50km from Jasper at the end of a stunning road that bears its name, 22km-long Maligne Lake is the recipient of a lot of hype. It's the largest lake in the national park and there's no denying its appeal: the baby-blue water and a craning circle of rocky, photogenic peaks are a feast for the eyes.

Horseshoe Lake Lake

This idyllic, blue-green horseshoe-shaped lake just off the Icefields Parkway is missed by many visitors, making a stopover here all the more alluring. A choice spot for a bracing summer swim or a short stroll around the perimeter, the lake is surrounded by steep cliffs and is frequented by cliff divers. It's probably safer to watch than join in.

> *"especially enjoyable when the fall snow is drifting down"*

ACTIVITIES

Maligne Canyon Hiking

One of Jasper's most spectacular hikes is the easy amble through this steep, narrow gorge shaped by the torrential waters of the Maligne River. The canyon at its narrowest is only a few meters wide and drops a stomach-turning 50m beneath your feet. Crossed by six bridges, it's most easily accessed from the parking area on Maligne Lake Rd.

Sulphur Skyline Trail Hiking

If you're not easily daunted by the sustained two-hour climb, this trail above Miette Hot Springs offers some of Jasper's most unforgettable views. After initially following a creek valley, the trail switchbacks relentlessly up into open high country, with near-aerial views over the heart-achingly wild and beautiful Fiddle River valley. Soak in the hot springs on your way back out.

Bald Hills Loop Hiking

The first two-thirds of this 10.4km hike, climbing relentlessly through the forest on a rather drab fire road, may have you wondering what all the fuss is about. Once you emerge above tree line, however, this is one of Jasper's most spectacular hikes, with wraparound views of Maligne Lake, several mountain ranges and the pristine wilderness surrounding Evelyn Creek.

TOURS

SunDog Tour Company Tours

(☎780-852-4056; www.sundogtours.com; 414 Connaught Dr; ⏰8am-5pm) SunDog Tour Company runs a whole host of tours, including trips to the Icefields, train rides, boat rides, wildlife viewing, canoeing, horseback riding and more.

Jasper Walks & Talks Hiking

(☎780-852-4994; www.walksntalks.com; 626 Connaught Dr; walks per adult $65-90, per child $45-50) Longtime local resident and former Parks Canada guide Paula Beauchamp leads small groups on three- to six-hour tours with a focus on such local attractions as Maligne Canyon and Mt Edith Cavell Meadows. Bring a picnic lunch, good walking shoes, your camera and lots of questions for your very knowledgeable guide. Winter snowshoe adventures are also offered.

EATING & DRINKING

Other Paw Bakery Cafe $

(☎780-852-2253; www.bearspawbakery.com; 610 Connaught Dr; mains $5-13; ⏰7am-6pm) An offshoot of the original Bear's Paw bakery around the corner, the Other Paw offers the same addictive mix of breads, pastries, muffins and coffee – while also serving up tasty sandwiches, salads, soups and well-stuffed wraps.

On the Sulphur Skyline Trail (p195)

MORITZ WOLF / GETTY IMAGES ©

Olive Bistro Mediterranean $$
(780-852-5222; www.olivebistro.ca; Pyramid Lake Rd; mains $14-35; 4-10pm May-Oct, 5-9pm Nov-Apr;) This casual restaurant with big booths has a classy menu. Main dishes such as slow-braised organic lamb shank, elk rigatoni or a vegan 'dragon bowl' come sandwiched between appetizers of white truffle scallops and indulgent desserts like a gourmet banana split. In summer, enjoy excellent cocktails during the 4pm to 6pm happy hour; in winter, there's live music twice monthly.

Raven Bistro Mediterranean $$$
(780-852-5151; www.theravenbistro.com; 504 Patricia St; lunch mains $16-27, dinner mains $28-46; 11:30am-11pm;) This cozy, tastefully designed bistro offers vegetarian dishes, encourages shared plates and earns a loyal clientele with sublime offerings like Kaffir lime and coconut seafood pot or lamb shank glazed with fresh mint, horseradish, honey and Dijon mustard. Not in a lunch-dinner mood? Try the 'late riser' breakfast skillet, or come for happy hour (3pm to 5:30pm daily).

Downstream Lounge Bar
(780-852-9449; www.facebook.com/DSjasper; 620 Connaught Dr; 5pm-2am) This is likely the best-stocked bar in town, with a wide array of whiskeys, vodkas and other alcoholic indulgences – and a bar staff who know how to use them. There's some awesome food to keep your head above water and, often, live music.

Jasper Brewing Co Brewery
(780-852-4111; www.jasperbrewingco.ca; 624 Connaught Dr; 11:30am-1am) This brewpub was the first of its kind in a Canadian national park, using glacial water to make its fine ales, including the signature Rockhopper IPA and Jasper the Bear honey beer. It's a perennial favorite hangout for locals and tourists alike, with TVs and a good food menu.

INFORMATION

Parks Canada Jasper Information Centre
(780-852-6176; www.pc.gc.ca/jasper; 500 Connaught Dr, Jasper Town; 9am-7pm mid-May–early Oct, to 5pm rest of year) In the city center, Parks Canada operates a well-staffed and helpful info desk in a beautiful historic building dating to 1913.

Tourism Jasper (780-852-6236; www.jasper.travel; 500 Connaught Dr; 9am-7pm mid-May–early Oct, to 5pm rest of year) Jasper's municipal tourist office, directly adjacent to the Parks Canada desk, offers a wealth of information about area activities and accommodations.

GETTING THERE & AWAY

BUS

SunDog Tour Company offers daily bus service year-round to Edmonton airport ($99, 5½ hours), along with winter service (late October through April) to Lake Louise ($69, four hours), Banff Town ($79, five hours) and Calgary airport ($135, seven hours).

From May through mid-October, **Brewster Express** (877-625-4372; www.banffjaspercollection.com/brewster-express) runs its own daily express bus to Lake Louise ($97, 3½ hours), Banff ($120, 4¾ hours), Canmore ($144, 5¾ hours) and Calgary airport ($167, eight hours).

TRAIN

VIA Rail (888-842-7245; www.viarail.ca) offers tri-weekly train services west to Vancouver (from $148, 23½ hours) and bi-weekly services east to Toronto (from $367, 72 hours). In addition, there is a tri-weekly service to Prince Rupert, BC (from $156, 33 hours, with obligatory overnight stop in Prince George). Call or check in at the **train station** (607 Connaught Dr) for exact schedule and fare details.

GETTING AROUND

Maligne Valley Hikers Express Shuttle
(780-852-3331; www.maligneadventures.com; one way adult/child $35/17.50; late Jun-late Sep) Runs a daily 45-minute shuttle from Jasper Town to Maligne Lake, stopping en route at the North Skyline trailhead, then returning from Maligne Lake to Jasper at 10am.

Caribou Cabs (780-931-2334; www.facebook.com/cariboucabs) offers dependable taxi service.

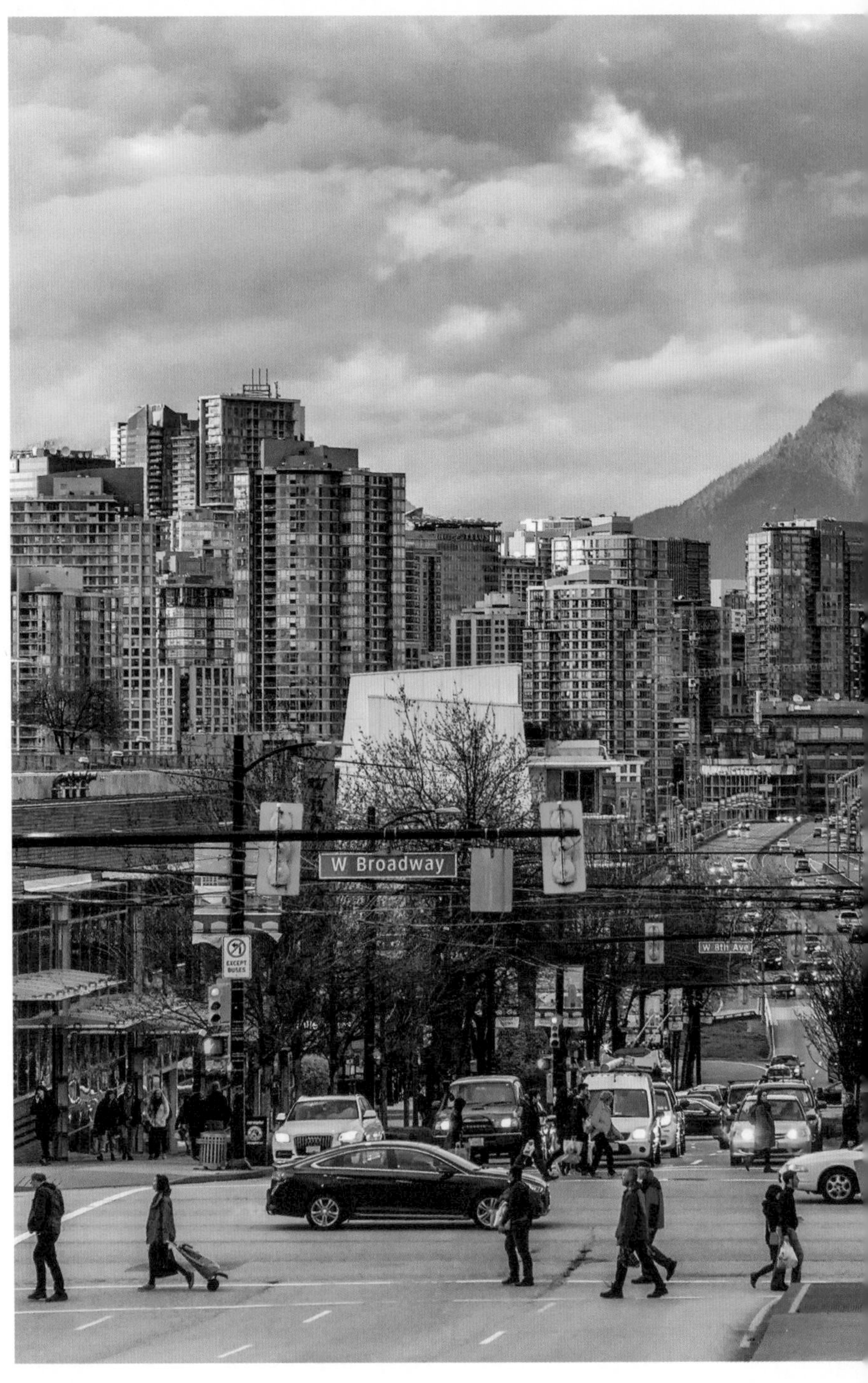
W Broadway
W 8th Ave
EXCEPT
BUSES

VANCOUVER

In this Chapter

Vancouver at a glance...

Tucked in between snowy peaks and the wild Pacific Ocean, Vancouver boasts forest trails, sandy beaches, kayaking routes, seawall bike lanes and the mighty green jewel of Stanley Park. Downtown is thus just the start of Vancouver – walk or hop on public transit and within minutes you'll be in one of the city's many diverse and distinctive 'hoods. Whether discovering the coffee shops of Commercial Dr, the hipster haunts of Main St, the indie bars and restaurants of Gastown, the heritage-house beachfronts and browsable stores of Kitsilano, or the great natural landscapes beyond, you'll find plenty to fall in love with.

One Day in Vancouver

Get to **Stanley Park** before the crowds to stroll the seawall and explore the Lost Lagoon. Stump up for a sustainable lunch at **Forage** (p218), then head to **English Bay Beach** (p210). Give your credit card a workout along Robson St (p216) and stop in at **Vancouver Art Gallery** (p210). Head to **Campagnolo** (p219) in Chinatown for rustic Italian *cibo* and end the day with a live show at the **Commodore Ballroom** (p224).

Two Days in Vancouver

Start your wander at **Granville Island**. Peruse the cool shops and fill your belly in the market before heading to Chinatown to spend some time exploring the aromatic grocery and apothecary stores on Keefer St. End your afternoon at the **Dr Sun Yat-Sen Classical Chinese Garden** (p211). Continue east to Commercial Drive for brews at **Powell Brewery** (p221) and an art-house movie at the **Rio Theatre** (p224).

Previous page: Downtown view

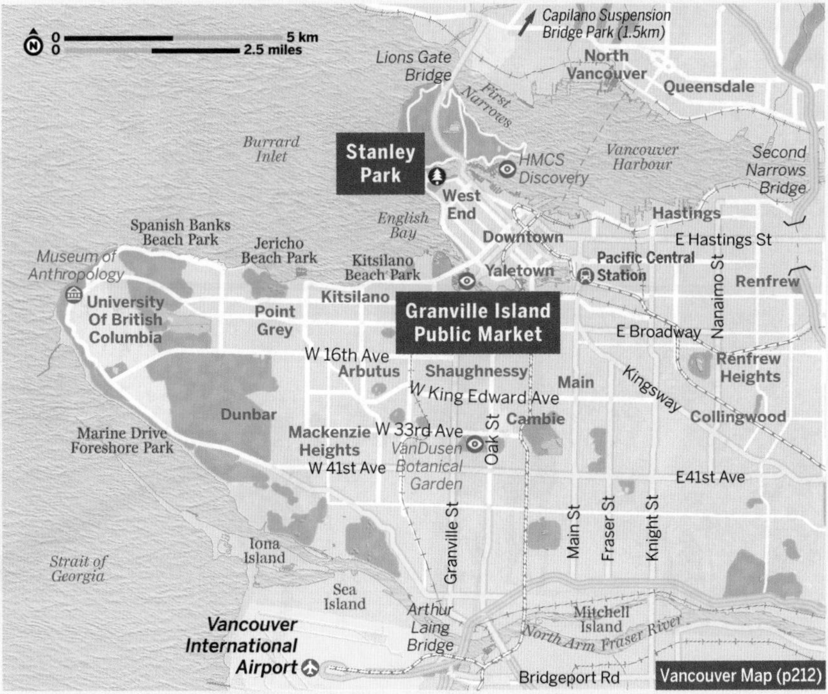

Vancouver Map (p212)

Arriving in Vancouver

Vancouver International Airport Take a Canada Line train downtown ($8 to $9.25, 25 minutes) or grab a cab (up to $45).

Pacific Central Train Station SkyTrain it from the Main St-Science World Station downtown ($3, five minutes).

BC Ferries Services arrive at Tsawwassen, an hour south of Vancouver, and at Horseshoe Bay. Both are accessible by regular transit bus services.

Where to Stay

Metro Vancouver is home to more than 23,000 hotel, B&B and hostel rooms, the majority in or around the downtown core. Airbnb also operates here, although a regulatory crackdown has reduced their number in recent years. Book far ahead for summer or you may struggle to find a place to lay your head. Rates peak in July and August, but there are good spring and fall deals here (alongside increased rainy days).

For more information on the best neighborhood to stay in, see p227.

Seawall trail

MARC BRUXELLE / SHUTTERSTOCK ©

Stanley Park

One of North America's largest urban green spaces, 400-hectare Stanley Park is revered for its dramatic forest-and-mountain oceanfront views, nature-hugging trails, family-friendly attractions and tasty places to eat.

Great For...

☑ Don't Miss

The family of beavers who currently reside on Beaver Lake; you'll likely spot them swimming around their large den.

Seawall

Built in stages between 1917 and 1980, the park's 8.8km seawall trail is Vancouver's favorite outdoor hangout. Encircling the park, it offers spectacular waterfront vistas on one side and dense forest on the other.

The seawall delivers you to some of the park's top highlights. You'll pass alongside the stately **HMCS Discovery** (1200 Stanley Park Dr, Deadman's Island; 19) naval station and, about 1.5km from the W Georgia St entrance, you'll come to the ever-popular Totem Poles. Remnants of an abandoned 1930s plan to create a First Nations 'theme village,' the bright-painted poles were joined by three exquisitely carved Coast Salish welcome arches a few years back.

Lost Lagoon

A few steps from the park's W Georgia St entrance lies Lost Lagoon, which was

Totem poles

SVETLANASF / GETTY IMAGES ©

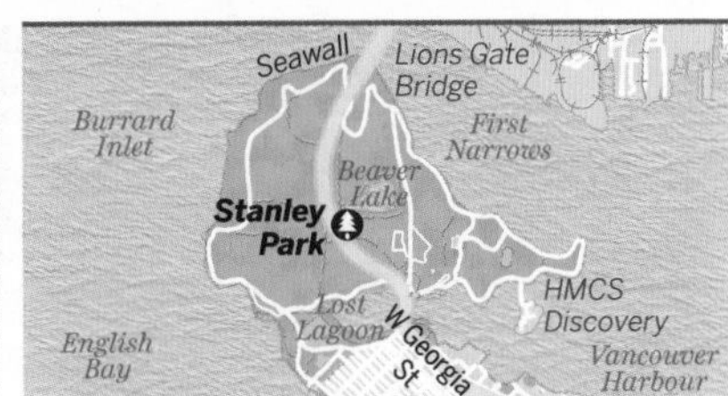

Need to Know

It typically takes around three hours to walk the 8.8km seawall; bike rentals are also available on nearby Denman St.

Take a Break

The park's **Stanley's Bar & Grill** (604-602-3088; www.stanleysbargrill.com; 610 Pipeline Rd; 11am-5pm; 19) is a great spot for a patio beer among the trees.

★ Top Tip

Head to Ceperley Meadows in the summer for wildly popular free outdoor movie screenings by Fresh Air Cinema (www.freshaircinema.ca).

originally part of Coal Harbour. After a causeway was built in 1916, the new body of water was renamed, transforming itself into a freshwater lake a few years later. Today it's a bird-beloved nature sanctuary – keep your eyes peeled for blue herons – and its perimeter pathway is a favored stroll for wildlife nuts. Plunging deeper into the park's more secluded trails, you'll also likely spot wrens, hummingbirds and chittering little Douglas squirrels. And while they mostly give humans a wide berth, you might also come across a coyote or two; treat them with respect and give them a wide berth as well. The **Stanley Park Nature House** (604-257-8544; www.stanleyparkecology.ca; north end of Alberni St; 10am-5pm Tue-Sun Jul & Aug, 10am-4pm Sat & Sun Sep-Jun; ; 19) FREE here has exhibits on the park's wildlife, history and ecology – ask about the fascinating and well-priced guided walks.

Beaches & Views

Second Beach is a family-friendly area on the park's western side, with a grassy playground, an ice-cream stand and a huge outdoor **swimming pool** (604-257-8371; www.vancouverparks.ca; cnr N Lagoon Dr & Stanley Park Dr; adult/child $6.10/3.05; 10am-8pm Jun-Aug, reduced hours in low season; ; 19). For a little more tranquility, try Third Beach, a favored summer-evening destination for Vancouverites. The sky often comes alive with pyrotechnic color, while chilled-out locals munch through their picnics.

Perhaps the most popular vista is at Prospect Point. One of Vancouver's best lookouts, this lofty spot is located at the park's northern tip. In summer, you'll be jostling for elbow room with tour parties; heading down the steep stairs to the viewing platform usually shakes them off. Also look out for scavenging raccoons here (don't pet them).

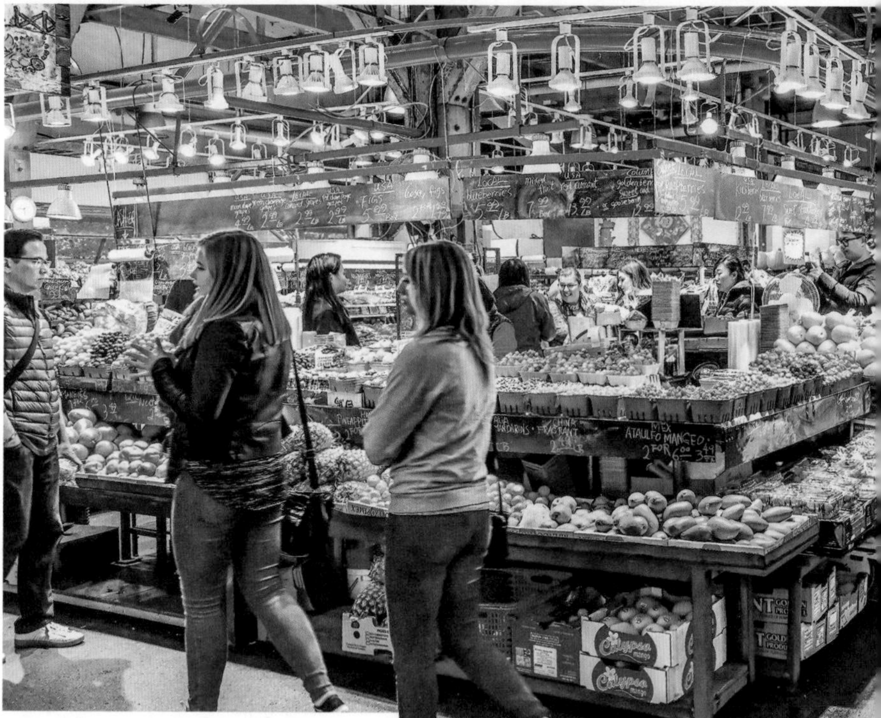

Granville Island Public Market

A multisensory smorgasbord of fish, cheese, fruit and bakery treats, this is one of North America's finest public markets.

Great For...

☑ Don't Miss

The alfresco farmers market outside (June to September) with BC cherries, peaches and blueberries.

The market is ideal for whiling away an afternoon, snacking on goodies in the sun among the buskers outside or sheltering from the rain with a market tour. You'll also find cool arts and crafts.

Forgotten Past

The Public Market is the centerpiece of one of Canada's most impressive urban regeneration projects – and the main reason it has been so successful. Built as a district for small factories in the early part of the last century, Granville Island – which has also been called Mud Island and Industrial Island over the years – had declined into a paint-peeled no-go area by the 1960s. But the abandoned sheds began attracting artists and theater groups by the 1970s, and the old buildings slowly started springing back to life with some much-needed

repairs and upgrades. Within a few years, new theaters, restaurants and studios had been built and the Public Market quickly became an instantly popular anchor tenant. One reason for the island's popularity? Only independent, one-of-a-kind businesses operate here.

Taste-Tripping

Come hungry: there are dozens of food stands to weave your way around at the market. Among the must-see stands are **Oyama Sausage Company**, replete with hundreds of smoked sausages and cured meats; **Benton Brothers Fine Cheese**, with its full complement of amazing curdy goodies from British Columbia and around the world; and **Granville Island Tea Company**, with its tasting bar and more than 150 steep-tastic varieties to choose from.

Need to Know

604-666-6655; www.granvilleisland.com/public-market; Johnston St; 9am-7pm; 50, miniferries

Take a Break

All that eating may just deserve a drink or two – take a load off at Liberty Distillery (p223).

★ Top Tip

For local insights and plenty of samples, join a delicious market tour run by Vancouver Foodie Tours (p215).

Baked goodies also abound: abandon your diet at **Lee's Donuts** or stop by **Siegel's Bagels**, where the cheese-stuffed baked bagels are not to be missed. And don't worry: there's always room for a wafer-thin album-sized 'cinnamon record' from **Stuart's Baked Goods**. French-themed **L'Epicerie Rotisserie and Gourmet Shop** has also been a popular addition to the market in recent years. It sells vinegars, olive oils and Babapapa pop bottles, alongside delicious, fresh-cooked picnic-friendly takeout chicken and sausages.

In the unlikely event you're still hungry, there's also a small **international food court** if you want to snag a table and indulge in a good-value selection that runs from Indian curries to German sausages. And if you want to dive into some regional, seasonal produce, there's even a **farmers market** just outside the market building between June and October where you can, due to a recent law change, also sample BC-made booze (look out for brews by Brassneck, Powell and Main Street).

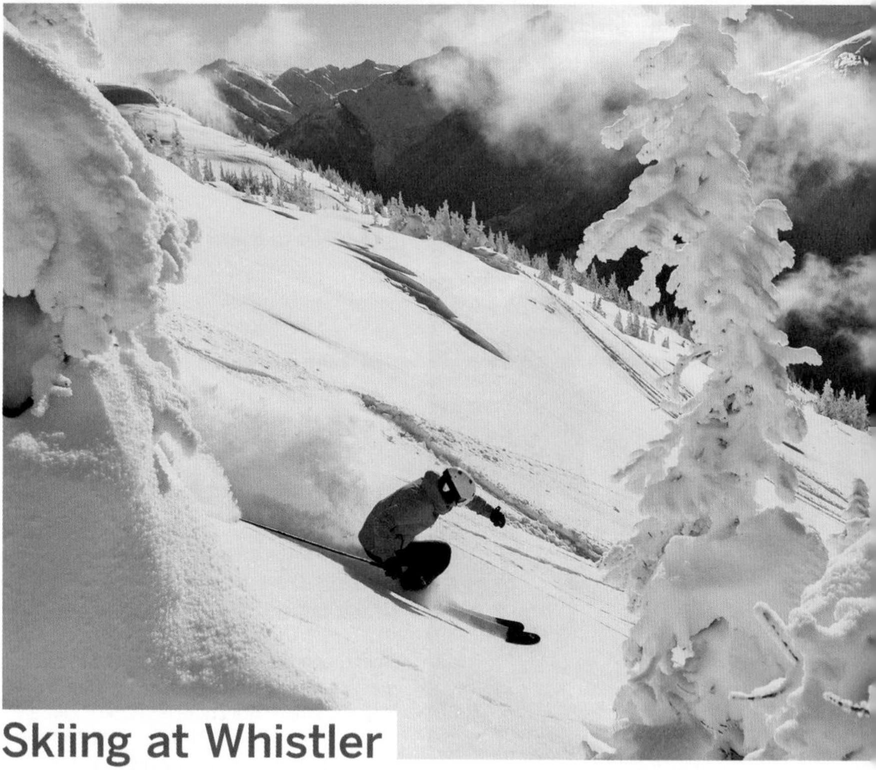

Skiing at Whistler

Named for the furry marmots that populate the area and whistle like deflating balloons, this gabled alpine village is one of the world's largest, best-equipped and most popular ski resorts.

Great For...

☑ Don't Miss

Skiing the Saddle run, for top views and the feeling of soaring down the mountain.

Skiing & Snowboarding

The eminently skiable Whistler-Blackcomb sister mountains were combined into one resort in 1997 and linked by a **Peak 2 Peak Gondola** (www.whistlerblackcomb.com/discover/360-experience; 4545 Blackcomb Way; adult/child $63/32; ⏰10am-5pm) in 2008, meaning you no longer have to return to the village to switch peaks. Whistler Mountain can also be accessed from a base-station at Creekside, 4km south of the main village.

Both mountains have their fans. Blackcomb has a greater vertical drop, steeper runs and the best on-mountain dining in the shape of **Christine's** (☎604-938-7437; Rendezvous Lodge; mains $26-34; ⏰11am-3pm). Whistler has more skiable hectares, a sunnier aspect (especially in the mornings) and is better for beginners.

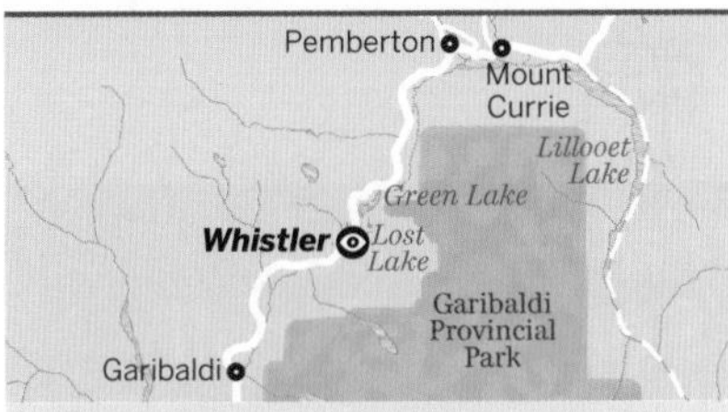

Need to Know

☎604-967-8950; www.whistlerblackcomb.com; day pass adult/child $178/89

Take a Break

Purebread (☎604-962-1182; www.purebread.ca; 4338 Main St; baked goods $3-6; ⌚8am-6pm) will satisfy your cravings, from salted caramel bars to homity pie.

★ Top Tip

Beat the crowds with an early-morning Fresh Tracks ticket ($23.95) for an extra hour on the slopes and breakfast at the Roundhouse Lodge.

Helpfully, there's no need to lug your own gear here, as you can **rent online** (www.whistlerblackcomb.com/rentals; skis & boots per day $62; ⌚8am-6pm) and pick up from one of several locations on arrival.

Cross-Country Skiing & Snowshoeing

Whistler has 120km of cross-country skiing trails spread over two areas: **Lost Lake Park** (☎604-905-0071; www.crosscountryconnection.ca; day pass adult/child $22/11; ⌚8am-8pm mid-Dec–Mar), a short walk from the Village, and the interlinked **Olympic Park–Callaghan Country** (☎604-964-0060; www.whistlersportlegacies.com; 5 Callaghan Valley Rd; trail pass skiing/snowshoeing $28/17; ⌚9am-4:30pm mid-Dec–late Mar) network, 25km by road to the west. Both areas offer groomed trails appropriate for classic and skate skiing and are graded easy (green) to advanced (black). Lost Lake is a pretty area with placid vistas and 30km of trails that partially utilize the snowed-in Chateau Whistler golf course. The Olympic Park has more technical terrain including the Nordic and Biathlon Olympic courses. The adjacent Callaghan Valley has a wilder flavor, including an opportunity to ski to the backcountry **Journeyman Lodge**, where you can dine and/or spend the night.

Getting There & Away

While most visitors arrive by car from Vancouver via Hwy 99, there are several economical buses from Vancouver, including Skylynx (www.yvrskylynx.com), with seven services a day (from $58.50, three hours), and the winter-only Snowbus (www.snowbus.com), with two buses a day from Vancouver Airport ($40) via Vancovuer's Hyatt Hotel, including a crack-of-dawn service that gets you to the slopes before 8am.

False Creek Seawall Stroll

Vancouver's shimmering waterfront has a spectacular seawall trail linking more than 20km of coastline. Don't miss this False Creek stretch; it's crammed with public art and water-to-city views.

Start David Lam Park
Distance 6km
Duration 3 hours

1 Start on the north side of False Creek at Yaletown's **David Lam Park** and head east alongside several public artworks before passing under Cambie Bridge.

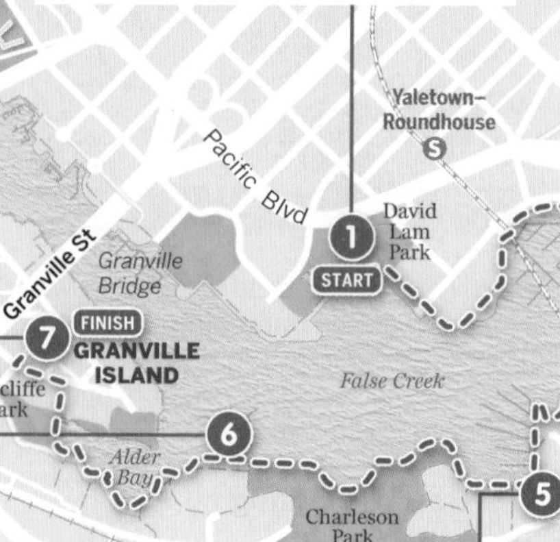

7 Enter **Granvillle Island** from the hidden back route few visitors know about. Look out for the totem pole as you step onto the island. It was carved by hundreds of people and was erected in 1999, recalling the First Nations residents who once fished and lived in this area.

6 Passing through the neighborhood and alongside Charleson Park, you'll arrive at **Spruce Harbour Marina**, a live-aboard boat community. Within a few minutes, Granville Island will appear on the shoreline ahead.

5 Continuing on, pass under the Cambie Bridge again before reaching **Leg-in-Boot Sq**. The cozy waterfront neighborhood here is worth a quick poke around. Built in the 1980s, the low-rise homes and condos are a stark contrast to the high-as-possible residential towers on the opposite shoreline.

Classic Photo

The view of Science World from Habitat Island.

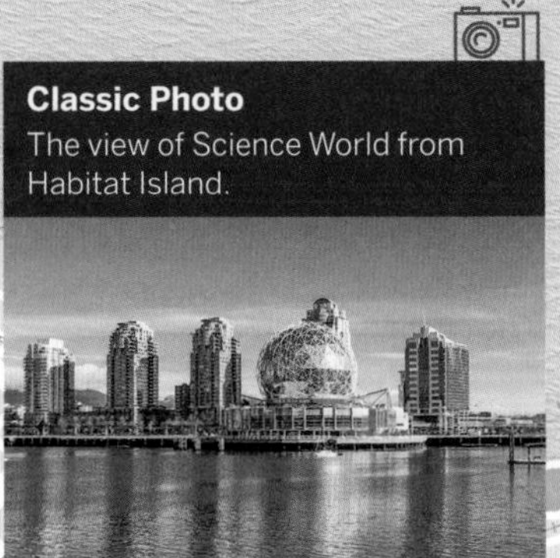

2 Continue on your weave and you'll pass into the area that once housed Expo '86, the giant world exposition that put the city on the international map. Several reminders of the big event remain including **Science World** (p211) and, in the distance, the SkyTrain line.

Take a Break

Bag a 'dirty burger' for lunch at Italian-tinged **Campagnolo** (p219).

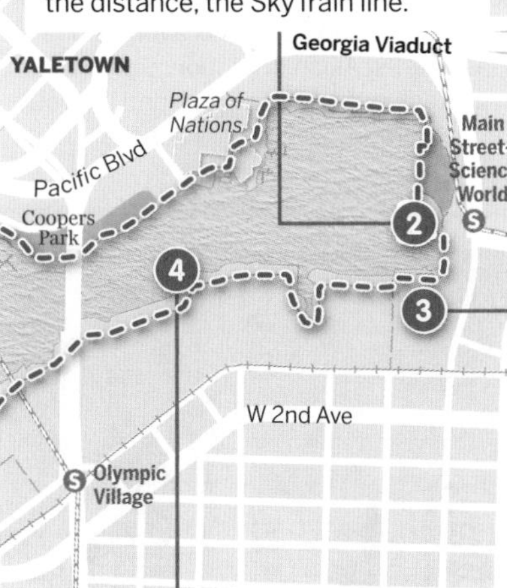

3 Follow the seawall trail past Science World to the **Olympic Village**, the high-rise housing development on the southeast corner of False Creek. Home to athletes during the 2010 Olympic and Paralympic Winter Games, it's now a slick city neighborhood containing bars, restaurants and two huge bird sculptures.

4 From here, continue west along the seawall, passing over a steel pedestrian bridge shaped like a canoe, and you'll soon come to an unlikely urban attraction. **Habitat Island** – an artificially constructed tree-and-shrub-lined creation – is a pit stop for cormorants and blue herons (plus the occasional falcon).

SIGHTS

Downtown & West End

Vancouver Art Gallery Gallery

(☎604-662-4700; www.vanartgallery.bc.ca; 750 Hornby St, Downtown; adult/child $24/6.50; ⏲10am-5pm Wed-Mon, to 9pm Tue; 🚌5) Combining blockbuster international shows with selections from its striking contemporary collection, the VAG is a magnet for art fans. There are often three or four different exhibitions on its public levels, but save time for the top-floor Emily Carr paintings, showcasing swirling nature-themed works from BC's favorite historic artist. Check ahead for **FUSE** (☎604-662-4700; www.vanartgallery.bc.ca/fuse; 750 Hornby St, Vancouver Art Gallery, Downtown; $29; ⏲8pm-midnight; 🚌5), a late-opening party with bars and live music. And if you're on a budget, consider the by-donation entry after 5pm on Tuesdays ($10 suggested); expect a queue.

English Bay Beach Beach

(cnr Denman St & Beach Ave, West End; 🚌5) Wandering south on Denman St, you'll spot a clutch of palm trees ahead announcing one of Canada's best urban beaches. Then you'll see one of Vancouver's most popular public artworks: a series of oversized laughing figures that makes everyone smile. Across the street is the beach, where a summertime party atmosphere has locals catching rays and panoramic ocean views... or just watching the volleyballers prancing around on the sand.

Fairview & South Granville

VanDusen Botanical Garden Gardens

(☎604-257-8335; www.vandusengarden.org; 5251 Oak St; adult/child $11.25/5.50; ⏲9am-8pm Jun-Aug, 9am-6pm Apr & Sep, 9am-7pm May, hours reduced Oct-Mar; P 👪; 🚌17) This highly popular green-thumbers' oasis is a 22-hectare, 255,000-plant idyll that offers a strollable web of pathways weaving through specialized garden areas: the Rhododendron Walk blazes with color in spring, while the Korean Pavilion is a focal point for a fascinating Asian collection. Save time to get lost in the hedge maze and look out for the herons, owls and turtles that call

English Bay Beach

the park and its ponds home. Informative guided tours are also offered here daily from April to October.

Gastown & Chinatown

Dr Sun Yat-Sen Classical Chinese Garden & Park — Gardens

(604-662-3207; www.vancouverchinesegarden.com; 578 Carrall St, Chinatown; adult/child $14/10; 9:30am-7pm mid-Jun–Aug, 10am-6pm May–mid-Jun & Sep, 10am-4:30pm Oct-Apr; Stadium-Chinatown) A tranquil break from bustling Chinatown, this intimate 'garden of ease' reflects Taoist principles of balance and harmony. Entry includes an optional 45-minute guided tour, in which you'll learn about the symbolism behind the placement of the gnarled pine trees, winding covered pathways and ancient limestone formations. Look out for the colorful carp and lazy turtles in the jade-colored water.

Kitsilano & University of British Columbia

Kitsilano Beach — Beach

(cnr Cornwall Ave & Arbutus St; 2) Facing English Bay, Kits Beach is one of Vancouver's favorite summertime hangouts. The wide, sandy expanse attracts buff Frisbee tossers and giggling volleyball players, and those who just like to preen while catching the rays. The ocean is fine for a dip, though serious swimmers should consider the heated **Kitsilano Pool** (604-731-0011; www.vancouverparks.ca; 2305 Cornwall Ave; adult/child $6.10/3.05; 7am-evening mid-Jun–Sep; ; 2), one of the world's largest outdoor saltwater pools.

Museum of Anthropology — Museum

(MOA; 604-822-5087; www.moa.ubc.ca; 6393 NW Marine Dr, UBC; adult/child $18/16; 10am-5pm Fri-Wed, 10am-9pm Thu, closed Mon Oct-May; P; 99B-Line, then 68) Vancouver's best museum is studded with spectacular Indigenous totem poles and breathtaking carvings – but it's also teeming with artifacts from cultures around the world, from intricate Swedish lace to bright Sri Lankan folk masks. Take one of the free daily tours (check ahead for times) for some context, but give yourself at least a couple of hours to explore on your own; it's easy to immerse yourself here. On a budget? Thursday evening entry is $10 (after 5pm).

Skiing & Snowboarding

If you can't make it out to **Whistler**, you'll find excellent alpine skiing and snowboarding areas as well as cross-country skiing trails less than 30 minutes from downtown – it's where you'll find most locals when the powder arrives. The season typically runs from late November to early April, and the main ski areas are **Grouse Mountain** (604-980-9311; www.grousemountain.com; 6400 Nancy Greene Way, North Vancouver; lift ticket adult/child $47/42; 9am-10pm mid-Nov–mid-Apr; ; 236), **Cypress Mountain** (604-926-5612; www.cypressmountain.com; 6000 Cypress Bowl Rd, West Vancouver; lift ticket adult/youth/child $79/56/36; 9am-10pm mid-Dec–Mar, to 4pm Apr;) and **Mt Seymour** (604-986-2261; www.mountseymour.com; 1700 Mt Seymour Rd, North Vancouver; adult/youth/child $51/44/24; 9:30am-10pm Mon-Fri, from 8:30am Sat & Sun Dec-Apr).

Mt Seymour

Main Street

Science World — Museum

(604-443-7440; www.scienceworld.ca; 1455 Quebec St; adult/child $27.15/18.10; 10am-6pm Jul & Aug, reduced hours off-season; P; Main St-Science World) Under Vancouver's favorite

Vancouver

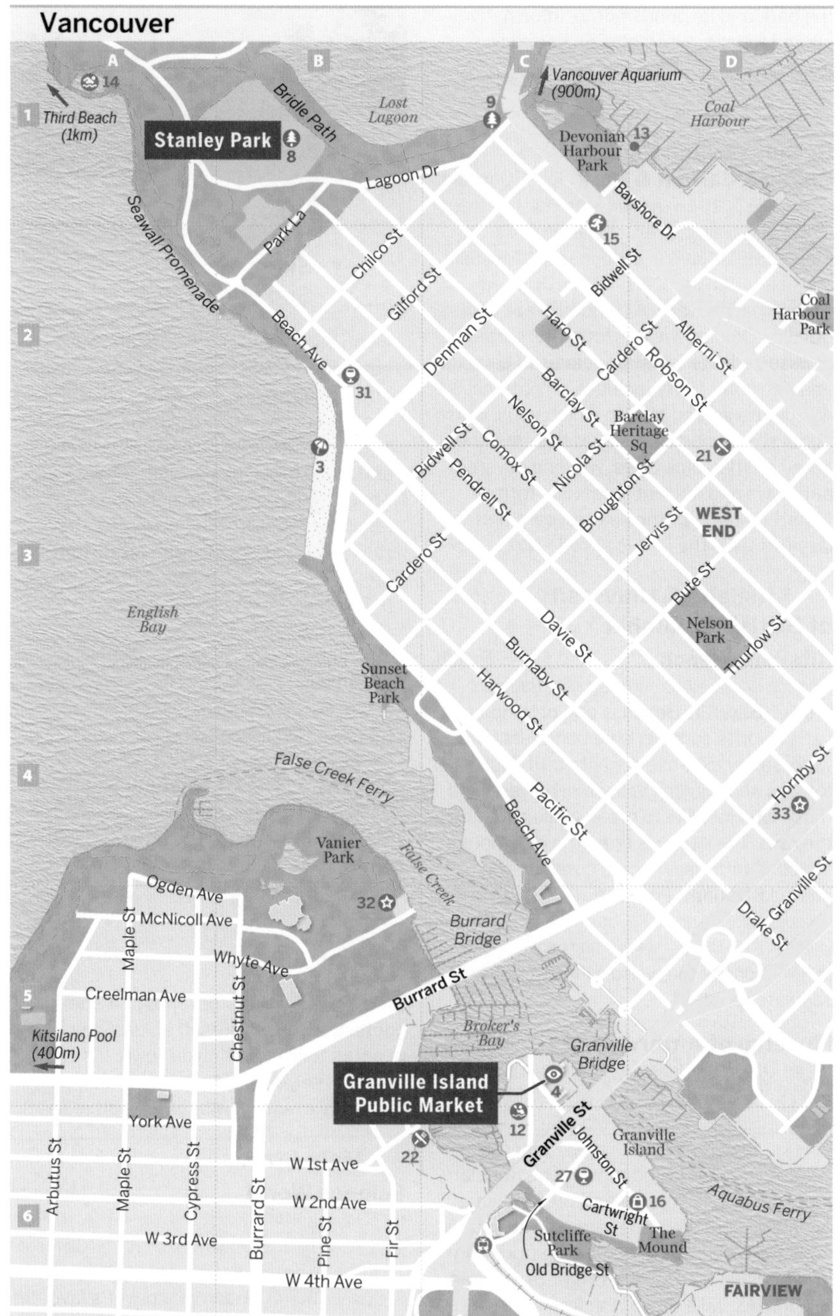

A
B
C
D
1
2
3
4
5
6
Third Beach (1km)
Vancouver Aquarium (900m)
Stanley Park
Lost Lagoon
Coal Harbour
Devonian Harbour Park
Bridle Path
Lagoon Dr
Park La
Seawall Promenade
Chilco St
Gilford St
Denman St
Bayshore Dr
Bidwell St
Haro St
Cardero St
Robson St
Alberni St
Coal Harbour Park
Beach Ave
Barclay St
Nelson St
Comox St
Nicola St
Barclay Heritage Sq
Pendrell St
Broughton St
Jervis St
WEST END
Bute St
Nelson Park
Thurlow St
English Bay
Davie St
Burnaby St
Harwood St
Sunset Beach Park
Pacific St
Hornby St
Granville St
Drake St
False Creek Ferry
False Creek
Vanier Park
Ogden Ave
McNicoll Ave
Maple St
Whyte Ave
Burrard Bridge
Burrard St
Creelman Ave
Chestnut St
Kitsilano Pool (400m)
Broker's Bay
Granville Bridge
Granville Island Public Market
York Ave
Granville Island
Johnston St
Aquabus Ferry
Arbutus St
Cypress St
W 1st Ave
W 2nd Ave
Cartwright St
The Mound
Sutcliffe Park
W 3rd Ave
Pine St
Fir St
Old Bridge St
W 4th Ave
FAIRVIEW

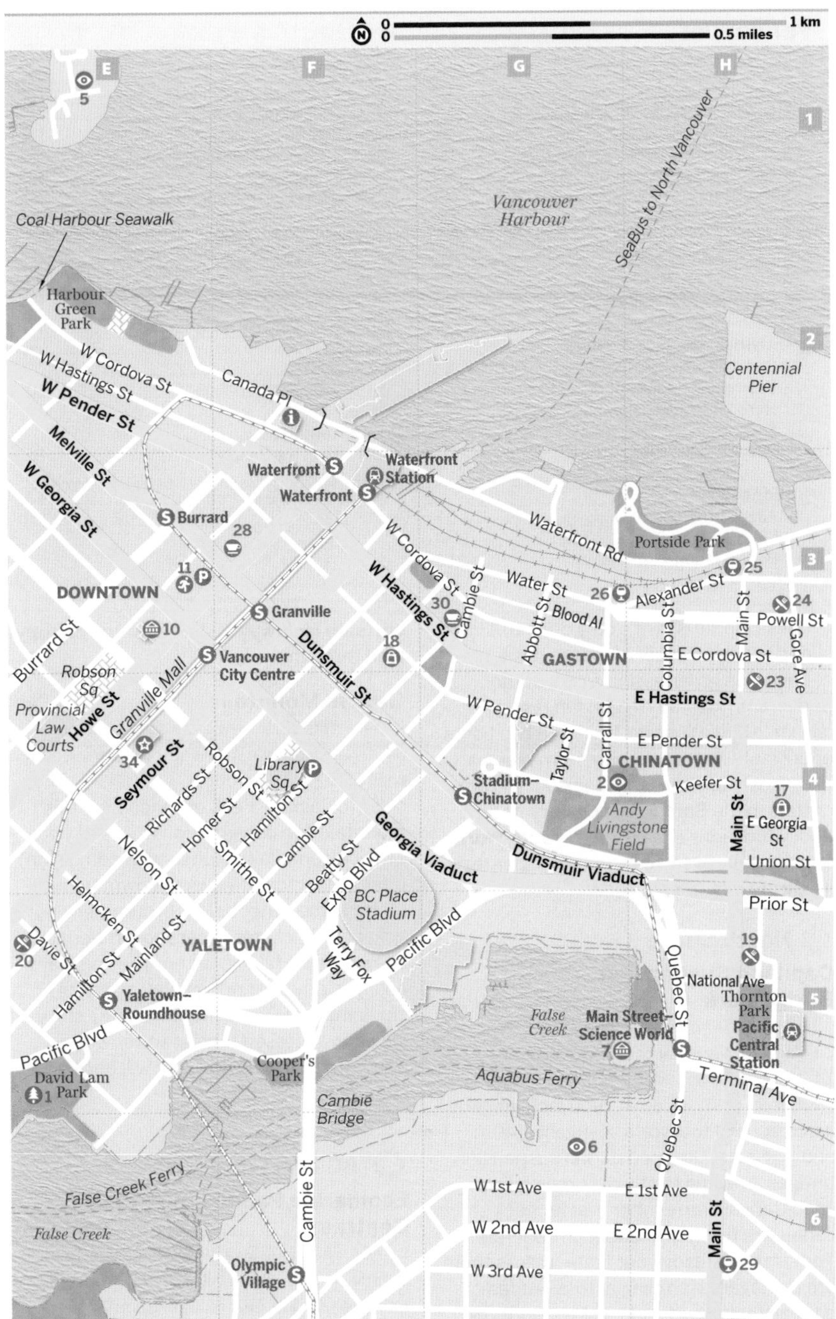

0 1 km
0 0.5 miles
E
F
G
H
1
2
3
4
5
6
Vancouver Harbour
SeaBus to North Vancouver
Coal Harbour Seawalk
Harbour Green Park
Centennial Pier
W Cordova St
W Hastings St
W Pender St
Canada Pl
Melville St
W Georgia St
Waterfront
Waterfront Station
Burrard
28
Waterfront Rd
Portside Park
11
DOWNTOWN
Granville
W Cordova St
W Hastings St
30
Cambie St
Water St
26
Alexander St
25
24
Powell St
Blood Al
Abbott St
Columbia St
Main St
Gore Ave
10
Burrard St
Robson Sq
Vancouver City Centre
Dunsmuir St
18
GASTOWN
E Cordova St
23
E Hastings St
Provincial Law Courts
Howe St
Granville Mall
W Pender St
Carrall St
Taylor St
E Pender St
CHINATOWN
34
Seymour St
Robson St
Library Sq
Hamilton St
Stadium–Chinatown
2
Keefer St
17
Andy Livingstone Field
E Georgia St
Richards St
Homer St
Smithe St
Cambie St
Beatty St
Expo Blvd
Georgia Viaduct
Dunsmuir Viaduct
Main St
Union St
Nelson St
BC Place Stadium
Prior St
Helmcken St
Mainland St
YALETOWN
Terry Fox Way
Pacific Blvd
19
Davie St
20
Hamilton St
Quebec St
National Ave
Yaletown–Roundhouse
Thornton Park
False Creek
Main Street–Science World
Pacific Central Station
7
Pacific Blvd
Cooper's Park
Aquabus Ferry
Terminal Ave
David Lam Park
1
Cambie Bridge
Quebec St
6
Cambie St
False Creek Ferry
W 1st Ave
E 1st Ave
False Creek
W 2nd Ave
E 2nd Ave
Main St
Olympic Village
W 3rd Ave
29

Vancouver

Sights

1 David Lam Park ... E5
2 Dr Sun Yat-Sen Classical Chinese Garden & Park ... G4
3 English Bay Beach ... B3
4 Granville Island Public Market ... C5
5 HMCS Discovery ... E1
6 Olympic Village ... G6
7 Science World ... G5
8 Stanley Park ... B1
9 Stanley Park Nature House ... C1
10 Vancouver Art Gallery ... E3

Activities, Courses & Tours

11 Cycle City Tours ... E3
12 Ecomarine Paddlesport Centres ... C6
13 Harbour Cruises ... D1
14 Second Beach Pool ... A1
15 Spokes Bicycle Rentals ... C1

Shopping

16 Ainsworth Custom Design ... D6
17 Massy Books ... H4
18 Paper Hound ... F3

Eating

19 Campagnolo ... H5
20 Chancho Tortilleria ... E5
21 Forage ... D3
22 Go Fish ... B6
23 Ovaltine Cafe ... H4
24 St Lawrence Restaurant ... H3

Drinking & Nightlife

25 Alibi Room ... H3
26 Guilt & Co ... G3
27 Liberty Distillery ... C6
28 Mario's Coffee Express ... F3
29 Narrow Lounge ... H6
30 Revolver ... G3
31 Sylvia's Bar & Lounge ... B2

Entertainment

32 Bard on the Beach ... B5
33 Cinematheque ... D4
34 Commodore Ballroom ... E4
FUSE ... (see 10)

geodesic dome (OK, it's only one), this ever-popular science showcase has tonnes of hands-on galleries and a cool outdoor park crammed with rugged fun (yes, you *can* lift 2028kg). Inside, there are two floors of brilliant educational play, from plasma balls to whisper dishes. Check out the live critters in the **Sara Stern Gallery**, the bodily functions exhibits in the **BodyWorks** area, then fly over a city on the virtual-reality **Birdly** ride ($8 extra).

North Shore

Capilano Suspension Bridge Park — Park

(☎604-985-7474; www.capbridge.com; 3735 Capilano Rd, North Vancouver; adult/child $47/15; ⏰8am-8pm May-Aug, reduced hours off-season; P 👪; 🚌236) As you inch gingerly across one of the world's longest (140m) and highest (70m) pedestrian suspension bridges, swaying gently over roiling Capilano Canyon, remember that its thick steel cables are firmly embedded in concrete. That should steady your feet – unless there are teenagers stamping across. Added park attractions include a glass-bottomed **cliffside walkway** and an elevated **canopy trail** through the trees.

Grouse Mountain — Park

(☎604-980-9311; www.grousemountain.com; 6400 Nancy Greene Way, North Vancouver; adult/child $56/29; ⏰9am-10pm; P 👪; 🚌236) The self-proclaimed 'Peak of Vancouver,' this mountain-top playground, accessed via Skyride gondola (included with admission), offers spectacular views of downtown glittering in the water below. In summer, your ticket also includes access to lumberjack shows, alpine hiking, bird-of-prey displays and a grizzly bear refuge. Pay extra for zip-lining and Eye of the Wind, a 20-story, elevator-accessed turbine tower with a panoramic viewing pod that will have your camera itching for action.

ACTIVITIES

Ecomarine Paddlesport Centres — Kayaking

(☎604-689-7575; www.ecomarine.com; 1668 Duranleau St, Granville Island; kayak/paddleboard rental per 2hr $39/30; ⏰10am-8pm mid-May–Aug, 10am-6pm Tue-Sun Sep–mid-May; 🚌50)

Headquartered on Granville Island, the friendly folks at Ecomarine offer kayak (single and double) plus stand-up paddleboard (SUP) rentals, as well as popular guided tours, including the magical Urban Sunset Kayak ($79). Fancy exploring further? They also arrange multiday tours around some of BC's most magical marine regions.

Harbour Cruises Boating

(604-688-7246; www.boatcruises.com; 501 Denman St, West End; adult/child from $39/12; May–mid-Oct; 19) View Vancouver – and some unexpected wildlife – from the water on a one-hour narrated harbor tour, weaving past Stanley Park, Lions Gate Bridge and the North Shore mountains. There's also a popular 2½-hour sunset dinner cruise (adult/child $87/73) plus a long, languid lunch trek to lovely Indian Arm ($76) that makes you feel like you're a million miles from the city.

Spokes Bicycle Rentals Cycling

(604-688-5141; www.spokesbicyclerentals.com; 1798 W Georgia St, West End; adult bicycle rental per hr/day from $8.57/34.28; 8am-9pm, reduced hours in low season; ; 5) On the corner of W Georgia and Denman streets, this is the biggest of the bike shops servicing the Stanley Park cycling trade. It can kit you and your family out with all manner of bikes, from cruisers to tandems to kiddie one-speeds. Ask for tips on riding the Seawall; it extends far beyond Stanley Park.

TOURS

Cycle City Tours Cycling

(604-618-8626; www.cyclevancouver.com; 648 Hornby St, Downtown; tours from $65, bicycle rentals per hour/day $9.50/38; 9am-6pm, reduced hours in winter; Burrard) Striped with bike lanes, Vancouver is a good city for two-wheeled exploring. But if you're not great at navigating, consider a guided tour with this popular operator. Its Grand Tour ($90) is a great city intro, while the Craft Beer Tour ($90) includes brunch and three breweries. Alternatively, go solo with a rental; there's a bike lane outside the store.

Grouse Grind

If you really want a workout, try North Vancouver's **Grouse Grind** (www.grousemountain.com; Grouse Mountain, North Shore; 236), a steep, sweat-triggering slog up the side of Grouse Mountain that's been nicknamed 'Mother Nature's Stairmaster.' Reward yourself at the top with free access to the resort's facilities. Many grinders then pay the $15 fee to get down the mountain via the Skyride gondola.

Vancouver Foodie Tours Tours

(604-295-8844; www.foodietours.ca; tours from $65) A popular culinary-themed city stroll operator running three tasty tours in Vancouver; choose between Best of Downtown, Gastronomic Gastown and Granville Island tours. Friendly red-coated guides lead you on belly-pleasing ventures with plenty to eat and drink; the trick is not to dine before you arrive.

Architectural Institute of British Columbia Walking

(604-683-8588; www.aibc.ca; tours $10; Tue-Sun Jul & Aug) Local architecture students conduct these excellent two-hour wanders, focusing on the buildings, history and heritage of several key Vancouver neighborhoods. There are six tours in all, covering areas including Gastown, Strathcona, Yaletown, Chinatown, downtown and

MICHAEL WHEATLEY / AGE FOTOSTOCK ©

Kitsilano Farmers Market

Kitsilano's best excuse to get out and hang with the locals

the West End. If you're visiting Victoria, tours operate there as well.

SHOPPING

Vancouver's retail scene has developed dramatically in recent years. Hit Robson St's mainstream chains, then discover the hip, independent shops of Gastown, Main St and Commercial Dr. Granville Island is stuffed with artsy stores and studios, while South Granville and Kitsilano's 4th Ave serve up a wide range of tempting boutiques.

Paper Hound Books
(☎604-428-1344; www.paperhound.ca; 344 W Pender St, Downtown; ⏰10am-7pm Sun-Thu, to 8pm Fri & Sat; 🚌14) Proving the printed word is alive and kicking, this small but perfectly curated secondhand bookstore is a dog-eared favorite among locals. A perfect spot for browsing, you'll find tempting tomes (mostly used but some new) on everything from nature to poetry to chaos theory. Ask for recommendations; they really know their stuff here. Don't miss the bargain rack out front.

Massy Books Books
(☎604-721-4405; www.massybooks.com; 229 E Georgia St, Chinatown; ⏰10am-6pm Sun-Wed, 10am-8pm Thu-Sat; 🚌3) A former pop-up favorite with a now-permanent Chinatown location, this delightful bookstore is lined with tall stacks of well-curated, mostly used titles. There's an impressively large selection of Indigenous-themed books, alongside good selections covering travel, history and literature – plus a bargain $1 cart outside. Love mysteries? Try finding the store's secret room, hidden behind a pushable bookcase door.

Pacific Arts Market Arts & Crafts
(☎778-877-6449; www.pacificartsmarket.ca; 1448 W Broadway, South Granville; ⏰noon-5:30pm Tue & Wed, noon-7pm Thu & Fri, 11am-7pm Sat, 1-5pm Sun; 🚌9) Head upstairs to this

large, under-the-radar gallery space and you'll find a kaleidoscopic array of stands showcasing the work of 40+ Vancouver and BC artists. From paintings to jewelry and from fiber arts to handmade chocolate bars, it's the perfect spot to find authentic souvenirs to take back home. The artists change regularly and there's something for every budget here.

Kitsilano Farmers Market Market

(www.eatlocal.org; 2690 Larch St, Kitsilano Community Centre, Kitsilano; 10am-2pm Sun May-Oct; 9) This seasonal farmers market is one of the city's most popular and is Kitsilano's best excuse to get out and hang with the locals. Arrive early for the best selection and you'll have the pick of freshly plucked local fruit and veg, such as sweet strawberries or spectacularly flavorful heirloom tomatoes. You'll likely never want to shop in a mainstream supermarket again.

Regional Assembly of Text Arts & Crafts

(604-877-2247; www.assemblyoftext.com; 3934 Main St; 11am-6pm Mon-Sat, noon-5pm Sun; 3) This ironic antidote to the digital age lures ink-stained locals with its journals, handmade pencil boxes and T-shirts printed with typewriter motifs. Check out the tiny under-the-stairs gallery showcasing global zines and don't miss the monthly Letter Writing Club (7pm, first Thursday of every month), where you can hammer on vintage typewriters, crafting erudite missives to far-away loved ones.

Red Cat Records Music

(604-708-9422; www.redcat.ca; 4332 Main St; 11am-7pm Mon-Thu, to 8pm Fri & Sat, to 6pm Sun; 3) Arguably Vancouver's coolest record store and certainly the only one named after a much-missed cat... There's a brilliantly curated collection of new and used vinyl and CDs, and it's co-owned by musicians; ask them for tips on where to see great local acts such as Loscil and Nick Krgovich or peruse the huge list of shows in the window.

Mountain Equipment Co-Op Sports & Outdoors

(604-872-7858; www.mec.ca; 130 W Broadway; 10am-7pm Mon-Wed, 10am-9pm Thu & Fri, 9am-6pm Sat, 10am-6pm Sun; 9) Grown hikers weep at the amazing selection of clothing (including lifestyle wear for urban hipsters), kayaks and clever camping gadgets at this cavernous store. You'll need to be a member to buy, but that costs just $5. At the time of research, a new store was being built at 111 E 2nd Ave to replace this one.

Ainsworth Custom Design Arts & Crafts

(604-682-8838; www.ainsworthcustomdesign.com; 1243 Cartwright St, Granville Island; 10am-6pm Mon-Fri, noon-6pm Sat, noon-5pm Sun; 50) Ostensibly a design studio working to commission, its two-story front-of-shop area showcases a kaleidoscopic array of quirky arts and crafts by mostly local artists. It's an amazing selection, with bright-colored cartoon-monster paintings competing with Mexican wrestler-mask purses for your attention. You'll also find lots of ideas for furnishing rooms that belong to cool kids who love Roald Dahl.

EATING

Vancouver has an eye-popping array of generally good-value dine-out options: authentic Asian restaurants, finger-licking brunch spots, fresh-catch seafood joints and a locally sourced farm-to-table scene are all on the menu here. You don't have to be a local to indulge: just follow your taste buds and dinner will become the most talked-about highlight of your Vancouver visit.

Chancho Tortilleria Mexican $

(604-428-8494; www.chancho.ca; 1206 Seymour St, Downtown; mains $8-12; 11:30am-7pm Mon-Sat, to 5:30pm Sun; ; 10) Look for the pig-and-pineapple sign outside this authentic Mexican hole-in-the-wall, which has painted walls, plastic garden chairs and a super-friendly welcome. It's the food

Denman Dining Street

This West End thoroughfare is crammed like a United Nations food court with Vancouver's best midrange dining from around the world. From authentic *izakayas* (Japanese neighbourhood pubs) and noodle shops to Mexican joints and fancy French restaurants, you can eat in a different country here every night.

TRACEY KUSIEWICZ / FOODIE PHOTOGRAPHY / GETTY IMAGES ©

that'll keep you smiling, though; order meat or vegetarian fillings by weight, all served with beans, salsa, pickled red cabbage and housemade tortillas.

Go Fish Seafood $

(☎604-730-5040; 1505 W 1st Ave; mains $8-14; ⏰11:30am-6pm Mon-Fri, noon-6pm Sat & Sun; 🚌50) A short stroll westward along the seawall from the Granville Island entrance, this almost-too-popular seafood stand is one of the city's fave fish-and-chip joints, offering halibut, salmon and cod encased in crispy golden batter. The smashing fish tacos are also recommended, while changing daily specials – brought in by the nearby fishing boats – often include scallop burgers or ahi tuna sandwiches.

Paul's Omelettery Breakfast $

(☎604-737-2857; www.paulsomelettery.com; 2211 Granville St, South Granville; mains $6-19; ⏰7am-3pm; 🖉; 🚌10) You'll be jostling for space with chatty locals at this breakfast and lunch joint near the south side of Granville Bridge. But it's worth it: the cozy, friendly place is superior to most bacon-and-eggs destinations. The menu is grounded on signature omelets, while also offering excellent eggs Benedict and heaping 'lumberjack breakfasts.' Reservations are not accepted; arrive early on weekends.

Caffè La Tanna Italian $

(☎604-428-5462; www.caffelatana.ca; 635 Commercial Dr; mains $12-16; ⏰8am-6pm; 🚌20) Like a 1950s neighborhood cafe in Rome, this handsome little hidden gem looks like it's been here for decades. But it's a new addition to this quiet stretch of the Drive, luring delighted locals with its delicate housemade pastries and fresh pastas (watch the mesmerizing pasta production at the counter). Check the daily special and peruse the shelves of Italian groceries, too.

Ovaltine Cafe Diner $

(☎604-685-7021; www.facebook.com/ovaltinecafe; 251 E Hastings St, Chinatown; mains $7-10; ⏰6:30am-3pm Mon-Sat, 6:30am-2pm Sun; 🚌14) Like being inside Edward Hopper's *Nighthawks* diner painting, this time-capsule greasy spoon instantly transports you to the 1940s. Snag a booth alongside the hospital-green walls or, better yet, slide onto a tape-repaired spinning stool at the long counter. Truck-stop coffee is de rigueur here, alongside burgers, sandwiches and fried breakfasts that haven't changed in decades (yes, that's liver and onions on the menu).

Forage Canadian $$

(☎604-661-1400; www.foragevancouver.com; 1300 Robson St, West End; mains $16-35; ⏰6:30-10am & 5-11pm Mon-Fri, 7am-2pm & 5-11pm Sat & Sun; 📶; 🚌5) 🌿 A popular farm-to-table eatery, this sustainability-focused restaurant is the perfect way to sample regional flavors. Brunch has become a firm local favorite (the halibut eggs Benedict is recommended), and for dinner there's everything from bison steaks to slow-cooked salmon. Add a flight of BC craft beers, with top choices from the likes of Four Winds, Strange Fellows and more. Reservations advised.

Salmon n' Bannock Northwestern US $$

(☎604-568-8971; www.facebook.com/SalmonNBannockBistro; 1128 W Broadway, Fairview; mains $16-32; ⏰5-10pm Mon-Sat; 🚌9) Vancouver's only First Nations restaurant is an utterly delightful art-lined little bistro on an unassuming strip of Broadway shops. It's worth the easy bus trip, though, for fresh-made Indigenous-influenced dishes made with local ingredients. The juicy salmon 'n' bannock burger has been a staple here for years but more elaborate, feast-like options include game sausages and bison pot roast.

Acorn Vegetarian $$

(☎604-566-9001; www.theacornrestaurant.ca; 3995 Main St; mains $18-22; ⏰5:30-10pm Sun-Thu, to 11pm Fri & Sat, brunch 10am-2:30pm Sat & Sun; 🌿; 🚌3) One of Vancouver's hottest vegetarian restaurants – hence the sometimes long wait for tables – the Acorn is ideal for those craving something more inventive than mung-bean soup. Consider seasonal, artfully presented treats such as beer-battered halloumi or vanilla-almond-beet cake and stick around at night: the bar serves until midnight if you need to pull up a stool and set the world to rights.

Anh & Chi Vietnamese $$

(☎604-878-8883; www.anhandchi.com; 3388 Main St; mains $16-25; ⏰11am-11pm; 🌿; 🚌3) You'll find warm and solicitous service at this delightful contemporary Vietnamese restaurant whose authentic, perfectly prepared dishes are a must for local foodies. Not sure what to order? Check out the menu's 'bucket list' dishes, including the highly recommended prawn-and-pork-packed crunchy crepe. Reservations are not accepted and waits here can be long; consider mid-afternoon weekday dining instead.

Campagnolo Italian $$

(☎604-484-6018; www.campagnolorestaurant.ca; 1020 Main St, Chinatown; mains $18-25; ⏰11:30am-2:30pm Mon-Fri, plus 5:30-10pm daily; 🌿; 🚌3) Eyebrows were raised when this contemporary, rustic-style Italian restaurant opened in a hitherto sketchy part of town. But Campagnolo has lured locals and inspired a mini-wave of other restaurants in the vicinity. Reserve ahead and dive into

Elk shank dish at Salmon n' Bannock

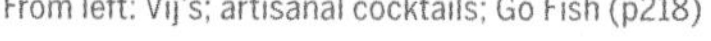

From left: Vij's; artisanal cocktails; Go Fish (p218)

reinvented comfort dishes such as shrimp gnocchetti and a fennel-sausage-topped pizza that may induce you to eat your body weight in thin-crust.

Vij's Indian $$$

(604-736-6664; www.vijs.ca; 3106 Cambie St, Cambie Village; mains $23-36; 5:30-10pm; ; 15) Spicy aromas scent the air as you enter this warmly intimate dining space for Vancouver's finest Indian cuisine. Exemplary servers happily answer menu questions, while bringing over snacks and chai tea. There's a one-page array of tempting dishes but the trick is to order three or four to share (mains are all available as small plates and orders come with rice and naan).

St Lawrence Restaurant French $$$

(604-620-3800; www.stlawrencerestaurant.com; 269 Powell St, Railtown; mains $34-44; 5:30-10:30pm Tue-Sun; 4) Resembling a handsome wood-floored bistro that's been teleported straight from Montréal, this sparkling, country-chic dining room is a Railtown superstar. The Québecois approach carries over onto a small menu of elevated, perfectly prepared old-school mains such as the utterly delicious duck-leg confit with sausage. French-Canadian special-occasion dining at its finest.

DRINKING & NIGHTLIFE

Sylvia's Bar & Lounge Bar

(604-681-9321; www.sylviahotel.com; 1154 Gilford St, West End; 7am-11pm Sun-Thu, to midnight Fri & Sat; 5) Part of the permanently popular Sylvia Hotel, this was Vancouver's first cocktail bar when it opened in the mid-1950s. Now a comfy, wood-lined neighborhood bar favored by in-the-know locals (they're the ones hogging the window seats as the sun sets over English Bay), it's a charming spot for an end-of-day wind down. There's live music on Wednesdays, Thursdays and Sundays.

Mario's Coffee Express Coffee

(604-608-2804; www.facebook.com/marioscoffeeexpress; 595 Howe St, Downtown; 6:30am-4pm Mon-Fri; S Burrard) A java-lover's favorite that only downtown office workers seem to know about. You'll wake

CANADA / ALAMY STOCK PHOTO ©

up and smell the coffee long before you make it through the door here. The rich aromatic brews served up by the man himself are the kind of ambrosia that makes Starbucks' drinkers weep. You might even forgive the 1980s Italian pop percolating through the shop.

Powell Brewery Microbrewery

(www.powellbeer.com; 1357 Powell St; ⏲2-9pm Mon-Thu, noon-10pm Fri & Sat, noon-9pm Sun; 📶; 🚌4) One of the finest of Vancouver's surfeit of tasty artisan breweries, popular Powell Brewery relocated to larger premises soon after launching. The tasting room is also much larger now, with a window so you can overlook production. Aim for renowned tipples like Dive Bomb Porter and Old Jalopy Pale Ale and you may well discover you've found your new favorite beermaker.

Grapes & Soda Wine Bar

(☎604-336-2456; www.grapesandsoda.ca; 1541 W 6th Ave, South Granville; ⏲5:30-11pm Tue-Sat; 🚌10) A warm, small-table hangout that self-identifies as a 'natural wine bar' (there's a well-curated array of options from BC, Europe and beyond). This local favorite also serves excellent cocktails: from the countless bottles behind the small bar, they can seemingly concoct anything your taste buds desire, whether or not it's on the menu. Need help? Slide into a Scotch, ginger and walnut Cortejo.

Storm Crow Alehouse Pub

(☎604-428-9670; www.stormcrowalehouse.com; 1619 W Broadway, South Granville; ⏲11am-1am Sun-Thu, 11am-2am Fri & Sat; 📶; 🚌9) The larger sibling of Commercial Dr's excellent nerd bar, this pub welcomes everyone from the Borg to beardy *Lord of the Rings* dwarves. They come to peruse the memorabilia-studded walls (think Millennium Falcon models and a TARDIS washroom door), check out the role-playing games and dive into refreshments including Romulan Ale and Pangalactic Gargleblaster cocktails. Hungry? Miss the chunky chickpea fries at your peril.

Alibi Room Pub

(☎604-623-3383; www.alibi.ca; 157 Alexander St, Gastown; ⏲5-11:30pm Mon-Thu, 5pm-12:30am Fri, 10am-12:30am Sat, 10am-11:30pm Sun; 📶; 🚌4) Vancouver's best craft-beer tavern pours a near-legendary roster of 50-plus drafts, many from celebrated BC breweries including Four Winds, Yellow Dog and Dageraad. Hipsters and veteran-ale fans alike love the 'frat bat': choose your own four samples or ask to be surprised. Check the board for new guest casks and stick around for a gastropub dinner at one of the long communal tables.

Guilt & Co Bar

(www.guiltandcompany.com; 1 Alexander St, Gastown; ⏲7pm-late; S Waterfront) This cavelike subterranean bar, beneath Gastown's brick-cobbled sidewalks, is also a brilliant venue to catch a tasty side dish of live music. Most shows are pay-what-you-can and can range from trumpet jazz to heartfelt singer-songwriters. Drinks-wise, there's a great cocktail list plus a small array of draft beers (and many more in cans and bottles). Avoid weekends when there are often long queues.

"Gastown's coolest see-and-be-seen coffee shop"

Revolver

Brassneck Brewery Microbrewery

(☎604-259-7686; www.brassneck.ca; 2148 Main St; ⏲2-11pm Mon-Fri, noon-11pm Sat & Sun; 🚌3) A beloved Vancouver microbrewery with a small, wood-lined tasting room. Peruse the ever-changing chalkboard of intriguing libations with names such as Pinky Promise, Silent Treatment and Faux Naive, or start with a delicious, highly accessible Passive Aggressive dry-hopped pale ale. It's often hard to find a seat here, so consider a weekday afternoon visit for a four-glass $8 tasting flight.

Key Party Bar

(www.keyparty.ca; 2303 Main St; ⏲5pm-1am Mon-Thu, to 2am Fri & Sat, to 1am Sun; 🚌3) Walk through the doorway of a fake storefront that looks like an accountancy office and you'll find yourself in a candlelit, boudoir-red speakeasy dominated by a dramatic mural of frolicking women and animals. Arrive early to avoid the queues, then fully explore the entertaining cocktail program (Kir Royale champagne jello shooters included).

Liberty Distillery Distillery

(☎604-558-1998; www.thelibertydistillery.com; 1494 Old Bridge St, Granville Island; ⏰11am-9pm; 🚌50) Gaze through internal windows at the shiny, steampunk-like booze-making equipment when you visit this handsome saloon-like tasting room. It's not all about looks, though. During happy hour (Monday to Thursday, 3pm to 6pm and after 8pm), sample housemade vodka, gin varieties and several whiskeys plus great $6 cocktails. Tours are also available ($10, 11:30am and 1:30pm Saturday and Sunday).

Revolver Coffee

(☎604-558-4444; www.revolvercoffee.ca; 325 Cambie St, Gastown; ⏰7:30am-6pm Mon-Fri, 9am-6pm Sat; 📶; 🚌14) Gastown's coolest see-and-be-seen coffee shop, Revolver has never lost its hipster crown. But it's remained at the top of the Vancouver coffee-mug tree via a serious commitment to serving expertly prepared top-quality java. Aim for a little booth table or, if they're taken (they usually are), hit the large communal table next door.

Narrow Lounge Bar

(☎778-737-5206; www.narrowlounge.com; 1898 Main St; ⏰5pm-1am Mon-Fri, to 2am Sat & Sun; 🚌3) Enter through the doorway on 3rd Ave – the red light tells you if it's open or not – then descend the graffiti-lined stairway into one of Vancouver's coolest small bars. Little bigger than a train carriage and lined with taxidermy and junk-shop pictures, it's an atmospheric nook where it always feels like 2am. In summer, try the hidden alfresco bar out back.

Shameful Tiki Room Bar

(www.shamefultikiroom.com; 4362 Main St; ⏰5pm-midnight Sun-Thu, to 1am Fri & Sat; 🚌3) This windowless snug instantly transports you to a Polynesian beach. The lighting – including glowing puffer-fish lampshades – is permanently set to dusk and the walls are lined with tiki masks and rattan coverings under a straw-shrouded ceiling. But it's the drinks that rock; seriously well-crafted classics from zombies to blue Hawaiis to a four-person Volcano Bowl (don't forget to share it).

Bard on the Beach

Watching Shakespeare performed at **Bard on the Beach** (☎604-739-0559; www.bardonthebeach.org; 1695 Whyte Ave, Vanier Park, Kitsilano; tickets from $24; ⏰Jun-Sep; 👪; 🚌2) while the sun sets over the mountains beyond the tented main stage is a Vancouver summertime highlight. There are usually three Shakespeare plays, plus one Bard-related work (*Rosencrantz and Guildenstern are Dead*, for example), to choose from during the season. Q&A talks are staged after some Tuesday performances; also opera, fireworks and wine-tasting special nights are held throughout the season.

✪ ENTERTAINMENT

Stanley Theatre Theatre

(☎604-687-1644; www.artsclub.com; 2750 Granville St, South Granville; tickets from $29; ⏰Sep-Jul; 🚌10) Popular musicals dominate early summer (usually the last show of the season) at this heritage theater, but first half of the year sees new works and adaptations of contemporary hits from around the world. Officially called the Stanley Industrial Alliance Stage (a moniker that not a single Vancouverite uses), the Stanley is part of the Arts Club Theatre Company, Vancouver's biggest.

Cinematheque Cinema

(☎604-688-8202; www.thecinematheque.ca; 1131 Howe St, Downtown; tickets $12, double bills $16; 🚌10) This beloved cinema operates like an ongoing film festival with a daily-changing program of movies. A $3 annual membership is required – organize it at the door – before you can skulk in the dark with other chin-stroking movie buffs

Performance at Commodore Ballroom

SERGEI BACHLAKOV / SHUTTERSTOCK ©

who probably named their children (or pets) after Fellini and Bergman.

Commodore Ballroom Live Music
(☎604-739-4550; www.commodoreballroom.com; 868 Granville St, Downtown; tickets from $30; 🚌10) Local bands know they've made it when they play Vancouver's best mid-sized venue, a restored art-deco ballroom that still has the city's bounciest dance floor – courtesy of tires placed under its floorboards. If you need a break from moshing, collapse at one of the tables lining the perimeter, catch your breath with a bottled brew and then plunge back in.

Rio Theatre Live Performance
(☎604-879-3456; www.riotheatre.ca; 1660 E Broadway; tickets from $5; 🅢Commercial-Broadway) A huge public fundraising campaign in 2018 saved this beloved theater and cinema venue from possible redevelopment, proving just how important it's become in the cultural lives of locals. But alongside art-house movie screenings, there's a seriously eclectic array of entertainment here, from burlesque to stand-up and from live music to cult films. Check the calendar to see what's on during your visit.

Theatre Under the Stars Performing Arts
(TUTS; ☎604-631-2877; www.tuts.ca; 610 Pipeline Rd, Malkin Bowl, Stanley Park; tickets from $30; ⏲Jul & Aug; 🚌19) The charming **Malkin Bowl** (www.malkinbowl.com; 🚌19) provides an atmospheric alfresco stage for the summertime TUTS season, usually featuring two interchanging Broadway musicals. It's hard to find a better place to catch a show, especially as the sun fades over the surrounding Stanley Park trees. The troupe's production values have massively increased in recent years, and these productions are slick, professional and energetic.

INFORMATION

Tourism Vancouver Visitor Centre (☎604-683-2000; www.tourismvancouver.com; 200 Burrard St, Downtown; ⏲9am-5pm; 🅢Waterfront) provides free maps, visitor guides, accommodations and tour bookings, plus brochures on the city and the wider BC region.

GETTING THERE & AWAY

AIR

Canada's second-busiest airport, **Vancouver International Airport** (YVR; ☎604-207-7077; www.yvr.ca; 3211 Grant McConachie Way, Richmond;) is 13km south of downtown in the city of Richmond.

BOAT

BC Ferries (☎250-386-3431; www.bcferries.com) services arrive at Tsawwassen, an hour south of Vancouver, and at Horseshoe Bay, 30 minutes from downtown in West Vancouver.

Main services to Tsawwassen arrive from Vancouver Island's Swartz Bay, near Victoria, and Duke Point, near Nanaimo. Services also arrive from the Southern Gulf Islands.

Services to Horseshoe Bay arrive from Nanaimo's Departure Bay. Services also arrive here from Bowen Island and from Langdale on the Sunshine Coast.

BUS

Intercity buses trundle into Vancouver's neon-signed Pacific Central Station. BC Connector (www.bcconnector.com) operates bus services from Kelowna, Kamloops and Whistler as well as Victoria (via BC Ferries). Cross-border services from Bolt Bus (www.boltbus.com) and Quick Shuttle (www.quickcoach.com) also arrive here.

TRAIN

Pacific Central Station (1150 Station St, Chinatown; S Main St-Science World) is the city's main terminus for long-distance trains from across Canada on VIA Rail (www.viarail.com), and from Seattle (just south of the border) and beyond on Amtrak (www.amtrak.com).

GETTING AROUND

TO/FROM THE AIRPORT

SkyTrain's 16-station Canada Line (see the route maps at www.translink.ca) operates a rapid-transit train service from the airport to downtown (tickets $8 to $10.75, depending on your destination and the time of day). Trains run every few minutes from early morning until after midnight and take around 25 minutes to reach downtown's Waterfront Station.

A taxi to most downtown Vancouver destinations costs $35.

BICYCLE

- Vancouver is a relatively good cycling city, with more than 300km of designated routes crisscrossing the region.
- Cyclists can take their bikes for free on SkyTrains, SeaBuses and transit buses, which are all now fitted with bike racks. Cyclists are required by law to wear helmets.

BOAT

The iconic SeaBus shuttle is part of the TransLink transit system (regular transit fares apply) and it operates throughout the day, taking around 15 minutes to cross Burrard Inlet between Waterfront Station and North Vancouver's Lonsdale Quay.

BUS

Vancouver's TransLink (www.translink.ca) bus network is extensive. Exact change (or more) is required; buses use fare machines and change is not given. Fares are adult/child $3/1.95 and are valid for up to 90 minutes of transfer travel.

TRAIN

TransLink's SkyTrain rapid-transit network is a great way to move around the region, especially beyond the city center. Compass tickets for SkyTrain trips can be purchased from station vending machines. SkyTrain journeys cost $3 to $5.75, depending on how far you are journeying.

TAXI

At the time of research, Vancouver was in the process of paving the way for ride-hailing schemes such as Uber and Lyft. Until then, try **Yellow Cab** (☎604-681-1111; www.yellowcabonline.com;).

HELIRY / GETTY IMAGES ©

Where to Stay

Be aware that there will be some significant additions to most quoted room rates. You'll pay an extra 8% Provincial Sales Tax (PST) plus 5% Goods and Services Tax (GST) and an additional 3% Hotel Room Tax.

Neighborhood	Atmosphere
Downtown	Walking distance to stores, restaurants, nightlife and some attractions; great transit links to wider region; good range of hotels; can be pricey; some accommodations overlook noisy traffic areas.
West End	Walking distance to Stanley Park; many midrange restaurants nearby; heart of the gay district; quiet residential streets; mostly high-end B&Bs with a couple of additional chain hotels; can be a bit of a hike to the city center.
Yaletown & Granville Island	Close to shops and many restaurants; good transport links to other areas; few accommodation options to choose from.
Fairview & South Granville	Quiet residential streets; well-priced heritage B&B sleepovers; good bus and SkyTrain access to downtown; few local nightlife options.
Kitsilano & UBC	Comfy heritage houses and good UBC budget options; direct transit to downtown; on the doorstep of several beaches; scant nightlife options; can feel a bit too quiet and laid-back.
North Shore	Better hotel rates than city center; handy access to downtown via SeaBus; close to popular attractions such as Grouse Mountain and Capilano Suspension Bridge; takes time to get to other major attractions.

VANCOUVER ISLAND

In this Chapter

Vancouver Island at a glance...

Comparable in size to Taiwan or the Netherlands, Vancouver Island is just a short ferry hop from the mainland, but feels worlds away. Victoria, the charming provincial capital, has a distinctive English feel with double-decker buses and high tea, while the rest of the island is studded with colorful communities and a lot of rugged wilderness. Witness a salmon run, surf Tofino's endless Long Beach, sample local wine and cheese, and see the biggest trees of your life. Vancouver Island is not shy of wowing visitors.

Two Days on Vancouver Island

Spend a day exploring Victoria (p236), taking in **Craigdarroch Castle** (p236) and the **Royal BC Museum** (p232) before wandering through Chinatown. Divert over to **Miniature World** (p236) to see some modeling marvels before venturing out on the water on a **whale-watching tour** (p237). On day two, rent a bike and head along the **Galloping Goose Trail** (p237) to get a taste of the forest. End the day with a live show at the **Royal Theatre** (p241).

Four Days on Vancouver Island

Head up island to Port Alberni (p243) stopping on the way at **Cathedral Grove** (p243) to admire the giant trees. Peruse the exhibits at **Alberni Valley Museum** (p243) and stock up on baked goods at **Mountain View Bakery & Deli** (p243). On day three, cross the island to **Tofino**. Take a long walk on Long Beach or test your surfing skills in Cox Bay. Visit the **Roy Henry Vickers Gallery** (p235) and then chill in a wood-paneled cafe.

Previous page: Pacific Rim National Park
ADAM ZIHLA / SHUTTERSTOCK ©

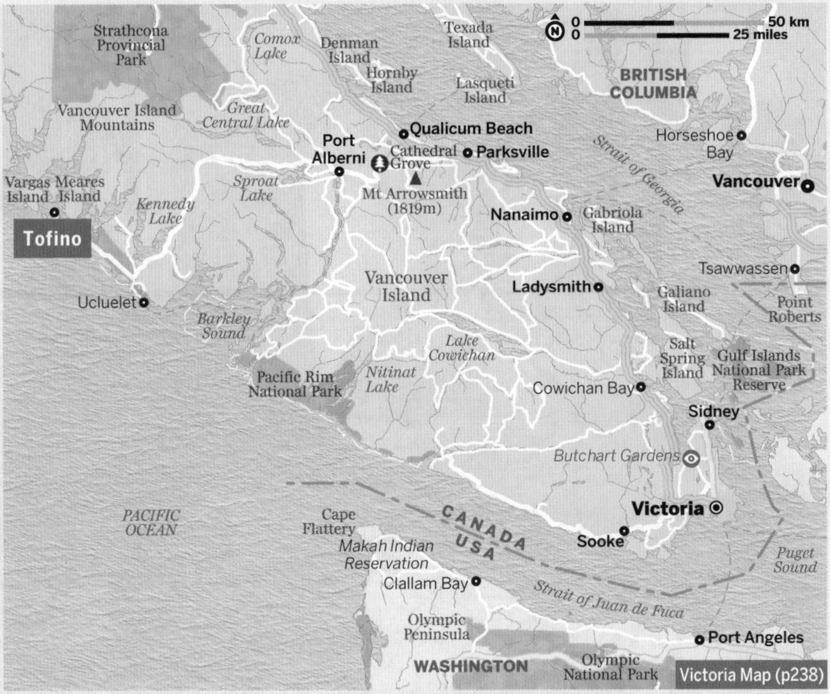

Strathcona Provincial Park
Comox Lake
Denman Island
Texada Island
Hornby Island
Lasqueti Island
BRITISH COLUMBIA
50 km
25 miles
Vancouver Island Mountains
Great Central Lake
Qualicum Beach
Port Alberni
Cathedral Grove
Parksville
Strait of Georgia
Horseshoe Bay
Vancouver
Vargas Island
Meares Island
Sproat Lake
Mt Arrowsmith (1819m)
Kennedy Lake
Nanaimo
Gabriola Island
Tofino
Tsawwassen
Vancouver Island
Ladysmith
Ucluelet
Galiano Island
Point Roberts
Barkley Sound
Lake Cowichan
Salt Spring Island
Gulf Islands National Park Reserve
Pacific Rim National Park
Nitinat Lake
Cowichan Bay
Sidney
Butchart Gardens
Victoria
PACIFIC OCEAN
Cape Flattery
CANADA
USA
Sooke
Makah Indian Reservation
Puget Sound
Clallam Bay
Strait of Juan de Fuca
Olympic Peninsula
Port Angeles
WASHINGTON
Olympic National Park

Victoria Map (p238)

Arriving on Vancouver Island

Victoria International Airport YYJ Airport Shuttle (www.yyjairportshuttle.com) buses run to downtown Victoria ($25, 30 minutes). A taxi costs around $50.

BC Ferries (www.bcferries.com) Arrive from mainland Tsawwassen at Swartz Bay, 27km north of Victoria (take bus 70 or 72).

Harbour Air (www.harbourair.com) Floatplane services arrive into Victoria's Inner Harbour.

Where to Stay

The island is awash with accommodation options, from the heritage B&Bs and swank hotels of Victoria to the luxe boutique resorts of the west coast. Tofino is notoriously pricey, but Ucluelet up the road offers better deals. Elsewhere, you'll find campgrounds, boutique spa hotels and some of BC's best hostels.

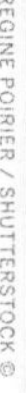

Royal BC Museum

Located in the provincial capital, Victoria, BC's most illustrious museum provides a definitive overview of the province's natural and human history.

Great For...

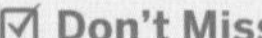

☑ Don't Miss

Stopping by St Ann's Schoolhouse – perhaps the oldest building still standing in Victoria.

Imax & Temporary Exhibitions

Carrier of a 'royal' prefix since 1987, Victoria's flagship sight mixes its provincial exhibits with a revolving lineup of world-class temporary exhibitions. Recent shows have included Egyptian pharaohs, the Mesoamerican Maya civilization and BC's 19th-century gold rush.

The onsite **IMAX Theatre** (☎250-480-4887; www.imaxvictoria.com; 675 Belleville St; tickets $11.95; 🚌70) shows larger-than-life documentaries and Hollywood blockbusters.

Permanent Collection

Permanent fixtures inside the museum are split into natural history (2nd floor) and human history (3rd floor). Both focus almost exclusively on British Columbia.

The permanent collection is known for its recreations of various Pacific Northwest

Performer at the Victoria Indigenous Cultural Festival

Need to Know

250-356-7226; www.royalbcmuseum.bc.ca; 675 Belleville St; adult/child $17/11, incl IMAX $26.95/21.25; 10am-5pm daily, to 10pm Fri & Sat mid-May–Sep; 70

Take a Break

Sequoia Coastal Coffee is the museum's on-site coffee shop. Food carts congregate on the museum's back patio in the summer.

★ Top Tip

Check the website beforehand to see what temporary exhibits are showing.

ecosystems both prehistoric and contemporary. The biggest head-turner is a life-size model of a woolly mammoth complete with meter-long fur, but you'll also spy bears, cougars and marine life. As the human history section unfolds, you're taken down a diorama of a Victoria street from the early 20th century, complete with cinema, hotel and mini-Chinatown. There's also a full-scale replica of George Vancouver's 1789 ship, HMS *Discovery*.

The exhaustive First Nations collection is extensive, with room for only a fraction of it to be displayed. Look out for a recreated Kwakwaka'wakw clanhouse and a sonic exhibit that greets you in 34 different Indigenous languages.

Thunderbird Park

In adjacent Thunderbird Park, behind a line of weathered totem poles, lie two of the province's oldest buildings. **St Ann's Schoolhouse** is a small log cabin that dates from 1844, when it served as a fur trading post. Next door, the **Helmcken House** (1852) is the former home of fur trade era doctor, John Helmcken.

What's Nearby?

Colonizing part of the Inner Harbour's landmark Steamship Terminal building, the **Robert Bateman Centre** (250-940-3630; www.batemancentre.org; 470 Belleville St; adult/child $10/6; 10am-5pm daily, to 9pm Fri & Sat Jun-Aug; 70) showcases the photo-realistic work of Canada's most celebrated nature painter, the eponymous Bateman, along with a revolving roster of works by other artists. Start with the five-minute intro movie, then check out the dozens of achingly beautiful paintings showing animals in their natural surroundings in BC and beyond.

Tofino

From resource outpost to hippie enclave to resort town and surfers' paradise, Tofino remains Vancouver Island's favorite outdoor retreat.

Great For...

☑ Don't Miss

Spending time at the beach – either with a board in the water or strolling the magnificent sands.

Surfing

Tofino's quartet of Pacific beaches are the pinnacle of surfing in Canada. They run north to south: Mackenzie Beach, North and South Chesterman, Cox Bay (*the* surfing beach in Tofino) and Long Beach. Check out **Pacific Surf School** (www.pacificsurfschool.com; 430 Campbell St; board rental 6/24hr $20/25) or **Surf Sister** (☎250-725-4456; www.surfsister.com; 625 Campbell St; lessons $89) for lessons and equipment.

Whale-Watching

The waters around Tofino are a great place to experience these graceful giants of the sea. Whale-watching trips run year-round, but they're ramped up between March and October. Gray and humpback whales are common in Tofino's waters, with the occasional orca also sighted. Other mammals

BLAKE81 / GETTY IMAGES ©

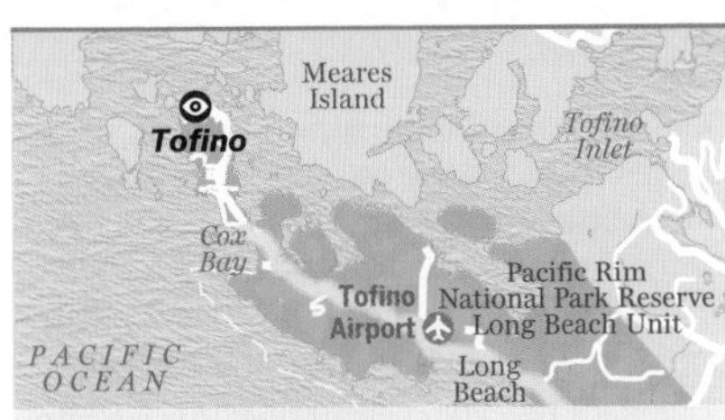

Need to Know

Tourism Tofino Visitor Centre (250-725-3414; www.tourismtofino.com; 1426 Pacific Rim Hwy; 9am-8pm Jun-Aug, reduced hours Sep-May)

Take a Break

Seasonally focused **Wolf in the Fog** (250-725-9653; www.wolfinthefog.com; 150 Fourth St; mains $21-45; 10am-late, dinner from 5pm) is destination dining at its finest.

Top Tip

The drive here is spectacular, but if you're pressed for time, Pacific Coastal Airlines (www.pacificcoastal.com) has flights from Vancouver.

include sea lions and – along the island's shorelines – black bears.

Prices hover at around $109 for three-hour trips. **Jamie's Whaling Station** (250-725-3919; www.jamies.com; 606 Campbell St; adult/child $109/79) is an established operator.

Storm-Watching

Started as a clever marketing ploy to lure off-season visitors, storm-watching has become a popular reason to visit the island's wild west coast between November and March. View spectacularly crashing winter waves, then scamper back inside for hot chocolate with a face freckled by sea salt. The best spots to catch a few crashing spectacles are Cox Bay, Chesterman Beach, Long Beach, Second Bay and Wickaninnish Beach.

Meares Island

Visible through the mist and accessible via kayak or tour boat from the Tofino waterfront, Meares Island is home to the Big Tree Trail, a 4.2km loop through old-growth forest that includes a stunning 1500-year-old red cedar. The island was the site of the key 1984 Clayoquot Sound anti-logging protest that kicked off the region's latter-day environmental movement.

Roy Henry Vickers Gallery

Showcasing the work of world-renowned First Nations artist Roy Henry Vickers, this dramatic, longhouse-style **gallery** (250-725-3235; www.royhenryvickers.com; 350 Campbell St; 10am-5pm) FREE is a downtown landmark. Inside you'll find beautifully presented paintings and carvings as well as occasional opportunities to meet the man himself.

Victoria

Double-decker buses, afternoon tea, homes that look like castles, and pubs with names like the Sticky Wicket and the Penny Farthing... Victoria has long traded on its British affiliations. But while the fish and chips remain first class and summer cricket games still enliven Beacon Hill Park, the days when Victoria was more British than Britain are long gone. In Victoria 2.0, the food culture embraces fusion, the beer leans toward craft brews and the abundance of bicycles seems to have more in common with Holland than England.

SIGHTS

Craigdarroch Castle Museum

(250-592-5323; www.thecastle.ca; 1050 Joan Cres; adult/child $14.60/5.10; 9am-7pm mid-Jun–early Sep, 10am-4:30pm early Sep–mid-Jun; P; 14) More ostentatious country mansion than fortified castle, Craigdarroch, with its turrets, stained-glass windows and palatial interior, looks like it might have been teleported over from the Scottish Highlands. Beautifully preserved by a local historical society, the interior is filled with rich period detail and is notable for its spectacular wood-paneled staircase, which ascends from the entry vestibule. You'll need at least an hour to admire the four floors of rooms, including a dining room, smoking room, billiard room and dance hall.

Miniature World Museum

(250-385-9731; www.miniatureworld.com; 649 Humboldt St; adult/child $16/8; 9am-9pm mid-May–mid-Sep, to 5pm mid-Sep–mid-May; ; 70) Tucked along the side of the Fairmont Empress Hotel, this huge collection of skillfully crafted models depicting important battles, historic towns and popular stories is far more fascinating than it sounds. Lined with dozens of diminutive diorama scenes, divided into themes ranging from Camelot to space and from fairyland to Olde England, it has plenty of push-button action, several trundling trains and the chance to see yourself on a miniature movie-theater screen. An immaculately maintained reminder of innocent yesteryear attractions.

Craigdarroch Castle

Parliament Buildings Historic Building
(☎250-387-3046; www.leg.bc.ca; 501 Belleville St; ⊙tours 9am-5pm mid-May–Aug, from 8:30am Mon-Fri Sep–mid-May; 🚌70) FREE This dramatically handsome confection of turrets, domes and stained glass is British Columbia's working legislature and is also open to visitors. You can go behind the facade on a free 45-minute guided tour then stop for lunch at the 'secret' politicians' **restaurant** (☎250-387-3959; mains $9-18; ⊙8am-3pm Mon-Thu, to 2pm Fri; 🚌70) inside. Return in the evening when the elegant exterior is illuminated like a Christmas tree.

Victoria Bug Zoo Zoo
(☎250-384-2847; www.victoriabugzoo.com; 631 Courtney St; adult/child $12/8; ⊙10am-5pm Mon-Fri, to 6pm Sat & Sun, reduced hours Sep-May; 👪; 🚌70) It's not big, nor are its resident critters (although some of them are alarmingly colossal by insect standards); however, this diminutive indoor 'zoo' is a small marvel thanks to the enthusiasm and knowledge of its guides. Atlas beetles, dragon-headed crickets and thorny devils are all explained, admired and – on occasion – lifted out of their tanks to be handed around for closer inspection. Children are the main audience, but this is a hugely entertaining and educational experience on any level.

TOURS

Pedaler Cycling
(☎778-265-7433; www.thepedaler.ca; 321 Belleville St; tours from $50, rentals per day $30; ⊙9am-6pm, reduced hours Nov–mid-Mar) Pedaler offers bike rentals and several guided two-wheeled tours around the city, including the 'Hoppy Hour Ride' with its craft-beer-sampling focus. Get kitted out with a sturdy hybrid at the office in the 'olde' Huntingdon Manor building and go explore the Galloping Goose Trail. Helmets, locks and rain ponchos are thrown in.

Galloping Goose Trail

Victoria's best-loved **trail** follows the grade of an old railway line and is named for a train carriage that rattled through these parts in the early 20th century. As a result, the trail is flat, passable on a hybrid bike, and flecked with remnants of Vancouver Island's pioneering railroad history, including several trestles and a smattering of explanatory boards.

The first 13km is on concrete and relatively urban. Further west, the trail becomes increasingly rural, with pastoral sections interspersing with woodland and regular glimpses of water (both bays and lakes).

GENE LEE / SHUTTERSTOCK ©

Eagle Wing Tours Whale-Watching
(☎250-384-8008; www.eaglewingtours.ca; 12 Erie St, Fisherman's Wharf; adult/child from $115/75; ⊙Mar-Oct) Popular and long-established operator of whale-watching boat tours.

Discover the Past Walking
(☎250-384-6698; www.discoverthepast.com; adult/child $20/15; ⊙Fri-Sun Nov-May, daily Jun-Oct) This outfit's Chinatown Walks tour is the best way to explore the stories behind one of the city's oldest neighborhoods. It also offers ghost-walk and other history-walk options.

Harbour Air Scenic Flights
(☎250-384-2215; www.harbourair.com; 950 Wharf St; tours from $119) For a bird's-eye

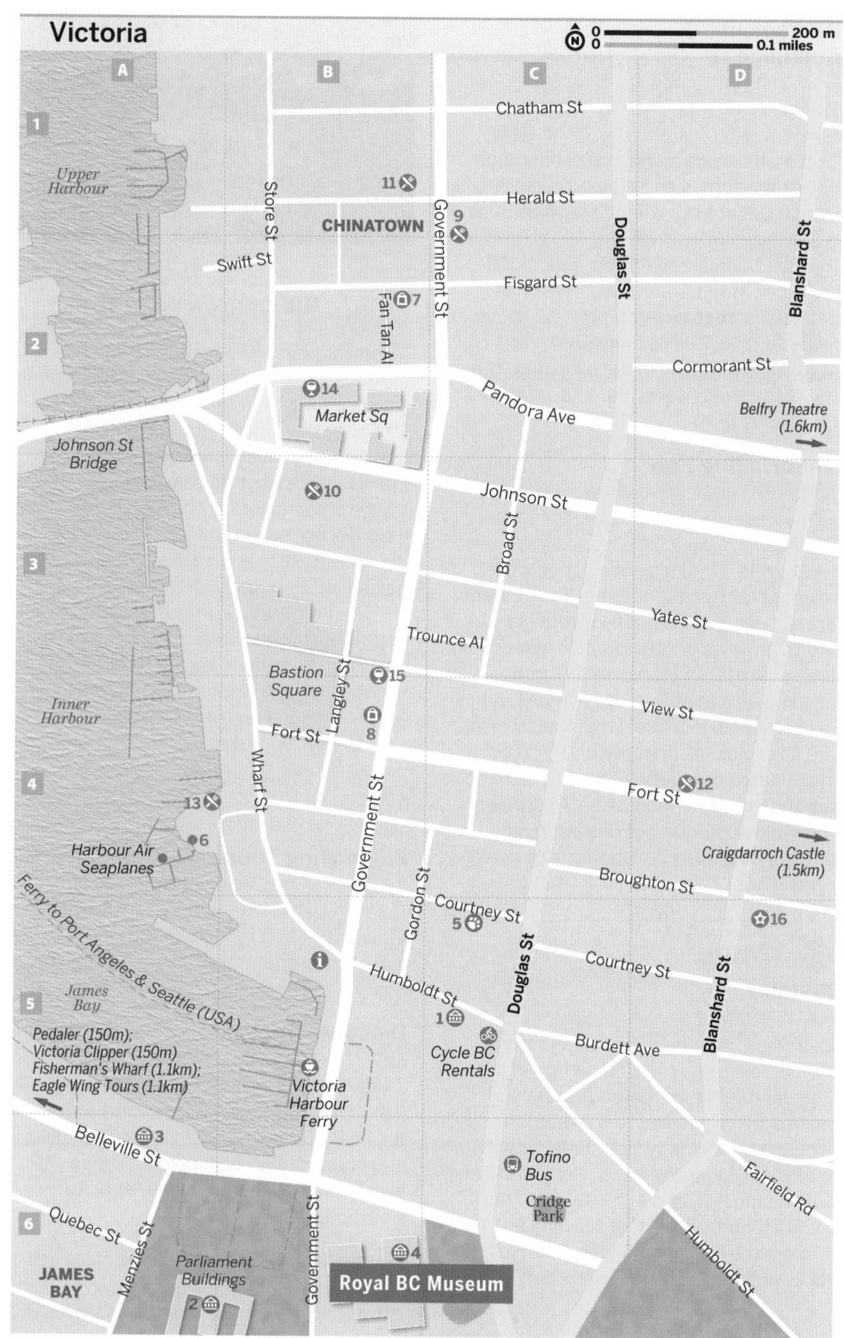
Victoria
0 200 m
0 0.1 miles
A
B
C
D
1
2
3
4
5
6
Chatham St
Upper Harbour
11
Herald St
Store St
CHINATOWN
Government St
9
Douglas St
Blanshard St
Swift St
Fisgard St
7
Fan Tan Al
Cormorant St
14
Pandora Ave
Belfry Theatre (1.6km)
Market Sq
Johnson St Bridge
10
Johnson St
Broad St
Yates St
Trounce Al
Bastion Square
15
Langley St
View St
Inner Harbour
Fort St
8
Wharf St
12
Fort St
13
6
Harbour Air Seaplanes
Craigdarroch Castle (1.5km)
Broughton St
Gordon St
Courtney St
5
16
Ferry to Port Angeles & Seattle (USA)
Courtney St
Humboldt St
James Bay
1
Cycle BC Rentals
Burdett Ave
Pedaler (150m);
Victoria Clipper (150m)
Fisherman's Wharf (1.1km);
Eagle Wing Tours (1.1km)
Victoria Harbour Ferry
3
Belleville St
Tofino Bus
Cridge Park
Fairfield Rd
Quebec St
Menzies St
Government St
4
Humboldt St
JAMES BAY
Parliament Buildings
2
Royal BC Museum

Victoria

Sights
1 Miniature World C5
2 Parliament Buildings A6
3 Robert Bateman Centre A6
4 Royal BC Museum B6
5 Victoria Bug Zoo C5

Activities, Courses & Tours
6 Harbour Air A4

Shopping
7 Fantan Trading Ltd B2
8 Munro's Books B4

Eating
9 Brasserie L'École C1
10 Il Terrazzo B3
11 Jam Cafe B1
12 La Taqueria D4
Legislative Dining Room .... (see 2)
13 Red Fish Blue Fish A4

Drinking & Nightlife
14 Drake B2
15 Garrick's Head Pub B3

Entertainment
IMAX Theatre .... (see 4)
Pacific Opera Victoria .... (see 16)
16 Royal Theatre D5

Victoria view, these floatplane tours from the Inner Harbour are fab, especially when they dive-bomb the water on landing.

SHOPPING

Munro's Books Books

(250-382-2464; www.munrobooks.com; 1108 Government St; 9am-6pm Mon-Wed, to 9pm Thu-Sat, 9:30am-6pm Sun; 70) The name is no coincidence. Victoria's cathedral to reading was established in 1963 by Nobel-prize-winning Canadian author Alice Munro and her husband Jim. Encased in a heritage building on the city's famous Government St, it's an obligatory pilgrimage for bibliophiles with its high ceilings, wide array of local-interest tomes and well-read staff, some of whom have worked here for decades.

Fantan Trading Ltd Homewares

(250-381-8882; 551 Fisgard St; 11am-5pm; 70) A labyrinthine Chinatown store hawking everything from paper lanterns to fake bonsai trees. It's hard not to find something to buy here.

EATING

Red Fish Blue Fish Seafood $

(250-298-6877; www.redfish-bluefish.com; 1006 Wharf St; mains $6-18; 11am-7pm Mar-Oct; 70) On the waterfront boardwalk at the foot of Broughton St, this freight-container takeout shack serves fresh-made, finger-licking sustainable seafood. Highlights include jerk fish poutine, amazing chowder and tempura-battered oysters (you can also get traditional fish and chips, of course). Expanded new seating has added to the appeal but watch out for hovering gull mobsters as you try to eat. Closed in winter.

La Taqueria Mexican $

(778-265-6255; www.lataqueria.com; 766 Fort St; tacos up to $3; 11am-8:30pm Mon-Sat, noon-6pm Sun; ; 14) A huge, aquamarine-painted satellite of Vancouver's popular and authentic Mexican joint, this ultra-friendly spot specializes in offering a wide array of soft-taco options (choose four for $10.50, less for vegetarian), including different specials every day. Quesadillas are also available and you can wash everything down with margaritas, Mexican beer or mezcal – or all three.

Jam Cafe Breakfast $$

(778-440-4489; http://jamcafes.com; 542 Herald St; breakfast $13-17; 8am-3pm; ; 70) No need to conduct an opinion poll: the perennial lines in the street outside Jam suggest that this is the best breakfast spot in Victoria. The reasons? Tasteful vintage

Butchart Gardens

Far more than just another pretty flower arrangement, **Butchart** (☎250-652-5256; www.butchartgardens.com; 800 Benvenuto Ave; adult/teen/child $33.80/16.90/3; ⏲8:45am-10pm Jun-Aug, reduced hours Sep-May; 🚌75) is a National Historic Site and a triumph of early-20th-century gardening aesthetics. With its well-tended blooms, ornate fountains and diverse international flavor (from Japanese to Italian), it's hard to imagine that this land was once an abandoned limestone quarry.

The gardens were the brainchild of Jennie Butchart, whose husband founded the quarry. She began planting and landscaping over the old quarry site in 1912. Expanded and manicured throughout the course of a century, the site now counts over one million blooms to cater for its one million annual visitors. Passed down through several generations, the gardens are still owned by the Butchart family.

Food outlets and gift shops crowd the entrance, including the **Dining Room Restaurant**, which serves a smashing afternoon tea.

Located in Brentwood Bay, a 30-minute drive from Victoria, Butchart is open year-round, although summer is, arguably, the best (and busiest) season to visit: there are Saturday-night fireworks in July and August. The Christmas-lights season from early December to early January is another highlight.

decor (if you'll excuse them the moose's head); fast, discreet service; and the kind of creative breakfast dishes that you'd never have the energy or ingenuity to cook yourself.

Jam classics include the 'cracker jack' (a banana-and-nutella brioche sandwich), the 'three pigs' (sausages fried in pancake batter) and the naan burrito (eggs, goat's cheese, avocado and spices). It's first-come, first-served, so join the line.

Brasserie L'École French $$$

(☎250-475-6260; www.lecole.ca; 1715 Government St; mains $20-50; ⏲5:30-10pm Tue-Thu, to 11pm Fri & Sat; 🚌70) *Bonsoir!* You may have just arrived at the best restaurant in Victoria, a small but wonderfully elegant bistro discreetly furnished in *la mode français,* but without any of the infamous Parisian pretension. Service is warm and impeccable, and the renditions of classic French dishes are exquisitely executed. *Moules frites* (mussels and fries), duck confit and superb Bordeaux wines all hit the spot.

Il Terrazzo Italian $$$

(☎250-361-0028; www.ilterrazzo.com; 555 Johnson St; mains $21-44; ⏲11:30am-3pm & 5pm-late Mon-Fri, 5pm-late Sat & Sun; 🚌24) Authentic Italian flavors melded with a laid-back Victoria spirit make a devastatingly good combo. If you don't believe us, come to Il Terrazzo, a restaurant that's as much about its atmosphere and service as it is about its Italian-inspired, locally nurtured food. Aside from the usual suspects (seafood linguine, margherita pizza), there is a handful of more unusual renditions.

DRINKING & NIGHTLIFE

Drake Bar

(☎250-590-9075; www.drakeeatery.com; 517 Pandora Ave; ⏲11:30am-midnight; 📶; 🚌70) Victoria's best tap house, this redbrick hangout has more than 30 amazing craft drafts, typically including revered BC producers Townsite, Driftwood and Four Winds. Arrive on a rainy afternoon and you'll find yourself still here several hours later. Food-wise, the smoked tuna club is a top seller but the cheese and meat boards are ideal for grazing.

Garrick's Head Pub Pub
(250-384-6835; www.garrickshead.com; 66 Bastion Sq; 11am-late; 70) A great spot to dive into BC's brilliant craft-beer scene. Pull up a seat at the long bar with its 55-plus taps – a comprehensive menu of beers from Driftwood, Phillips, Hoyne and beyond. There are always 10 rotating lines with intriguing tipples (ask for samples) plus a comfort-grub menu of burgers and such to line your boozy stomach.

ENTERTAINMENT

Belfry Theatre Theater
(250-385-6815; www.belfry.bc.ca; 1291 Gladstone Ave; 22) The celebrated Belfry Theatre showcases contemporary plays in its lovely former church-building venue, a 20-minute stroll from downtown.

Royal Theatre Theater
(888-717-6121; www.rmts.bc.ca; 805 Broughton St; 70) The Royal Theatre hosts mainstream stage productions in its rococo interior, and is home to the **Victoria Symphony** (250-385-6515; www.victoriasymphony.ca) and **Pacific Opera Victoria** (250-385-0222; www.pov.bc.ca).

INFORMATION

Tourism Victoria Visitor Centre (250-953-2033; www.tourismvictoria.com; 812 Wharf St; 8:30am-8:30pm mid-May–Aug, 9am-5pm Sep–mid-May; 70) Tons of brochures, plenty of staff, ample help.

GETTING THERE & AWAY

AIR

Harbour Air (250-384-2215; www.harbourair.com; 950 Wharf St) flies into the Inner Harbour from downtown Vancouver ($242, 30 minutes) throughout the day.

Red Fish Blue Fish (p239)

Cathedral Grove

CHRISTIAN KOBER / SHUTTERSTOCK ©

> *centuries-old Douglas firs more than 3m in diameter*

Victoria International Airport (☎250-953-7500; www.victoriaairport.com) is 26km north of the city via Hwy 17. Frequent Air Canada (www.aircanada.com) flights arrive from Vancouver ($193, 25 minutes) and Calgary ($285, 1¾ hours). WestJet (www.westjet.com) offers similar services. Alaska Airlines (www.alaskaair.com) links to Seattle (US$246, 45 minutes) five times a week.

BOAT

BC Ferries (☎250-386-3431; www.bcferries.com) Runs large car ferries from mainland Tsawwassen (adult/vehicle $17.20/57.50, 1½ hours) to Swartz Bay, 33km north of Victoria via Hwy 17. Services run eight to 12 times a day.

Victoria Clipper (☎250-382-8100; www.clippervacations.com) Has a dock in the Inner Harbour from where it runs a passenger-only catamaran to and from Seattle (adult/child US$124/74, three hours, up to two daily).

BUS

With Greyhound no longer serving Vancouver Island, the best transportation company is **Tofino Bus** (☎250-725-2871; www.tofinobus.com), which runs three daily services via Nanaimo ($33, two hours) to all points north as far as Campbell River ($65, 5¼ hours) with bus 1 carrying on to Port Hardy ($115, nine hours). A separate service runs to and from Tofino ($75, 6½ hours, one daily) via Port Alberni ($60, 4½ hours, two daily).

Frequent **BC Ferries Connector** (☎778-265-9474; www.bcfconnector.com) services, via the ferry, arrive from Vancouver (from $49.50, 3½ hours) and Vancouver International Airport ($58, four hours).

GETTING AROUND

BICYCLE

Victoria is a great cycling capital, with routes crisscrossing the city and beyond. Check the website of the Greater Victoria Cycling Coalition (www.gvcc.bc.ca) for local resources. Bike rentals are offered by **Cycle BC Rentals** (☎250-380-2453; www.cyclebc.ca; 685 Humboldt St;

per hour/day $8/28; 10am-4pm; 1) or Pedaler (p237).

BOAT

Victoria Harbour Ferry (250-708-0201; www.victoriaharbourferry.com; fares from $7; Mar-Oct) calls in at over a dozen docks around the Inner Harbour and beyond with its colorful armada of little boats.

BUS

Victoria Regional Transit (www.bctransit.com/victoria) buses (single fare/day pass $2.50/5) cover a wide area from Sidney to Sooke, with some routes served by modern-day double-deckers. Children under five travel free.

Buses 70 and 72 link downtown with the Swartz Bay Ferry Terminal. Bus 75 goes to Butchart Gardens. Bus 61 goes to Sooke.

Port Alberni

With resource jobs declining, Alberni – located on Hwy 4 between the island's east and west coasts – has been dipping its toe into tourism in recent years. And while the downtown core is a little run-down, there are some good historical attractions and outdoor activities to consider before you drive on through.

SIGHTS

Alberni Valley Museum Museum

(250-723-2181; www.alberniheritage.com; 4255 Wallace St; by donation; 10am-5pm Tue-Sat, to 8pm Thu) Don't be put off by the unassuming concrete exterior: this is one of Vancouver Island's best community museums. Studded with fascinating First Nations displays – plus an eclectic array of vintage exhibits ranging from bottle caps to dresses and old-school toys – it's worth an hour of anyone's time.

History buffs should also hop aboard the summertime **Alberni Pacific Railway steam train** (www.alberniheritage.com/alberni-pacific-railway), likewise operated by the Alberni Valley Heritage Network, for a trundle to McLean Mill; it's a National Historic Site.

Cathedral Grove Park

(www.bcparks.ca; MacMillan Provincial Park; P) This spiritual home of tree-huggers is the mystical highlight of **MacMillan Provincial Park**. Located between Parksville and Port Alberni, it's often overrun with summer visitors – try not to knock them down as they scamper across the highway in front of you. Short accessible trails on either side of the road wind through a dense canopy of vegetation, offering glimpses of some of BC's oldest trees, including centuries-old Douglas firs more than 3m in diameter. Only huggable in groups.

ACTIVITIES

MV Frances Barkley Cruise

(250-723-8313; www.ladyrosemarine.com; 5425 Argyle St; round-trip Bamfield/Ucluelet $84/88) This historic boat service is a vital link for the region's remote communities, ferrying freight, supplies and passengers between Alberni and Bamfield thrice weekly. In summer, with its route extended to Ucluelet and the utterly beautiful Broken Group Islands, it lures kayakers and mountain bikers – as well as those who just fancy an idyllic day cruise up Barkley Sound.

EATING

Mountain View Bakery & Deli Bakery $

(250-724-1813; 4561 Gertrude St; snacks $4-10; 7:30am-6pm Tue-Sat) If you're making a transportation connection in Port Alberni, pray you have time to dash across the road to this traditional bakery with a huge selection of pies, samosas, wraps, sandwiches, pastries, brownies, cheesecakes, muffins, buns and...there goes your bus!

GETTING THERE & AWAY

Tofino Bus (866-986-3466; www.tofinobus.com; 4541 Margaret St) services arrive here from Victoria ($60, 4½ hours, two daily) and Tofino ($36, 2½ hours, two daily), among other places.

HAIDA GWAII

In this Chapter

Haida Gwaii at a glance...

The bewitching Haida Gwaii is a lush archipelago of some 450 islands lying 80km west of the BC coast. The number-one attraction is remote Gwaii Haanas National Park, nicknamed 'Canada's Galápagos' and brimming with unique species of flora and fauna. The real soul of the islands, however, is the Haida culture itself. Haida reverence for the environment is protecting the last stands of superb old-growth rain forests, where the spruce and cedars are some of the world's largest. Amid this sparsely populated, wild and rainy place are bald eagles and bears, while offshore, sea lions, whales and orcas abound.

One Day in Haida Gwaii

Get your culture fix at the **Haida Heritage Centre** in Skidegate. Head north through the dense forest toward Masset, exploring the small towns of Tlell and Port Clements en route and hiking along the **Golden Spruce Trail** (p252). In Masset, explore the **Dixon Entrance Maritime Museum** (p252) and check out local artwork. Nail a beer and some pub grub at **Daddy Cool's Public House at Mile Zero** (p252).

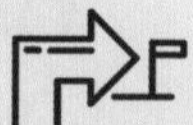

Two Days in Haida Gwaii

Start your second day with some breakfast and your caffeinated beverage of choice from **Jags Beanstalk Bistro & Beds** (p252), then join a full-day boat tour with **Haida Style Expeditions** (p251) to see the highlights of **Gwaii Haanas National Park Reserve**, including cultural sites and a traditional Haida feast.

Previous page: Haida Gwaii forest stream

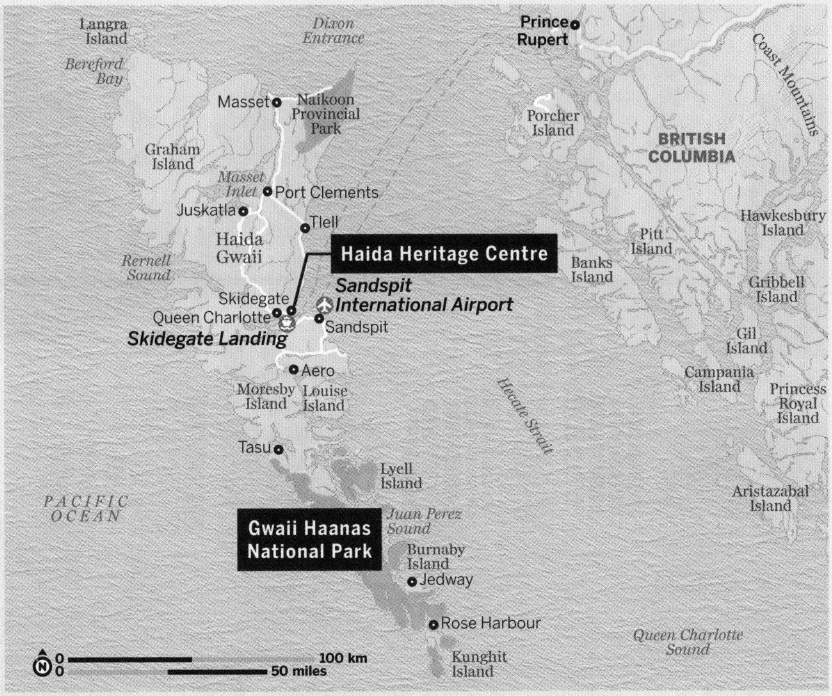

Arriving in Haida Gwaii

Sandspit International Airport Located on Moresby Island, 12km east of the ferry landing at Aliford Bay. There are daily Air Canada flights from Vancouver.

Skidegate Landing BC Ferries from Prince Rupert dock here on Graham Island.

Where to Stay

Small inns and B&Bs are mostly found on Graham Island. There are numerous choices in Queen Charlotte (QCC) and Masset, with many in between and along the spectacular north coast. Naikoon Provincial Park has two campgrounds, including a dramatic, windswept one on deserted Agate Beach, 23km east of Masset.

Haida Heritage Centre

One of the top attractions in the north, the marvelous Heritage Centre at Kay Llnagaay celebrates the rich traditions and living culture of the Haida.

Great For...

☑ Don't Miss

The remarkable model of Skidegate before colonial times.

Totem Poles

Even if you're not lucky enough to see one being carved, a tour of the center's iconic totem poles will fill you in on the animals, crests and stories that they tell.

Endangered Language

The Haida language, X̱aayda Kil, is both tricky and beautiful. One of the 52 First Nations languages in Canada, it is unique in both its sound and construction and not closely related to any other language. Originally it was spoken only by the Haida on Haida Gwaii, but it spread with those who moved north to Prince of Wales Island in southeast Alaska.

A century ago, virtually all Haida were fluent in X̱aayda Kil. These days, it is believed that there are fewer than 50 fluent

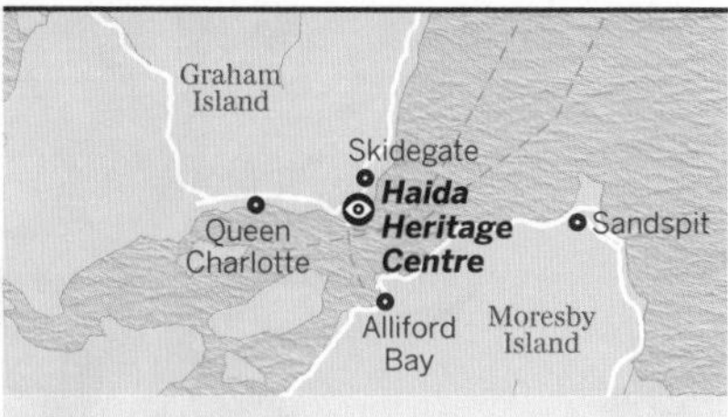

Need to Know

250-559-7885; www.haidaheritagecentre.com; Second Beach Rd. Hwy 16, Skidegate; adult/child $16/5; 9am-5pm Jul & Aug, reduced hours Sep-Jun

Take a Break

Stop for lunch at the center's Kay Bistro, where the food rivals the sea views.

★ Top Tip

In summer, join worthwhile free tours of the collection, and talks and walks by Parks Canada rangers.

speakers left, the majority of whom are 70 years of age or older. Recently, there has been a resurgence of interest by younger Haidas to learn their language, with classes, camps and dictionaries being created. The Heritage Centre works hard to both preserve, use and share the language and you'll have ample opportunity to encounter it in the displays and on tours.

Canoe-Building

For the Haida, creating a canoe is more than just boat-building. It reflects their connection with the sea and is a revered art. The giant cedars of Haida Gwaii make excellent vessels and the Haida were known up and down the coast for their seafaring canoes. The tree would need to be large enough to fit numerous men and selection was incredibly important. The outside was first carved, then the inside burned away. Hot water was used to make the wood more malleable for shaping. The beauty of the canoes made them prized possessions sought after by chiefs of other tribes. For the Haida, the canoes brought great strength for transportation, trade, fishing and war.

With the catastrophic arrival of smallpox to Haida Gwaii in 1862, up to 70% of the Haida population was obliterated. With them went much of the cultural knowledge. The revival of canoe building in the 1990s was done through knowledge passed down through oral storytelling, through photographs, and with the discovery of a partially dug out canoe deep in the Haida Gwaii rainforest. Today you can witness the creation of canoes at the Heritage Centre and join a Canoe Chat to learn about the cultural significance of these stunning vessels.

Skedans

Gwaii Haanas National Park Reserve

This huge Unesco World Heritage site – also a marine reserve and Haida heritage site – encompasses Moresby and 137 smaller islands at its southern end.

Great For...

☑ Don't Miss

G̱andll K'in Gwaayaay (Hot-Water Island) with its stunning hot springs along the coast.

The park combines a time-capsule look at abandoned Haida villages alongside hot springs, amazing natural beauty and some of the continent's best kayaking.

Cultural Heritage

Archaeological finds have documented more than 500 ancient Haida sites, including villages and burial caves throughout the islands. The most famous village is SGang Gwaay (Ninstints) on Anthony Island, where rows of weathered totem poles stare eerily out to sea. Other major sights include the ancient village of Skedans, on Louise Island, and Hotspring Island, the natural hot springs of which are back on after being disrupted by earthquakes in 2012. The sites are protected by Haida Gwaii caretakers, who live on the islands in summer.

NATIONAL GEOGRAPHIC IMAGE COLLECTION / ALAMY STOCK PHOTO ©

Need to Know

250-559-8818; www.pc.gc.ca/en/pn-np/bc/gwaiihaanas

Take a Break

Bring everything you need to stay nourished and pack out your garbage; there are no food outlets in the reserve.

★ Top Tip

Parks Canada can provide plenty of information, along with lists of local tour operators.

Legacy Pole

In 2013 the magnificent Gwaii Haanas Legacy Pole was raised at Windy Bay, the first new pole in the protected area in 130 years.

Visiting

Access to the park is by boat or plane only. To visit independently, you must make a reservation, pay a visitor use fee (adult/child $20/free per day) and attend a 90-minute orientation. The number of daily reservations is limited, so plan well in advance, especially for the busiest period of July to mid-August. Details of the requirements are on the excellent Parks Canada website, which has links to the essential annual trip planner. The Parks Canada office is next to the Haida Heritage Centre at Kay Llnagaay.

Joining a Tour

Many people visit the park with a guide. Tours last from one day to two weeks. Many operators can also set you up with rental kayaks (average per day/week $60/300) and gear for independent travel.

Haida Style Expeditions (250-637-1151; www.haidastyle.com; Second Beach Rd/Hwy 16, Skidegate; tours per person from $250; Apr-Sep) lets you buzz through the reserve in a large inflatable boat. This Haida-run outfit runs four different one-day tours (eight to 12 hours) that together take in the most important sights in the park.

Archipelago Ventures (250-652-4913, 888-559-8317; www.tourhaidagwaii.com; 6-day tours from $3360) runs multiday kayak trips that fully explore the reserve. Guests are housed on the mothership MV *Island Bay*, which is run like a small community. Itineraries are flexible.

Queen Charlotte, Skidegate & Masset

Haida Gwaii, which means 'Islands of the People,' lies 80km west of the BC coast, and about 50km from the southern tip of Alaska. The principal town is Graham Island's Queen Charlotte (previously Queen Charlotte City and still known by its old QCC acronym), 6km west of the ferry dock at Skidegate Landing. Graham Island is linked to Moresby Island to the south by ferry from Skidegate Landing.

Haida Gwaii was formerly known as the Queen Charlotte Islands, the name of which was officially dropped in 2010.

SIGHTS

Monumental poles (*gyaa'aang*) can be seen all over Haida Gwaii. One of the newest and most impressive was raised outside the new Haida Gwaii Hospital in Queen Charlotte in 2018. After the Haida carve, dance and raise them, the *gyaa'aang* are considered to be living community members.

The Haida Gwaii portion of the **Yellowhead Hwy** (Hwy 16) heads 110km north from Queen Charlotte past Skidegate, Tlell and Port Clements. Officially, Mile 0 for the Yellowhead Hwy is at Masset and it runs all the way to Winnepeg, Manitoba.

Near Port Clements was where a golden spruce tree, famous for its color, was cut down by a demented forester in 1997. The incident is detailed in the best-selling *The Golden Spruce* by John Vaillant, an excellent book on the islands and Haida culture.

Just south of Port Clements is the excellent **Golden Spruce Trail** (30 minutes return) through moss-covered forest featuring huge red cedar and Sitka spruce to the Yakoun River. Across the river is where the legendary Golden Spruce used to stand. To get to the trailhead, carry on through Port Clements on Bayview Dr, then for 3.5km on the gravel road.

Naikoon Provincial Park Park

(☎250-626-5115; www.env.gov.bc.ca/bcparks; off Hwy 16) Much of the island's northeastern side is devoted to the beautiful 726-sq-km Naikoon Provincial Park, which combines sand dunes and low sphagnum bogs, surrounded by stunted and gnarled lodgepole pine, and red and yellow cedar. The starkly beautiful **beaches** on the north coast feature strong winds, pounding surf and flotsam from across the Pacific. They can be reached via the stunning 26km-long Tow Hill Rd, east of Masset.

Dixon Entrance Maritime Museum Museum

(☎250-626-6066; www.massetbc.com/visitors/maritime-museum; 2183 Collinson Ave, Masset; adult/child $3/free; ⏱1-6pm daily Jun-Aug, 2-4pm Sat & Sun Sep-May) Housed in what was once the local hospital, the museum features exhibits on the history of this seafaring community, with displays on shipbuilding, medical pioneers, military history, and nearby clam and crab canneries. Local artists also exhibit work here.

EATING & DRINKING

The best selection of restaurants is in Queen Charlotte, and there are also a few in Skidegate and Masset. There is a simple pub with food in Port Clements. Good supermarkets are found in QCC and Masset.

Jags Beanstalk Bistro & Beds Canadian $

(☎250-559-8826; www.jagsbeanstalk.com; 100 16 Hwy, Skidegate; mains from $10; ⏱7:30am-4pm Mon-Fri, 9am-4pm Sat) Fresh, wholesome food delivered with speedy, friendly service about 1.5km north of the ferry terminal. Great coffee, pizzas, tacos and salads, with an effort to source ingredients locally. It also has cozy guest rooms above the coffee shop.

Daddy Cool's Public House at Mile Zero Pub

(☎250-626-3210; www.daddycools.ca; Collison Ave, Masset; ⏱9am-2am, hours can vary) You can't go wrong at Daddy Cool's in Masset, with a popular pub on one side and a quiet dining room specializing in pub grub on the other. The eating side is family-friendly, while the pub side usually stays open until everyone has gone home. These guys are onto it and also run a liquor store and a taxi service.

 INFORMATION

Download, browse online or pick up a free copy of the encyclopedic annual *Haida Gwaii Visitors Guide* (www.gohaidagwaii.ca). Cell-phone coverage is good in some locations, iffy in others and nonexistent on much of Haida Gwaii.

Parks Canada (250-559-8818, reservations 877-559-8818; www.pc.gc.ca/en/pn-np/bc/gwaiihaanas; Haida Heritage Centre at Kay Llnagaay, Skidegate; 8:30am-noon & 1-4:30pm Mon-Fri) Main Parks Canada office for Haida Gwaii. Download the Gwaii Haanas National Park trip planner from the website.

Queen Charlotte Visitor Centre (250-559-8316; www.queencharlottevisitorcentre.com; 3220 Wharf St, QCC; 9am-7pm Mon-Sat, noon-6pm Sun May-Sep, shorter hours other times;) Handy visitor center that can make advance excursion bookings by phone.

 GETTING THERE & AWAY

AIR

The main airport for Haida Gwaii is at Sandspit on Moresby Island, 12km east of the ferry landing at Aliford Bay. Note that reaching the airport from Graham Island is time-consuming: eg if your flight is at 3:30pm, you'll need to line up at the car ferry at Skidegate Landing at 12:30pm (earlier in summer). Air Canada (www.aircanada.com) flies daily between Sandspit and Vancouver.

There's also a small airport 2km east of Masset that has daily flights from Vancouver with Pacific Coastal Air (www.pacificcoastal.com). Daily seaplane services between Prince Rupert and Masset are flown by Inland Air (www.inlandair.bc.ca).

FERRY

BC Ferries (250-386-3431; www.bcferries.com) is the most popular way to reach the islands. Mainland ferries dock at Skidegate Landing on Graham Island, which houses 80% of residents. Services run between Prince Rupert and Skidegate Landing five times a week in summer and three times a week in winter (adult $39 to $48, children half-price, cars $139 to $169; six to seven hours). Cabins are useful for overnight schedules (from $90).

 GETTING AROUND

The main road on Graham Island is Hwy 16, the first part of the Yellowhead Hwy, which is fully paved. It links Skidegate with Masset, 101km north, passing the small towns of Tlell and Port Clements. Off paved Hwy 16, most roads are gravel or worse. There is no public transit.

BC Ferries, with its MV *Kwuna* car ferry, links Graham and Moresby Islands at Skidegate Landing and Alliford Bay (adult/child $11/5.50, cars from $25, 20 minutes, from 7am to 6pm).

Eagle Transit (250-559-4461, 877-747-4461; www.eagletransit.net; airport shuttle adult/child $30/15) buses meet Sandspit flights and serve Skidegate and Queen Charlotte.

Renting a car can cost roughly the same ($60 to $100 per day) as bringing one over on the ferry. Local companies include **Budget** (250-637-5688; www.budget.com; Sandspit Airport). There are several small, locally owned firms, but the number of rental cars on Haida Gwaii is limited, so think ahead.

You can rent bikes at the small **Sandspit Airport Visitor Center** (250-637-5362; Sandspit Airport; 9:30-11:30am & 1.30-4pm) for $30 per day. **Green Coast** (250-637-1093; www.gckayaking.com; 3302 Oceanview Dr, QCC; per day $30) rents bikes in Queen Charlotte, while **Masset Bikes** (250-626-8939; www.massetbikes.com; 1900 Towhill Rd, Masset; per day from $30) has a good selection of rentals at Masset Airport.

THE YUKON

In this Chapter

The Yukon at a glance...

This vast and thinly populated wilderness, where most four-legged species far outnumber humans, has a grandeur and beauty that needs to be seen up close. Few places in the world today have been so unchanged over the course of time.

Any visit to the Yukon will mean spending plenty of time outdoors: Canada's five tallest mountains and the world's largest ice fields below the Arctic are all within Kluane National Park. Get set to appreciate the bustle of Whitehorse and the offbeat vibe of Dawson City before you head off into the wilds beyond.

Two Days in the Yukon

Spend a day exploring Whitehorse (p262), taking in the museums and galleries, then indulge in some fantastic, locally sourced and creatively prepared food at **Antoinette's** (p262). On day two, get a taste of adventure and join a paddling excursion out onto the **Yukon River**. You'll feel like you've earned that pizza and beer at the **Dirty Northern Public House** (p263), and you may be lucky enough to catch a live act there as well.

Four Days in the Yukon

Head north to Dawson City and take in the **Klondike sites**. Join a **Goldbottom Tour** (p265) to try your hand at gold panning or immerse yourself in *Call of the Wild* lore at the **Jack London Museum** (p264). Stop by **Alchemy Cafe** (p265) for delicious vegetarian food and spend an evening (or two) at **Diamond Tooth Gertie's Gambling Hall** (p259) for some honky-tonk piano and dancing.

Previous page: Yukon River

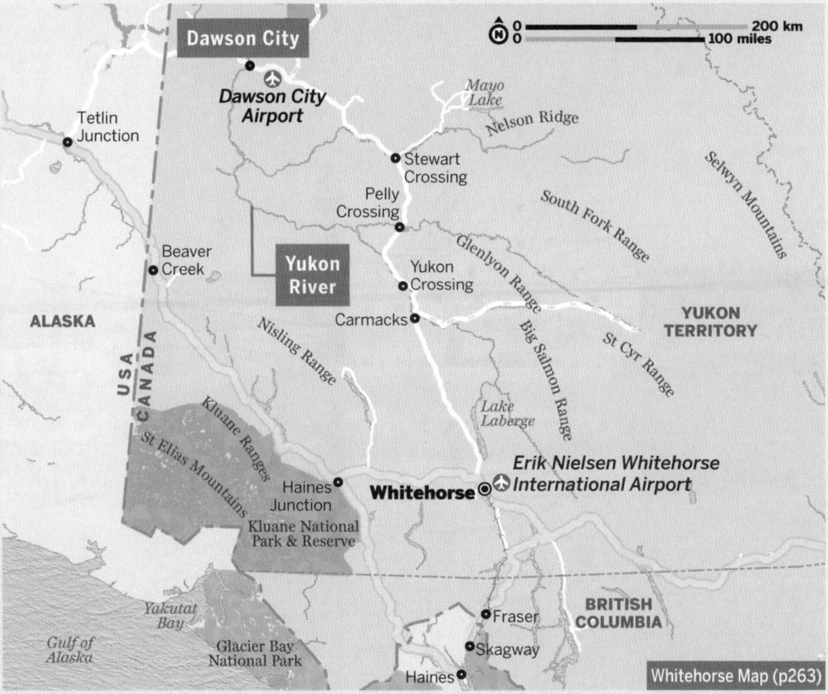

Whitehorse Map (p263)

Arriving in the Yukon

Erik Nielsen Whitehorse International Airport Services from Vancouver and Calgary; a taxi to the center (10 minutes) will cost around $22.

Dawson City Airport Air North serves Whitehorse and Old Crow, and Inuvik in the NWT.

Bus Husky Bus runs from Whitehorse to Dawson City thrice-weekly.

Train White Pass & Yukon Route offers a jaw-droppingly scenic daily 10-hour rail and bus connection between Whitehorse and Skagway, AK in season.

Where to Stay

Basic sleeping accommodations can be found at strategic points along the Alaska Hwy and other major roads. Whitehorse and Dawson have a range of good choices, including plenty of midrange motels, but both can get almost full during the peak of summer – book ahead. Many places in Dawson City will pick you up at the airport; ask in advance.

Gold dredge

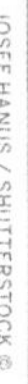

Dawson's Klondike History

The Klondike Gold Rush continues to be the defining moment for the Yukon. Certainly it was the population high point. Between 1896 and 1899, around 40,000 gold seekers hoped to strike it rich in the gold fields of Dawson City.

Great For...

☑ **Don't Miss**

Stopping in at **Harrington's Store** (cnr 3rd Ave & Princess St; 9:30am-8:30pm) FREE to see photos from Dawson's heyday.

The Gold Rush

From 1896, gold seekers washed ashore (some literally) in Skagway and made their way to Dawson City, some 700km north. To say that most were ill-prepared for the enterprise is an understatement. Although some were veterans of other gold rushes, a high percentage were American men who thought they'd just pop up North and get rich. The reality was different. Prospectors had to contend with scammers, trips over the frozen Chilkoot Pass with their 1000lb of gear, and building their own boats to cross the lakes and Yukon River to Dawson. Scores died trying.

There was another harsh reality awaiting in Dawson: by the summer of 1897 when the news of the discoveries on Bonanza Creek reached the US, the best sites had all been claimed. The Klondike gold-rush mobs were

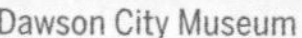
Dawson City Museum

PECOLD / SHUTTERSTOCK ©

mostly too late to the action by at least a year. Sick and broke, the survivors glumly made their way home.

Klondike National Historic Sites

It's easy to relive the gold rush at myriad preserved and restored **National Historic Sites** (☎867-993-7210; www.pc.gc.ca/dawson; Parks Canada passes adult $7-31). Parks Canada runs walking tours (p265) that allow access into various examples of the 26 restored buildings. Take several tours so you can see a wide variety. Outside of tours, various buildings, including the Palace Grand Theatre, are open for free on a rotating basis, usually from 4:30pm to 5:30pm.

Bonanza Creek Discovery Site

Up the valley from Dredge No 4, the **Bonanza Creek** (Bonanza Creek Rd) FREE National Historic Site is roughly where gold was first found in 1896. A fascinating 500m-long walk passes interpretive displays. Pick up a guide at the Visitor Center (p265).

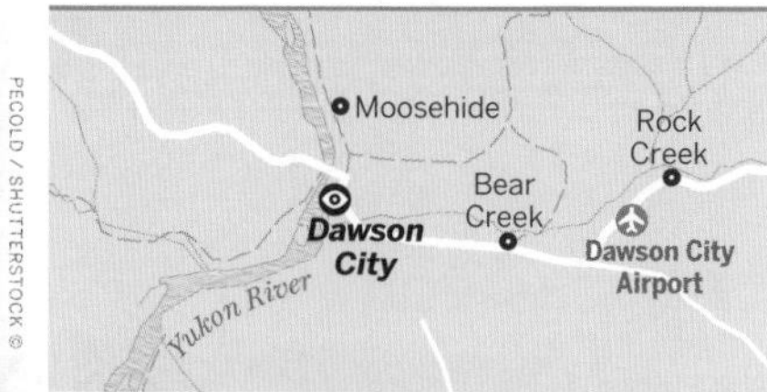

Need to Know

Unless noted otherwise, Dawson City sights, attractions and many businesses are closed outside of the summer high season.

Take a Break

Stop in at Klondike Kate's (p265) for top-notch home-cooking.

★ Top Tip

To really get a feel for those gold-rush days, join a Goldbottom Tour (p265) and try your hand at gold panning.

Diamond Tooth Gertie's Gambling Hall

A popular recreation of an 1898 saloon, **Gertie's** (☎867-993-5575; www.dawsoncity.ca; cnr Queen St & 4th Ave; $15; ⏰7pm-2am) is complete with small-time gambling, a honky-tonk piano and dancing girls. The casino helps promote the town and fund culture. Each night there are three different floor shows with singing and dancing.

Dawson City Museum

Make your own discoveries among the 25,000 gold-rush artifacts at this **museum** (☎867-993-5291; www.dawsonmuseum.ca; 595 5th Ave; adult/child $9/7; ⏰10am-6pm May-Aug). Engaging exhibits walk you through the grim lives of the miners. The museum is housed in the landmark 1901 Old Territorial Administration building.

Paddle the Yukon River

Canoe expeditions down the Yukon River are epic. Paddle past Klondike-era cabins, gold dredges on the banks, bears fishing, and moose lapping up the cold water.

Great For...

☑ **Don't Miss**

Trying your luck with a fishing rod – perhaps you'll hook an arctic grayling or a great northern pike.

Most canoeing and kayaking trips begin in Whitehorse and head to Carmacks or on to Dawson City, ranging from eight to 16 days of wilderness camping. Outfitters offer gear of all kinds (canoes and kayaks are about $40 to $50 per day), guides, tours, lessons and planning services, and can arrange transportation back to Whitehorse.

Thirty-Mile Section

A Canadian Heritage site, this narrow river channel flows from Lake Laberge, 96km north of Whitehorse, to the confluence of the Teslin River. With clear, blue-green waters and perpendicular bluffs stretching 100m up from the river, it's one of the most scenic stretches of the Yukon River. An important salmon migration area, this region is also home to bald and golden

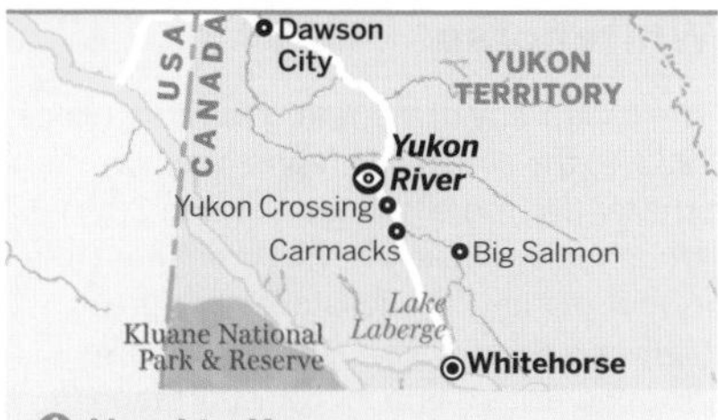

Need to Know

See outfitters' websites for details.

Take a Break

Other than fish straight from the river, you or your guide will need to bring all supplies.

★ Top Tip

Most paddlers use the map *The Yukon River: Marsh Lake to Dawson City*; available at www.yukonbooks.com.

eagles, trumpeter swans, wolverines and grizzly bears that prowl the riverside.

While paddling may seem easy in this stretch, with the current pulling your canoe on an almost effortless journey, this was the most difficult part of the run for gold seekers traveling to Dawson City. The strong currents and shifting shoals claimed more ships than any other stretch of the Yukon River. Along the way, you'll see simple graves and pass locations named after wrecked boats, such as Tanana Reef and Domville Creek. Also watch for abandoned cabins, a dilapidated shipyard and the abandoned village of Hootalinqua.

Big Salmon

Further north, Big Salmon River meets the Yukon River, widening the course. At the confluence is an abandoned turn-of-the-century First Nations village and a trading post on the riverbanks.

Outfitters

Kanoe People (867-668-4899; www.kanoepeople.com; cnr 1st Ave & Strickland St, Whitehorse; half-day from $70) At the river's edge. Can arrange any type of trip including paddles down Teslin and Big Salmon rivers. Gear, maps and guidebooks for sale.

Up North Adventures (867-667-7035; www.upnorthadventures.com; 103 Strickland St, Whitehorse; canoeing half-day from $70; 9am-7pm) Offers guided tours, rentals and transportation on the major rivers. Also paddling lessons to get you started.

Klondike Canoeing Rentals (867-334-2889; www.klondikecanoe.yk.ca; 409 Alexander St, Whitehorse; canoe/kayak per day $40/50; 9am-5pm) Can supply all canoeing and kayaking needs plus arrange transport to/from river locations.

Whitehorse

The capital city of the Yukon Territory (since 1953, to the continuing regret of much smaller and more isolated Dawson City), Whitehorse will likely have a prominent role in your journey. The territory's two great highways – the Alaska and the Klondike – cross here; it's a hub for transportation (it was a terminus for the White Pass & Yukon Route railway from Skagway in the early 1900s, and during WWII was a major center for work on the Alaska Hwy). You'll find all manner of outfitters and services for explorations across the territory.

SIGHTS

MacBride Museum of Yukon History Museum

(☎867-667-2709; www.macbridemuseum.com; 1124 Front St; adult/child $10/5; ⊙9:30am-5pm) This is the Yukon's pre-eminent museum, preserving and presenting the region's history since 1952. Recently expanded, the museum offers a comprehensive view of the resilient people and groundbreaking events that have shaped the Yukon Territory's history and should not be missed.

SS Klondike National Historic Site Historic Site

(☎867-667-4511; www.pc.gc.ca; cnr South Access Rd & 2nd Ave; ⊙9:30am-5pm May-Aug) FREE Carefully restored, this was one of the largest stern-wheelers used on the Yukon River. Built in 1937, it made its final run upriver to Dawson in 1955 and is now a National Historic Site.

Whitehorse Waterfront Area

One look at the surging Yukon River and you'll want to spend time strolling its bank. The beautiful **White Pass & Yukon Route Station** (1109 1st Ave) has been restored and anchors an area that's in the midst of a revitalization. **Rotary Peace Park** (off 2nd Ave) at the southern end is a great picnic spot, the **Kwanlin Dün Cultural Centre** (☎867-456-5322; www.kwanlindunculturalcentre.com; 1171 1st Ave; by donation; ⊙10am-6pm Mon-Sat) is a dramatic addition in the middle, and **Shipyards Park** (off 2nd Ave) at the northern end has a growing collection of historic structures moved here from other parts of the Yukon.

SHOPPING

Mac's Fireweed Books Books

(☎867-668-2434; www.macsbooks.ca; 203 Main St; ⊙8am-9pm Mon-Sat, from 10am Sun) Mac's has an unrivaled selection of Yukon titles. It also stocks topographical maps, road maps and periodicals.

EATING & DRINKING

Deli Yukon Deli $

(☎867-667-6077; 203 Hanson St; sandwiches from $7; ⊙9am-5:30pm Mon-Fri) The smell of smoked meat wafts out to the street; inside there's a huge selection of prepared items and custom-made sandwiches. Offers great picnic fare, or dine in the simple table area. The spicy elk sausage rolls for $3.95 are addictive. Attached to Yukon Meat & Sausage.

Klondike Rib & Salmon Canadian $$

(☎867-667-7554; www.klondikerib.com; 2116 2nd Ave; mains from $14; ⊙11am-9pm May-Sep) The food is superb at this sprawling casual half-tent restaurant in a place originally opened as a tent-frame bakery in 1900. Besides the namesakes (the salmon skewers and smoked pork ribs are tops), there are other local faves. Great place to try bison steak ($34) or Yukon Arctic char ($28). It's half-tent, so closed when winter temperatures turn up.

Antoinette's Fusion $$$

(☎867-668-3505; www.antoinettesrestaurant.com; 4121 4th Ave; dinner mains from $22; ⊙3:30-10pm Mon-Sat) Antoinette Greenoliph runs one of the most creative kitchens in the Yukon. Her eponymous restaurant has an ever-changing, locally sourced menu. Many dishes have a Caribbean flair. There is often live bluesy, loungey music on weekends.

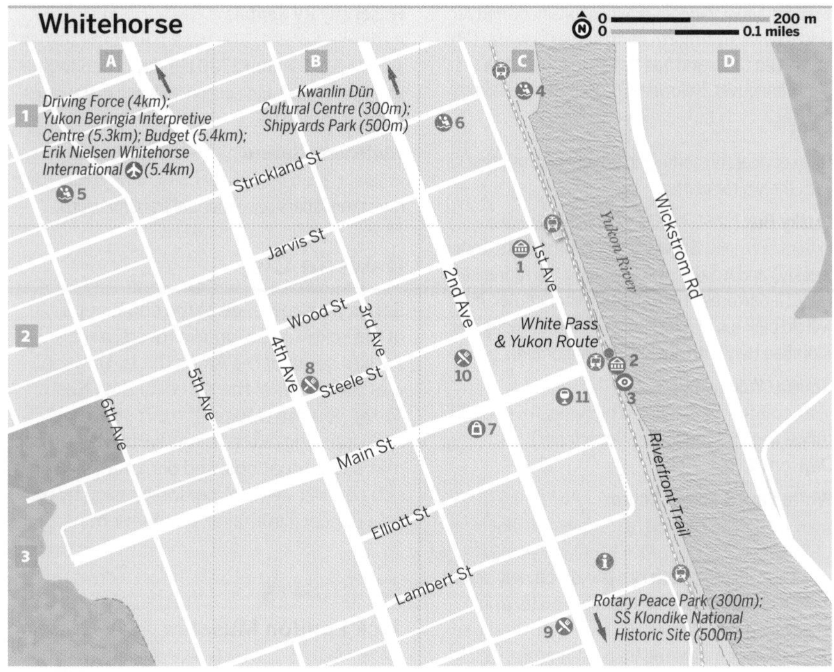

Whitehorse

Sights
1 MacBride Museum of Yukon History ... C2
2 White Pass & Yukon Route Station ... C2
3 Whitehorse Waterfront ... C2

Activities, Courses & Tours
4 Kanoe People ... C1
5 Klondike Canoeing Rentals ... A1
6 Up North Adventures ... C1

Shopping
7 Mac's Fireweed Books ... C2

Eating
8 Antoinette's ... B2
9 Deli Yukon ... C3
10 Klondike Rib & Salmon ... C2

Drinking & Nightlife
11 Dirty Northern Public House ... C2

Dirty Northern Public House Pub
(☎867-633-3305; www.facebook.com/dirtynorthernpublichouse; 103 Main St; 3pm-late) There are hints of style at this upscale pub, which has a great draft-beer selection and makes excellent mixed drinks. Grab a booth and chase the booze with a wood-fired pizza such as the Chris Brother's Pepperoni. Top local acts perform many nights and the food comes from the sister-restaurant next door, **Miner's Daughter** (5-10pm Mon-Thu, 5pm-late Fri & Sat).

INFORMATION

Whitehorse Visitor Center (☎867-667-3084; www.travelyukon.com; 2nd Ave & Lambert St; 8am-8pm) An essential stop with vast amounts of territory-wide information.

GETTING THERE & AWAY

AIR

Erik Nielsen Whitehorse International Airport (YXY; ☎867-667-8440; www.hpw.gov.yk.ca/whitehorse_airport.html; off Alaska Hwy; wi-fi) is five minutes west of downtown. Air Canada and

WestJet serve Vancouver, while locally owned Air North (www.flyairnorth.com) serves Dawson City, Mayo, Old Crow and has flights to Inuvik, NWT, plus Vancouver, Kelowna, Edmonton and Calgary.

BUS

Bus services, er, come and go; check the latest with the visitor center.

Husky Bus (☎867-993-3821; www.klondikeexperience.com) Serves Dawson City ($119, thrice weekly) and makes all stops along the Klondike Hwy. Departures are from the visitor center. It will do pickups of paddlers and canoes along the Klondike Hwy with advance arrangement.

Alaska/Yukon Trails (☎907-479-2277; www.alaskashuttle.com) Serves Fairbanks, AK (US$385, thrice weekly June to mid-September), via Dawson City.

White Pass & Yukon Route (☎867-633-5710; www.wpyr.com; 1109 1st Ave; adult/child one way US$144/72; ⊙ticket office 9am-5pm Mon-Sat mid-May–mid-Sep) Offers a jaw-droppingly scenic daily 10-hour rail and bus connection to/from Skagway, AK, via Fraser, BC, in season. On some days, the bus meets the train in Carcross, which maximizes the beautiful train ride (this is the preferred option).

 GETTING AROUND

BUS

Whitehorse Transit System (☎867-668-7433; www.whitehorse.ca; $2.50; ⊙Mon-Sat) runs through the center. Route 3 serves the airport, Route 5 passes the Robert Service Campground.

CAR & RV

Check your rental rate very carefully, as it's common for a mileage charge to be added after the first 200km per day, which will not get you far in the Yukon. Also understand your insurance coverage and ask whether windscreen and tire damage from Yukon's rugged roads is included.

Budget (☎867-667-6200; www.budget.com; Erik Nielsen Whitehorse International Airport) The only worldwide rental car company in Whitehorse.

Driving Force (☎867-322-0255; www.drivingforce.ca; Erik Nielsen Whitehorse International Airport; ⊙8am-6pm) These guys have cars, trucks, vans and SUVs.

Fraserway RV Rentals (☎867-668-3438; www.fraserway.com; 9039 Quartz Rd) Rents all shapes and sizes of RV from $200 per day depending on size (it matters) and season. Mileage extra; rates can quickly add up.

Whitehorse Subaru (☎867-393-6550; www.whitehorsesubaru.com; 17 Chilkoot Way) Has good rates; most cars have manual transmissions.

Dawson City

Set on a narrow shelf at the confluence of the Yukon and Klondike Rivers, a mere 240km south of the Arctic Circle, Dawson was the center of the Klondike Gold Rush. Today, you can wander the dirt streets of town, passing old buildings with dubious permafrost foundations, and discover Dawson's rich cultural life (that person passing by may be a dancer, filmmaker, painter or miner).

 SIGHTS

Jack London Museum Museum

(☎867-993-5575; www.jacklondonmuseum.ca; 600 Firth St; adult/child $5/free; ⊙11am-6pm May-Aug) In 1898 Jack London lived in the Yukon, the setting for his most popular stories, including *The Call of the Wild* and *White Fang*. At the writer's cabin there are excellent daily interpretive talks. A labor of love by the late historian Dick North, Dawne Mitchell and others, this place is a treasure trove of stories – including the search for the original cabin.

Robert Service Cabin Historic Site

(☎867-993-7200; www.pc.gc.ca; cnr 8th Ave & Hanson St; Parks Canada admission $7; ⊙several events daily May-Aug) The 'Bard of the Yukon,' poet and writer Robert W Service, lived in this typical gold-rush cabin from 1909 to 1912. Each day in season there are dramatic readings, guided walks and tours.

 ACTIVITIES

Dawson City River Hostel Canoeing

(www.yukonhostels.com; bike rental per day from $25; ⊙May-Sep) Arranges all manner of canoe rentals, trips and transportation from

Whitehorse and points further downstream to Dawson and from Dawson to the Alaskan towns of Eagle and Circle. Canoe rental for the 16-day trip from Whitehorse to Dawson City costs $395 plus freight; you can also rent bicycles by the day. On the far side of the Yukon River from downtown Dawson City.

TOURS

Goldbottom Tours History

(867-993-5023; www.goldbottom.com; 966 Front St; tours with/without transport from Dawson $55/45; May-Sep) Run by the legendary Millar mining family. Tour the placer mine 15km up Hunker Creek Rd, which meets Hwy 2 just north of the airport. The three-hour tours include a gold-panning lesson; you get to keep what you find. You can also just pan for gold on the site for $20. The ticket office is on Front St.

Parks Canada Walking Tours Walking

(867-993-7200; www.pc.gc.ca; single tour $7, unlimited tours $31; May-Aug) Parks Canada docents, often in period garb, lead excellent walking tours. On each tour, learn about a few of the 26 restored buildings and the characters that walked the streets (many of whom could be called 'streetwalkers'). There are also self-guided 90-minute audio tours (adult $7, 9am to 5pm).

EATING & DRINKING

Alchemy Cafe Cafe $

(867-993-3831; www.alchemycafe.ca; 878 3rd Ave; mains from $8; 9am-4pm;) Groovy in the best sense of the word, Alchemy combines fantastic vegetarian food with a life-affirming green ethos. The coffees are way cool (in a hot sort of way), and special events include music, talks and, yes, rap sessions. The vintage-style building has an alluring porch.

Klondike Kate's Canadian $$

(867-993-6527; www.klondikekates.ca; cnr King St & 3rd Ave; dinner mains from $14; 11am-10pm Mon-Fri, from 8am Sat & Sun May-Oct) Two ways to know spring has arrived: the river cracks up and Kate's reopens. Locals in the know prefer the latter. The long and inventive menu has fine sandwiches, pastas and fresh Yukon fish. Look for great specials. Excellent list of Canadian craft brews.

Joe's Wood-fired Pizza Pizza $$

(867-993-5326; 978 2nd Ave; pizzas from $15; 4-9:30pm Mon-Fri) Surprisingly authentic Italian in downtown Dawson City. Pizza options include Italian favorites and house specialties, the wine list has bottles from all over the globe, while the atmosphere is friendly, relaxed and comfortable.

Bombay Peggy's Pub

(867-993-6969; www.bombaypeggys.com; cnr 2nd Ave & Princess St; 11am-11pm Mar-Nov) There's always a hint of pleasures to come swirling around the tables of Dawson's most inviting bar. Enjoy good beers, wines and mixed drinks inside or out.

INFORMATION

Visitor Center (867-993-5566; www.travelyukon.com; cnr Front & King Sts; 8am-8pm May-Sep) A veritable mine of tourist and Parks Canada information (buy activity tickets and passes here). It also has essential schedules of events and activities.

GETTING THERE & AWAY

Dawson City is 527km from Whitehorse. Public transportation to/from Whitehorse is often in flux.

Yukon Dawson Airport (Km 694 Klondike Hwy) is 15km east of Dawson. **Air North** (800-661-0407; www.flyairnorth.com) serves Whitehorse and Old Crow in the Yukon, Inuvik in the NWT and flies to Vancouver, Calgary, Edmonton and other cities.

Alaska/Yukon Trails (www.alaskashuttle.com) runs buses to Fairbanks, AK ($315, thrice weekly June to mid-September).

Husky Bus (867-993-3821; www.huskybus.ca) serves Whitehorse ($119, thrice weekly) and makes all stops along the Klondike Hwy. Also does airport transfers. Departures are from the visitor center.

Old Québec (p120)

In Focus

Hiking in Québec

MARIDAV / SHUTTERSTOCK ©

Canada Today

Canada is clearly a country where change is in the air. Cannabis legalization in 2018 has brought a green, skunky gold rush, with ubiquitous wafts of weed on city streets. A basketball win by the Toronto Raptors in 2019 means Canada is soaring high in all kinds of ways. Climate change is still a political discussion here, but whether it's wildfires or storm surges, scientific agreement is widespread.

Economy

With the oil and gas future looking less rosy, cannabis may come through as Canada's next cash cow. In Ontario alone, legal cannabis sales doubled after marijuana was legalized and retail shops opened in 2019. Overall, Canada's economy is solid, with its currency holding well against the American dollar, and it was one of the seven major industrialized democracies to return to surplus in 2015, following the global financial crisis. The Conservative government of the time focused on federal job cuts that impacted many departments, including Parks Canada and Indigenous Affairs. In their first full year back in office, the Liberals planned for a $30 billion deficit in 2016–17, claiming investment in job creation, support for the middle class and infrastructure would build a brighter, more sustainable future.

Oil Between Neighbors

Voltaire may have written off Canada as 'a few acres of snow' back in the mid-18th century, but those few acres have yielded vast amounts of oil, timber and other natural resources, and propelled Canada to an enviable standard of living.

Extracting and developing the resources has, however, come with an ecological price. Northern Alberta's Athabasca Oil Sands are among the world's biggest oil reserves, and they've done an excellent job boosting the economy. But as the world's fourth-largest oil producer, Canada is the 10th highest greenhouse gas emitting country. Its oil and gas industry accounts for 27% of these emissions. The pro-industry camp says improvements are being made.

The controversial Keystone XL pipeline plays into these themes. Aiming to funnel Alberta's crude oil to refineries on the Texas and Louisiana coast, much of it was already built when the US State Department refused approval for the pipeline's completion in late 2015, saying Canada could be doing more to curb carbon emissions. The project was also contentious within Canada, with environmentalists and Indigenous communities voicing their concerns regarding damage to sacred sites and water contamination. Back across the border, the project received a boost when President Trump enacted approval legislation shortly after taking office in 2017, and again when he signed a new permit for the development in 2019. The battle is ongoing.

Politics

After being under Conservative rule for almost 10 years, Canada went to the polls in record numbers in 2015 in an election that strongly divided the population. Resource-based communities backed the Conservatives, while many others felt the party had sold out to big business and was being short-sighted in supporting industry over the environment. Many also feared that a split in votes between the leftist New Democratic Party (NDP) and the Liberals would return the Conservatives to power.

The Liberals took back the reigns, with a majority leadership headed by the 43-year-old Justin Trudeau, who became the second-youngest prime minister in Canadian history. Trudeau's support of women, children, immigrants, same-sex marriage, marijuana legalization and environmentalism was welcomed by many Canadians disheartened by Conservative rule. But the fairy tale ended with widely publicized scandals, including allegations that Trudeau violated federal conflict-of-interest rules in trying to influence the outcome of a corporate corruption case. In the election of October 2019, many Canadians again headed to the polls looking for change; the Liberal Party won enough seats to form a minority government, with Trudeau retaining the prime-ministership, but lost the popular vote to the Conservatives.

Old Montréal (p100)

History

The human story of Canada begins around 15,000 years ago, when Indigenous locals began carving thriving communities from the abundant wilderness. Everything changed, though, when the Europeans rolled in from the late 15th century onward, staking claims that triggered rumbling conflicts and eventually shaped a vast new nation. Much of this colorful heritage is accessible to visitors, with more than 950 National Historic Sites.

c 25,000 BCE

The first humans arrive in Canada by crossing the land bridge that once connected Siberia to North America.

1000 CE

Viking Leif Erikson and crew wash up at L'Anse aux Meadows, becoming the first Europeans in North America.

1497

John Cabot sails from Britain and finds Newfoundland instead of China.

Performance at Royal BC Museum (p232)

GTS PRODUCTIONS / SHUTTERSTOCK ©

Early Locals & Viking Visitors

The first Canadians came from Asia, chasing down caribou and bison across the one-time land link between Siberia and Alaska and eventually settling throughout the Americas. The north proved particularly popular for its abundance of tasty fish and seal dinners, and these early Indigenous communities eventually spread to four main regions in what would become Canada: the Pacific, the Plains, southern Ontario/St Lawrence River, and the northeast woodlands.

About 2500 BCE, a second major wave of migration from Siberia brought the ancestors of the Inuit to Canada. These early Inuit were members of the Dorset Culture, named after Cape Dorset on Baffin Island, where its remains were first unearthed. Around 1000 CE, a separate Inuit cultural group – the whale-hunting Thule of northern Alaska – began making its way east through the Canadian Arctic. As these people spread, they overtook the Dorset Culture. The Thule are the direct ancestors of Canada's modern-day Inuit.

1534
Jacques Cartier sails into what is now Québec and claims the land for France.

1608
Samuel de Champlain puts down stakes at Québec City and gives New France its first permanent settlement.

1610
Merchant John Guy builds a plantation at Cupids, Newfoundland. It's England's first colony in Canada.

★ Best Historic Neighborhoods

Gastown, Vancouver

Old Québec

Old Montréal

Downtown Halifax, Nova Scotia

Old Québec (p120)

PRI MA / SHUTTERSTOCK ©

Also around 1000, Viking explorer Leif Erikson and his hairy posse poked around the eastern shores, sticking around long enough to establish winter settlements and a few hardy outposts. Life was tough for these interlopers and the hostile reception from the locals eventually sent them back where they came from. Without a glowing recommendation from these first European visitors, it was several centuries before anyone else bothered to make the epic journey across the Atlantic.

Return of the Europeans

After Christopher Columbus made heading west from Europe across the ocean fashionable again with his 1492 journey in search of Asia, avaricious European monarchs began queuing up to sponsor expeditions. In 1497 Giovanni Caboto – better known as John Cabot – sailed under a British flag as far west as Newfoundland and Cape Breton. His great discovery turned out to be a surfeit of cod stocks, triggering a hungry rush of boats from Europe, including Spanish whaling vessels.

King François I of France looked over the fence at his neighbors, stroked his beard, and ordered Jacques Cartier to appear before him. By this time, the hunt was on not only for the fabled Northwest Passage route but also for gold, given the shiny discoveries made by Spanish conquistadors among the Aztec and Inca civilizations.

But upon arrival in Labrador, Cartier found only 'stones and horrible rugged rocks.' He kept exploring, though, and soon went ashore on Québec's Gaspé Peninsula to claim the land for France. The local Iroquois thought he was a good neighbor at first, until he kidnapped two of the chief's sons and took them to Europe. Rather surprisingly, Cartier returned them a year later when sailing up the St Lawrence River.

Fur: the New Gold

While these early explorers were always looking for gold to please their royal sponsors back home, it eventually became clear that the riches of the new land were not quite so

1670
King Charles II creates the Hudson's Bay Company to shore up the local fur trade for the British.

1755
The English deport some 14,000 French Acadians from the Bay of Fundy region during the Great Expulsion.

1759
The French and English come to blows on the Plains of Abraham at Québec City. The battle lasts less than an hour; France loses.

sparkly. With fur the latest fashion of the French court, the New World's lustrous and abundant pelts were suddenly in huge demand across Europe.

In 1588 the French crown granted the first trading monopoly in Canada, only to have other merchants promptly challenge the claim. And so the race for control of the fur trade was officially on. The economic value of this enterprise and, by extension, its role in shaping Canadian history, cannot be underestimated. It was the main reason behind the country's European settlement, at the root of the struggle for dominance between the French and the British, and the source of strife and division between various Indigenous groups.

To support their claims, French pioneers established a tentative foothold on Île Ste-Croix (a tiny islet in the river on the present border with Maine) in 1604. They soon moved to Port Royal (today's Annapolis Royal) in Nova Scotia. Exposed and difficult to defend, neither site was ideal for controlling the inland fur trade. As the would-be colonists moved up the St Lawrence River, they came upon a spot their leader, Samuel de Champlain, considered prime real estate – where today's Québec City now stands. It was 1608 and 'New France' had landed.

Pirates

Atlantic Canada had a notorious history of pirates. Peter Easton was the first in 1602, plundering around Newfoundland. Black Bart, aka Bartholomew Roberts, was another, c 1720. He disliked booze and gambling and encouraged prayer among his employees. In Halifax pirates were called 'privateers' and were sanctioned by the government.

Brits Take Over

While the French enjoyed their plush fur monopoly for several decades, the Brits mounted a challenge in 1670 when King Charles II formed the Hudson's Bay Company. He granted it a trade monopoly over a vast northern area that would today encompass about 40% of Canada.

As both countries reaffirmed and expanded their claims, skirmishes broke out between groups of colonizers, mirroring the wars that were engulfing Europe in the first half of the 18th century. Things came to a head with the Treaty of Utrecht, which forced the French to recognize British claims in the region.

But the enmity and military skirmishes between the two continued for several decades, culminating in a 1759 battle on Québec's Plains of Abraham that is remembered today as one of Canada's most important military events. Besieging the city in a surprise and bloody attack that left both commanding generals dead, the Brits eventually won the day and the French were forced to hand over control of Canada in the resulting 1763 Treaty of Paris.

1763
The Treaty of Paris expels France from Canada after France loses the Seven Years' War.

1775
American rebels invade Canada and try to entice Québec to join the revolt against the British in the American Revolution.

1793
Explorer Alexander Mackenzie makes the first transcontinental journey across the land.

★ Best History Museums

Canadian War Museum (p82), Ottawa

Pointe-à-Callière Cité d'archéologie et d'histoire de Montréal (p101)

Royal BC Museum (p232), Victoria

Western Development Museum (p175), Saskatoon

Canadian War Museum (p82)

TODAMO / SHUTTERSTOCK ©

Managing their newly acquired territory was a tricky challenge for the Brits, who had to contend with Indigenous uprisings as well as resentment from French Canadians. Next, the restless American colonies started rumbling from the south. To keep the French Canadians on side, the Québec Act of 1774 confirmed the French Canadians' right to their religion, allowed them to assume political office and restored the use of French civil law. It worked: during the American Revolution (1775–83) most French Canadians refused to take up arms in support of the American cause.

After the revolution, the English-speaking population exploded when some 50,000 settlers from the newly independent USA migrated north. Called United Empire Loyalists due to their presumed allegiance to Britain, the majority ended up living in Nova Scotia and New Brunswick, while a smaller group settled along the northern shore of Lake Ontario and in the Ottawa River Valley (forming the nucleus of what became Ontario). About 8000 settlers moved to Québec, creating the first sizeable Anglophone community in the French-speaking bastion.

Canada Splits…then Unites

Accommodating the interests of Loyalist settlers, the British government passed the Constitutional Act of 1791, which divided the colony into Upper Canada (today's southern Ontario) and Lower Canada (now southern Québec). Lower Canada retained French civil laws, but both provinces were governed by the British criminal code. These divisions didn't help matters, with rising tensions and arguments caused by the clear dominance of the British over the French in administrative matters across the two regions. Two French rebellions kicked off in the 1830s and although each was swiftly quelled, it was an indication that the ill-conceived division was unsustainable. The Brits then tried a different approach.

The Union Act of 1840 sought to crush French nationalism by legislating that British laws, language and institutions were superior across both regions, now joined together as the Province of Canada. If anything, the union's clear underlying objective of destroying

1858
Prospectors discover gold along the Fraser River in BC, spurring thousands of hopefuls to move north and start panning.

1867
The British North America Act unites the colonies under the Dominion of Canada, a card-carrying member of the British Empire.

1885
Canada's first national park opens in Banff, Alberta; meanwhile, in Craigellachie, BC, the Canadian Pacific Railway is completed.

French identity made Francophones cling together even more tenaciously – the wounds can still be seen in Canada today.

With the rise of the USA after the American Civil War (1861–65), fragile Canada, whose border with the USA was established on the 49th parallel in 1818, sought to further solidify its status and prevent annexation. In 1864 Charlottetown, Prince Edward Island, became the birthing room for modern Canada when the 'Fathers of Confederation' – a group of representatives from Nova Scotia, New Brunswick, Prince Edward Island, Ontario and Québec – got together and hammered out the framework for a new nation. The British North America Act was passed in 1867, creating a modern, self-governing nation originally known as the Dominion of Canada. The day the act became official, July 1, is now celebrated across the country as Canada's national holiday.

The Maple Leaf Symbol

It's on the penny, on Air Canada planes, on Toronto hockey-team jerseys – you can't escape the maple leaf. The leaf has been considered a national symbol for almost two centuries. In 1836, *Le Canadien* newspaper, published in Lower Canada, wrote about it as a suitable emblem for the nation. Ontario and Québec both were using it on their coat of arms by 1868. The Canadian Armed Forces used it during the world wars. And finally, after much wrangling over the design (one leaf? three leaves? 13 points?), the current 11-point leaf was granted national-symbol status and went on the flag in 1965.

Creating Confederation

Under Canada's first prime minister, John A Macdonald, land and colonies were slowly added to the confederation. The government acquired a vast northern swathe, now called the Northwest Territories (NWT), in 1869 for the paltry sum of £300,000 – about $11.5 million in today's money – from the Hudson's Bay Company. The land was sparsely populated, mostly by Plains First Nations and several thousand Métis, a blend of Cree, Ojibwe or Saulteaux and French-Canadian or Scottish fur traders, who spoke French as their main language. Their biggest settlement was the Red River Colony around Fort Garry (today's Winnipeg).

The Canadian government immediately clashed with the Métis people over land-use rights, causing the latter to form a provisional government led by the charismatic Louis Riel. He sent the Ottawa-appointed governor packing and, in November 1869, seized control of Upper Fort Garry, thereby forcing Ottawa to the negotiating table. However, with his delegation already en route, Riel impulsively executed a Canadian prisoner he was holding at the fort.

Although the murder caused widespread uproar in Canada, the government was so keen to bring the west into the fold it agreed to most of Riel's demands, including special

1896
Prospectors find more gold, this time in the Yukon. The Klondike Gold Rush is on, with 40,000 aspirants heading to Dawson City.

1913
Immigration to Canada crests, with more than 400,000 people embracing the maple leaf.

1931
First Nations, Inuit and Métis children are removed from their communities and forced to attend schools to 'assimilate.'

★ Canadian Inventions

Foghorn (1854)

Basketball (1892)

Egg carton (1911)

Insulin (1922)

IMAX (1967)

NORTONRSX / GETTY IMAGES ©

language and religious protections for the Métis. As a result, the then-pint-sized province of Manitoba was carved out of the NWT and entered the dominion in July 1870. Macdonald sent troops after Riel but he narrowly managed to escape to the USA. He was formally exiled for five years in 1875.

Rail Link to the West

Despite the progress toward confederation, the west coast remained a distant and forbidding frontier. British Columbia (BC), created in 1866 by merging the colonies of New Caledonia and Vancouver Island, finally joined in 1871 in exchange for the Canadian government assuming all its debt and promising to link it with the east within 10 years via a vast transcontinental railroad.

The Canadian Pacific Railway's construction is one of the most impressive and decisive chapters in Canada's history. Though essential in uniting the nation, it was a costly proposition, made even more challenging by the rough and rugged terrain the tracks had to traverse. To entice investors, the government offered major benefits, including massive land grants in western Canada. Workers drove the final spike into the track at Craigellachie, BC, on November 7, 1885.

Canada rang in the 20th century on a high note. Industrialization was in full swing, prospectors had discovered gold in the Yukon, and Canadian resources – from wheat to lumber – were increasingly in demand. In addition, the new railroad opened the floodgates to immigration. Between 1885 and 1914 about 4.5 million people arrived in Canada. This included large groups of Americans and Eastern Europeans, especially Ukrainians, who went to work cultivating the prairies.

By the time the guns of WWI fell silent in 1918, most Canadians were fed up with sending their sons and husbands to fight in distant wars for Britain. Under the government of William Lyon Mackenzie King, Canada made it clear that Britain could no longer automatically draw upon the Canadian military and even sent its own ambassador to Washington. This

1961
Saskatchewan introduces the country's first universal health-care plan, an idea that soon spreads to the rest of Canada.

1967
The Great Canadian Oil Sands plant opens at Fort McMurray, Alberta, and starts pumping out black gold.

1982
Queen Elizabeth II signs the Canada Act, giving Canada complete sovereignty.

forcefulness led to the Statute of Westminster, passed by the British Parliament in 1931. It formalized the independence of Canada and other Commonwealth nations, although Britain retained the right to pass amendments to those countries' constitutions – a right only removed with the 1982 Canada Act. The British monarch remains Canada's head of state, although this is predominantly a ceremonial role and does not diminish the country's sovereignty.

French Islands

France retains a token of its early exploits in Canada: St Pierre and Miquelon, two small islands off Newfoundland's coast, remain staunchly French to this day.

Modern-Day Canada

The period after WWII brought another wave of economic expansion and immigration, especially from Europe. The one province left behind during the 1950s boom years was Québec, caught in the grip of ultraconservative leader Maurice Duplessis. Only after his death did the province finally start getting up to speed during the 'Quiet Revolution' of the 1960s. Still, progress wasn't swift enough for radical nationalists, who claimed independence was the only way to ensure Francophone rights. Québec has spent the ensuing years flirting with separatism, culminating in a cliffhanger 1994 referendum when a majority of less than 1% voted that the province should remain a part of Canada.

In 1960 Canada's Indigenous peoples were finally granted Canadian citizenship. Issues involving land rights and discrimination played out in the decades that followed. In 1985 Canada became the first country in the world to pass a national multicultural act. Today, more than 20% of Canada's population is foreign-born. BC has a long history of welcoming Japanese, Chinese and South Asian immigrants. The prairie provinces have traditionally been the destination of large numbers of Ukrainians, and Ontario, which has sizable Caribbean and Russian populations, is also home to 60% of Canada's Muslims.

The new millennium has been kind to Canada. The Canadian dollar took off around 2003 – thanks to oil, diamonds and other natural resources fueling the economy – and tolerance marches onward, with medical marijuana legalized and marriage equality achieved. The country showed off its abundant assets to the world when it successfully hosted the 2010 Winter Olympics in Vancouver. The nation shone again for its 150th birthday in 2017, with royal visits and its arms of open wide to tourists.

1999
Nunavut, Canada's newest province, is chiseled from the icy eastern Arctic.

2013
Calgary is hit by epic floods; four people die and 100,000 others are forced from their homes.

2018
Anti-independence Coalition Avenir Québec party wins a landslide victory in the Québec assembly, gaining 74 of the 125 seats.

Roy Henry Vickers Gallery (p235)

Arts & Culture

Looking specifically at artistic output, overseas visitors might be forgiven for thinking that culture in Canada simply means Celine Dion, Drake, Margaret Atwood and a few totem poles. But while Canadians rarely shout about it, the country's creative and artistic scenes are rich and vibrant across the nation, offering a deep well of creativity for visiting culture vultures to sink their beaks into.

Literature

Canada's earliest inhabitants built their cultures on storytelling, passing important tales from generation to generation. Later authors created a written body of Canadian literature – the phrase 'Canlit' is still used here – that defined the struggles of creating a new life in a vast, sometimes barren wilderness. These often deeply affecting novels are the ideal accompaniment for an epic train ride across the prairies. Recommended authors for the long haul include Margaret Laurence and Robertson Davies, while many will also enjoy Lucy Maud Montgomery's *Anne of Green Gables*.

If you want to hit an adult page-turner during your travels, there are three main authors to focus on. If you read Mordecai Richler's *The Apprenticeship of Duddy Kravitz* while hanging around in Montréal's Plateau district, you'll almost feel the story on the streets around you (his later epic, *Barney's Version*, was made into a 2010 movie). Short-story writer Alice Munro won the 2013 Nobel Prize for Literature. Her work often focuses on small-town life in western Ontario; *The View from Castle Rock* provides a good sampler. And, of course, a trip to Canada that doesn't include a Margaret Atwood novel is like visiting a bar without having a drink. Consider top titles such as *Oryx and Crake, The Blind Assassin, Surfacing, The Handmaid's Tale* or *The Testaments*, Atwood's *Handmaid's* sequel, which (jointly) won the Booker Prize in 2019.

Other Canadian authors to look out for include Carol Shields, Douglas Coupland, William Gibson and Michael Ondaatje. If you time your visit well, you can join the local bookworms at literary events including the Vancouver Writers Fest (www.writersfest.bc.ca), Toronto's International Festival of Authors (www.ifoa.org) and the annual five-city Word on the Street (www.thewordonthestreet.ca).

Indigenous Artists

There was little outside recognition of the art produced by local Indigenous communities until the 20th century. But over the last 50 years or so, there's been a strong and growing appreciation of this body of work, led initially by the paintings, sculptures and carvings of revered Haida artist Bill Reid (1920–98), whose work used to appear on the back of the $20 bill. Also look out for colorful paintings by Norval Morrisseau; mixed-media works by Saskatchewan-born Edward Poitras; and challenging younger artists such as Marianne Nicolson and Brian Jungen, who explore political and environmental themes in their art.

Visual Arts

Canada's artistic bent was founded thousands of years ago when early Indigenous inhabitants began adorning their homes with visual representations of the natural world. Later, European painters continued to use nature as their muse, often adding images of the (to them) mysterious Indigenous locals to their canvases.

But the most famous artistic school in Canadian cultural history is the Group of Seven, a clutch of painters who banded loosely together in the early 1920s, creating bold, stylized representations of the striking Canadian landscape that still seem fresh and vibrant today. Members of the group – which included famed luminaries such as Tom Thomson, Lawren Harris and Arthur Lismer, and which later expanded beyond the original seven – would often disappear into the wilderness for months on end. It's during one of these trips that Thomson met his demise, drowning in a lake in 1917, just as he was at the height of his creative powers.

While Group of Seven paintings still attract huge prices and exhibitions of their work typically lure large crowds, Canada also has an energetic contemporary art scene. Internationally renowned latter-day stars include photo conceptualist Jeff Wall, painter and sculptor Betty Goodwin, and painter and avant-garde filmmaker Michael Snow – look out for their works at galleries across the country. And don't forget to check out the celebrated public-art scenes on the streets of Vancouver, Toronto and Montréal.

Music

Ask visitors to name a few Canadian musicians and they'll stutter to a halt after Drake, Justin Bieber, Celine Dion and Bryan Adams. But ask the locals to do the same and they'll hit you with a roster of performers you've probably never heard of as well as a few that you always assumed were US-born. For the record, this is the homeland of classic legends such

★ Best Art Galleries

National Gallery of Canada (p82), Ottawa

Art Gallery of Ontario (p45), Toronto

Musée des Beaux-Arts de Montréal (p101)

Vancouver Art Gallery (p210)

Roy Henry Vickers Gallery (p235), Tofino

Vancouver Art Gallery (p210)

DEYMOSHR / SHUTTERSTOCK ©

as Neil Young, Leonard Cohen and Joni Mitchell as well as Michael Bublé, Diana Krall and modern superstars like Shawn Mendes, Arcade Fire, The Weeknd and Carly Rae Jepsen.

Working their list into a lather, it won't be long before most Canadians also mention the Tragically Hip, Barenaked Ladies, Blue Rodeo, Guess Who, Feist, New Pornographers, Sarah McLachlan, Oscar Peterson, Great Big Sea, Gordon Lightfoot and Bruce Cockburn: seminal Canadian musicians past and present that define the country's musical soundscape, yet some have little profile outside the country. The Hip, for example, easily packed stadiums in Canada but would have struggled to fill a midsized venue in most other countries.

To tap into the scene on your visit, drop into a local independent record store and ask for some recommendations. They'll likely point you to the area's best live-music venues and offer you some tips on who to look out for. And if you're a true die-hard traveling muso, consider timing your visit for a music festival. The Montréal Jazz Festival (www.montreal jazzfest.com) is one of the biggest in the world, while Toronto's North by Northeast (www. nxne.com) draws music industry executives hoping to find the rock stars of tomorrow. If you make it to Calgary, don't miss the super-modern National Music Centre (p166), which takes you on a musical journey across the country.

Film

There are two distinct sides to Canada's burgeoning movie industry. As a production hot spot, it's often used as a visual stand-in for US cities, which means you usually don't know you're watching a Canadian-made flick when you sit down to *X-Men* or *Twilight: New Moon*. But aside from being a busy back-lot for Hollywood – the nickname Hollywood North is frequently used here – there's a healthy independent Canadian movie-making scene with a flavor all its own.

Celebrated films made here over the years (and which are about as far from Hollywood blockbusters as you can imagine) include *Incendies* (2010, directed by Denis Villeneuve), *Anthropocene: The Human Epoch* (2018, directed by Edward Burtynsky, Jennifer Baichwal and Nicholas de Pencier), *Away from Her* (2006, directed by Sarah Polley), *The Sweet Hereafter* (1997, directed by Atom Egoyan), *Thirty Two Short Films About Glenn Gould* (1993, directed by Francois Girard) and *The Red Violin* (1998), co-written by Don McKellar, who has often seemed like a one-man movie industry unto himself. Guy Maddin is another well-known local filmmaker. He typically films around his hometown of Winnipeg; see *Keyhole* (2011) for an example of his offbeat style.

You can dip into both sides of the Canadian film industry at the country's two main movie festivals. The Toronto International Film Festival (www.tiff.net) is a glitzy affair where Hollywood megastars drop by to promote their new offerings. In contrast, the Vancouver International Film Festival (www.viff.org) showcases art-house and independent flicks from Canada and around the world.

Digby scallops

Canadian Cuisine

Canadian cuisine has moved well beyond the doughnut, and cities such as Montréal, Toronto and Vancouver now offer world-leading dining scenes. Regions across the country have rediscovered distinctive local ingredients produced on their doorsteps, and chefs transform these into an impressive plateful.

Local Flavors

If you're starting from the east, the main dish of the Maritime provinces is lobster – boiled in the pot and served with a little butter – and the best place to sample it is a community hall 'kitchen party' on Prince Edward Island. Dip into some chunky potato salad and hearty seafood chowder while waiting for your crustacean to arrive, but don't eat too much; you'll need room for the mountainous fruit pie coming your way afterwards.

Next door, Nova Scotia visitors should save their appetites for butter-soft Digby scallops and rustic Lunenburg sausage, while the favored meals of nearby Newfoundland and Labrador often combine rib-sticking dishes of cod cheeks and sweet snow crab. If you're feeling really ravenous, gnaw on a slice of seal-flipper pie – a dish you're unlikely to forget in a hurry.

★ Best Restaurants

Damas Restaurant (p108), Montréal

Beckta Dining & Wine Bar (p88), Ottawa

Lee (p53), Toronto

Chez Boulay (p129), Québec City

Salmon n' Bannock (p219), Vancouver

Chez Boulay

Québec is the world's largest maple syrup producer, processing an annual 6.5 million gallons of the syrup used on pancakes and as an ingredient in myriad other dishes. In this French-influenced province, fine food is a lifeblood for the locals, who happily sit down to lengthy dinners where the accompanying wine and conversation flow in equal measures.

The province's cosmopolitan Montréal has long claimed to be the nation's fine-dining capital, but there's an appreciation of food here at all levels that also includes hearty pea soups, exquisite cheeses and tasty pâtés sold at bustling markets. In addition, there's also that national dish, poutine, waiting to clog your arteries, plus smoked-meat deli sandwiches so large you'll have to dislocate your jaw to fit them in your mouth.

Ontario – especially Toronto – is a microcosm of Canada's melting pot of cuisines. Like Québec, maple syrup is a super-sweet flavoring of choice here, and it's found in decadent desserts such as beavertails (fried, sugared dough) and on breakfast pancakes the size of Frisbees. Head south to the Niagara Peninsula wine region and you'll also discover restaurants fusing contemporary approaches and traditional local ingredients, such as fish from the Great Lakes.

Far north from here, Nunavut in the Arctic Circle is Canada's newest territory, but it has a long history of Inuit food, offering a real culinary adventure for extreme-cuisine travelers. Served in some restaurants (but more often in family homes – make friends with locals and they may invite you in for a feast), regional specialties include boiled seal, raw frozen char and *maktaaq* – whale skin cut into small pieces and swallowed whole.

In contrast, the central provinces of Manitoba, Saskatchewan and Alberta have their own deep-seated culinary ways. The latter, Canada's cowboy country, is the nation's beef capital – you'll find top-notch Alberta steak on menus at leading restaurants across the country. If you're offered 'prairie oysters' here, though, you might want to know (or maybe you'd prefer not to!) that they're bull's testicles, prepared in a variety of ways designed to take your mind off their origin. In the Rockies things get wilder – try elk, bison and even moose.

There's an old Eastern European influence over the border in Manitoba, where immigrant Ukrainians have added comfort food staples such as pierogi and thick, spicy sausages. Head next door to prairie-land Saskatchewan for dessert. The province's heaping fruit pies are its most striking culinary contribution, especially when prepared with tart Saskatoon berries.

In the far west, British Columbians have traditionally fed themselves from the sea and the fertile farmlands of the interior. Okanagan Valley peaches, cherries and blueberries – best purchased from seasonal roadside stands throughout the region – are the staple of many summer diets. But it's the seafood that attracts the lion's share of culinary fans. Tuck into succulent wild salmon, juicy Fanny Bay oysters and velvet-soft scallops and you may decide you've stumbled on foodie nirvana. There's also a large and ever-growing influence of Asian food in BC's Lower Mainland.

Top Dining Neighborhoods

Ask anyone in Toronto, Montréal or Vancouver to name Canada's leading foodie city and they'll likely inform you that you've just found it. But while each of the big three claims to be at the top table when it comes to dining, their strengths are so diverse they're more accurately defined as complementary courses in one great meal.

First dish on the table is Montréal, which was Canada's sole dine-out capital long before the upstarts threw off their fried-meat-and-mashed-potato shackles. Renowned for bringing North America's finest French-influenced cuisine to local palates, it hasn't given up its crown lightly. Chefs here are often treated like rock stars as they challenge old-world conventions with daring, even artistic, approaches – expect clever, fusion-esque gastronomy. You should also expect a great restaurant experience: Montréalers have a bacchanalian love for eating out, with lively rooms ranging from cozy old-town restaurants to the animated patios of Rue Prince Arthur and the sophisticated, often funky eateries of the Plateau.

If Montréal serves as an ideal starter, that makes Toronto the main course – although that's a reflection of its recent elevation rather than its prominence. Fusion is also the default approach in Canada's largest city, although it's been taken even further here, with a wave of contemporary immigration adding modern influences from Asia to a foundation of European cuisines. With a bewildering 7000 restaurants to choose from, it can be a tough choice figuring out where to unleash your top-end dining budget. The best approach is to hit the neighborhoods: both the Financial District and Old Town are studded with classy, high-end joints.

And while that appears to make Vancouver the dessert, it could be argued this glass-towered, west-coast metropolis is the best of the bunch. In recent years, some of the country's most innovative chefs have set up shop here, inspired by the twin influences of an abundant local larder and Canada's most cosmopolitan population. Fusion is the starting point here in fine-dining districts such as Yaletown and Kitsilano. But there's also a high level of authenticity in the top-notch Asian dining: the best sushi bars and *izakayas* outside Japan jostle for attention with superb Vietnamese and Korean eateries.

Tasty Blogs

- Dinner with Julie (www.dinnerwithjulie.com)
- Seasonal Ontario Food (www.seasonalontariofood.blogspot.com)
- Vancouver Foodster (www.vancouverfoodster.com)
- Food Bloggers of Canada (www.foodbloggersofcanada.com)

Wine Regions

While many international visitors – especially those who think Canadians live under a permanent blanket of snow – are surprised to learn that wine is produced here, their suspicion is always tempered after a drink or two. Canada's wines have gained ever-greater kudos in recent years and, while their small-scale production and the industry dominance of other wine regions mean they will never be global market leaders, these wines could definitely hold their own in an international taste-off.

Okanagan Valley, British Columbia

The rolling hills of this lakeside region are well worth the five-hour drive from Vancouver. Studded among the vine-striped slopes are more than 100 wineries enjoying a diverse climate that fosters both crisp whites and bold reds. With varietals including pinot noir, pinot gris, pinot blanc, merlot and chardonnay, there's a wine here to suit almost every palate. Most visitors base themselves in Kelowna, the Okanagan's wine capital, before fanning out to well-known blockbuster wineries, such as Mission Hill, Quail's Gate, Cedar Creek and Summerhill Pyramid Winery (yes, it has a pyramid). Many of them also have excellent restaurants.

Further south in the valley, the small town of Oliver has cunningly trademarked its slogan, 'Wine Capital of Canada,' and controversially registered the website www.winecapitalofcanada.com, much to the chagrin of its rivals. There are huge signs emphasizing the point at the entrance to town.

Niagara Peninsula, Ontario

This picture-perfect region of country inns and charming old towns offers more than 60 wineries and grows more than three quarters of Canada's grapes. Neatly divided between the low-lying Niagara-on-the-Lake area and the higher Niagara Escarpment, its complex mix of soils and climates – often likened to France's Loire Valley – is ideal for chardonnay, riesling, pinot noir and cabernet-franc varietals. This is also the production center for Canadian ice wine, that potently sweet dessert libation. Although it's home to some of Canada's biggest wineries, including Inniskillin, Jackson-Triggs and Peller Estates, don't miss smaller pit stops such as Magnotta, Cave Spring Cellars and Tawse.

Wine Festivals

Canada is dripping with palate-pleasing wine events, which makes it especially important to check the dates of your trip: raising a few glasses with celebratory locals is one of the best ways to encounter the country.

If you're in BC, it's hard to miss one of the Okanagan's three main festivals – see www.thewinefestivals.com for dates. If you prefer not to leave the big city, check out February's Vancouver International Wine Festival (www.vanwinefest.ca).

Across the country in Ontario, Niagara also stages more than one annual event to celebrate its winey wealth, including January's Niagara Icewine Festival and September's giant Niagara Grape and Wine Festival. For information, visit www.niagarawinefestival.com.

Eating Out Basics

It's worth booking ahead for popular places, especially on the weekend – which, in the Canadian restaurant world, includes Thursdays. Most cafes and budget restaurants don't accept reservations.

Restaurants Diverse selection, from steakhouses to vegan raw food joints. Many are family-friendly and casual; some are not.

Cafes Often serve sandwiches, soups and baked goods, as well as coffee, and offer counter service.

Bistros Small and often classy, with home-cooked food.

Delis Choose your food, have it wrapped and take it with you. Usually have sandwiches and wraps.

Diners Brunches and lunches, sometimes served 24 hours; often family-friendly.

Pubs Home-cooked fish and chips, burgers and salads.

Skiing in British Columbia

Outdoor Activities

Canada's endless variety of landscapes makes for a fantastic playground. Whether it's snowboarding Whistler's mountains, surfing Nova Scotia's swells or kayaking the white-frothed South Nahanni River in the Northwest Territories, adventures abound.

Skiing & Snowboarding

It seems like almost everyone in Canada was born to ski. Visitors will find some of the world's most renowned resorts here – British Columbia (BC), Alberta and Québec host the premier ones – but it's also worth asking the locals where they like to hit the slopes: for every big-time swanky resort, there are several smaller spots where the terrain and the welcome can be even better.

Québec boasts some big slopes – Le Massif, near Québec City, has a vertical drop of 770m – located handily close to the cities. Most of these lower-elevation resorts, such as Mont-Tremblant, are a day's drive from Toronto and less than an hour from Québec City and Montréal. Ski areas in Québec's Eastern Townships offer renowned gladed runs that weave through a thinned forest.

★ Outdoors Resources

Parks Canada (www.pc.gc.ca) National park action.

Canada Trails (www.canadatrails.ca) Hiking, biking and cross-country skiing.

Paddle Canada (www.paddlecanada.com) Kayaking and canoeing.

Toronto Islands (p47)

HONESTTRAVELLER / GETTY IMAGES ©

Head west and you'll hit the big mountains and vast alpine terrains. Glide down gargantuan slopes at Whistler-Blackcomb, which has North America's highest vertical drop and most impressive terrain variation. You'll also slide through stunning postcard landscapes in the Canadian Rockies, especially at Sunshine in Banff National Park.

In BC's Okanagan Valley, resorts such as Apex and Big White boast good snow year after year. The snowpack ranges from 2m to 6m-plus, depending on how close the resort is to the Pacific Ocean. The deepest, driest snow in the world piles up in BC's Kootenay region. Ski it at Nelson's Whitewater, Rossland's Red Mountain or Fernie's Alpine Resort.

For cross-country skiing, Canmore (www.canmorenordic.com) in Alberta offers popular trails that were part of that Calgary's Winter Olympics in 1988.

For further information and resources covering the national scene, check the website of the Canadian Ski Council (www.skicanada.org).

Hiking

You don't have to be a hiker to hike in Canada. While there are plenty of multiday jaunts for those who like tramping through the wilderness equipped only with a Swiss Army knife, there are also innumerable opportunities for those who prefer a gentle stroll around a lake with a pub at the end.

The country's hiking capital is Banff National Park, crisscrossed with stupefying vistas accessible to both hard and soft outdoor adventurers. Near Lake Louise, for example, you can march through dense spruce and pine forests, then ascend into alpine meadows carpeted with wildflowers and surrounded by rugged glaciers and azure lakes. Also in the Rockies region, Wilcox Ridge and Parker Ridge offer breathtaking glacier views.

In BC's provincial parks system (www.bcparks.ca), you'll have a choice of more than 100 parks, each with distinct landscapes to hike through: check out Garibaldi Park's landscape of ancient volcanoes (not far from Whistler) and Mt Robson Park's popular Berg Lake alpine trail. Vancouver's North Shore is home to the Grouse Grind, a steep forest hike that's also known as 'Mother Nature's Stairmaster.' Across the water in Vancouver Island's Pacific Rim Park, the lush 75km West Coast Trail (www.westcoasttrail.com) is undoubtedly one of the country's most breathtaking, combining traditional First Nations trails and life-saving routes used by shipwreck survivors.

Out east, awe-inspiring trails pattern the landscape. In southern Ontario, the Bruce Trail (www.brucetrail.org) tracks from Niagara Falls to Tobermory. It's the oldest and longest continuous footpath in Canada and spans more than 850km. Though portions are near cities such as Hamilton and Toronto, it's surprisingly serene. Cape Breton Highlands National Park offers exquisite hiking over stark, dramatic coastline. Newfoundland's trails make for fantastic shoreline hiking and often provide whale views. The East Coast Trail (www.eastcoasttrail.ca) on the Avalon Peninsula is particularly renowned for its vistas, and

Skerwink Trail in eastern Newfoundland has been named one of the best walks in North America.

And don't forget the cities. Canada's major metropolises offer some great urban hikes, an ideal way to get to know the communities you're visiting. Slip into your runners for a stroll (or a jog) with the locals in Montréal's Parc du Mont Royal or in Vancouver's gemlike Stanley Park, where the idyllic seawall winds alongside towering trees and lapping ocean.

Fishing

Built on its Indigenous and pioneer past, Canada has a strong tradition of fishing and you can expect to come across plenty of opportunities to hook walleye, pike, rainbow or lake trout on your travels. Among the best fishing holes to head for are Lunenburg in Nova Scotia and the Miramichi River in New Brunswick. And while salmon are the usual draw on the Pacific coastline, hopping aboard a local vessel for some sea fishing off Haida Gwaii can deliver the kind of giant catches you'll be bragging about for years to come.

Kayaking & Canoeing

The Canadian Arctic, kayaking's motherland, still remains one of its special places: cruise the polar fjords of Ellesmere Island and watch narwhals and walruses during the short summer. In the Yukon, paddle down the Yukon River from Whitehorse and spot bald eagles. Further south, slide silently past ancient forests and totem poles in BC's Gwaii Haanas National Park Reserve, or watch orcas breaching in the province's Johnstone Strait. The east coast has sea kayaking galore: the seaside adjunct of Kejimkujik National Park is a superb place to paddle. Paddlers in Witless Bay or Gros Morne, Newfoundland, often glide alongside whales.

If you're on a tight schedule and don't have time for multiday odysseys, there are plenty of more accessible ways to get your kayaking fix. Big cities such as BC's Vancouver and Victoria offer tours and lessons near town, while the province's Sunshine Coast and Salt Spring Island have crenulated coastlines combined with tranquil sea inlets.

As old as kayaking, and equally as Canadian, is the canoe. Experienced paddlers can strike out on one of 33 Canadian Heritage Rivers (www.chrs.ca). Some of the best include the Northwest Territories' South Nahanni River (near Fort Simpson) and Ontario's French River (near Sudbury).

Mountain Biking & Cycling

Mountain biking is a big deal in Canada. While cycling enthusiasts in Europe might be into trundling around town or along a gentle riverside trail, in Canada you're more likely to find them hurtling down a mountainside covered in mud. Given the landscape, of course, it was just a matter of time before the wheels went off-road here.

If you need to ease yourself in, start gently with BC's Kettle Valley Rail Trail (www.kettlevalleyrailway.ca), near Kelowna. This dramatic segment of converted railway barrels across picturesque wooden trestle bridges and through canyon tunnels.

Looking for more of an adrenaline rush? In Vancouver's North Shore area, you'll be riding on much narrower and steeper trestles. The birthplace of freeride mountain biking (which combines downhill and dirt jumping), this area offers some unique innovations: elevated bridges, log rides and skinny planks that loft over the wet undergrowth. It's a similar story up at Whistler where the melted ski slopes are transformed into a summertime bike park that draws thousands every year – especially during the annual Crankworx Mountain Bike Festival (www.crankworx.com/whistler) in August.

For road touring, Canada's east coast, with more small towns and less emptiness, is a fantastic place to pedal, either as a single-day road ride or a multiday trip. Circle Québec's Lac St-Jean; try any part of the 4000km Route Verte (www.routeverte.com), the longest network of bicycle paths in the Americas; or follow Prince Edward Island's bucolic red roads and its Confederation Trail (www.tourismpei.com/pei-cycling).

Rock Climbing & Mountaineering

All those inviting crags you've spotted on your trip are an indication that Canada is a major climbing capital, ideal for both short sport climbs and epic big-wall ascents.

BC's Squamish region, located between Vancouver and Whistler, is a climbing center, with dozens of accessible (and not so accessible) cracks, faces, arêtes and overhangs. Tap into the scene via **Squamish Rock Guides** (☎604-892-7816; www.squamishrockguides.com; guided rock climbs half-day/day from $100/140). Canmore, near Banff, is another ideal destination for rock climbers, no matter what your skill level. For the adventure of a lifetime, the Northwest Territories' Cirque of the Unclimbables is certainly near the top of the list. If your trip takes you out east instead, Ontario's favorite climbing havens dot the Bruce Peninsula.

If mountaineering is more your thing, the Rockies are the recommended first stop. Yamnuska (www.yamnuska.com) is one company that offers ice climbing, ski mountaineering and avalanche training in the region. The Matterhorn of Canada is BC's Mt Assiniboine, located between the Kootenay and Banff National Parks. Other western classics include Alberta's Mt Edith Cavell, in Jasper; BC's Mt Robson and Sir Donald in the Rockies; and Garibaldi Peak, in Garibaldi Provincial Park, near Whistler. If you need a guide, check in with the excellent Alpine Club of Canada (www.alpineclubofcanada.ca).

Surfing & Windsurfing

If you're aiming to become a beach bum on your Canada trip, head to the wild west coast of BC's Vancouver Island and hang out on the beaches around Tofino. Surfing schools and gear-rental operations stud this region and you'll have an awesome time riding the swells (or just watching everyone else as you stretch out on the sand). Backed by verdant rainforest, it's an idyllic spot to spend some time.

June to September is the height of the season here, but serious surfers also like to drop by in winter to face down the lashing waves. Check Surfing Vancouver Island (www.surfingvancouverisland.com) for a taste of what to expect.

Some 6000km away, the east coast of Nova Scotia can also dish out some formidable swells. The US south coast's hurricane season (August to November) brings Canadians steep fast breaks, snappy right and left point breaks, and offshore reef and shoal breaks in areas such as Lawrencetown, just outside Halifax, as well as across the entire South Shore region. There are also a couple of surf schools here. SANS (Surfing Association of Nova Scotia; www.surfns.com) is a good place to start your research on the swells.

Windsurfers set their sails for Howe Sound in Squamish, BC, and for Québec's Îles de la Madeleine (Magdalen Islands), a small chain in the Gulf of St Lawrence.

Polar bears in Manitoba

ANDREANITA / GETTY IMAGES ©

Wildlife

On land, in the water and in the air, Canada is teeming with the kind of critters that make visitors wonder if they've stepped into a zoo by mistake. And when we say 'critters,' we're not talking small fry: this is the home of grizzlies, polar bears, wolverine, moose and bald eagles, and the coast offers perfect whale-watching spots. Extra camera batteries are heartily recommended.

Grizzly Bears & Black Bears

Grizzly bears – *Ursus arctos horribilis* to all you Latin scholars out there – are commonly found in the Rocky Mountain regions of British Columbia (BC) and Alberta, though they are now moving up further into the Arctic. Standing up to 3m tall, they have a distinctive shoulder hump and labrador-like snout. Solitary animals with no natural enemies (except humans), they enjoy crunching on elk, moose and caribou, but they're usually content to fill their bellies with berries and, if available, fresh salmon. Keep in mind that you should never approach any bear. And in remote areas, be sure to travel in groups.

In 1994, coastal BC's Khutzeymateen Grizzly Bear Sanctuary (near the northern town of Prince Rupert) was officially designated with protected status. More than 50 grizzlies

★ **Best Moose-Viewing**

Northern Peninsula, Newfoundland

Cape Breton Highlands National Park, Nova Scotia

Algonquin Provincial Park, Ontario

Maligne Lake, Jasper National Park, Alberta

Moose in Newfoundland

WILDNERDPIX / GETTY IMAGES ©

currently live on this 450-sq-km refuge. A few ecotour operators have permits for viewing the animals.

Just to confuse you, grizzlies can be brown or black, while their smaller, more prevalent relative, the black bear, can be brown. Canada is home to around half a million black bears and they're spread out across the country, except for Prince Edward Island, southern Alberta and southern Saskatchewan. In regions such as northern BC, as well as in Banff and Jasper National Parks, seeing black bears feasting on berries or dandelions as you drive past on the highway is surprisingly common.

The world's only white-colored black bears roam in northern BC. Born with a recessive gene, there are approximately 400 of these 'spirit bears', living in mostly coastal areas.

Polar Bears

Weighing less than a kilogram at birth, the fiercest member of the bear clan is not quite so cute when it grows up to be a hulking 600kg. But these mesmerizing animals still pack a huge visual punch for visitors. If your visit to Canada won't be complete until you've seen one, there's really only one place to go: Churchill, Manitoba, on the shores of Hudson Bay (late September to early November is the viewing season). About 900 of the planet's roughly 20,000 white-furred beasts prowl the tundra here.

Just remember: the carnivorous, ever-watchful predators are not cuddly cartoon critters. Unlike grizzlies and black bears, polar bears actively prey on people.

Moose

Canada's iconic shrub-nibbler, the moose is a massive member of the deer family that owes its popularity to its distinctively odd appearance: skinny legs supporting a humongous body and a cartoonish face that looks permanently inquisitive and clueless at the same time. And then there are the antlers: males grow a spectacular rack every summer, only to discard them come November.

Adding to their *Rocky and Bullwinkle Show* appeal, a moose can move at more than 50km/h and easily outswim two adults paddling a canoe – all on a vegetarian diet comprised mostly of tasty leaves and twigs.

You'll spot moose foraging for food near lakes, muskegs and streams, as well as in the forests of the western mountain ranges in the Rockies and the Yukon. Newfoundland is perhaps the moosiest place of all. In 1904, the province imported and released four beasts into the wild. They evidently enjoyed the good life of shrub-eating and hot sex, ultimately spawning the 120,000 inhabitants that now roam the woods.

During mating season (September), the males can become belligerent, as can a mother with her calves, so keep your distance.

Elk, Deer & Caribou

Moose are not the only animals that can exhibit a Mr Hyde personality change during rutting season. Usually placid, male elk have been known to charge vehicles in Jasper National Park, believing their reflection in the shiny paintwork to be a rival for their harem of eligible females. It's rare, though, and Jasper is generally one of the best places in Canada to see this large deer species, which you'll see wandering around attracting camera-toting travelers on the edge of town.

White-tailed deer can be found anywhere from Nova Scotia's Cape Breton to the Northwest Territories' Great Slave Lake. Its bigger relative, the caribou, is unusual in that both males and females sport enormous antlers. Barren-ground caribou feed on lichen and spend most of the year on the tundra from Baffin Island to Alaska. Woodland caribou roam further south, with some of the biggest herds trekking across northern Québec and Labrador. These beasts, which have a reputation for not being especially smart, also show up in the mountain parks of BC, Alberta and Newfoundland, which is where many visitors see them. In 2009, the small herd in Banff National Park set off an avalanche that ultimately wiped out the population. Also known as reindeer, the caribou is on the Canadian 25-cent coin.

Whales

More than 22 species of whale and porpoise lurk offshore in Atlantic Canada, including superstars such as the humpback whale, which averages 15m and 36 tons; the North Atlantic right whale, the world's most endangered leviathan, with an estimated population of just 350; and the mighty blue whale, the largest animal on earth at 25m and around 100 tons. Then there's the little guy, the minke, which grows to 10m and often approaches boats, delighting passengers with acrobatics as it shows off. Whale-watching tours are very popular throughout the region: the Bay of Fundy and Cape Breton are both whale-watching hot spots.

You can also spot humpbacks and gray whales off the west coast, but it's the orca that dominates viewing here. Their aerodynamic bodies, signature black-and-white coloration and incredible speed (up to 40km/h) make them the Ferraris of the aquatic world, and their diet includes fish, seals and other whales (hence the 'killer whale' nickname). The waters around Vancouver Island, particularly in the Strait of Juan de Fuca, teem with orcas every summer. Whale-watching tours depart from points throughout the region; Tofino and Victoria are particularly packed with operators. It's also not uncommon to see whales from the decks of the BC ferries.

Belugas glide in Arctic waters to the north. These ghostly white whales are one of the smallest members of the whale family, typically measuring no more than 4m and weighing about 1 ton. They are chatty fellows who squeak, chirp and peep while traveling in close-knit family pods. Churchill, Manitoba, is a good place to view them, as is Tadoussac, Québec (the only population outside the Arctic resides here).

Birds

Canada's wide skies are home to 462 bird species, with BC and Ontario boasting the greatest diversity. The most famous feathered resident is the common loon, Canada's national bird – if you don't spot one in the wild, you'll see it on the back of the $1 coin. Rivaling it in the ubiquity stakes are Canada geese, a hardy fowl that can fly up to 1000km per day and seems to have successfully colonized parks throughout the world.

★ Whale Hot Spots

Witless Bay, Newfoundland

Digby Neck, Nova Scotia

Victoria, British Columbia

Tofino, British Columbia

Cabot Trail, Nova Scotia

Humpback whale near Vancouver Island

DANIEL BEARHAM / GETTY IMAGES ©

The most visually arresting of Canada's birds are its eagles, especially the bald variety, whose wingspan can reach up to 2m. Good viewing sites include Brackendale, between Vancouver and Whistler in BC, where up to 4000 eagles nest in winter. Also train your binoculars on Bras d'Or Lake on Cape Breton Island, Nova Scotia and on Vancouver Island's southern and western shorelines.

Seabirds flock to Atlantic Canada to breed. Think razorbills, kittiwakes, Arctic terns, common murres and, yes, puffins. Everyone loves these cute little guys, a sort of waddling penguin-meets-parrot, with black-and-white feathers and an orange beak. They nest around Newfoundland in particular. The preeminent places to get feathered are New Brunswick's Grand Manan Island and Newfoundland's Witless Bay and Cape St Mary's (both on the Avalon Peninsula near St John's). The best time is May through August, before the birds fly away for the winter.

Watching Wildlife

Seeing a bear foraging alongside the road or happening upon a moose swimming in a remote lake are the highlights of many visitors' trips to the parks. Keep in mind, however, that you're a guest in their home. A number of guidelines and laws exist to protect both you and the animals. Approaching or interfering with wildlife is a crime taken very seriously is this corner of the world – penalties are steep.

- Keep your distance – at least 10 bus lengths from bears, cougars and wolves and three bus lengths from elk, deer, sheep, goats and moose. If a bedded animal gets up or a feeding animal stops chewing, you're too close. Animals don't like the spotlight and those that feel threatened can (and do!) charge.

- If you see a female elk on her own, there's a calf nearby. If there's a bear cub, a mama bear is not far. *Never* get between a wild animal and her young. You will be viewed as a threat and treated likewise.

- Wildlife-watching is a spectator sport only: do not approach, entice or in any way disturb wildlife. Many people move closer and closer in an attempt to get a photo, frightening the animal and putting the photographer in a dangerous position.

- Never feed wildlife. Park rangers are almost always forced to put down animals that become accustomed to people, as the animals generally turn aggressive over time.

- If you see an animal from your car, slow down – it could dart in front of you at any moment. If you decide to stop, stay inside your car.

- Be particularly wary of animals that appear indifferent to your presence; they may appear cuddly and even docile, but they're not.

The Moncton Wildcats play the Québec Remparts

Spectator Sports

While Canadians have a solid reputation for being mild-mannered, that all changes when it comes to watching sports. Peace-loving most of the time, locals will paint their faces, down a few too many Molsons and chant, scream and sing at the top of their lungs at hockey games. For visitors, watching sports with these passionate locals is an eye-opening cultural experience.

Hockey

While Canada is a multi-faith country, there's one religion that rises above all others. Hockey – don't even bother calling it ice hockey here – rouses rabid emotions in die-hard fans and can trigger group hugging and uncontrollable sobbing at the drop of a puck, especially when the local team has just lost (like they have always done lately) in the annual Stanley Cup play-offs.

Canada has seven teams in the elite, US-dominated National Hockey League (NHL): the Vancouver Canucks, Calgary Flames, Edmonton Oilers, Ottawa Senators, Montréal Canadiens, Winnipeg Jets and Toronto Maple Leafs (don't make the mistake of calling them 'the Leaves'). The CBC Television website (www.cbc.ca/sports/hockey/nhl) has the details.

Although Canadians make up nearly half of all NHL players, no Canadian team has won the revered Stanley Cup in over quarter of a century (since the Montréal Canadiens in 1993).

While tickets for games in some areas can be hard to come by – Vancouver Canucks games routinely sell out, for example, and booking as far ahead as possible for the September to June season is essential – you don't have to hit a stadium to catch a game. For a glimpse at what it feels like to be unreservedly in love with a Canadian hockey side, head to any local pub on game night and you'll be swept up in the emotion. And the beer will be better than the overpriced plastic cups of fizz on offer at the games themselves.

Minor pro teams and junior hockey clubs also fill arenas with fans. Check the Canadian Hockey League (www.chl.ca) and American Hockey League (www.theahl.com) for local stick wielders.

Football

We're not talking about soccer and we're not even talking about American Football here. With nine major teams across the country, the Canadian Football League (CFL) is second only to hockey in the hearts and minds of many north-of-the-border sports nuts. And while it's similar to American Football – think hefty padding, an egg-shaped ball and the kind of crunching tackles that would stop a grizzly bear – the Canadian version involves teams of 12 players and is fought out on a larger pitch.

Like hockey, the main annual aim of the Hamilton Tiger-Cats, Montréal Alouettes, Toronto Argonauts, Ottawa Redblacks, Winnipeg Blue Bombers, Saskatchewan Roughriders, Calgary Stampeders, Edmonton Eskimos and BC Lions is to win that elusive trophy, this one called the Grey Cup. Play-off games trigger raucous street celebrations in host cities, with fans from visiting teams parading around in team shirts hollering their undying love for their side.

Soccer

Canada's most popular participation sport, soccer – you won't get very far calling it football here – has traditionally mirrored the US experience by never quite reaching the heights of the continent's more established professional sports. But things are slowly changing, buoyed by the recent success of MLS team Toronto FC (who won the 'double' of MLS Cup and Supporters Shield in 2017) and the 2019 launch of the new Canadian Premier League.

Canada currently has three teams in the US-based top level Major League Soccer (MLS) class: Toronto FC and Montreal Impact who compete in the Eastern Conference, and Vancouver Whitecaps, who play in the Western Conference. Since the MLS's inception in 1996, only Toronto FC has bagged major honors.

The fully professional Canadian Premier League consists of seven clubs spread across five provinces although there are plans to expand it. Forge FC from Hamilton, Ontario and Calvary FC from Calgary, Alberta were early front-runners.

Soccer is growing in popularity as a spectator sport in Canada, but tickets for top-level games are still relatively easy to buy – book ahead via club websites, though, if you have a particular date in mind.

Baseball

Following the 2004 relocation of the Montréal Expos to Washington (they're now called the Washington Nationals), Canada's only Major League Baseball (MLB) team is the Toronto Blue Jays, a member of the American League's Eastern Division. Founded in 1977 and playing in the city's cavernous downtown Sky Dome – now known as the Rogers Centre – they are the only non-US team to win the World Series (in 1993). Follow the team and check out ticket options for the April to early October season at www.bluejays.com.

There is also one professional minor league side in Canada: the Vancouver Canadians (www.milb.com/vancouver), affiliated with the Blue Jays and playing in the Northwest League. Their recently refurbished outdoor stadium with mountain views is one of the best diamonds in Canada, so hit the bleachers and feel the nostalgic ambiance of old-school summertime baseball.

Additional lower level teams across the country – including the Winnipeg Goldeyes (www.goldeyes.com) – offer a similar family-friendly feel, while college teams are also popular if you want to catch the atmosphere of a game without paying Blue Jay prices.

Women's National Soccer Team

With two Olympic bronze medals from 2012 and 2016, Canada's Women's National Soccer Team has gained a huge following. In 2002, Canada hosted FIFA's first U-19 Championship where the team won silver and thousands of fans woke up to the fact that Canada is good at sports other than hockey. The 2015 FIFA Women's World Cup was held in Vancouver. While the national team was eliminated in the quarter finals, the tournament drew in 1,353,506 fans – setting a new record.

Canadian Pacific Railway in Banff National Park

FERRANTRAITE / GETTY IMAGES ©

Survival Guide

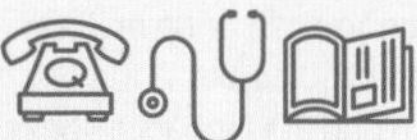

Directory A–Z

Accessible Travel

Canada is making progress when it comes to easing the challenges facing people with disabilities, especially the mobility-impaired.

- Many public buildings have access ramps and/or lifts. Most public restrooms feature extra-wide stalls equipped with handrails. Many pedestrian crossings have sloping curbs.
- Newer and recently remodeled hotels, especially chain hotels, have rooms with extra-wide doors and spacious bathrooms.
- Interpretive centers at national and provincial parks are usually accessible, and many parks have trails that can be navigated in wheelchairs.
- Car rental agencies offer hand-controlled vehicles and vans with wheelchair lifts at no additional charge, but you must reserve them well in advance.
- Download Lonely Planet's free Accessible Travel guides from http://lptravel.to/AccessibleTravel.
- For accessible air, bus, rail and ferry transportation, check Access to Travel (www.accesstotravel.gc.ca), the federal government's website. In general, most transportation agencies can accommodate people with disabilities if you make your needs known when booking.

Other organizations specializing in the needs of travelers with disabilities:

Mobility International (www.miusa.org) Advises travelers with disabilities on mobility issues and runs an educational exchange program.

Society for Accessible Travel & Hospitality (www.sath.org) Travelers with disabilities share tips and blogs.

Accommodations

In popular destinations, such as Ottawa, Banff and Jasper, it pays to book ahead in the height of the summer, especially during major festivals, and for ski season.

B&Bs From purpose-built villas to heritage homes or someone's spare room, they are often the most atmospheric lodgings.

Camping Campgrounds are plentiful; private grounds often have fancier facilities.

Hostels Young backpacker hangouts, but favored by outdoor adventurers in remoter regions.

Hotels From standard to luxurious with a burgeoning number of boutique options.

Motels Dotting the highways into town, these are often family-fun affairs that offer the most bang for your buck.

Seasons

- Peak season is summer, basically June through August; prices are highest.
- It's best to book ahead during summer, as well as during ski season at winter resorts, and during holidays and major events, as rooms can be scarce.
- Some properties close down altogether in the off-season.

Amenities

- At many budget properties (campgrounds, hostels, simple B&Bs) bathrooms are shared.
- Midrange accommodations, such as most B&Bs, inns (*auberges* in French), motels and some hotels, generally offer the best value for money. Expect a private bathroom, cable TV and, in some cases, free breakfast.
- Top-end accommodations offer an international standard of amenities.

Book Your Stay Online

For more accommodation reviews by Lonely Planet authors, check out http://hotels.lonelyplanet.com/canada. You'll find independent reviews, as well as recommendations on the best places to stay. Best of all, you can book online.

Climate

Halifax

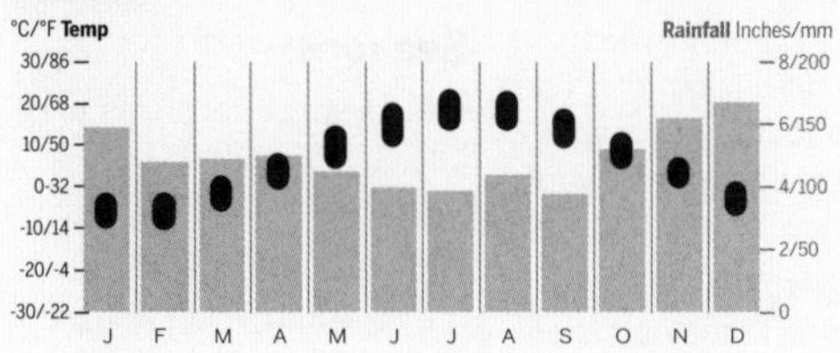

Toronto

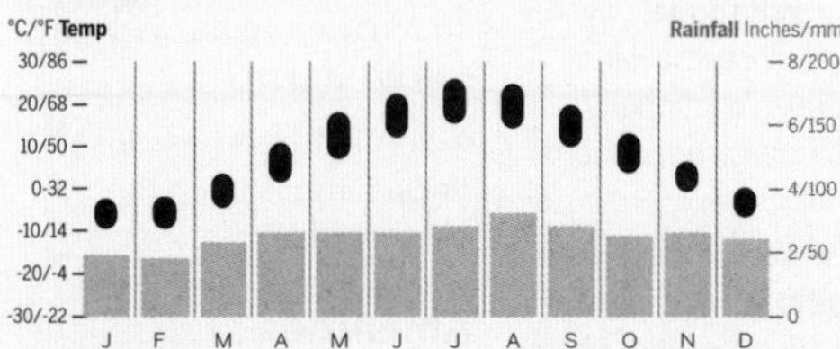

Vancouver

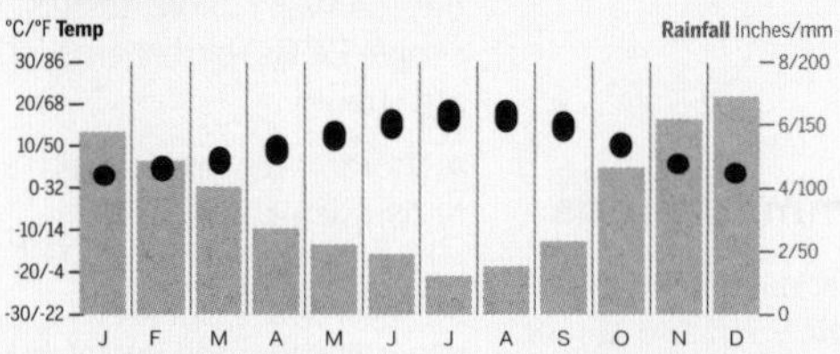

- Most properties offer in-room wi-fi. It's typically free in budget and midrange lodgings, while top-end hotels occasionally charge a fee.
- Air-conditioning is not a standard amenity at most budget and midrange places; ask before you book.

Customs Regulations

The Canada Border Services Agency (www.cbsa-asfc.gc.ca) website has the customs lowdown. A few regulations to note:

Alcohol You can bring in 1.5L of wine, 1.14L of liquor or 24 355mL beers duty-free.

Money You can bring in/take out up to $10,000; larger amounts must be reported to customs.

Pets You must carry a signed and dated certificate from a veterinarian to prove your dog or cat has had a rabies shot in the past 36 months.

Prescription drugs You can bring in/take out a 90-day supply for personal use (though if you're taking it to the USA, know it's technically illegal, but overlooked for individuals).

Tobacco You can bring in 200 cigarettes, 50 cigars, 200g of tobacco and 200 tobacco sticks duty-free.

Discount Cards

Discounts are commonly offered for seniors, children, families and people with disabilities, though no special cards are issued (you get the savings on-site when you pay). AAA and other automobile association members can also receive various travel-related discounts.

International Student Identity Card (www.isic.org) Provides students with discounts on travel insurance and admission to museums and other sights. There are also cards for those who are under 26 but not students, and for full-time teachers.

Parks Canada Discovery Pass (adult/family $68/137; www.pc.gc.ca) Provides access to more than 100 national parks and historic sites for a year. Can pay for itself in as few as seven visits; also provides quicker entry into sites. Note that there's no charge for kids under 18, and a 'family' can include up to seven people in a vehicle, even if they're unrelated.

Many cities have discount cards for local attractions, such as the following:

Montréal Museum Pass (www.museesmontreal.org; $75)

Ottawa Museums Passport (www.museumspassport.ca; $35)

Toronto CityPASS (www.citypass.com/toronto; adult/child $73/50)

Vanier Park ExplorePass (Vancouver; www.spacecentre.ca/explore-pass; adult/child $42.50/36.50)

Electricity

Type A
120V/60Hz

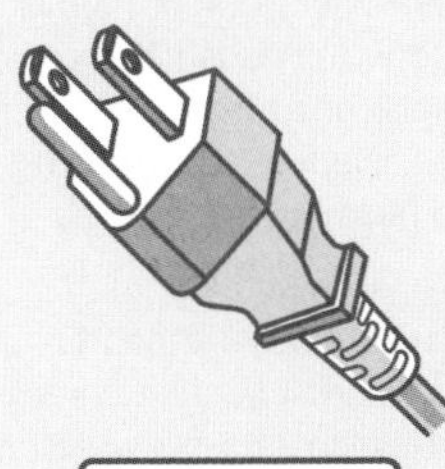

Type B
120V/60Hz

Food

The following price ranges are for main dishes:

$ less than $15

$$ $15–25

$$$ more than $25

Health

Availability & Cost of Health Care

Medical services are widely available. For emergencies, the best bet is to find the nearest hospital and go to its emergency room. If the problem isn't urgent, call a nearby hospital and ask for a referral to a local physician, which is usually cheaper than a trip to the emergency room (where costs can be $500 or so before any treatment).

Pharmacies are abundant, but prescriptions can be expensive without insurance. However, Americans may find Canadian prescription drugs to be cheaper than drugs at home. You're allowed to take out a 90-day supply for personal use (it's technically illegal to bring them into the USA, but often overlooked for individuals).

Environmental Hazards

Cold exposure This can be a significant problem, especially in the northern regions. Be sure to keep all body surfaces covered, including the head and neck. Watch out for the 'Umbles' – stumbles, mumbles, fumbles and grumbles – which ould be signs of impending hypothermia.

Heat exhaustion Dehydration is the main contributor. Symptoms include feeling weak, headache, nausea and sweaty skin. Lay the victim flat with their legs raised; apply cool, wet cloths to the skin; and rehydrate.

Infectious Diseases

Most are acquired by mosquito or tick bites, or environmental exposure. The Public Health Agency of Canada (www.phac-aspc.gc.ca) has details on all listed below.

Giardiasis Intestinal infection. Avoid drinking directly from lakes, ponds, streams and rivers.

Lyme Disease Occurs mostly in southern Canada. Transmitted by deer ticks in late spring and summer. Perform a tick check after you've been outdoors.

Severe Acute Respiratory Syndrome (SARS) At the time of writing, SARS had been brought under control in Canada.

West Nile Virus Mosquito-transmitted in late summer and early fall. Prevent by keeping covered (wear long sleeves, long pants, hats, and shoes rather than sandals) and applying a good insect repellent, preferably one containing

DEET, to exposed skin and clothing.

Medical Checklist

Bring medications you may need clearly labeled in their original containers. A signed, dated letter from your physician that describes your medical conditions and medications, including generic names, is also a good idea.

Also consider packing: insect repellent; permethrin-containing insect spray for clothing, tents and bed nets; sunblock; and motion-sickness medication.

Recommended Vaccinations

No special vaccines are required or recommended for travel to Canada. All travelers should be up to date on routine immunizations.

Useful Websites

Government travel-health websites are available for Australia (www.smarttraveller.gov.au), the United Kingdom (www.nhs.uk/healthcareabroad) and the United States (www.cdc.gov/travel).

MD Travel Health (http://redplanet.travel/mdtravelhealth) General health resources.

Public Health Agency of Canada (www.phac-aspc.gc.ca) Canadian health resources.

World Health Organization (www.who.int) General health resources.

Insurance

Make sure you have adequate travel insurance, whatever the length of your trip. At a minimum, you need coverage for medical emergencies and treatment, including hospital stays and an emergency flight home. Medical treatment for non-Canadians is expensive.

Also consider insurance for luggage theft or loss. If you already have a homeowners or renters policy, check what it will cover and get only supplemental insurance to protect against the rest. If you have prepaid a large portion of your vacation, trip cancellation insurance is worthwhile.

Worldwide travel insurance is available at www.lonelyplanet.com/travel-insurance. You can buy, extend and claim online at anytime – even if you're already on the road.

Internet Access

- It's easy to find internet access. Libraries and community agencies in practically every town provide free wi-fi and computers for public use. The only downsides are that usage time is limited (usually 30 minutes), and some facilities have erratic hours.
- Internet cafes are scarce, limited to the main tourist areas in only certain towns; access generally starts around $2 per hour.
- Wi-fi is widely available. Most lodgings have it (in-room, with good speed), as do many restaurants, bars and Tim Hortons coffee shops.

Legal Matters

- If you are arrested or charged with an offense, you have the right to keep your mouth shut and to hire any lawyer you wish (contact your embassy for a referral, if necessary). If you cannot afford one, ask to be represented by public counsel. There is a presumption of innocence.
- The blood-alcohol limit is 0.08% federally, but can be 0.06% or lower provincially, and driving cars, motorcycles, boats and snowmobiles while drunk or high is a criminal offense. If you are caught, you may face stiff fines, license suspension and possibly prison.
- Consuming alcohol anywhere other than at a residence or licensed premises is also a no-no, which puts parks, beaches and the rest of the great outdoors off-limits.
- Avoid illegal drugs, as penalties may entail heavy fines, possible jail time and a criminal record. While cannabis for personal and medical use is legal, driving

while high is certainly not, and police can stop you and request a breathalyzer even if you're behind the wheel of a parked vehicle.

LGBTIQ+ Travelers

Gay and lesbian travelers will generally find Canada a welcoming destination, especially the big cities. Same-sex marriage is legal throughout the country (Canada was one of the first countries to change their laws on this, back in 2005).

Montréal, Toronto and Vancouver are by far Canada's gayest cities, each with a humming nightlife scene, publications and lots of associations and support groups. All have sizeable Pride celebrations, too, which attract big crowds.

Attitudes remain more conservative in rural areas, as well as in the northern regions. Throughout Nunavut, and to a lesser extent in the Indigenous communities of the Northwest Territories, there are some retrogressive attitudes toward homosexuality. The Yukon, in contrast, is more like British Columbia, with a live-and-let-live West Coast attitude.

The following are good resources for LGBTIQ+ travel; they include Canadian information, though not all are exclusive to the region:

Damron (www.damron.com) Publishes several travel guides, including *Men's Travel Guide, Women's Traveller* and *Damron Accommodations;* gay-friendly tour operators are listed on the website, too.

Out Traveler (www.outtraveler.com) Gay travel magazine.

Purple Roofs (www.purpleroofs.com) Website listing queer accommodations, travel agencies and tours worldwide.

Queer Events (www.queerevents.ca) A general resource for finding events to attend that are aimed at the gay community.

Xtra (www.xtra.ca) Source for gay and lesbian news nationwide.

Maps

- Most tourist offices distribute free provincial road maps.
- For extended hikes or multiday backcountry treks, it's a good idea to carry a topographic map. The best are the series of 1:50,000 scale maps published by the government's Centre for Topographic Information. These are sold by bookstores and parks around the country.
- You can also download and print maps from GeoBase (http://geogratis.gc.ca).

Money

- All prices quoted are in Canadian dollars ($), unless stated otherwise.
- Canadian coins come in 5¢ (nickel), 10¢ (dime), 25¢ (quarter), $1 (loonie) and $2 (toonie or twoonie) denominations. The gold-colored loonie features the loon, a common Canadian waterbird, while the two-toned toonie is decorated with a polar bear. Canada phased out its 1¢ (penny) coin in 2012.
- Paper currency comes in $5 (blue), $10 (purple), $20 (green) and $50 (red) denominations. The $100 (brown) and larger bills are less common. The newest bills in circulation – which have enhanced security features – are actually a polymer-based material; they feel more like plastic than paper.
- For changing money in the larger cities, currency exchange offices may offer better conditions than banks.

ATMs

- Many grocery and convenience stores, airports and bus, train and ferry stations have ATMs. Most are linked to international networks, the most common being Cirrus, Plus, Star and Maestro.
- Most ATMs also spit out cash if you use a major credit card. This method tends to be more expensive because, in addition to a service fee, you'll be charged interest immediately (in other words, there's no interest-free period as with purchases). For exact fees,

check with your own bank or credit card company.

- Visitors heading to Canada's truly remote regions won't find an abundance of ATMs, so it is wise to cash up beforehand.
- Scotiabank, common throughout Canada, is part of the Global ATM Alliance. If your home bank is a member, fees may be less if you withdraw from Scotiabank ATMs.

Cash

Most Canadians don't carry large amounts of cash for everyday use, relying instead on credit and debit cards. Still, carrying some cash, say $100 or less, comes in handy when making small purchases. In some cases, cash is necessary to pay for rural B&Bs and shuttle vans; inquire in advance to avoid surprises.

Credit Cards

Major credit cards such as MasterCard, Visa and American Express are widely accepted in Canada, except in remote, rural communities, where cash is king. You'll find it difficult or impossible to rent a car, book a room or order tickets over the phone without having a piece of plastic. Note that some credit card companies charge a 'transaction fee' (around 3% of whatever you purchased); check with your provider to avoid surprises. If you are given an option to pay in your home currency, it is usually better to NOT accept, as they charge a higher interest rate for the point-of-sale transaction.

For lost or stolen cards, these numbers operate 24 hours:

American Express (800-869-3016; www.americanexpress.com)

MasterCard (800-307-7309; www.mastercard.com)

Visa (416-367-8472; www.visa.com)

Practicalities

Newspapers The most widely available newspaper is the Toronto-based *Globe and Mail*. Other principal dailies are the *Montréal Gazette, Ottawa Citizen, Toronto Star* and *Vancouver Sun*. *Maclean's* is Canada's weekly news magazine.

Radio & TV The Canadian Broadcasting Corporation (CBC) is the dominant nationwide network for both radio and TV. The CTV Television Network is its major competition.

Smoking Banned in all restaurants, bars and other public venues nationwide. This includes tobacco, vaping and cannabis.

Weights & Measures Canada officially uses the metric system, but imperial measurements are used for many day-to-day purposes.

Taxes

Canada's federal goods and services tax (GST), aka the 'gouge and screw' or 'grab and steal' tax, adds 5% to just about every transaction. Most provinces also charge a provincial sales tax (PST) on top of it. Several provinces have combined the GST and PST into a harmonized sales tax (HST). Expect to pay 10% to 15% in most cases.

Tipping

Tipping is a standard practice. Generally you can expect to tip:

Bar staff $1 per drink

Hotel bellhop $1 to $2 per bag

Hotel room cleaners From $2 per day (depending on room size and messiness)

Restaurant waitstaff 15% to 20%

Taxis 10% to 15%

Opening Hours

Opening hours vary throughout the year. We've provided high-season opening hours; hours will generally decrease in the shoulder and low seasons.

Banks 10am–5pm Monday to Friday; some open 9am–noon Saturday

Restaurants breakfast 8–11am, lunch 11:30am–2:30pm Monday to Friday, dinner 5–9:30pm daily; some open for brunch 8am–1pm Saturday and Sunday

Bars 5pm–2am daily

Clubs 9pm–2am Wednesday to Saturday

Shops 10am–6pm Monday to Saturday, noon–5pm Sunday; some open to 8pm or 9pm Thursday and/or Friday

Supermarkets 9am–8pm; some open 24 hours

Public Holidays

Canada observes 10 national public holidays and more at the provincial level. Banks, schools and government offices close on these days.

Kids break for summer holidays in late June and don't return to school until early September. University students get even more time off, usually from May to early or mid-September. Most people take their big annual vacation during these months.

National Holidays

New Year's Day January 1

Good Friday March or April

Easter Monday March or April

Victoria Day Monday before May 25; called National Patriots Day in Québec

Canada Day July 1; called Memorial Day in Newfoundland

Labour Day First Monday of September

Thanksgiving Second Monday of October

Remembrance Day November 11

Christmas Day December 25

Boxing Day December 26

Provincial Holidays

Some provinces observe local holidays, with Newfoundland leading the pack.

Family Day Third Monday of February in Alberta, Ontario, Saskatchewan, Manitoba and British Columbia; known as Louis Riel Day in Manitoba

St Patrick's Day Monday nearest to March 17

St George's Day Monday nearest to April 23

National Day Monday nearest to June 24 in Newfoundland; June 24 in Québec (aka St-Jean Baptiste Day)

Orangemen's Day Monday nearest to July 12 in Newfoundland

Civic Holiday First Monday of August everywhere except Newfoundland, Québec and Yukon Territory

Discovery Day Third Monday of August in Yukon Territory

Canadian Celebrations

Victoria Day (late May) This day was established in 1845 to observe the birthday of Queen Victoria and now celebrates the birthday of the British sovereign, who's still Canada's titular head of state. Victoria Day marks the official beginning of the summer season (which ends with Labour Day on the first Monday of September). Some communities put on fireworks shows.

National Indigenous Peoples Day (June 21) Created in 1996, it celebrates the contributions of Indigenous peoples to Canada. Coinciding with the summer solstice, festivities are organized locally and may include traditional dancing, singing and drumming; storytelling; arts and crafts shows; canoe races; and lots more.

Canada Day (July 1) Known as Dominion Day until 1982, Canada Day was created in 1869 to commemorate the creation of Canada two years earlier. All over the country, people celebrate with barbecues, parades, concerts and fireworks.

Canadian Thanksgiving Day (mid-October) First celebrated in 1578 in what is now Newfoundland by explorer Martin Frobisher to give thanks for surviving his Atlantic crossing, Thanksgiving became an official Canadian holiday in 1872 to celebrate the recovery of the Prince of Wales from a long illness. These days, it's essentially a harvest festival involving a special family dinner of roast turkey and pumpkin, very much as it is practiced in the US.

Safe Travel

Canada is one of the safest countries in the world. Pickpocketing and muggings are rare, especially if you take common sense precautions. Panhandling is common, but usually not dangerous or aggressive.

- Stay in your car at all times when photographing wildlife.
- Drink spiking is rare, but solo travelers should be cautious.
- With the exception of cannabis, recreational drug use in Canada is illegal, including magic mushrooms, and police can stop you any time you're behind the wheel.
- Forest fires, though rare, are a possible threat and should be treated seriously, as they can shift and turn quickly into unexpected areas.

Telephone

Canada's phone system is extensive and landlines reach most places; however, cell service can be spotty. Truly remote areas may not have any phone service at all.

Cell Phones

- If you have an unlocked GSM phone, you should be able to buy a SIM card from local providers such as Telus (www.telus.com), Rogers (www.rogers.com) or Bell (www.bell.ca). Bell has the best data coverage.
- US residents can often upgrade their domestic cell phone plan to extend to Canada. Verizon (www.verizonwireless.com) provides good results.
- Reception is poor and often nonexistent in rural areas no matter who your service provider is. Some companies' plans do not reach all parts of Canada, so check coverage maps prior to purchase.
- SIM cards that work for a set period, such seven, 14, 20 or 30 days, can be purchased online, often with United States and Canada voice, SMS and data bundled together.

Domestic & International Dialing

- Canadian phone numbers consist of a three-digit area code followed by a seven-digit local number. In many parts of Canada, you must dial all 10 digits preceded by ☎1, even if you're calling across the street. In other parts of the country, when you're calling within the same area code, you can dial the seven-digit number only, but this is slowly changing.
- For direct international calls, dial ☎011 + country code + area code + local phone number. The country code for Canada is ☎1 (the same as for the USA, although international rates still apply for all calls made between the two countries).
- Toll-free numbers begin with ☎800, ☎877, ☎866, ☎855, ☎844 or ☎833 and must be preceded by ☎1. Some of these numbers are good throughout Canada and the USA, others only work within Canada, and some work in just one province.

Emergency Numbers

Dial ☎911. This is *not* the emergency number in the Northwest Territories, which is usually the regional three-digit code and then ☎2222 for fire, or ☎1111 for police.

Phonecards

- Prepaid phonecards usually offer the best per-minute rates for long-distance and international calling.
- Cards come in denominations of $5, $10 or $20 and are widely sold in drugstores, supermarkets and convenience stores.
- Beware of cards with hidden charges, such as 'activation fees' or a per-call connection fee.
- A surcharge ranging from 30¢ to 85¢ for calls made from public pay phones is common.

Public Phones

Coin-operated public pay phones are fewer than previously, but still out there. Local calls cost 50¢; many phones also accept prepaid phonecards and credit cards. Dialing the operator (☎0) or directory assistance (☎411 for local calls, ☎1 + area code + 555-1212 for long-distance calls) is free of charge from public phones; it may incur a charge from private phones.

Time

- Canada spans six of the world's 24 time zones. The Eastern zone in Newfoundland is unusual in that it's only 30 minutes different from the adjacent zone. The time difference from coast to coast is 4½ hours.
- Canada observes daylight saving time, which comes into effect on the second Sunday in March, when clocks are put forward one hour, and ends on the first Sunday in November. Saskatchewan and small pockets of Québec, Ontario and British Columbia are the only areas that do not switch to daylight saving time.
- In Québec especially, times for shop hours, train schedules, film screenings etc are usually indicated by the 24-hour clock.

Tourist Information

- The Canadian Tourism Commission (www.canada.travel) is loaded with general information, packages and links.
- All provincial tourist offices maintain comprehensive websites packed with information helpful in planning your trip. Staff also field telephone inquiries and, on request, will mail out free maps and directories about accommodations, attractions and events. Some offices can also help with making hotel, tour or other reservations.
- For detailed information about a specific area, contact the local tourist office, aka visitor center. Just about every city and town has at least a seasonal branch with helpful staff, racks of free pamphlets and books and maps for sale.

Visas

Currently, visas are not required for citizens of 46 countries – including most EU members, Australia and New Zealand – for visits of up to six months.

To find out if you need an Electronic Travel Authorisation (eTA) or are required to apply for a formal visa, go to www.cic.gc.ca/english/visit/visas.asp.

Visitor visas – aka Temporary Resident Visas (TRVs) – can now be applied for online at: www.cic.gc.ca/english/information/applications/visa.asp. Single-entry TRVs ($100) are usually valid for a maximum stay of six months from the date of your arrival in Canada. In most cases your biometric data (such as fingerprints) will be taken. Note that you don't need a Canadian multiple-entry TRV for repeated entries into Canada from the USA, unless you have visited a third country.

A separate visa is required for all nationalities if you plan to study or work in Canada.

Visa extensions ($100) need to be filed with the **CIC Visitor Case Processing Centre** (☎888-242-2100; ⏲8am-4pm Mon-Fri) in Alberta at least one month before your current visa expires.

Visiting the USA

Admission requirements are subject to rapid change. The US State Department (http://travel.state.gov) has the latest information; you can also check with a US consulate in your home country.

Under the US visa-waiver program, visas are not required for citizens of 38 countries – including most EU members, Australia and New Zealand – for visits of up to 90 days (no extensions allowed), as long as you can present a machine-readable passport and are approved under the Electronic System for Travel Authorization (www.cbp.gov/esta). Note that you must register at least 72 hours before arrival with an e-passport, and there's a

$14 fee for processing and authorization.

Canadians do not need visas to enter the USA, though they do need a passport or document approved by the Western Hemisphere Travel Initiative (http://www.cbp.gov/travel/us-citizens/western-hemisphere-travel-initiative). Citizens of all other countries need to apply for a US visa in their home country before arriving in Canada.

All foreign visitors (except Canadians) must pay a US$6 processing fee when entering at land borders.

Women Travelers

Canada is generally a safe place for women to travel, even alone and even in the cities. Simply use the same common sense as you would at home.

In bars and nightclubs, solo women are likely to attract a lot of attention, but if you don't want company, most men will respect a firm 'no, thank you.' If you feel threatened, protesting loudly will often make the offender slink away – or will at least spur other people to come to your defense. Note that carrying mace or pepper spray is illegal in Canada.

Physical attacks are unlikely, but if you are assaulted, call the police immediately – dial 911 except in the Northwest Territories (p304) – or contact a rape crisis center. A complete list is available from the **Canadian Association of Sexual Assault Centres** (☎604-876-2622; www.casac.ca).

Resources for women travelers include:

Her Own Way (www.travel.gc.ca/travelling/publications/her-own-way) Published by the Canadian government for Canadian travelers, but contains a great deal of general advice.

Journeywoman (www.journeywoman.com) Travel links and tips for women with a section on Canada.

Transport

Getting There & Away

Flights, cars and tours can be booked online at www.lonelyplanet.com/bookings.

Entering the Country

Visitors to Canada must hold a valid passport with at least six months remaining before its expiration. Visitors from visa-exempt countries (with the exception of the US; see p305) are required to purchase an Electronic Travel Authorization (eTA; $7), similar to the USA's ESTA visa waiver, before departing their home country. Visitors from non-visa-waiver countries must apply for the appropriate visa prior to arriving in Canada.

Note that questioning may be more intense at land border crossings and your car may be searched.

For updates (particularly regarding land-border crossing rules), check the websites for the US State Department (http://travel.state.gov) and Citizenship & Immigration Canada (www.cic.gc.ca).

Passports

Most international visitors require a passport to enter Canada. US citizens at land and sea borders have other options, such as an enhanced driver's license, permanent resident card or NEXUS card. See Canada Border Services Agency (www.cbsa-asfc.gc.ca) for approved identification documents.

Air

Toronto is far and away Canada's busiest airport, followed by Vancouver. Air Canada (www.aircanada.com), the national flagship carrier, is considered one of the world's safest airlines. All major global airlines fly to Canada. Other companies based in the country and serving international destinations:

WestJet (www.westjet.com) Calgary-based low-cost carrier serving destinations throughout Canada as well as across the US and Caribbean.

Porter Airlines (www.flyporter.com) Flies around eastern Canada and to US cities, including

Boston, Chicago, Washington, DC, and New York.

Land

Border Crossings

There are around 25 official border crossings along the US–Canadian border, from New Brunswick to British Columbia.

The website of the Canadian Border Services Agency (www.cbsa-asfc.gc.ca) shows current wait times at each. You can also access it via Twitter (@CBSA_BWT).

In general, waits rarely exceed 30 minutes, except during the peak summer season, and on Friday and Sunday afternoons, especially on holiday weekends. Some entry points are especially busy:

- Windsor, Ontario, to Detroit, Michigan
- Fort Erie, Ontario, to Buffalo, New York
- Niagara Falls, Ontario, to Niagara Falls, New York
- St Bernard de Lacolle, Québec to Rouse's Point/ Champlain, New York
- Surrey, British Columbia, to Blaine, Washington

Organize your Canadian visa or Electronic Travel Authorization (eTA) in advance. When returning to the USA, check the website for the US Department for Homeland Security (http://bwt.cbp.gov) for border wait times.

All foreign visitors (except Canadians) must pay a $6 processing fee when entering the USA by land.

Bus

Greyhound (www.greyhound.com) and its Canadian equivalent, Greyhound Canada (www.greyhound.ca), operate the largest bus network in North America, but the latter has cut service drastically in recent years. There are direct connections between some cities in the USA and Canada, but you usually have to transfer to a different bus at the border (where it takes a good hour for all passengers to clear customs and immigration). Most international buses have free wi-fi on board. Western Canada has no Greyhound service save a Vancouver–Seattle route.

Other notable international bus companies (with free wi-fi) include:

Megabus (www.megabus.com) Runs between Toronto and US cities, including New York City, Philadelphia and Washington, DC; usually cheaper than Greyhound. Tickets can only be purchased online.

Quick Coach (www.quickcoach.com) Runs between Seattle and Vancouver; typically a bit quicker than Greyhound.

Car & Motorcycle

The highway system of the continental USA connects directly with the Canadian highway system at numerous points along the border. These Canadian highways then meet up with the east–west Trans-Canada Hwy further north. Between the Yukon Territory and Alaska, the main routes are the Alaska, Klondike and Haines Hwys.

If you're driving into Canada, you'll need the vehicle's registration papers, proof of liability insurance and your home driver's license. Cars rented in the USA can usually be driven into Canada and back, but make sure your rental agreement says so. If you're driving a car registered in someone else's name, bring a letter from the owner authorizing use of the vehicle in Canada.

Train

Amtrak (www.amtrak.com) and VIA Rail Canada (www.viarail.ca) run three routes between the USA and Canada: two in the east and one in the west. Customs inspections happen at the border, not upon boarding.

Sea

Various ferry services on the coasts connect the USA and Canada:

- Bar Harbor, Maine, to Yarmouth, NS: Bay Ferries Limited (www.ferries.ca/thecat)
- Eastport, Maine, to Deer Island, NB: East Coast Ferries (www.eastcoastferriesltd.com)
- Seattle, WA, to Victoria, BC: Victoria Clipper (www.clippervacations.com)
- Ketchikan, Alaska, to Prince Rupert, BC: Alaska Marine Highway System (www.ferryalaska.com)
- Sandusky, Ohio, to Pelee Island, ON: Pelee Island

Transportation Service (www.ontarioferries.com)

Getting Around

Air

Air Canada operates the largest domestic-flight network in the country, serving some 150 destinations.

The Canadian aviation arena also includes many independent regional and local airlines, which tend to focus on small, remote regions, mostly in the north. Depending on the destination, fares in such noncompetitive markets can be high.

Bicycle

Much of Canada is great for cycling. Long-distance trips can be done entirely on quiet back roads, and many cities (including Edmonton, Montréal, Ottawa, Toronto, Vancouver and Victoria) have designated bike routes.

- Cyclists must follow the same rules of the road as vehicles, but don't expect drivers to always respect your right of way.
- Helmets are mandatory for all cyclists in British Columbia, New Brunswick, Prince Edward Island and Nova Scotia, as well as for anyone under 18 in Alberta and Ontario.
- The Better World Club (www.betterworldclub.com) provides emergency roadside assistance. Membership costs $40 per year, plus a $12 enrollment fee; it entitles you to two free pickups, and transport to the nearest repair shop, or home, within a 50km radius of where you're picked up.

Rental

- Outfitters renting bicycles exist in most tourist towns.
- Rentals cost around $20 per day for touring bikes and $35 or more per day for mountain bikes. The price usually includes a helmet and lock.
- Most companies require a security deposit of $20 to $200.

Transportation

By air Most airlines will carry bikes as checked luggage without charge on international flights, as long as they're in a box. On domestic flights they usually charge between $30 and $65. Always check details before you buy the ticket.

By bus You must ship your bike as freight on Greyhound Canada. In addition to a bike box ($10), you'll be charged an oversize fee and GST. Bikes only travel on the same bus as the passenger if there's enough space. To ensure that yours arrives at the same time as (or before) you do, ship it a day early.

By train VIA Rail will transport your bicycle for $25, but only on trains offering checked-baggage service (which include all long-distance and many regional trains).

Boat

Ferry services are extensive, especially throughout the Atlantic provinces and in British Columbia.

Walk-ons and cyclists should be able to get aboard at any time, but call ahead for vehicle reservations or if you require a cabin berth. This is especially important during summer peak

Climate Change & Travel

Every form of transport that relies on carbon-based fuel generates CO_2, the main cause of human-induced climate change. Modern travel is dependent on aeroplanes, which might use less fuel per kilometre per person than most cars but travel much greater distances. The altitude at which aircraft emit gases (including CO_2) and particles also contributes to their climate change impact. Many websites offer 'carbon calculators' that allow people to estimate the carbon emissions generated by their journey and, for those who wish to do so, to offset the impact of the greenhouse gases emitted with contributions to portfolios of climate-friendly initiatives throughout the world. Lonely Planet offsets the carbon footprint of all staff and author travel.

season and holidays. Main operators:

Bay Ferries (877-762-7245; www.ferries.ca) Year-round service between Saint John, New Brunswick, and Digby, Nova Scotia.

BC Ferries (250-386-3431; www.bcferries.com) Huge passenger-ferry systems with 25 routes and 47 ports of call, including Vancouver Island, the Gulf Islands, the Sechelt Peninsula along the Sunshine Coast and the islands of Haida Gwaii – all in British Columbia.

CTMA Ferries (418-986-3278; www.ctma.ca/en) Daily ferries to Québec's Îles de la Madeleine from Souris, Prince Edward Island.

Labrador Marine (709 535 0811; www.labradormarine.com) Connects Newfoundland to Labrador.

Marine Atlantic (902-794-5254; www.marineatlantic.ca) Connects Port aux Basques and Argentia in Newfoundland with North Sydney, Nova Scotia.

Northumberland Ferries (902-566-3838; www.ferries.ca) Connects Wood Islands (PEI) and Caribou, Nova Scotia.

Provincial Ferry Services (888-638-5454; www.tw.gov.nl.ca/ferryservices) Operates coastal ferries throughout Newfoundland.

Bus

Greyhound Canada (www.greyhound.ca) has cut service dramatically, offering only a handful of connections, primarily in the east and to Vancouver. Regional carriers pick up the slack.

Buses are generally clean, comfortable and reliable. Amenities may include on-board toilets, air-conditioning (bring a sweater), reclining seats, free wi-fi and on-board movies. Smoking is not permitted. On long journeys, buses make meal stops every few hours, usually at highway service stations.

Car & Motorcycle

Automobile Associations

Autoclub membership is a handy thing to have in Canada. The Canadian Automobile Association (www.caa.ca) offers services, including 24-hour emergency roadside assistance, to members of international affiliates, such as AAA in the USA, AA in the UK and ADAC in Germany. The club also offers trip-planning advice, free maps, travel-agency services and a range of discounts on hotels, car rentals etc.

The Better World Club (www.betterworldclub.com), which donates 1% of its annual revenue to environmental cleanup efforts, has emerged as an alternative. It offers service throughout the USA and Canada, and has a roadside-assistance program for bicycles.

Bring Your Own Vehicle

There's minimal hassle driving into Canada from the USA, as long as you have your vehicle's registration papers, proof of liability insurance and your home driver's license.

Fuel

Gas is sold in liters. Prices are higher in remote areas, with Yellowknife usually setting the national record; drivers in Calgary typically pay the least for gas.

Fuel prices are usually lower in the USA, so fill up south of the border if that's an option.

Insurance

Canadian law requires liability insurance for all vehicles, to cover you for damage caused to property and people.

- The minimum requirement is $200,000 in all provinces except Québec, where it is $50,000.
- Americans traveling to Canada in their own car should ask their insurance company for a Nonresident Interprovince Motor Vehicle Liability Insurance Card (commonly known as a 'yellow card'), which is accepted as evidence of financial responsibility anywhere in Canada. Although not mandatory, it may come in handy in an accident.
- Car-rental agencies offer liability insurance. Collision Damage Waivers (CDW) reduce or eliminate the amount you'll have to reimburse the rental company if there's damage to the car itself. Some credit cards cover CDW for a certain rental period if you use the

Car Sharing

Car2Go (www.car2go.com) operates in Vancouver, Calgary, Montreal and Toronto. It costs $5 to join and then 41¢ per minute or $15 per hour to use a vehicle. You locate the cars with a smartphone app and then can park and leave them anywhere within the designated downtown zone.

card to pay for the rental and decline the policy offered by the rental company. Always check with your card issuer to see what coverage it offers in Canada.

- Personal accident insurance (PAI) covers you and any passengers for medical costs incurred as a result of an accident. If your travel insurance or your health-insurance policy at home does this as well (and most do, but check), then this is one expense you can do without.

Rental

Car

To rent a car in Canada you generally need to:

- be at least 25 years old (some companies will rent to drivers between the ages of 21 and 24 for an additional charge);
- hold a valid driver's license (an international one may be required if you're not from an English- or French-speaking country);
- have a major credit card.

You should be able to get an economy-size vehicle for about $45 to $75 per day. Child safety seats are compulsory (reserve them when you book) and cost about $15 per day.

Major international car-rental companies usually have branches at airports, train stations and in city centers.

In Canada, on-the-spot rentals often are more expensive than pre-booked packages (ie cars booked with a flight).

Motorcycle

Several companies offer motorcycle rentals and tours. A Harley Heritage Softail Classic costs about $210 per day, including liability insurance and 200km mileage. Some companies have minimum rental periods, which can be as much as seven days. Riding a hog is especially popular in British Columbia.

Cycle BC (☎604-709-5663; http://cyclebc.ca) Tours and rentals out of Victoria and Vancouver in British Columbia.

McScoots Motorcycle & Scooter Rentals (☎250-763-4668; www.mcscoots.com) Big selection of Harleys; also operates motorcycle tours. It's based in Kelowna, British Columbia.

Recreational Vehicle

The RV market is biggest in the west, with specialized agencies in Calgary, Edmonton, Whitehorse and Vancouver. For summer travel, book as early as possible. The base cost is roughly $250 per day in high season for smaller vehicles, although insurance, fees and taxes add a hefty chunk to that. Diesel-fueled RVs have considerably lower running costs.

Canadream Campers (☎925-255-8383; www.canadream.com) Based in Calgary, with rentals (including one-way rentals) in eight cities, including Vancouver, Whitehorse, Toronto and Halifax.

Cruise Canada (☎403-291-4963; www.cruisecanada.com) Offers three sizes of RVs. Locations in Halifax, and in central and western Canada; offers one-way rentals.

Road Rules

- Canadians drive on the right-hand side of the road.
- Seat belt use is compulsory. Children who weigh less than 18kg must be strapped into child-booster seats, except infants, who must be in a rear-facing safety seat.
- Motorcyclists must wear helmets and drive with their headlights on.
- Distances and speed limits are posted in kilometers. The speed limit is generally 40km/h to 50km/h in cities and 90km/h to 110km/h outside town.
- Slow down to 60km/h when passing emergency vehicles (such as police cars and ambulances) stopped

on the roadside with their lights flashing.

- Turning right at red lights after coming to a full stop is permitted in all provinces (except where road signs prohibit it, and on the island of Montréal, where it's always a no-no). There's a national propensity for running red lights, however, so don't assume 'right of way' at intersections.
- Driving while using a hand-held cell phone is illegal in Canada. Fines are hefty.
- Radar detectors are not allowed in most of Canada (Alberta, British Columbia and Saskatchewan are the exceptions). If you're caught driving with a radar detector, even one that isn't being operated, you could receive a fine of $1000 and your device may be confiscated.
- The blood-alcohol limit for drivers is 0.08%, but provincial limits can be lower. Driving while drunk or high is a criminal offense.

Local Transportation

Bicycle

Cycling is a popular means of getting around during the warmer months, and many cities have hundreds of kilometers of dedicated bike paths. Bicycles typically can be taken on public transportation (although some cities have restrictions during peak travel times). All the major cities have shops renting bikes. Vancouver, Toronto and Montréal have bike-share programs.

Bus

Buses are the most common form of public transportation, and practically all towns have their own systems. Most are commuter-oriented, and offer only limited or no services in the evenings and on weekends.

Taxi

Most of the main cities have taxis, and smaller towns have one or two. They are usually metered, with an initial fee of roughly $3.50 and a per-kilometer charge of around $1.75. Drivers expect a tip of between 10% and 15%. Taxis can be flagged down or ordered by phone.

Train

Toronto and Montréal are the two Canadian cities with subway systems. Vancouver's version is mostly an above-ground monorail. Calgary, Edmonton and Ottawa have efficient light-rail systems. Route maps are posted in all stations.

Train

VIA Rail (www.viarail.ca) operates most of Canada's intercity and transcontinental passenger trains, chugging over 14,000km of track. In some remote parts of the country, such as Churchill, Manitoba, trains provide the only overland access.

- Rail service is most efficient in the corridor between Québec City and Windsor, Ontario – particularly between Montréal and Toronto, the two major hubs.
- The rail network does not extend to Newfoundland, Prince Edward Island or the Northwest Territories.
- Free wi-fi is available on most trains.
- Smoking, including vaping and smoking cannabis, is prohibited on all trains.

Classes

There are four main classes:

- Economy class buys you a fairly basic, if indeed quite comfortable, reclining seat with a headrest. Blankets and pillows are provided for overnight travel.
- Business class operates in the southern Ontario/Québec corridor. Seats are more spacious and have outlets for plugging in laptops. You also get a meal and priority boarding.
- Sleeper class is available on shorter overnight routes. You can choose from compartments with upper or lower pullout berths, and private single, double or triple roomettes, all with a bathroom.
- Touring class is available on long-distance routes and includes sleeper-class accommodations plus meals, access to the sightseeing car and sometimes a tour guide.

Costs

Taking the train is more expensive than the bus and

often comparable to flying, but most people find it a fun, comfortable way to travel. June to mid-October is peak season, when prices are about 40% higher. Buying tickets in advance (even just five days before) can yield significant savings.

Long-Distance Routes

VIA Rail has several classic trains:

Canadian A 1950s stainless-steel beauty between Toronto and Vancouver, zipping through the northern Ontario lake country, the western plains via Winnipeg and Saskatoon, and Jasper in the Rockies over three days.

Hudson Bay From the prairie (slowly) to the subarctic: Winnipeg to polar-bear hangout Churchill.

Ocean Chugs from Montréal along the St Lawrence River through New Brunswick and Nova Scotia.

Jasper to Prince Rupert An all-daylight route from Jasper, Alberta, to coastal Prince Rupert, British Columbia; there's an overnight stop in Prince George (you make your own hotel reservations).

Privately run regional train companies offer additional rail-touring opportunities:

Algoma Central Railway (www.agawatrain.com) Access to northern Ontario wilderness areas.

Ontario Northland (www.ontarionorthland.ca) Operates the seasonal *Polar Bear Express* from Cochrane to Moosonee on James Bay (round-trip $119).

Royal Canadian Pacific (☎403-319-4690; www.royalcanadianpacific.com) A cruise-ship-like luxury line running between and around the Rockies via Calgary.

Rocky Mountaineer Railtours (www.rockymountaineer.com) Gape at Canadian Rockies scenery on swanky trains between Vancouver, Kamloops and Calgary (two days from $1247).

White Pass & Yukon Route (www.wpyr.com) Gorgeous route paralleling the original White Pass trail from Whitehorse, Yukon, to Fraser, British Columbia (round-trip $175).

Reservations

Seat reservations are highly recommended, especially in summer, on weekends and around holidays. During peak season (June to mid-October), some of the most popular sleeping arrangements are sold out months in advance, especially on long-distance trains such as the *Canadian*. The *Hudson Bay* often books solid during polar-bear season (around late September to early November).

Train Passes

VIA Rail offers a variety of passes that provide good savings, but the 'System' Canrailpass ($649 to $1518) is often the best for travelers. It's good for six, 12 or unlimited trips on all trains during a 15-, 30- or 60-day period. All seats are in economy class; upgrades are not permitted. You must book each leg at least three days in advance (which you can do online).

Language

English and French are the official languages of Canada. You'll see both on highway signs, maps, tourist brochures, packaging etc. In Québec the preservation of French is a major concern. Here, road signs and visitor information is often in French only.

New Brunswick is the only officially bilingual province but French is widely spoken, particularly in the north and east. Nova Scotia also has a significant French-speaking population, and there are pockets in most other provinces.

The French spoken in Canada is essentially the same as in France. Although many English-speaking (and most French-speaking) students in Québec are still taught the French of France, the local tongue is known as 'Québecois' or joual.

French sounds can almost all be found in English. The exceptions are nasal vowels (represented in our pronunciation guides by o or u followed by an almost inaudible nasal consonant sound m, n or ng), the 'funny' *u* (ew in our guides) and the deep-in-the-throat *r*. Bearing this in mind and reading the pronunciation guides here as if they were English, you'll be understood just fine.

Basics

Hello.	*Bonjour.*	bon·zhoor
Goodbye.	*Au revoir.*	o·rer·vwa
Excuse me.	*Excusez-moi.*	ek·skew·zay·mwa
Sorry.	*Pardon.*	par·don
Yes./No.	*Oui./Non.*	wee/non
Please.	*S'il vous plaît.*	seel voo play
Thank you.	*Merci.*	mair·see

How are you?
Comment allez-vous? ko·mon ta·lay·voo

Fine, and you?
Bien, merci. Et vous? byun mair·see ay voo

My name is ...
Je m'appelle ... zher ma·pel ...

What's your name?
Comment vous appelez-vous? ko·mon voo·za·play voo

Do you speak English?
Parlez-vous anglais? par·lay·voo ong·glay

I don't understand.
Je ne comprends pas. zher ner kom·pron pa

Directions

Where's ...?
Où est ...? oo ay ...

What's the address?
Quelle est l'adresse? kel ay la·dres

Could you write the address, please?
Est-ce que vous pourriez écrire l'adresse, s'il vous plaît? es·ker voo poo·ryay ay·kreer la·dres seel voo play

Can you show me (on the map)?
Pouvez-vous m'indiquer (sur la carte)? poo·vay·voo mun·dee·kay (sewr la kart)

Eating & Drinking

A table for (two), please.
Une table pour (deux), s'il vous plaît. ewn ta·bler poor (der) seel voo play

What would you recommend?
Qu'est-ce que vous conseillez? kes·ker voo kon·say·yay

What's in that dish?
Quels sont les ingrédients? kel son lay zun·gray·dyon

I'm a vegetarian.
Je suis végétarien/végétarienne. zher swee vay·zhay·ta·ryun/vay·zhay·ta·ryen (m/f)

I don't eat ...
Je ne mange pas ... zher ner monzh pa ...

That was delicious.
C'était délicieux! say·tay day·lee·syer

The check, please.
L'addition, s'il vous plaît. la·dee·syon seel voo play

Behind the Scenes

Acknowledgements

Climate map data adapted from Peel MC, Finlayson BL & McMahon TA (2007) 'Updated World Map of the Köppen-Geiger Climate Classification', *Hydrology and Earth System Sciences*, 11, 1633–44.

Cover photograph: Aerial view of trees growing in forest, Vancouver, Michael Wu/EyeEm/Getty Images ©

This Book

This 2nd edition of Lonely Planet's *Best of Canada* guidebook was curated by Brendan Sainsbury and researched and written by Ray Bartlett, Oliver Berry, Gregor Clark, Shawn Duthie, Steve Fallon, Anna Kaminski, Adam Karlin, John Lee, Craig McLachlan, Liza Prado, Brendan and Phillip Tang. This guidebook was produced by the following:

Destination Editor Ben Buckner

Senior Product Editors Grace Dobell, Martine Power, Saralinda Turner

Regional Senior Cartographer Corey Hutchison

Product Editor Hannah Cartmel

Book Designer Wibowo Rusli

Cartographer Julie Dodkins

Assisting Editors Sarah Bailey, James Bainbridge, Judith Bamber, Michelle Bennett, Samantha Cook, Joel Cotterell, Melanie Dankel, Carly Hall, Jennifer Hattam, Anne Hayden, Gabrielle Innes, Kellie Langdon, Lou McGregor, Christopher Pitts, Sarah Reid, Tamara Sheward, James Smart, Simon Williamson

Cover Researcher Naomi Parker

Thanks to Jessica Boland, Andrea Dobbin, Bailey Freeman, Paul Gatward, Karen Henderson, Kate James, Kate Kiely, Chris Oh, Kirsten Rawlings, Vicky Smith

Send Us Your Feedback

We love to hear from travelers – your comments keep us on our toes and help make our books better. Our well-traveled team reads every word on what you loved or loathed about this book. Although we cannot reply individually to postal submissions, we always guarantee that your feedback goes straight to the appropriate authors, in time for the next edition. Each person who sends us information is thanked in the next edition, the most useful submissions are rewarded with a selection of digital PDF chapters.

Visit lonelyplanet.com/contact to submit your updates and suggestions or to ask for help. Our award-winning website also features inspirational travel stories, news and discussions.

Note: We may edit, reproduce and incorporate your comments in Lonely Planet products such as guidebooks, websites and digital products, so let us know if you don't want your comments reproduced or your name acknowledged. For a copy of our privacy policy visit lonelyplanet.com/privacy.

Index

A

B

C

D

E

F

G

H

I

J

K

L

M

W

Z

Symbols & Map Key

Look for these symbols to quickly identify listings:

- Sights
- Activities
- Courses
- Tours
- Festivals & Events
- Eating
- Drinking
- Entertainment
- Shopping
- Information & Transport

These symbols and abbreviations give vital information for each listing:

Sustainable or green recommendation

FREE No payment required

- Telephone number
- Opening hours
- Parking
- Nonsmoking
- Air-conditioning
- Internet access
- Wi-fi access
- Swimming pool
- Bus
- Ferry
- Tram
- Train
- English-language menu
- Vegetarian selection
- Family-friendly

Find your best experiences with these Great For... icons.

- Art & Culture
- Beaches
- Budget
- Cafe/Coffee
- Cycling
- Detour
- Drinking
- Entertainment
- Events
- Family Travel
- Food & Drink
- History
- Local Life
- Nature & Wildlife
- Photo Op
- Scenery
- Shopping
- Short Trip
- Sport
- Walking
- Winter Travel

Sights

- Beach
- Bird Sanctuary
- Buddhist
- Castle/Palace
- Christian
- Confucian
- Hindu
- Islamic
- Jain
- Jewish
- Monument
- Museum/Gallery/Historic Building
- Ruin
- Shinto
- Sikh
- Taoist
- Winery/Vineyard
- Zoo/Wildlife Sanctuary
- Other Sight

Points of Interest

- Bodysurfing
- Camping
- Cafe
- Canoeing/Kayaking
- Course/Tour
- Diving
- Drinking & Nightlife
- Eating
- Entertainment
- Sento Hot Baths/Onsen
- Shopping
- Skiing
- Sleeping
- Snorkelling
- Surfing
- Swimming/Pool
- Walking
- Windsurfing
- Other Activity

Information

- Bank
- Embassy/Consulate
- Hospital/Medical
- Internet
- Police
- Post Office
- Telephone
- Toilet
- Tourist Information
- Other Information

Geographic

- Beach
- Gate
- Hut/Shelter
- Lighthouse
- Lookout
- Mountain/Volcano
- Oasis
- Park
- Pass
- Picnic Area
- Waterfall

Transport

- Airport
- BART station
- Border crossing
- Boston T station
- Bus
- Cable car/Funicular
- Cycling
- Ferry
- Metro/MRT station
- Monorail
- Parking
- Petrol station
- Subway/S-Bahn/Skytrain station
- Taxi
- Train station/Railway
- Tram
- Underground/U-Bahn station
- Other Transport

contributed to Lonely Planet guides, with a focus on Europe and the Americas. He has also worked on cycling guides to Italy and California and coffee-table pictorials such as *Food Trails*, the *USA Book* and the *Lonely Planet Guide to the Middle of Nowhere*.

Shawn Duthie

Originally from Canada, Shawn has been traveling, studying and working around the world for the past 13 years. A love of travel merged with an interest in international politics, which led to several years of lecturing at the University of Cape Town and now working as a freelance political risk consultant specializing in African countries. Shawn lives in South Africa and takes any excuse to travel around this amazing continent.

Steve Fallon

A native of Boston, Massachusetts, Steve graduated from Georgetown University with a Bachelor of Science in modern languages. After working for several years for an American daily newspaper and earning a master's degree in journalism, his fascination with the 'new' Asia led him to Hong Kong, where he lived for over a dozen years, working for a variety of media and running his own travel bookshop. Steve lived in Budapest for three years before moving to London in 1994. He has written or contributed to more than 100 Lonely Planet titles. Visit his website on www.steveslondon.com.

Anna Kaminski

Originally from the Soviet Union, Anna grew up in Cambridge, UK. She graduated from the University of Warwick with a degree in Comparative American Studies, a background in the history, culture and literature of the Americas and the Caribbean, and an enduring love of Latin America. Her restless wanderings led her to settle briefly in Oaxaca and Bangkok and her flirtation with criminal law saw her volunteering as a lawyer's assistant in the courts, ghettos and prisons of Kingston, Jamaica. Anna has contributed to almost 30 Lonely Planet titles. When not on the road, Anna calls London home.

Adam Karlin

Adam has contributed to dozens of Lonely Planet guidebooks, covering an alphabetical spread that ranges from the Andaman Islands to the Zimbabwe Border. As a journalist, he has written on travel, crime, politics, archeology and the Sri Lankan Civil War, among other topics. He has sent dispatches from every continent barring Antarctica (one day!) and his essays and articles have featured in the BBC, NPR and multiple nonfiction anthologies. Adam is based out of New Orleans, which helps explain his love of wetlands, food and good music. Learn more at www.walkonfine.com or follow on Instagram @adamwalkonfine.

John Lee

Born and raised in the historic UK city of St Albans, John grew up in London, gorging on the capital's rich diet of museums and galleries. Slowly succumbing to the lure of overseas exotica, he arrived on Canada's West Coast in 1993 to begin an MA in Political Science at the University of Victoria. After stints living in Tokyo and Montreal he returned to British Columbia to become a full-time freelance writer in 1999. Now living in Vancouver, John specializes in travel writing and has contributed to more than 150 different publications around the world, including around 25 Lonely Planet books. You can read some of his stories (and see some of his videos) online at www.johnleewriter.com.

Craig McLachlan

Craig has covered destinations all over the globe for Lonely Planet for two decades. Based in Queenstown, New Zealand for half the year, he runs an outdoor activities company and a sake brewery, then moonlights overseas for the other half, leading tours and writing for Lonely Planet. Craig has completed a number of adventures in Japan and his books are available on Amazon. Describing himself as a 'freelance anything', Craig has an MBA from the University of Hawai'i and is also a Japanese interpreter, pilot, hiking guide, tour leader, karate instructor, marriage celebrant and budding novelist. Check out www.craigmclachlan.com

Liza Prado

Liza has been a travel writer since 2003, when she made a move from being a corporate lawyer to travel writing (and never looked back). She's written dozens of guidebooks and articles as well as apps and blogs to destinations throughout the Americas. She takes decent photos too. Liza is a graduate of Brown University and Stanford Law School. She lives very happily in Denver, Colorado, with her husband and fellow Lonely Planet writer, Gary Chandler, and their two kids.

Phillip Tang

Phillip grew up on a typically Australian diet of pho and fish'n'chips before moving to Mexico City. A degree in Chinese- and Latin-American cultures launched him into travel and then writing about it for Lonely Planet's *Canada*, *China*, *Japan*, *Korea*, *Mexico*, *Peru* and *Vietnam* guides. You can see more of his writing at hellophillip.com, photos @mrtangtangtang and tweets @philliptang

Contributing Writers

Carolyn B Heller researched and wrote about Gatineau Park in Québec, and Korina Miller researched and wrote about the Fundy National Park in New Brunswick.

Our Story

A beat-up old car, a few dollars in the pocket and a sense of adventure. In 1972 that's all Tony and Maureen Wheeler needed for the trip of a lifetime – across Europe and Asia overland to Australia. It took several months, and at the end – broke but inspired – they sat at their kitchen table writing and stapling together their first travel guide, *Across Asia on the Cheap*. Within a week they'd sold 1500 copies. Lonely Planet was born. Today, Lonely Planet has offices in Franklin, London, Melbourne, Oakland, Dublin, Beijing, and Delhi, with more than 600 staff and writers. We share Tony's belief that 'a great guidebook should do three things: inform, educate and amuse'.

Our Writers

Brendan Sainsbury

Born and raised in the UK, Brendan spent the holidays of his youth caravanning in the English Lake District and didn't leave Blighty until he was 19. Making up for lost time, he's since squeezed 70 countries into a sometimes precarious existence as a writer and professional vagabond. His rocking chair memories will probably include staging a performance of *A Comedy of Errors* at a school in war-torn Angola and hitchhiking from Cape Town to Kilimanjaro with an early, dog-eared copy of *Africa on a Shoestring*. In the last 11 years, he has written over 40 books for Lonely Planet.

Ray Bartlett

Ray has been travel writing for nearly two decades, bringing Japan, Korea, Mexico, Tanzania, Guatemala, Indonesia and many parts of the United States to life in rich detail for top publishers, newspapers and magazines. His debut novel, *Sunsets of Tulum*, was a Midwest Book Review 2016 Fiction pick. Among other pursuits, he surfs regularly and is an accomplished Argentine tango dancer. Follow him on Facebook, Twitter, Instagram, or contact him for questions or speaking opportunities via www.kaisora.com, his website.

Oliver Berry

Oliver is a writer and photographer from Cornwall. He has worked for Lonely Planet for more than a decade, covering destinations from Cornwall to the Cook Islands, and has worked on more than 30 guidebooks. He is also a regular contributor to many newspapers and magazines, including Lonely Planet magazine. His writing has won several awards, including the *Guardian* Young Travel Writer of the Year and the *TNT Magazine* People's Choice Award. His latest work is published at www.oliverberry.com.

Gregor Clark

Gregor is a US-based writer whose love of foreign languages and curiosity about what's around the next bend have taken him to dozens of countries on five continents. Chronic wanderlust has also led him to visit all 50 states and most Canadian provinces on countless road trips through his native North America. Since 2000, Gregor has regularly

More Writers

STAY IN TOUCH LONELYPLANET.COM/CONTACT

AUSTRALIA The Malt Store, Level 3, 551 Swanston St, Carlton, Victoria 3053 ☎03 8379 8000, fax 03 8379 8111

IRELAND Digital Depot, Roe Ln (off Thomas St), Digital Hub, Dublin 8, D08 TCV4, Ireland

USA 155 Filbert St, Suite 208, Oakland, CA 94607 ☎510 250 6400, toll free 800 275 8555, fax 510 893 8572

UK 240 Blackfriars Rd, London SE1 8NW ☎020 3771 5100, fax 020 3771 5101

 twitter.com/lonelyplanet

 facebook.com/lonelyplanet

 instagram.com/lonelyplanet

 youtube.com/lonelyplanet

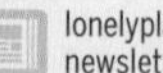 lonelyplanet.com/newsletter